Shaping Early Childhood

Shaping Early Childhood

LEARNERS, CURRICULUM AND CONTEXTS

Glenda Mac Naughton

Open University Press

Open University Press
McGraw-Hill Education
McGraw-Hill House
Shoppenhangers Road
Maidenhead
Berkshire
England
SL6 2QL

email: enquiries@openup.co.uk
world wide web: www.openup.co.uk

First published 2003

A catalogue record of this book is available from the British Library

ISBN 0 335 21106 2

Library of Congress Cataloging-in-Publication Data
CIP data applied for

Typeset by RefineCatch Limited, Bungay, Suffolk
Printed in the UK by Bell & Bain Ltd, Glasgow

Contents

Foreword   vii

Acknowledgements   x

INTRODUCTION
Critical reflection in early childhood teaching and learning   1

PART 1
Models of the learner   7

  1 Reflecting on the learner   9

  2 Models of the learner: conforming to nature, conforming to culture   14

  3 Models of the learner: reforming through interaction between
nature and culture   40

  4 Models of the learner: transforming culture and nature   70

  5 Models of the learner: critical reflections   93

PART 2
Positions on the early childhood curriculum   111

  6 Reflecting on the early childhood curriculum   113

  7 Curriculum position: conforming to society   121

  8 Curriculum position: reforming society   155

  9 Curriculum position: transforming society   182

10 Curriculum positions: critical reflections   213

PART 3
Curriculum contexts 245

11 Reflecting on contexts 247

12 Curriculum contexts: parents and communities 255

13 Curriculum contexts: becoming an early childhood professional 282

14 Curriculum contexts: critical reflections 302

References 320
Index 341

Foreword

This book is designed to support novice and more experienced early childhood educators to be critically reflective in their curriculum work. It is a 'ways to think' book more than a 'ways to do' book.

This is because the book has been written against a background of increasing calls for reflective teachers (Imel 1998; Bennett and Wood 2000) and a changing landscape of ideas about children's learning and development and about the role of early childhood education in society. This changing landscape has placed new demands on early childhood educators to be accountable for their ideas and their methods. There is increased evidence that governments around the world are keenly interested in how the outcomes of childhood education can achieve broader social and political goals, such as improvements in literacy and reduction in crime rates (see, for example, McCain and Mustard 1999).

As early childhood educators in many countries face increased accountability for the outcomes of their work with young children, early childhood researchers and academics are engaged in debate about what the knowledge base that drives work with young children should be. This debate is unsettling many taken-for-granted assumptions about what programmes for young children should aim to achieve, what ideas should inform them, and what they should look like in practice.

Sat among these increasing expectations that early childhood education will improve life chances for children and this 'unsettling' of the taken-for-granted is the early childhood educator who is often left with little guidance or support on how to navigate through these changing professional landscapes. This book is offered as a guide and a support for early childhood educators in these changing and unsettling times. It attempts to guide early childhood educators through the 'big ideas' that have influenced how we think about children as learners, early childhood curriculum and the contexts of the curriculum. It attempts to support early childhood educators to reflect critically on the 'big ideas' and the practices that they have given rise to. It also attempts to support early childhood educators to build their own critically informed positions on how they will understand and practice early childhood curriculum.

In this book education is understood as a process and not a place or specific type of early childhood setting. The term 'early childhood educators' is used to refer to all of those who are involved in teaching and learning with young children in early childhood settings. It is therefore used as an inclusive, rather than as an exclusive term. 'Early childhood education' is similarly used to include all of those settings in which teaching and learning occurs with young children. They include home based and non-home based, sessional and full day, services for children between birth and 8 years of age.

This book's structure and content is built from the insights of my research in several areas critical to curriculum work in early childhood education including:

- creating and sustaining critical reflection in the curriculum;
- creating and sustaining parent involvement;
- creating and sustaining equity.

It also includes several research case studies contributed by practitioner researchers involved in action research and critical reflection on their curriculum work in early childhood education.

What this book offers

This book's content and structure draws on insights from early childhood practitioner researchers into what they believe would help them to critically reflect on their work. Their suggestions include:

- offering more than one perspective on 'how to do' and 'how to think about' the early childhood curriculum;
- using a readily accessible conceptual framework for recognizing, reflecting on and choosing between different perspectives on making early childhood curriculum (for this reason I have settled on the conceptual framework of conforming, reforming and transforming approaches to a topic to position different perspectives on each topic);
- providing a sense of where the 'big ideas' within each perspective have come from;
- exploring the equity implications of different perspectives on each topic.

Each section has been designed to honour these suggestions and it also includes Ideas clarification exercises, Reflection sheets, Ideas samplers, research-based case studies of curriculum-in-action and Ideas galleries to support early childhood educators to engage in critical reflection on their work and the 'big ideas' underpinning it.

What this book can't offer

This book does not offer a set of guides or recipes for implementing a specific early childhood curriculum. Given that the demand on early childhood staff in many countries is to implement specific, state-mandated curriculum this may seem foolish. However, the book is premised on the idea that early childhood educators are professionals who can be supported in their work by having access to research-based tools with which to think about curriculum that both position current curriculum documents that they work with and transcend them.

Acknowledgements

If this book achieves its goals, it will in no small measure be due to the practitioner researchers and colleagues who have contributed so generously to it, to research projects and to discussions with me about what it could and should look like. My specific thanks go to:

- Patrick Hughes for his long conversations about, generous proofreading of, help with restructuring of and unflinching support for this project. Without the intellectual, practical and political support that he has given to me throughout this project it could not have come to fruition. Patrick also contributed to Part 3 and to Chapter 10, in particular.
- Sheralyn Campbell and Jane Page for their contributions to Chapter 11. I know for each of them the writing demands of this project came at a difficult time and for their determined effort to meet my deadlines, I thank them. Sheralyn's long-standing ethical, intellectual and political commitment to social justice is evident in her work in this chapter, and Jane's strong commitment to children's rights and advocacy for children is apparent throughout it.
- Diana Hetherich for her case study on building meaningful curriculum with children and their families. Her openness and critical insights about her own journey to becoming more knowing about cultural diversity and about children and families shows that curriculum work changes as teachers change their ways of thinking and understandings. Diana's work continues through her Masters research with families that explores the intersections between her own knowledge as a teacher and those of children and their families.
- Heather Lawrence for her insights about and deep commitment to honouring children in all that they do in early childhood and for being a colleague and friend who believes in the place of ideas and social change in our work with young children. Heather contributed several Ideas clarification exercises to Part 1 and conversations with her during the book's writing helped me to clarify my own thinking.
- Brian Newman, Yarrow Andrew and Denise Rundle for the case study on

rethinking curriculum planning. I know that this work is not yet finished and it began well before this book. My thanks to them for sharing with others through this case study where they have reached in their journey.

- Sharon Saitta for her case study from her own curriculum research journeys. Her critical insights and questions about her own journey are generously shared with others through this case study and raise questions that are not just relevant to her specific case study but to any early childhood educator concerned, as Sharon is, with social justice and fairness in their classroom.

- Kylie Smith for her case study on observing and assessing children, which comes from her doctoral studies on reconceptualizing observation in early childhood education. Kylie's work has inspired many early childhood educators to rethink their ways of seeing children, because her reflection on the equity intents and effects of her work with children and families links so clearly with their own issues and practices.

- Margaret Trembarth, Early Childhood Research and the Faculty of Education of the University of Melbourne, for their funding of the research project 'Creating and sustaining critical reflection in early childhood settings'. The University of Melbourne and the Australian Research Council for funding research projects that have been drawn on in this book including: 'Staff perspectives on parent involvement in early childhood' (with Patrick Hughes) and 'Preschool children's perspectives on equity and social diversity'.

INTRODUCTION
Critical reflection in early childhood teaching and learning

The new problem situation cannot be handled with the old theoretical means.
(Habermas 1989: 302)

All early childhood educators work within a specific social and political context. For some early childhood educators local, state, regional or national governments will have clear mandates about the curriculum goals and learning outcomes that guide their interactions with young children. Some mandated curriculum contains explicit perspectives of the child as a learner. For example, in South Australia early childhood practitioners are advised to base their pedagogy on a constructivist view of the learner. However, not all mandated curriculum explicitly labels its underpinning perspectives on the child as a learner. For instance, in the Swedish national early childhood curriculum there is an emphasis on learning through 'play and social interactions' (Alvestad and Samuelsson 1999: 4) and an implicit socio-cognitive view of the child as a learner.

Some early childhood educators may face mandated curricula because they work within a specific organization, such as a chain of commerically run childcare centres, or a philosophically linked organization, such as a Montessori programme or Steiner programme. The curriculum goals, nature of the planning that they do and their approach to assessment may each be mandated. Yet other early childhood educators may have considerable autonomy over how they plan their curriculum work. For instance, in the Australian state of Victoria early childhood staff are not mandated to draw on specific theories of the child in their work. This produces an ever-shifting and debated curriculum landscape in which visions of the child as a learner, approaches to building curriculum for the child and relationships within the curriculum are highly context-bound and value-based.

It is against that background of differing curriculum landscapes that this book is written. It intends to enable early childhood educators to explore the different ways in which early childhood curriculum can be constructed, to engage them in critical reflection on their own curriculum possibilities, and to support them to shape curriculum that is meaningful to the children and communities that they work with. It is written from the position that central to shaping the curriculum for young children must be a commitment to equity, fairness, a respect for diversity and a concern with peace, and that critical reflection can support shaping such curricula. The drive to do this has become even more urgent with events since 11 September 2001, as the world feels less safe to many children and their families. Many early childhood educators touched by the effects of 11 September are asking how early childhood education in the here and now can contribute to making a safer and respectful world for all children and their families. This book is not a recipe for doing that. Rather, it is an attempt to provide early childhood educators with tools to help them to reflect critically on the equity effects of the 'big ideas' that they use to shape their daily deeds with young children.

Specifically, the book is built on the premise that critical reflection enables early childhood educators to make informed and careful choices about the ideas, processes and relationships that underpin their work with young children. It aims to assist early childhood educators in this process, mindful of the comments that follow:

> Which approach is the best one is a value decision that the individual educator must make . . . One cannot choose not to choose, because to accept the status quo is also to make a choice.
>
> (Sleeter and Grant 1999: 224)

> Governments, as well as international institutions, must be held accountable for their leadership in putting the rights and well-being of children above all other concerns. And those that fail to do so must also be held accountable.
>
> (Bellamy 2001: 4)

The book is structured on several understandings about early childhood educators and their work that became clearly apparent in a recent research project (Mac Naughton *et al.* 2002):

- early childhood educators enjoy intellectual engagement;
- early childhood educators like thinking about the 'big ideas' behind their work;
- early childhood educators struggle to find resources that discuss and contextualize the 'big ideas' in ways that help them form their own positions on them.

Critical reflection: what is it?

There is a keen debate about how to define critical reflection (Mackintosh 1998). Researchers generally agree that critical reflection is an intellectually engaged activity geared to changing practices by transforming knowledge (for example, Yost *et al.* 2000). However, they disagree over the goals of critical reflection (Ecclestone 1996) and the conditions in which it can transform knowledge.

Some researchers (for example, Boud *et al.* 1985; Mezirow 1990; Brookfield 1995; Cranton 1996) see critical reflection as a way to discover and transform an individual's understandings and practices (Bleakley 1999). In contrast, for researchers adopting critical approaches to knowledge (for example, Carr and Kemmis 1986;

Giroux 1991; Darder 2002), critical reflection is the collective examination of the social and political factors that produce knowledge and practices, together with the use of this knowledge to strategically transform education in socially progressive directions.

This second approach to critical reflection is associated with the critical social and political theory of Jürgen Habermas, and it regards transformations as arising from critiquing the 'big ideas' that underpin our work. For Habermas, critical knowledge of the 'big ideas' is linked to our possibilities for a better world. Smith and Lovat (1990: 69–70) summarized Habermas's position on being critical:

> For Habermas, it is only when we have reached . . . [critical knowledge] . . . that we are guaranteed true knowledge because true knowledge demands that we be free . . . the information which comes from any subject can become a means of bondage, rather than emancipation, a way of oppressing people or keeping them in straitjackets.

More recently, postmodern perspectives on knowledge have introduced additional understandings of what critical reflection looks like (for example, Parker 1997; Ryan and Ochsner 1999; Campbell *et al.* 2000). Postmodern perspectives on critical reflection emphasize (Lather 1991; Campbell *et al.* 2000; Kessler and Hauser 2000):

- troubling (giving a hard time to) the 'big ideas' (truths) we take for granted;
- exploring where our 'big ideas' or 'truths' about how the world works have come from, who has generated them and whose interests they serve;
- seeking many perspectives on our 'truths';
- giving preference to ways of understanding the world that come from those groups who are consistently marginalized and silenced in it;
- attempting to politically reconstruct what we do and what we think so that it honours the understandings of groups who are marginalized or silenced.

Those who reflect critically on their work and on the understandings that drive it typically ask questions such as:

- How have I come to do things this way?
- How have I come to understand things this way?
- Who benefits from how I do and understand this?
- Who is silenced in how I do and understand this?
- How many other ways are there to do and understand this?
- Which of those ways might lead to more equitable and fair ways of doing things and understandings things?

Structuring content to support critical reflection

The book is in three parts, each of which links to a specific feature of the curriculum landscape:

- Part 1: the learner;
- Part 2: the curriculum – philosophy, planning, pedagogy and assessment;
- Part 3: the relationships – with the child, the parent, the community and the profession.

Each part explores three positions on its topic as a 'benchmark', source of inspiration and a 'test-point' for reflection. These positions are:

- conforming positions on the topic;
- reforming positions on the topic;
- transforming positions on the topic.

The decision to group ideas on each topic into conforming, reforming and trans-forming positions builds from the work of the German critical social theorist Jürgen Habermas on knowledge interests. Habermas, along with other members of what has become known as the Frankfurt School of critical theory, was interested in 'social consciousness' (Pinar *et al.* 1995: 248). Habermas argued that in a given area of knowledge there are three interests (Kemmis 1986; Bertens 1995; Lovat and Smith 1995; Pinar *et al.* 1995):

- *Technical* interests are concerned with finding out how things happen and how we can control what happens. They often lead to knowledge that conforms to existing understandings and practices.
- *Practical* interests are concerned with finding out what things mean to people and understanding events rather than controlling them. They often lead to knowledge that is reformed in the process of gaining new insights.
- *Critical* (or emancipatory) interests are concerned with finding out if what we know is in some way distorted or biased, in order to ensure that our knowledge is free from bias. They often lead to knowledge that is transformed in the process of critical questioning about whose interests are served by the knowledge we have and that allows us to emancipate ourselves and others.

Each part of the book explores the technical (conforming), practical (reforming) and critical (transforming) knowledge interests that have shaped and continued to shape the landscapes of early childhood curriculum and invites readers to critically reflect on each of those interests. They offer a way to build 'social consciousness' (Pinar *et al.* 1995: 248) about why we do what we do in early childhood and in doing so, enable early childhood educators to be critically informed about their intellectual and political curriculum choices.

Each position (or knowledge interest) is examined in terms of:

- an overview of its key ideas;
- where the ideas within each position have come from;
- how each position has influenced early childhood education;
- equity reflections on each position.

Each part also includes a series of reflective exercises to help readers develop their positions on the topic under scrutiny.

Using the book for critical dialogue

Critical reflection is dialogic. It requires social connections with others: conversations with others, support from others, colleagues willing to spend time with you and a chance to share ideas and possibilities with others. The participants in a study of critical reflection in the early childhood field known as the Margaret Trembarth Project (Mac Naughton *et al.* 2002) highlighted that critical reflection to them was 'dialogue' with others to scrutinize teaching. Their essentially social and dialogic understandings of critical reflection emerged most powerfully in their comments about what prevents them from reflecting critically on their work.

> Lack of knowledge – sometimes feel that I operate in a vacuum – not knowing how to take the next step, not having the tools to open up more ideas. Knowledge might be in form of reading, but I need to see how it might work.

> If people not around or problem no-one else is engaged with – working on my own is the hardest. I need other people or other forms of support.

> Time and also the opportunity to actually get together to have those conversations because staff meetings are about – not critical reflection – they are about the day to day running of a school.

> Time, the key word. Yes I think basically it is time and the availability of the other people around you, and even if I do find something, some other resource that I find that's really good, then basically I still talk to other professionals about it as well to see if they've tried it as well.

> More time for us to share but also to be able to share continually on that same curriculum area, instead of jumping.

> Yes, well most of our talking is not in staff meetings, so most of it's after school.

This book can't produce that dialogue but it is intended to help those interested in making a difference to their curriculum practices to enter into dialogue with others about it. Participants in the Trembarth Project showed that critical reflection is incredibly hard work unless there are structures, processes and strategies which enable early childhood staff to:

- be involved in a dialogic community whose role is to scrutinize their teaching and its effects;
- bring new knowledge and perspectives to bear on their teaching;
- create change in their teaching practices and knowledge base;
- reflect deeply on major issues connected to what they do and why.

This book hopes to assist early childhood professionals – novice and experienced, undergraduate and postgraduate – to engage in these processes. I hope through this book to contribute to creating and sustaining critical reflection within the early childhood profession in these unsettling times of increased accountability and changing ideas.

PART 1

Models of the learner

1

Reflecting on the learner

Part 1 explores different ways to understand the child as a learner. We start by examining the child as a learner because perspectives on children and on childhood are central to developing early childhood curriculum. Early childhood educators act in particular ways with young children and develop curriculum for them based on their understandings of how children learn, how they make sense of their surroundings and how they form relationships. However, there is not unanimity within the field about whose understandings of the child should inform practice in early childhood programmes. Should it be those of developmental theorists or of philosophers and social theorists? There is increasing debate within the early childhood field about the extent to which developmental theories should lead curriculum decisions (Alloway 1997; Cannella 1997; Mac Naughton 2000) and, if it should, which theories we should use (Lambert and Clyde 2000).

Different models give us different ways to 'see' children and childhood

Participants in that debate present ways to understand children and childhood that are sometimes so different from each other as to be contradictory, which can make the debate hard to follow. How can contradictory views about the child co-exist? The answer is that each view of children and childhood reflects the models within which theorists and researchers developed it; and different models compete for dominance in early childhood education – as they do in any field. A model is built within a specific paradigm or way of seeing and making sense of the world. Our ways of seeing and making sense of the child – our models of the child – have been influenced by several paradigms, including positivism, interpretivism, structuralism and poststructuralism. Later chapters in the book will introduce you to each of these paradigms (ways of seeing the child) and show how each one has led us to different understandings about the child as a learner.

The differences between the paradigms used to understand childhood and children have fuelled debates between early childhood educators as they grapple with questions central to curriculum decisions:

- Do young children learn differently from adults? Should early childhood educators teach children differently from adults? Should early childhood educators' expectations of the child as a learner differ from their expectations of themselves? Should programmes be different for children of different ages?

- What motivates young children to learn? Can adults motivate young children to learn? Does a child's motivation to learn come from within them and, if it does, what does this mean for the educator? Will children's internal drives motivate them to make sense of the world or should their efforts to learn be rewarded with devices such as elephant stamps or gold stars?

- How can adults design environments that maximize young children's learning? Is young children's learning maximized by tightly structured experiences or by open-ended, play-based experiences? What materials should educators offer children and how should educators structure children's time in their programme? Can educators provide too little structure? Can they provide too much structure?

- What is the role of genetics in children's capacity to learn? Is every child equally capable of learning or are some more capable than others? Are some children born as gifted learners? What does that mean for early childhood educators?

- What part do emotions and relationships play in children's learning? What sorts of relationships do children need for their learning?

Developing your own position

This first part of the book assists you to develop your own position statement(s) on young children and on how they learn – position statement(s) that can guide your work for equitable curriculum with young children. This first chapter invites you to explore your own beliefs and ideas about how young children learn. Chapters 2, 3 and 4 introduce you to some influential theories of childhood and of children as learners. Each theory is categorized according to its views on the learner in society:

- conforming to nature;
- conforming to culture;
- reforming through interaction between nature and culture;
- transforming through collaboration.

Each theory is explored as follows:

- an overview of its ideas;
- a history of where its ideas have come from;
- the implications of the theory for early childhood curriculum;
- equity reflections on the theory.

This section's final chapter (Chapter 6) invites you to reflect critically on your own position on the child as a learner. To assist you to do so, it includes the following items:

- case studies;
- reflection tasks on where you are now and where to go next;
- a gallery of ideas about learners and education.

Reflecting on learning

Learning is understood (in various ways) as the acquisition of knowledge about ourselves and our world. It is critical to our capacity to make sense of our world and to act in it. At birth, we know little of the language, ideas and meanings of the cultural world into which we are born and our capacity to move and act on that world is limited. Yet, very quickly young children move to a point where they have considerable knowledge of their world and capacity to act in it. For instance, by 6 years of age, many children have a vocabulary of over 10,000 words (Thompson 2001).

How do these changes happen? How does learning happen and how can we best foster it? These questions are at the heart of any educational programme. Early childhood educators often answer these questions using the ideas of child development theorists who explore and explain how we change over time and who develop principles on which we can act to support our growth to adulthood.

Reflecting on where you are now

You can begin to develop your own position in the debates by reflecting on your own and other people's beliefs and knowledge about children and childhood and by exploring their implications for an early childhood curriculum. In doing so, you will begin to create a coherent vision of who the child is, how the child learns, what the child should learn and what the adult's role in the child's learning should be (Katz 1995).

We start with beliefs and knowledge, because irrespective of whether you are an experienced or inexperienced early childhood educator, you will have views about how children learn. These views will influence how you work with young children, so this book invites and enables you to:

- reflect on your implicit and/or explicit theories of learning;
- reflect where they sit on a 'map' of classical learning theories;
- examine selected contemporary theories of children as learners, meaning makers and relationship builders;
- explore the implications of different views of the child as a learner for curriculum practices;
- build an informed position on children as learners on which to base your decisions about early childhood curriculum.

Ideas clarification exercise 1.1

Try to complete one or more of the following exercises to help you clarify your ideas about children as learners:

- *Reflect on your own learning.* Write a short story about a moment when you learnt something new. How did your learning happen? What made that learning possible? Did others play a role in your learning? What motivated you to learn? Could a 4-year-old child have learnt what you did? Would they have learnt it in the same ways?
- *Reflect on how two children you know learn.* Do they learn by themselves or with the help of others? What seems to motivate them to learn? What seems to prevent them from learning?
- *Draw an image of someone learning something.* What will you include? What won't you include?

Reflection points

- What are your current theories/beliefs about how young children learn? Specifically:
  - Are there differences in how children and adults learn?
  - What motivates children to learn?
  - What role do adults play in children's learning?
  - To what extent do genetics determine what children will and can learn?
  - Can children learn by themselves?
- What issues do you currently face or think you might face in understanding children, their learning, their meanings and their relationships?

Reflection sheet 1.1 My theories of how children learn

Reflection questions	Your ideas	What examples do you have from your experiences to support this?	Where have your ideas come from? (for example, experience, research, reading, family, the media, colleagues)
Are there differences in how children and adults learn?			
What motivates children to learn?			
What role do adults play in children's learning?			
To what extent do genetics determine what children will and can learn?			
What role do emotions play in children's learning?			
Can children learn by themselves?			
What other questions do you have about children's learning?			

2

Models of the learner: conforming to nature, conforming to culture

This chapter introduces you to the views and ideas of those who see the child as learning through conforming to nature or conforming to culture.

Definitions

- *Conforming*: following general rules, patterns or ideas (for example, following general biological rules and patterns or following the general rules and patterns of a particular culture).

- *Nature*: forces that exist before society or outside of culture, within us or within the material world; not made by us, but given to us (Williams 1976) (for example, forces that exist within the child, given to them by their biology, not by society).

- *Culture*: what we create beyond our biology. Not given to us, but made by us (Williams 1976) (for example, what the child creates beyond their biology and what we create of the child beyond their biology).

Conforming to nature: maturationism

Our understandings of nature's role in children's learning influences how we interact with them. If learning results from an innate internal drive, then the less that adults interfere with nature's timetable, the better the child will learn. Maturationism is the belief that we can maximize young children's learning by listening to nature.

A key thinker	Definition
Arnold Gesell (1880–1961), USA	Maturation: the movement towards an increasingly complete and fully developed state of being (for example, the movement from infancy towards adulthood).

The theory in overview

> Babies enter the world with an inborn schedule which is the product of at least three million years of biological evolution: they are pre-eminently 'wise' about their needs, and what they are ready and not ready to do . . . [we should take] cues from the children themselves.
>
> (Crain 1985: 20)

Maturationists believe that genetics drives our movement towards adulthood, a movement that proceeds through an orderly sequence of stages, each with its own characteristics or behavioural norms. Maturationist Arnold Gesell believed that we moved towards increasingly adult ways of knowing and being through genetically pre-programmed structures. There was an unchangeable normal path for the unfolding of these structures that we went against at our peril. Gesell mapped a range of age-based behavioural norms for our motor skills, personal hygiene, emotional expression, fears and dreams, self and sex, interpersonal relations, play and pastimes, school life, ethical sense and philosophical outlook.

Crain (1985) said of Gesell:

> Gesell believed that each individual temperament and growth style makes different demands on the culture, and that the culture should try to adjust to each child's uniqueness.
>
> (p.21)

Where have the ideas come from?

Maturationism's roots lie in the ideas of the Romantics, who believe in the value and innocence of childhood and see in the child our hope for authentic experiences of freedom. Strictly, a Romantic is someone who holds an idealized view of something (for example, childhood) that often appeals to emotion, rather than to reason. Romantics believe that children's natural disposition to play and to be playful illustrates our natural disposition to creativity, innovation, emotion and imagination, and that culture corrupts this disposition. The Romantics regard the child as closer than the adult to real freedom, truth and beauty because he or she is free from culture's effects. The younger the child, the closer he or she is and could be to nature and the freer he or she is and could be from culture. Culture undermines our capacity to think and live in liberated ways; and so to regain freedom, beauty, justice and truth, we must look to the child as the closest approximation to our true nature. Consequently, being in nature and away from culture is the best way to ensure that our natural dispositions flourish, and so we should educate children for as long as possible and in ways that keep them as close to their true nature and as far from culture as possible.

Jean-Jacques Rousseau (1712–78, Switzerland and France) was a key Romantic thinker, who argued that hurrying children into adult ways of thinking, such as the capacity to reason, risks harming the child. For Rousseau, reason (culture) begins at 7 years of age and until they reach that age, children should be carefully and naturally educated, preferably within the confines of the family. The family should carefully observe the child's natural unfolding and respond to the child's changing needs:

> Nature wants children to be children before being men . . . if we want to pervert this order, we shall produce precocious fruits which will be immature and insipid and will not be long in rotting.
>
> (Rousseau [1762] 1991: 90)

Romanticism was born in the period of European (primarily British, French and German) intellectual history between the late 1600s and the mid-1700s. This period is referred to as the Enlightenment and/or the Age of Reason and it is regarded as the beginning of modern times or modernity. In the Enlightenment, hopeful reformers created a 'new passion for argument, criticism and debate' (Spencer and Kruaze 2000: 3) about humankind, its possibilities and its aspirations, and philosophers began to explore children's particular characteristics as learners.

Enlightenment thinkers believed that reason is the key to human progress and reason was at the heart of the new Enlightenment ways to understand the world that we now know as science. In reason lay the promise of finding true happiness, freedom and equality, as Habermas explained:

> Enlightenment thinkers still had the extravagant expectation that the arts and sciences would promote not only the control of natural forces, but would also further understanding of the world and of the self, would promote moral progress, the justice of institutions, and even the happiness of human beings.
>
> (Habermas 1981: 22)

The intellectual ferment of the Enlightenment included a search for the conditions under which reason could be pursued, with the result that the child became a point of focus and interest. John Locke and Jean-Jacques Rousseau were Enlightenment philosophers, who each argued that the child's capacity to reason develops from birth and that how we dealt with that fact would determine its realization and thus the achievement of happiness, freedom and equality (Ariès 1962; Archard 1993; James *et al.* 1998; Cannella 1999).

The ideas of the Romantics continue to influence how people think about children, although in the twentieth century they became inflected with a scientific approach. While Romantics such as Rousseau had argued that we must follow nature's pattern with young children and emphasized that observation influenced our capacity to do this, twentieth-century maturationists such as Gesell used scientific methods to map nature's patterns very precisely. Gesell worked at the Yale Clinic of Child Development and was one of the first child development researchers to film children and to use these films to detail meticulously what children did and to identify fixed sequences in when they did what and how they did it (Crain 1985).

Gesell was part of a new research tradition (also including Piaget, Skinner and Erikson) that sought to ground our understandings of the child in science. In the 1920s, child psychology emerged as a scientific discipline in its own right. Its task was to study child and human development using scientific methods. In clinics and nursery schools, trained psychologists could, for the first time, observe large numbers of children under laboratory conditions (Rose 1999). As Bloch explained:

> there were attempts to use the 'hard' physical sciences, and psychology's definition of science (typically personified in experimental psychology) as the model for truth, definitions of valuable knowledge, a way to get factual information about 'normal' child development, and guidance for pedagogy ... Being 'scientific' in theory, method of research, and pedagogical applications was part of becoming or appearing more professional, especially as many associated with child development or early education were associated with home economics and what was thought to be a female field.
>
> (Bloch 1992: 9)

Science embodies a set of assumptions concerning the truth about the world and how we discover it. Scientists aim to develop theories that predict how the world works and, therefore, increase our control over it. They gather facts about the world and use them to generate theories (rules or ideas) about the world that are based on cause and effect relationships applicable in all places at all times. For example, scientific researchers gather facts about children (for example, about their physical development) and use them to generate theories about the child that predict how young children develop at all times and in all places. Scientists claim that scientific knowledge is the best form of knowledge because it tells us what is true and what is not. As Hughes (2001: 33) explained:

> Traditionally, scientists have claimed that scientific (positivist) knowledge is the only form of knowledge that can be proven true (or false). Other forms of knowledge (e.g. myths, dreams, intuition) may be very interesting, they say, but we can neither prove nor disprove them.

Implications of maturationism for early childhood curriculum

The Romantics' and maturationists' idea that our inner nature determines how we become human is remarkably persistent. The Romantics' view that observations should guide the natural education of the young child resonate through much early childhood thinking about the child and their learning from the early twentieth century onwards. Consider the following statements made by early childhood academics in the last 20 years:

> Because early experiences can enhance or diminish inborn potential, the environment of early experiences shapes the opportunities and risks that young children encounter.
>
> (Thompson 2001: 30)

> It is the task of the teacher to stand between the known and unknown. The teacher must see where students are and lay the stepping stones to new

knowledge surely and safely so that the students come to trust themselves, their teachers and the educational process.

(Jonquiere 1990: 292)

I try to stand aside and allow [the children] to speak for themselves. It is not easy to wait and listen.

(Vivienne Paley, an American early childhood teacher and author 1986: xv)

Similarly, popular wisdom continues to express Romantic and maturationist beliefs that to maximize learning we must conform to our inner nature and drives. For example, consider these popular beliefs:

- early experiences determine our futures;
- the developing child is an incomplete adult and is different from adults;
- we all progress through stages towards adulthood;
- our progression through stages towards adulthood is unvarying in its sequence and common to us all;
- our progression through stages towards adulthood is biologically driven and thus unchangeable;
- we cannot learn outside of the possibilities given to us at each stage of development;
- we cannot learn before we are ready to, learning cannot and should not be forced.

'Conforming to nature' models of the learner imply clear tasks for the educator that maximize the child's learning and chances of normal growth towards adulthood:

- observe the child to determine the stage of 'becoming adult' they have reached;
- listen to nature's prompts about what the child needs at each stage;
- trust and support nature to lead the child towards adulthood;
- don't intervene – offer nature a helping hand only when necessary;
- take your cues from the child;
- adjust the learning environment to the child, not the child to the learning environment.

Ideas summary 2.1 explores how you plan for time, materials, space and people if you adhere to the 'conforming to nature' view of how children learn. As you review Ideas clarification 2.1 (p. 23), reflect on which of the planning implications you would feel comfortable with and which would discomfort you.

Ideas summary 2.1 Implications for planning of 'conforming to nature'

Key ideas:

- Nature prompts learning and educators should look for and respond to nature's prompts.
- The natural unfolding of innate physical, emotional, cognitive and psychological patterns makes learning possible.
- Nature leads learning, culture is merely the context of learning.

Implications for planning:

MATERIALS

'The educator prepares a series of motives of cultural activity, spread over a specially prepared environment and then refrains from obtrusive interference' (Montessori, *Education for a New World*).

Materials:

- must be developmentally appropriate to the individual child;
- will be sequenced to follow normal developmental patterns;
- will be focused in the early years on the child's physical development.

TIME

'There are two kinds of time – organic and clock time. The former is based on the wisdom of the body, the latter on astronomical science and cultural inventions' (Gesell and Ilg 1943: 51).

Time and routines:

- should adjust to the child, and not vice versa;
- children can regulate their own sleeping, eating, and so on, and should be allowed to do this.

Timing for what children learn and when:

- will follow;
- rather than hurry nature's plan, allow children time to unfold in their own way, at their own pace.

PEOPLE

'Man is born free, and everywhere he is in chains' (Rousseau [1762]: i).

The educator's job is to aid nature by:

- observing nature's prompts;
- offering a helping hand when necessary;
- avoiding direct teaching until a child is ready;
- taking cues from the child;
- adjusting to the child, not adjusting the child to us.

SPACE

'Direct the attention of your child to the phenomena of nature, and you will soon awaken his curiosity' (Rousseau 1773: 296).

Space:

- allows children freedom to be and to move;
- keeps the child as close to nature as possible (Romantics);
- is arranged to stimulate the child's curiosity;
- is structured to the child's needs (Montessori).

CONTENT

'Put questions to him adapted to his capacity, and leave him to resolve them. Let him take nothing on trust from his (tutor), but on his own comprehension and convictions; he should not learn, but invent the sciences' (Rousseau 1773: 296).

Content:

- will emphasize the process of learning rather than specific, pre-set content;
- will be responsive to and based on children's interests and change with them.

Equity reflections

A 'conforming to nature' model of the learner is associated with two contradictory ideas about diversity – that it is abnormal and that it is natural. These ideas have specific implications for how an educator might seek to create equity, especially when working with children with disabilities.

Diversity is abnormal

The maturationists' belief that we can plot normal patterns of development for each child implies that children who do not conform to those patterns are abnormal, different or deviant. For instance, Landreth (1969: 15) talked of congenital 'abnormalities' resulting from an 'aberration or error' in nature. Thus, developmental diversity should be corrected, not celebrated. This process of 'correcting' developmental abnormalities – for instance, in children with disabilities – is often referred to as 'normalization'.

Attempts to normalize the child link to an assimilationist approach to equity. To assimilate something is to absorb it into a larger group and, by doing so, make it the same as the larger group. Thus, adherents to an assimilationist approach to equity believe that we can create an equitable social world by ensuring that everyone shares the same ideas and values – when we are the same, we are equal. Within an assimilationist approach to equity, developmental, cultural and social diversity is problematic – if we are different, we cannot be equal. An early childhood educator who took an assimilationist approach to equity would believe that his or her role is to support each and every child to become as normal as is possible.

Hulmes (1989: 2) suggested that assimilation amounts to 'the obliteration of cultural distinctions'. We could say that assimilationist approaches to developmental diversity attempt to create equity by obliterating developmental distinctions and by encouraging children to adapt to pre-existing physical, social and cultural norms. If a disability is 'aberrant' or 'abnormal' development, then equitable education for children with disabilities would aim to make them as normal as possible by ensuring that they have 'normal' experiences within the early childhood programme by, for example:

- encouraging all children to achieve the same goals at the same time;
- emphasizing the similarities between people;
- ensuring that all children conform to the educator's ideas about normal ways to think, act, feel and speak.

In summary, assimilationist approaches to equity attempt to create a common culture and/or set of norms for behaviour and actively work to ensure that everyone is a member of that common culture and/or adheres to those norms. Norms are not only physical but also social and cultural, so assimilationist approaches to equity emphasize the importance of children adhering to norms irrespective of their gender, 'race', ethnicity, language, culture, socio-economic or ability background. Sleeter and Grant (1999: 159) explain how assimilation works:

when minority cultural groups come into contact with a majority cultural group, over time the values and life styles of the minority groups are replaced by those of the majority groups.

Diversity is natural

If nature determines our development, then differences between children's ways of being and doing are just natural differences. For example, differences in boys' and girls' behaviour reflect natural differences between the genders. Numerous studies have identified gender norms for girls and boys, in which boys consistently appear more competent than girls in areas such as:

- ball-handling skills;
- grip strength;
- hopping;
- running;
- jumping;
- visuo-spatial ability.

(see Landreth 1969; Sayers 1987).

Similarly, gender differences in a variety of areas have been linked to girls' relative underperformance in areas such as science and mathematics in the school years (see Sayers 1987). If the differences in competence in these areas reflect biological differences between genders, trying to make girls as competent as boys in these areas is both futile and unnatural. Instead, early childhood educators who take this approach to equity merely need to note gender differences in children or to explain them as biological.

In areas where gender differences are not determined by developmental norms they may be explained as due to developmental immaturity. For example, some girls may fail to throw a ball as well as some boys because they are not yet developmentally ready to do so. Early childhood educators who take this approach to equity wait for the moment when a girl is developmentally ready and then support her as she practises her ball-handling skills. As Graue (1992: 64) explained:

> This orientation to readiness, exemplified by those affiliated with the Gesell Institute, is premised on the concept of physical or social maturation, which can be development only with the passage of time. Lack of readiness is related to an underdeveloped organism, which will be damaged if challenged by tasks that are posed at a higher developmental level.

In both approaches ('abnormal' and 'natural') to equity, the (maturationist) early childhood educator should follow nature rather than intervene in it – they should follow natural gender differences rather than intervene to change them. This leads to what Sleeter and Grant (1999) call a 'business as usual' approach to equity, which dismisses differences (such as gender differences) as normal ('boys will be boys') or ignores them until the child is ready or mature enough to work on them.

There is a long history of noting 'natural' difference (for example, in physical skills, cognitive ability, sociability and capacity with language) between children from different 'racial' groups, as Zack indicates: 'Until the 1920s, social scientists also assumed the cultural differences among racially designated groups were physically inherited' (Zack 1998: 76). To illustrate the persistence of these ideas, consider to whom the following statements might refer:

- he just has natural rhythm when it comes to music;
- he is just naturally good at football;
- she's a real natural when it comes to singing.

An early childhood educator who regards such differences as natural also takes a 'business as usual' approach to equity. He or she doesn't need to change the curriculum or his or her interactions in any way when children are performing differently. This approach can be highly problematic, as it discounts the possibility that differences in performance may result from discrimination and/or disadvantage.

New (1994a) cited research indicating that less than 10 per cent of studies of child development published in major child development journals concern children from culturally or linguistically diverse backgrounds. Many child development norms have been developed by studying white, middle class children, and so children outside these categories may well fail to meet the norms. Educators' response may well be to normalize these children, in other words, to try to make them more white and middle class. For instance:

> Attachment to the image of Australia as a classless society has meant a certain resistance to acknowledging class-based dialects, and yet such acknowledgement is vital in understanding educational disadvantage. SAE [Standard Australian English] is a middle class dialect . . . in which all official business is carried out, including education.
>
> (Barnett and Walsh 1999: 125)

Equity alerts

'Assimilationist' and 'business as usual' approaches to equity raise several equity 'alerts' because they ignore the following possibilities:

- diversity is something to celebrate.
- 'race' is not genetic but cultural: 'There are no clear, or obvious genetically based groups which lead to the identification of "races". The process of labelling certain groups as races is not based on genetics' (McConnochie *et al.* 1988: 16).
- diversity is a result of social and cultural experiences and expectations:
  > middle class parents had information and perceived power to make decisions about their children . . . social class provides cultural capital (such as language and knowledge of how to navigate their way with educational professionals) . . . This capital provided the middle class children with a home advantage as they went through school.
  >
  > (Graue 1992: 86)

- regarding differences as natural may disadvantage some children:

    we have not made substantial gains in teaching literacy to Aboriginal children, children from low socio-economic backgrounds, and certain children from ethnic minorities . . . We must confront the question of performance and we must question the valuing of process over product if it means not taking deliberate, affirmative action to get all students up to a reasonable mark.

    (Boomer 1989, cited in Barnett and Walsh 1999: 124)

Ideas clarification exercise 2.1 (*from Heather Lawrence*)

1 *Review Ideas summary 2.2* of relationships between educators and children. Would you add any additional features to this summary of relationships between educators and children in a maturationist programme?

Ideas summary 2.2 Relationships between educators and children in a maturationist programme

A programme drawing on maturationist ideas would have the following features:

The educator would:

- wait to teach children until the children show they are ready to learn;
- use his or her own child rearing experiences to guide practices;
- draw on previous experiences with children to guide practices.

The child would be:

- dependent and innocent;
- an empty vessel in need of preparation before the child can learn what is most important;
- a reproducer of knowledge;
- developing according to predetermined developmental pathways;
- seen as abnormal and needing to be fixed through teaching if the child deviates from developmental norms.

Equity reflections:

- cultural and gender differences are seen as natural, not needing to be strengthened;
- equity will be arrived at if differences are ignored.

---

2 *Read the following scenario* of relationships between educators and children. What did the teacher believe about Ben's development? In what ways did the teachers in this scenario draw on a maturationist view of the child? What are the equity implications in this scenario for making meaningful relationships between the educators and Ben?

    Ben was a Vietnamese child of 4.5 years of age. Both his parents and older brother spoke Vietnamese at home. Ben's mother was very homesick and had been very sad after Ben's birth. Ben was very interested in trains and he become annoyed when other children came to share his toys. He had very few toys at home and spent a lot of time watching television. He did not play cooperatively with the other children. His spoken English was poor and his spoken Vietnamese was also limited. The teachers believed he was delayed for his age. They planned to 'teach him how to play with others' by staying with him when he played. Furthermore, they believed that he understood what he was supposed to do but deliberately refused to do it. They believed that he should learn to use more materials so they helped him to paint by holding his hand on a paintbrush and guided his hands while he painted. The teachers believed he had a cognitive developmental delay.

Conforming to culture: behaviourism

Key thinkers	Definition
• Ivan Pavlov (1849–1936), USSR • John Watson (1878–1958), USA • B.F. Skinner (1904–1990), USA	Behaviourism: The ways in which someone acts (for example: the ways in which children act as they learn).

The theory in overview

> Give me a dozen healthy infants, well-formed, and my own specified world to bring them up in and I'll guarantee to take any one at random and train him to become any type of specialist I might select . . . regardless of his talents, penchants, tendencies, abilities, vocations, and race of his ancestors.
>
> (Watson 1924: 104)

Not all theories of the child as a learner are developmental. For some theorists, learning is determined not by some internal biological plan but by the child's physical and social environment. Behaviourists argue that learning is driven by social and physical conditioning, not by innate psychological or biological structures. 'Give me the child, and I'll give you the man' is an oft-repeated statement that captures the key idea within behaviourism. This idea has a long heritage and is as persistent in popular culture as it is in child development.

Behaviourists are not developmentalists. Most of them believe that the same principles of learning apply to adults and children and that differences in what children and adults can know and do are due to differences in their opportunities to learn (Salkind 1981). They believe that nature (for example, genetics) limits learning rather than enabling it, as the Romantics and maturationists believe (Crain 1995: 221). As Murray Thomas (1985: 378) put it:

> Child development is a process of the growing individual's learning increasingly complex and refined ways of acting as a result of the consequences that have followed the behaviour she or he has attempted.

From a behaviourist perspective, culture determines learning: a learner is more likely to repeat a particular behaviour if adults or the environment reinforce it. As Mac Naughton and Williams (1998: 257) explained:

> When a child's behaviour is reinforced they are made stronger or more likely to occur through the use of rewards (or reinforcers). Rewards can be social, such as praise, or can be material, such as food (Spodek and Saracho, 1994). It is also possible to negatively reinforce a child's behaviour to make it less strong or less likely to occur. As a teaching technique reinforcement is, therefore, used to increase or decrease the likelihood of a child displaying a particular behaviour.

Crain (1985: 226) explained how this links to children's learning:

> Consider, for example, a baby girl who drops a block, hears the sound, and drops it again and again, making this new and interesting sound last. In Skinner's theory, the sound is a reinforcer which controls her behaviour. However, this reinforcer will soon lose its effectiveness, for she will soon become interested in more complex outcomes.

Watson, who initiated behaviourist thinking in 1913, believed that children should be treated as adults. He wrote in 1928:

> There is a sensible way of treating children. Treat them as though they were young adults. Dress them, bathe them with care and circumspection. Let your behaviour always be objective and kindly firm . . . Give them a pat on the head if they have made an extraordinary good job of a difficult task.
>
> (Watson 1928: 81–2)

Behaviourism is often split into classical behaviourism and social learning theory. The rest of this section examines classical behaviourism; the next section examines social learning theory.

Where have the ideas come from?

Enlightenment thinkers John Locke and Jean-Jacques Rousseau each influenced behaviourism, but there is debate about the extent of each one's influence. John Locke believed that we must teach children to dampen their desires and their tendency to frivolity, so that reason can prevail. In other words, we must teach children to conform to culture, rather than make culture conform to children's nature. Locke wrote: 'children should be used to submit to their desires and go without their longings even from the very cradle' (Locke 1693, cited in Cranton 1996: 240). Rousseau is credited with being committed to the child's nature, but Singer (1992) argued that Rousseau showed a behaviourist view of the child when he wrote:

Let your pupil always believe that he is the master, but in fact be the master yourself. No other subjection is so complete as that which keeps up the pretence of freedom; in such a way one can even imprison the will.

(Rousseau 1983, cited in Singer 1992: 39)

Locke's and Rousseau's ideas resonate in the work of early behaviourists such as Ivan Pavlov, a Russian physiologist who is often seen as the founder of modern behaviourism. Pavlov was studying how the digestive system works when he discovered accidentally that dogs salivate in anticipation of food. He described this as a conditioned response to a stimulus. John Watson developed Pavlov's ideas on the role of reinforcement in learning. The interest in behaviourism was part of scientists' quest to predict and thus control human behaviour and it arose at the time when scientific studies of the child were increasing. Behaviourism directly affected thinking in developmental psychology in the 1950s and 1960s in the USA. At that time, the USA was reeling from the launch in 1957 of the USSR's first satellite and sought to use early childhood education to 'catch up' in the space race. The result was an emphasis on young children's intellectual performance and a search for guaranteed ways to improve long-term outcomes for the nation (see Henniger 1999).

Implications of behaviourism for early childhood curriculum

Behaviourism has had a powerful influence on many early childhood educators' view of learning. The ideas that we conform to our culture as we learn, and that praise, positive rewards such as 'gold stars' or a special role in the classroom can reinforce positive behaviours and assist children's learning are widespread and persist in various forms, including:

- we can determine our future, irrespective of where and to whom we are born;
- our physical and social environments influence our learning;
- people of all ages learn in the same way;
- positive reinforcement such as praise can motivate learning;
- learning can be controlled;
- with the right reinforcement, we can learn anything.

More specifically, the adult directs the programme for children's learning through the use of rote learning and 'drill tasks' (Decker and Decker 1992: 35) and through the use of programmed study booklets, activity sheets, CD-ROMs and other highly structured materials. As Crain explained:

Adult direction is pervasive ... Although it must seem that children work independently on the booklets, in fact an adult (the program developer) has structured each small response.

(Crain 1995: 224)

'Conforming to culture' models of the learner imply some clear tasks to maximize the child's learning and chances of success in life. The educator needs to:

- Decide who we want the child to become or what we want the child to learn. For instance, learning appropriate social behaviours:

    the key to changing anti-social behaviour in young children is to identify the purpose of the behaviour and then teach and reinforce skills which achieve the same goal but in an acceptable fashion.

    (Slee 1998: 9)

- Choose reinforcers most appropriate to the child's learning goals. For instance:

    Time out is viewed as an efficient means of providing space and time for the young child to mull over wrongdoings, refresh feelings of guilt, and ponder socially desirable responses in similar circumstances. Consequently, time out appears to remain a popular technique because of the positive reinforcement received by the adult when administering time out to a misbehaving child.

    (Readdick and Chapman 2000: 81)

    Gold stars, best-student awards, honor roles, pizzas for reading, and other reward-focused incentives systems have long been part of the currency of schools.

    (Deci *et al.* 2001: 1)

    The reinforcement catalogue says that Emma likes a glass of juice and helping you in the kitchen – Here, have a sip of juice and then come and help me to lay the table.

    (Wagner *et al.* 1995: 98)

- Actively teach the child what we want them to learn. For instance:

    Never assume a child knows how to behave appropriately, and don't expect them to learn it from cues in their immediate environment. It is necessary to teach each skill of social interaction as one would teach an academic skill.

    (Slee 1998: 9)

- Construct an environment that directly and indirectly reinforces what we want the child to learn. For instance if you want children to stay focused on specific tasks you can develop a tight 'clock bound' (Decker and Decker 1992: 35) schedule that controls how long children can spend on particular tasks. Or if you want children to learn that only two children are allowed at the art table, set it up so only two chairs, two brushes, and so on, are present. Children can learn if you: 'Set up activities so that the number of children is automatically limited' (Stephen 1993: 7).

Many of these ideas and tasks underpin programmed and teacher-directed approaches to learning. Ideas summary 2.3 explores how you plan for time, materials, space and people if you take a behaviourist view of how children learn. As you review this summary, reflect on which of the planning implications you would feel comfortable with and which would discomfort you.

Ideas summary 2.3 Behaviourism: implications for planning of 'conforming to culture'

Key ideas:

- Culture controls learning.
- Learning happens through reinforcing physical, emotional, cognitive and psychological behaviours.
- Culture leads learning, nature is merely what we have to begin with.

Implications for planning:

MATERIALS

In programmed instruction:

- Learning is orderly, so materials must be chosen and carefully organized from the most simple to the increasingly complex.
- Students work independently and at their own pace, so materials must be self-correcting and reinforcing for the child. They must show the child what the right answer is.

More broadly:

- Children are encouraged to use materials in specific ways so that specific and intended learning occurs.
- Materials will be closed-ended rather than open-ended to ensure that there is only one right way for children to use them.
- Materials will be 'narrowly focused and unidimensional' (Decker and Decker 1992: 35), so that it is clear what the child is learning and how.

TIME

'Watson recommended that . . . parents place babies on rigid schedules, and he insisted that they refrain from hugging, kissing, or caressing their babies . . . (because it leads them to prefer parental company to exploring the world on their own)' (Crain 1995: 212).

Time and routines:

- will be structured to meet specific learning goals;
- will be individualized to meet individual learning goals.

Timing what children learn and when:

- will be organized by the adult;
- will allow children the time they need to move to the next step.

PEOPLE

The educator's job is to aid culture by:

- setting clear goals for the child's learning;
- structuring a clear, step-by-step programme to reach those goals;
- encouraging children to stay on task;
- reinforcing the child for each step and/or providing materials that act as reinforcers;
- designing learning for the child.

SPACE

- is structured to achieve the goals you set for the child;
- is arranged to reinforce the child.

It may be 'less roomy . . . calculated to focus children's attention and to avoid distractions. Areas within the room are clearly defined – often with high dividers' (Decker and Decker 1992: 35).

CONTENT

- Adults choose the goals and the content through which specific goals will be achieved.
- Adults strongly direct learning and thus they strongly direct the content of what is learned. This content will often be organized in traditional subject areas or topics for study.

Equity reflections

The behaviourist idea that social norms can be taught through reinforcement leads to an individualist approach to equity, in other words, one that makes each individual educator responsible for creating equity. If one individual can influence another's behaviour by reinforcing it, then individual educators can influence individual children's behaviour (for example, around gender) by reinforcing it. An individual educator seeking to create, for example, gender equity in their programme can do so by actively reinforcing non-traditional ways of being masculine and feminine. Conversely, individual educators who neglect or ignore their role as a gender role reinforcer face certain consequences, outlined by Hetherington and Parke:

> Even in the preschool years boys and girls are responded to differently by teachers. Although boys and girls are encouraged to engage in quiet activities rather than aggression and rough-and-tumble play, they receive more criticism from teacher and peers for cross-sex behaviours. Girls are less likely to receive criticism from teachers and peers for engaging in cross-sex play. However, pre-school teachers are more likely to instruct and respond to boys than to girls who are involved in task-oriented activities. It is not surprising that children tend to perceive school and school activities as feminine.
>
> (Hetherington and Parke 1986: 361)

Equity alerts
Three key equity alerts emerge from within behaviourism:

- Some commonly used ways of negatively reinforcing children for inappropriate behaviour, such as 'time out', may be difficult for children with little English as their first language to understand. Educators should be aware that children can misunderstand 'time out' and see it as rejection, be puzzled by why it is occurring and be uncertain and anxious about it (Readdick and Chapman 2000).

- Positive reinforcers selected by adults working with cultural and ethnic groups different to their own may be culturally inappropriate or offensive.

- The authoritarianism that is implicit within behaviourist approaches to teaching and learning may create fear and anxiety in young children who may not feel that they can meet prespecified objectives, and it may alienate them from learning.

Ideas clarification exercise 2.2 (*from Heather Lawrence*)

1 *Review the following summary of relationships* between educators and children. Would you add any additional features to this summary of relationships between educators and children in a behaviourist programme?

Ideas summary 2.4 Summary of relationships between educators and children in a behaviourist programme

A programme drawing on behaviourist ideas would have the following features:

The educator would:

- know best, and be charged with the responsibility of transmitting predetermined knowledge and measuring outcomes with the aim of having childen reach predetermined standards;
- teach children to follow the rules;
- teach children how to fit in;
- direct children's learning;
- teach toward curriculum goals;
- present and teach particular kinds of knowledge which can be measured by scientific and/or objective methods;
- refine the child to achieve predetermined goals;
- encourage independence and competence.

The child would be:

- needy;
- dependent;
- unrefined, not cultured;
- desirous and frivolous;
- deliberately oppositional, in other words, naughty;
- get bored easily;
- complying with rules set by teachers;
- competent within parameters set by teachers;
- learning what the teacher decides is important when he or she thinks it is important;
- socialized successfully in groups;
- always ready and interested in what the teacher wants to do when he or she wants to do it (for example, joining a story group with whole group);
- learning in a way which can be measured.

Equity reflections:

- teacher uses a conforming hat dominant cultural paradigm to meet curriculum goals;
- stereotypical images of gender, class and culture and race will be implicit within curriculum content;
- teacher will be a controller of learning using autocratic, authoritarian and behaviourist methods;
- teacher will be seen as the holder of all important knowledge;
- there will be high expectations of children's learning outcomes, behaviour and emotions (in other words, learning to separate from loved ones, fit in, comply and prepare for school).

---

2   *Read the following scenario* of relationships between educators and children. What did the teacher believe about Jessica's development? In what ways did the

teachers in this scenario draw on a behaviourist view of the child? What are the equity implications in this scenario for making meaningful relationships between the educators and Jessica?

Jessica fidgeted during a long story read in English. It contained quite difficult language. The teacher called her name on several occasions and asked her to 'concentrate'. Jessica continued to fiddle with the hair of a girl sat in front of her. Each time the teacher said Jessica's name, the children around her scowled at her. After a few more failed attempts at encouraging Jessica to concentrate, the teacher asked the assistant to take Jessica away from the story group. As the assistant led her away the assistant commented, 'She must want to go to the toilet'. On Jessica's return from the toilet, the story was finished and the session had finished. Jessica stood alone by the door. When the door opened Jessica's grandfather came in and held her in his arms speaking to her in Chinese.

Reflect on the following questions

- How would you feel and how would you behave if you had no choice and no control over your life?
- How would you feel if you were forced to say goodbye to a friend when you hadn't finished your conversation?
- How would you feel if you were made to eat food you didn't like every day?
- How would you feel if you were forced to do something which your parent taught you was not polite or acceptable behaviour?

Review the ideas of the behaviourists and attempt to complete Reflection sheet 2.1. Use the online and text resources at the end of this chapter to explore programmed instruction and the ideas of the behaviourists. For example, even if we can engineer and control learning, should we do so?

Reflection sheet 2.1 Reviewing the ideas of the behaviourists

Reflection points	To what extent do you agree with this idea?
Conforming to culture – key ideas	
Adults can teach children anything	
Learning is the same for people of all ages	
Reinforcement can change people's behaviours	

Conforming to culture: social learning theory

Key thinker	Definition
• Albert Bandura (1925–), Canada	Social: being with others (for example, learning through being with others).

The theory in overview

> Social learning theory is a natural outgrowth of the S–R (Stimulus–Response) learning tradition. It has retained the spirit of the behaviourist movement: the experimentally rigorous study of how basic learning occurs as a result of environmental forces. The spotlight, however, switched from a hungry rat pressing a bar to a child interacting with other people.
>
> (Miller 1983: 243)

Social learning theorists are behaviourists, in that they believe that reinforcement is key to learning, but they broaden reinforcement to include cognitive processes. They argue that much of our learning happens through observing and imitating our role models; and that modelling is at the heart of the socialization process through which we learn to be with others in our society. For instance, observing the consequences of another person's behaviour could be what Bandura called 'vicarious' reinforcement in our minds (Crain 1995). The idea that children learn through role modelling has been used to explain how children learn sex roles. As Crain explained: 'Children frequently learn, through observation, the behaviour of both sexes, however, they usually perform only the behaviour appropriate to their own sex because this is what they have been reinforced to do' (Crain 1995: 232).

Sex roles may be reinforced directly (in the classical behaviourist sense of rewards or punishments) or vicariously, when the child notes the social consequences of not conforming to sex role norms.

Social learning theories have been used to map and explain pro-social (socially orientated) behaviour in young children such as sharing, helping and cooperating; and anti-social behaviour such as aggression. In each case, reinforcers can be 'real' people acting as role models, and they can also be characters in the media, books, video games, CD-ROMs, and so on. As Bandura stated: 'One can get people to engage in almost any course of action by having such conduct exemplified' (Bandura 1977: 88).

As Statham (1986: 97) indicates, many attempts at non-sexist approaches to work with young children have relied heavily on social learning theory:

> Groups explored the effects of women's early conditioning; studies documented the sex role stereotyping evident in the media through content analyses of children's books, television programmes and advertisements; pressure was put on publishers to provide non-sexist guidelines for their authors; and specifically anti-sexist reading and teaching material was produced, often by women's groups.

Early childhood educators who espouse social learning theory direct children's development firmly. They see themselves as models for children's sex role learning and ensure that they offer non-sexist role models to the children by behaving in non-sexist ways, selecting non-sexist stories, songs, and so on, and reinforcing the children's non-sexist behaviour.

Where have the ideas come from?

Social learning theory developed from behavourist theory. Albert Bandura and Richard Walters, who were key in developing social learning theory, built from the work of the classic behaviourists but departed from their understanding of how individuals participate in the learning process. They believed, unlike the classical behaviourists, that the individual is:

> an active mediator who operates on the environment in accord with certain expectancies and contigencies, but with foresight or knowledge as to what the consequences of his or her behaviour might be even before the behaviour occurs.
>
> (Salkind 1982: 168)

They also departed from the classic behaviourist in their understanding of how learning was reinforced, believing that it could be reinforced indirectly and vicariously by the child themselves.

Implications of social learning theories for the early childhood curriculum

Social learning theories have had a powerful influence on many early childhood educators' view of how young children learn social roles and behaviours. The idea that children learn through watching others and imitating positive role models in their environment is core to much early childhood teaching. It rests on the principle that social roles and behaviours are caught and not taught. To learn, children need to be able to attend to a social role model, remember what they have done, be able to reproduce it and be motivated to do so (Salkind 1985). This means that:

- Early childhood educators need to be aware of the social behaviours that they engage in and ensure that they are those that they wish the children to emulate. For instance, modelling appropriate ways of resolving conflicts:

  > Children should witness adults compromising and negotiating. For example, adults can have minor arbitrations in front of the children: 'Since I have a cold, I'd rather not take the children out to the playground today. I'll go out tomorrow if you go out today.' Answered by, 'Okay! We sure don't want that cold to get worse!'
  >
  > (Schreiber 1999: 25)

- Early childhood educators need to ensure that they offer children positive role models from literature and everyday life. For instance, if you want children to display non-sexist behaviours: 'Men in childcare present good role models of men caring for children' (Powderly and Westerdale 1998: 9).

- Early childhood educators need to provide opportunities for children to observe what they are modelling and time to remember and practice it. This is particularly important, because the degree of frequency with which a child observes a behaviour influences whether or not they will imitate that behaviour. The more often a child observes a behaviour the more likely they are to imitate it (Salkind 1982).

- Early childhood educators need to be able to motivate young children to model them through acting as positive and enjoyable role models for the child. They can do this by building a strong and positive relationship with the child. The more intense a relationship is, the more likely it is that we will model the person in that relationship.

- Early childhood educators can change children's behaviour merely through modelling desired behaviours and so early childhood educators do not have to directly teach what they want children to know. For instance: 'From a social learning theory perspective, people are more likely to do as the others do' (Salkind 1982: 169); 'Children develop a sense of valuing the physical environment when this is modelled by adults' (Eaton and Shephard 1998: 13).

Many of these ideas and tasks underpin less teacher-directed approaches to learning. Ideas summary 2.5 explores how you plan for time, materials, space and people if you take a social learning view of how children learn. As you review this Ideas summary, reflect on which of the planning implications you would feel comfortable with and which would discomfort you.

Ideas summary 2.5 Social learning theory: implications for planning of 'conforming to culture'

Key ideas:

- culture controls learning;
- learning happens through modelling and imitation;
- culture leads learning, nature is merely what we have to begin with.

Implications for planning:

MATERIALS

- Materials will contain social role messages consistent with the educator's objectives for the children. For instance, they will model pro-social behaviours and non-sexist roles.
- Materials will be regularly vetted and chosen because of the role models offered to the children.

TIME

Time and routines:

- will be organized to allow the child time to observe adults as role models, modelling specific skills to the child.

Timing what children learn and when:

- the adult will actively model what he or she wishes the child to learn, and act as a social reinforcer of the learning.

PEOPLE

The educator's job is to aid culture by:

- setting clear goals for the child's learning;
- modelling behaviours linked to those goals;
- allowing children to imitate behaviours that the child has observed;
- acting as a social reinforcer for desired behaviours and skills modelled by the child.

SPACE

- is structured to allow the child to observe the educator as he or she models social and other behaviours for the child.

CONTENT

- Adults choose the goals and thus they control the content to be learned.
- Adults indirectly control the learning through modelling and thus the content is often what is being modelled by the adult.

Equity reflections

Social learning theory has influenced our understandings of how young children learn social roles – especially gender roles. Adherents to social learning theory apply the same learning principles to the learning of social roles (including gender roles) that they apply to learning in general (such as reinforcement, punishment, reward and observational learning). They believe that since children learn attitudes that directly reflect a culture's values, manipulating a child's environment creates the desired gender role outcomes. Within that general approach, however, modelling and imitation are regarded as crucial to learning gender roles. For instance:

> through observation, children learn behaviours associated with both parents. They learn these behaviours without any direct reinforcement because they see their parents as powerful, effective, and as having control over their rewards. For example, by watching their mother put on lipstick and perfume and observing their father tell her that she looks nice, both sons and daughters learn how to dress up. The daughter may be rewarded for 'acting cute', while the son may be disapprovingly told 'boys don't wear lipstick'.
>
> (Kessler and McKenna 1982: 276)

Children learn how to behave in gender-appropriate ways by modelling themselves on significant adults within their world and by imitating significant and attractive adults in their world (Nasper 1981; Honig 1983; Davies 1989). Mischel (1966, 1970) explained most comprehensively how children learn gender role and gender identity, and Kessler and McKenna summarize Mischel's work thus:

> . . . they begin to value gender 'appropriate' behaviours because they are rewarded and to devalue gender 'inappropriate' behaviours because they are punished or ignored. The child learns the label ('boy' or 'girl') appropriate to the

rewarded behaviours, and learns to apply that label to her/himself . . . Gender identity . . . is just another name for this self-label.

(Kessler and McKenna 1982: 276–7)

From this perspective, adults can create equity (for example, between genders) by modelling behaviours that they want children to imitate. Indeed, a significant portion of advice on how to achieve gender equity in early childhood has rested on this theory of the learner. Educators have been advised to:

- institute equal opportunities policies so that girls have equal access to teacher time, resources, educational experiences, playspaces and play materials (see, for example, Cuffaro 1975; Cohen and Martin 1976; Guttenberg and Bray 1976; Robinson and Hobson 1978);
- read non-sexist stories;
- model non-sexist behaviours.

For instance, in Australia, Elliot (1984) told early childhood educators that they could challenge children's sex role stereotypes by modelling non-sexist behaviours:

In order to provide positive role models for young children we must be seen by children as performing a wide variety of roles . . . Always be cautious when choosing curriculum materials to ensure they depict an approximately equal quantitative representation of male and female characters.

(pp. 20, 21)

Early childhood educators who adopt this approach to equity try to be non-discriminatory in their own behaviours, to select non-discriminatory stories, songs, and so on, and to reinforce children's non-discriminatory behaviours. Davies (1988) has called this approach to gender role learning an 'osmosis theory' because within it, individuals absorb gender 'through their pores' just by being in non-sexist circumstances. Learning happens automatically and unthinkingly and norms are 'caught', not taught.

Equity alerts
These approaches to equity ignore the possibilities that:

- gender norms can be resisted; but
- gender norms have power that make resistance problematic.

Social learning theory presents the child as learning passively (through reinforcement) to behave in gender-appropriate ways, and the social environment as a powerful director and controller of gender appropriate behaviours. Like classical behaviourism, it allows little room for the child actively to make choices and so it ignores the possibility that children may resist the role models and social expectations that they encounter. Here are a couple of instances of such resistance:

Resistance occurred at several levels. Some children resisted cleaning up and listening to stories; occasionally they succeeded. One interesting form of resistance occurred frequently when children rejected the attempts of teachers to engage them in activities in which they had little interest . . . The children clearly had an agenda for their play that did not include the teacher's literacy focus.

(Kessler and Hauser 2000: 67)

Most people, often as part of a group, oppose on a daily basis what they see as unfair authority or restrictions imposed by someone else. In school, this may take countless forms, such as girls resisting being viewed as sex objects, students in wheelchairs ganging up against those who tease them, or students living below the poverty line who refuse to obey middle class teachers with low expectations of them.

(Sleeter and Grant 1999: 195)

People wishing to resist the dominant gender norms must acknowledge that these norms are powerful. Connell (1987) argued that there are very real material and ideological constraints that make raising children in non-traditional ways difficult. For example, work with parents involved in non-sexist child rearing (Statham 1986) and writings by lesbian parents (Alpert 1988) indicate that parents who try to raise children in non-traditional ways can create difficulties for their children. Everyday matters such as birthday parties, what clothes to wear, what toys to play with and how to play become points of contention and difference with other adults, other children and one's own children – it's not easy being different!

Girls and boys cannot and do not freely choose to be non-sexist just because educators offer them the chance to do so. Their choices are constrained by what are considered the best ways to be a boy or a girl by their peers and by their wider social networks. Some ways of being a boy or a girl will be considered more desirable, more normal and more pleasurable than others. In addition, some ways of being a girl/boy or woman/man are more widely understood as normal than others. As Ramazanoglu (1992: 340) writes: 'It is not only that there are different ways of "doing masculinity", but that different masculinities stand in different relationships to power'.

Therefore, understanding children's choice of gender roles involves under-standing the power effects of different ways of being female and male. We will return to this point in Chapter 4, with feminist poststructuralist views of how emotion, power and desire are linked to gendered practices. These views suggest that:

teachers need to do more than just role-model desirable gender behaviours or provide environments that present alternative gender images and messages to young children. Instead, teachers need to actively engage in the complex pro-cesses through which young children negotiate and produce gendered cultural meanings, so that teachers' understandings of gender identity become part of young children's experience in their classroom.

(Hughes and Mac Naughton forthcoming)

Ideas clarification exercise 2.3 (*from Heather Lawrence*)

1 *Read the following scenario of relationships* between educators and children. What did the teacher believe about Su's development? In what ways did the teachers in this scenario draw on a behaviourist view of the child? What are the equity implications in this scenario for making meaningful relationships between the educators and Su?

> A Chinese child, named Su, did not want to be leader in a game of follow the leader. The teacher planned an objective for her to take the role of leader because she believed it was important for children to experience a sense of leadership. The teacher took the child by the hand and led her to the front and modelled being a leader for the child by walking with her for a short time, and then letting go of her hand. Su began to whimper and held her head cast down towards the floor. In an irritated voice the teacher sent Su to sit back on the mat where she sat with her head hung for the rest of the 'mat session'.

2 *Reflect on the following responses by children to educators.* To what extent might these behaviours be a response to children being required to conform to rules?

- children behave in oppositional ways to the educator by being subversive and overtly aggressive and challenging;
- children refuse to comply with rules;
- children cry for attention;
- children do not separate from parents happily;
- children from culturally and linguistically diverse backgrounds spend time outside of many play situations.

Further reading and online resources

The reading lists that follow act as a guide to two forms of additional material: general introductions to the theories covered in this chapter, and material of a more difficult level on the same topic.

General child development texts and overviews

Berk, L. (1994) *Child Development*, 3rd edn. Boston, MA: Allyn and Bacon.
Boulton-Lewis, G. and Catherwood, D. (eds) (1994) *The Early Years: Development, Learning and Teaching*. Melbourne: Australian Council for Educational Research.
Keenan, T. (2001) *An Introduction to Child Development*. London: Paul Chapman Publications.
Miller, P.H. (1993) *Theories of Developmental Psychology*, 3rd edn. New York: Freeman.
Thomas Murray, R. (1992) *Comparing Theories of Child Development*, 3rd edn. California: Wadsworth Publishing.

Rousseau and Romanticism

Jean-Jacques Rousseau. An introduction to his writing with links to key texts and summaries of them. Some e-texts of his work can be accessed via links from this site: http://www2.lucidcafe.com/lucidcafe/library/96jun/rousseau.html

Gesell and maturationism

The Gesell Institute of Human Development. This homepage has background information on Gesell's work and links to books and research based on Gesell's theories: http://www.gesellinstitute.org/

Thelen, E. and Adolph, K. (1992) Arnold L. Gesell: the paradox of nature and nurture, *Developmental Psychology*, 28(3): 368–80.

Behaviourism

Homepage of the B.F. Skinner Foundation. This has extensive links to publications and summaries of his work: http://www.bfskinner.org/

Social learning theory

Albert Bandura. An introduction to his work with links to additional resources on his work. The PSI Café: A Psychology Resource Site: http://psy.pdx.edu/PsiCafe/KeyTheorists/Bandura.htm

Albert Bandura: Personality theories: http://www.ship.edu/~cgboeree/bandura.html

Reflections on equity in child development theory

Grieshaber, S. and Cannella, G.S. (eds) (2001) *Embracing Identities in Early Childhood Education: Diversity and Possibilities*. New York: Teachers College Press.

New, R. (1994) Culture, child development and DAP, in B. Mallory and R. New (eds) *Diversity and Developmentally Appropriate Practice*. New York: Teachers College Press.

Stone, J. (1996) Developmentalism: an obscure but pervasive restriction on educational improvement, *Education Policy Analysis Archives*, 4(8): 1–21.

3

Models of the learner: reforming through interaction between nature and culture

This chapter introduces you to the views and ideas of those who see the child as reforming through interaction between nature and culture.

Definitions

- *Reforming*: improving something through changing it (for example, improving ways of thinking through changing them).

- *Interaction*: relations between things, in which each influences the other (for example, relations between a child's mind and the environment, in which each influences the other).

Three schools of thought share the belief that the key to young children's learning lies in how we respond to the tense interaction between nature and culture:

- constructivism;
- psychodynamics;
- neuroscience.

Constructivism

Key thinkers

- Jean Piaget (1896–1980), Swiss theorist of intellectual development
- Lev Vygotsky (1893–1934), Russian theorist of socio-cultural learning
- Jerome Bruner (1915–), American psychologist

Definition

Construction: something that is built or made (for example, ideas or knowledge that are built or made by the child).

The theory in overview

> Constructivism's central idea is that human learning is constructed, that learners build new knowledge upon the foundations of previous learning. This view of learning sharply contrasts with one in which learning is the passive transmission of information from one individual to another, a view in which reception, not construction, is key.
>
> (SEDL 1996: 1)

From this view of how we learn comes the idea that we come to new understandings of the world by building on what we already know and that we are active in learning. In other words, we learn through our own actions of taking in information, working with that information and turning that information into new understandings or linking it with what we know. These processes of taking in and working with information are internal cognitive processes that we control as individuals.

The explanations of the precise ways in which we take in and work with information from our external world differs among the constructivists. They all tend to agree that we are born with some internal 'maps' or 'structures' in our mind that make it possible for us to take in and then to rework information into new knowledge and/or new ways of thinking in the world. They also tend to agree that for those processes to occur and for new ways of thinking to grow, we must have direct experience in the world. For some constructivists, we need lots of help from our social world to build new knowledge (social and cultural constructivists) and new ways of thinking; for others, we need time by ourselves to do it for ourselves (individual constructivists).

Where have the ideas come from?

Constructivist theories can be likened to members of a large extended family with several 'branches'. Each branch is linked to the others through common theoretical 'genes' but each also has its own look and feel. Each branch of the family arises from a different philosophical tradition with different political and pedagogical implications. The constructivist family has a long pedigree and its members include Jean Piaget and Lev Vygotsky. As Hanley explained:

> Constructivism is not a new concept. It has its roots in philosophy and has been applied to sociology and anthropology, as well as cognitive psychology and education. Perhaps the first constructivist philosopher, Giambatista Vico commented in a treatise in 1710 that 'one only knows something if one can explain it' (Yager 1991). Immanual Kant further elaborated this idea by asserting that human beings are not passive recipients of information. Learners actively take knowledge, connect it to previously assimilated knowledge and make it theirs by constructing their own interpretation.
>
> (Hanley 1994)

These philosophers believed that learning is meaningful if we own it – we must make it our own. With such a long history, it is not surprising that many branches of the family have evolved, but all the branches share the belief that learning is an individual pursuit of truth about our world and how it works, and that we learn something as we produce new knowledge and understandings about it that we know are true or accurate.

Jean Piaget is often described as the founder of constructivism. He is sometimes known as a cognitive interactionist and sometimes as an individual constructivist. The reasons for these labels will become clear shortly. Piaget was born in Switzerland in 1896, trained as a biologist and eventually studied logic, psychopathology, epistemology and the philosophy of science. His interest after these studies was in why children repeatedly gave incorrect answers on intelligence tests and he spent over 50 years studying children's cognitive development. He suggested that internal cognitive structures or ways of organizing information enable us to act on and make sense of the world in different ways. The structures are organized in a hierarchy in which each structure comes into play only in response to our experiences and/or age. Each new structure involves us organizing information in different ways, and our progress through the hierarchy of structures leads us to increasingly 'adult' or abstract ways of thinking, feeling and being.

Most cognitive interactionists believe that this innate, sequential hierarchy of internal cognitive structures drives our learning, although they give different weight to the environment's influence on our progress through that hierarchy. Consequently, adults play a relatively non-directive role in a child's learning. This was the case for Piaget, who believed that our biology was determining what we could know and that it was our biological adaptation to our environment that drove cognitive development.

Piaget believed that we learn about the world in two ways: we assimilate new knowledge that strengthens our existing knowledge; and we accommodate new knowledge that challenges our existing knowledge. Children drive assimilation and accommodation through physically manipulating their environment in active learning and in 'learning by doing'. As they do so, each one passes through four stages of intelligence: sensorimotor (0–2 years of age), preoperational (2–6 years of age), concrete operational (6–11 years of age), formal operational (11 years of age). He believed that movement between each stage of thinking was driven by maturation, experience, social interaction and the bringing together ('equilibration') of these three to create new ways of thinking (Miller 1993).

While Piaget is generally held to focus more on the individual's own role in this process (hence he is called an individual constructivist), he did also place emphasis on the place of language and social factors in it. He wrote of the process of reaching equilibration: 'The symbolism of individual images fluctuates far too much to lead to this result. Language is therefore necessary, and thus we come back to social factors' (Piaget 1995: 154). He believed that individuals alone cannot come to symbolic thought because language is essential to it and language is essentially gained through social interaction (Becker and Varelas 2001).

Lev Vygotsky, a Russian psychologist working in the early part of the twentieth century, is often referred to as a social constructivist. He believed that learning 'cannot be forced on the child from the outside' (Vygotsky 1929: 421). To that extent, Vygotsky shared with Piaget and others a belief that inner psychological structures control our learning. He also agreed with Piaget that the ways in which children and adults think are different. However, he also believed that the external environment, especially the social environment, was a key instructor, guiding and challenging the child to learn new and different ways of thinking. In particular, language was seen as a key tool for learning.

Vygotsky used the term 'zone of proximal development' (ZPD) to describe the gap between a child's capacity to achieve results with and without skilled (adult) support. Consequently, a Vygotskyan educator prioritizes learning with others and provides activities that challenge the child at the upper level of their ZPD. This process of the adult challenging a child at the upper level of their ZPD is often talked of as the adult 'scaffolding' the child's learning.

As Lambert and Clyde (2000) point out, Vygotsky's ideas were influenced by classical behaviorism and by Marxism, and for this reason some would see him as taking the position on how children learn of 'conforming to culture'. However, Vygotsky's work has been used as a basis for taking a interactive approach to thinking about children's learning and for this reason he has been placed here.

Vygotsky's idea of the role of scaffolding in learning developed from the work of another key constructivist, Jerome Bruner (see Lambert and Clyde 2000). Jerome Bruner was an American psychologist who wrote about children's cognition. He, like Vygotsky and Piaget, strongly believed that we actively construct our own knowledge and that we learn through problem solving. Trial and error in the real world was seen by each as central to our capacity to construct knowledge. Bruner also strongly believed that play was a risk-free way in which children could test out the world and engage in trial and error learning: 'play provides an excellent opportunity to try combinations of behaviour that would, under funcational pressure, never be tried' (Bruner 1972: 693).

Piaget and Bruner also shared a strong belief in the need for young children to be able to use their five senses in exploring the world, thus building new ways of thinking about it. Bruner was instrumental in the move from the then dominant behaviourist ways of thinking about children to a more cognitive-orientated focus in the 1950s and 1960s.

Implications of constructivism for early childhood curriculum

Constructivism has had a powerful influence on how many early childhood educators see learning. The ideas that children can construct their own meanings and that self-discovery or guided discovery can assist in this process are core to much contemporary thinking about early childhood. Consider the following statements made by early childhood professionals in the last 30 years:

- From a 1970s Australian early childhood curriculum text: 'Thinking proceeds from perceptual to conceptual understanding but does not necessarily proceed directly. The child requires time for his own personal construction of experience' (Solomon 1976: 44).
- From a 1980s UK early childhood text: 'Learning is an active process and it is done by the learner . . . You cannot make a child learn' (Laishley 1983: 66).

- From a 1990s Australian early childhood text: 'This approach [developmentally appropriate curriculum] capitalises on children's innate desire to experiment, manipulate and interact with their environment' (Ebbeck 1991: 33–4).

The idea that we can and do reform through our interactions with our culture persist as these views:

- children can construct their own meanings;
- active involvement is necessary to learning;
- problem solving and trial and error learning are important to cognitive development;
- internal cognitive structures make learning possible.

The Piagetian 'reforming through interactions between nature and culture' position on learning implies some clear tasks that maximize the child's learning and chances of success in life:

- allow the child time to discover and construct their own meanings;
- construct an environment that helps the child's open-ended discovery of meaning.

Piaget's ideas led to specific recommendations for educators about what their role should be at each stage of cognitive development. It was to understand the specific nature of the difference in children's thinking at each stage and to work with that:

> The teacher's job then is not so much to transmit facts or concepts to the child, but to get him to act on both physical and mental levels. These actions – far more than imposed facts or concepts – constitute real knowledge.
> (Ginsburg and Opper 1969: 222)

Piaget believed that educators should create the right environment for learning but then allow the child to problem solve and to learn through their own active discovery. The adult attends to the unfolding of these structures and provides social and physical environments that encourage a child's normal development. As Crain explained:

> For Piaget . . . true learning is not something handed down by the teacher, but something that comes from the child. It is a process of active discovery . . . Accordingly, the teacher should not try to impose knowledge on the child, but he or she should find materials that will interest and challenge the child and then permit the child to solve problems on his or her own.
> (Crain 1980, in Moncadu 1984: 32)

Consequently, a Piagetian educator prioritizes individual learning experiences in their daily work with children, whereas an educator who believes that learning is motivated and produced through the social environment will prioritize group experiences in their programme. As Henniger put it:

> In a constructivist learning environment, the child creates rather than receives knowledge, and the teacher guides or facilitates this process of discovery. Unlike a traditional classroom where the teacher might lecture or perform demonstrations in front of a group of passive students, the students in a constructivist classroom actively learn by doing.
>
> (Henniger 1999: 40)

Bruner's work also supported the idea that children need to actively interact with their environment to make sense of it. The key to successful education of the young child, for Bruner was the educator's capacity to match materials and experiences to the child's current level of cognitive functioning and to extend the child beyond this.

Ideas summary 3.1 explores how you plan for time, materials, space and people if you adhere to a Piagetian 'reforming through interactions between nature and culture' view of how children learn. As you review this Ideas summary, reflect on which of the planning implications you would feel comfortable with and which would discomfort you.

Ideas summary 3.1 Constructivism: implications for planning of 'reforming through interactions between nature and culture'

Key ideas:

- children learn by doing in the real world with concrete objects;
- children learn best when experiences are matched to and extend their current levels of understanding and skill.

Implications for planning:

MATERIALS

- are real world objects that the child can explore and manipulate;
- are diverse, so that the child can explore diverse representations of reality.

TIME

- is organized to allow time to explore and manipulate the physical world (Piaget);
- is organized to allow the educators to act as guides to learning, rather than as transmitters of knowledge.

PEOPLE

The educator's job is to:

- focus on child-centred learning;
- emphasize facilitating learning, rather than direct teaching;
- guide, stimulate and challenge thinking, rather than using rote learning to teach new thinking;
- be a co-learner with the child, rather than an expert who the child learns from.

SPACE

- is organized to support self-discovery learning and learning by trial and error;
- is organized to allow the educators to act as guides to learning, rather than as transmitters of knowledge.

CONTENT
- is individualized to support and extend individual children's ways of thinking;
- emphasizes cognitive processes rather, than content;
- is selected on the basis of student interest;
- is presented in a holistic, cross-disciplinary way through projects and topics, rather than through specific subjects.

Equity reflections

Constructivist models of the learner generate several interconnected ideas about diversity and equity:

- a child's cognitive stage of development will influence how and what they can understand about diversity and equity;
- a child's understandings of diversity and equity are inaccurate;
- a child's understandings of diversity and equity naturally become more accurate as they develop the capacity for rational and abstract thought.

Piaget believed (from exploring children's 'incorrect' answers to intelligence tests) that children think differently to adults. Children's thinking is emotional and context bound, whereas adults' thinking is rational and abstract. Consequently, constructivists believe that our way of thinking progresses from 'child-like' (emotional and context bound) to the more desired and correct 'adult-like' (logical and abstract) through a series of stages that are universal (in other words, applicable to everyone, irrespective of the culture or the time in which they live). To explore the implications of these ideas for equity, we will examine research on 'race' and young children, and on gender and young children.

Children's constructions of 'race'

Fifty years of international research on 'race' has shown consistently that young children can and do demonstrate racial prejudice (Doyle and Aboud 1995; Hirschfeld 1995) from as young as 3 years of age (Black-Gutman and Hickson 1996). For instance, both black children and white children consistently show a positive bias towards 'whiteness' and a negative bias towards 'blackness'. More specifically:

- black children consistently choose white dolls as their preferred doll to play with and as the most pretty doll (Gopaul-McNicol 1995);
- both black and white children showed a bias towards lighter skins (Averhart and Bigler 1997);
- both black and white children showed racial preference towards being white (Kelly and Duckitt 1995; Johnson 1996).

These findings have generally been explained from within a Piagetian framework and the explanations have emphasized that young children's cognitive incapacities produce these behaviours. For instance, 22 out of the 24 pieces of recent research on this topic from North America, Australia and Europe linked children's attitudes to racial and ethnic difference to:

- their inability to hold multiple perspectives; and
- their inability to conserve their natural need to sort and classify objects and people (see Black-Gutman and Hickson 1996).

From a 'Western', Piagetian standpoint on cognition, preschool children cannot view other 'races' as acceptable or desirable, so they become biased. As children's capacity to take multiple perspectives and to conserve grows, bias decreases. Bias also decreases as children begin to see other 'races' as similar to their own and to see differences between individuals of the same 'race'. From this standpoint, bias is a developmental phenomenon that naturally disappears as these skills develop in each individual child (Mac Naughton 2001).

Children and gender development

Cognitive interactionism also emphasizes the child's role in shaping their own gendering experiences. Kohlberg developed a detailed theory of gender development based on Piagetian theory and argued that children learn gender roles through the interaction between cultural patterns and innate cognitive structures. As Honig indicates: 'this means that children construct sex role concepts on the basis of individual experience with their own bodies and with their social environments' (1983: 59).

Within this theoretical account, children develop sex role attitudes and behaviours as a consequence of the interaction between biology, socializing forces and their own developing cognitive capacities. Children actively try to make sense of their own worlds, but their ability to do so is limited by pre-existing and developing cognitive structures. Children are influenced by the nature of the expectations placed on them to behave in particular ways as boys and girls. Their gender learning reflects the language they learn, the meanings of the words 'boy', 'girl', 'male', 'female', and the symbols they learn to associate with them through literature, songs and stories. However, they also interpret these expectations in their own ways and make their own choices about the expectations to which they will and won't conform. Smith states this position clearly:

> Children do not react passively to adult encouragement of stereotyped sex roles. The work of Kohlberg, Lewis, and Maccoby supports the notion that children use their observations to construct a set of roles which they then use to govern their own behaviour.
>
> (1982: 32)

So a constructivist perspective links an individual child's cognitive development with their learning about gender identity, ethnic identity and the diversity of others. This perspective leads educators to adopt a 'business as usual' approach to equity, because it is consistent with the following understandings and practices:

- children's negative statements about ethnic and 'racial' diversity or other forms of social diversity represent just a stage that children pass through;
- children's understandings are 'natural' for their stage of development;
- educators only raise equity and diversity issues when the child is cognitively ready to deal with the concepts involved.

Equity alerts

Constructivists' developmental approach to cognition can be challenged with the following arguments, which we will examine in turn:

- power relations affect which meanings we are able to construct;
- children's and adults' ways of thinking are equally correct;
- developmental stages in thinking always exist in specific times and cultures;
- so-called universal theories generally benefit those in power.

First, power relations affect which meanings we are able to construct. Critical constructivists (whose ideas are looked at in more detail in Chapter 4) believe that we cannot construct any meanings that we like because power relations get in the way of meaning construction (Young 1990). Until power relations are removed between people the meanings we construct will always be culturally distorted and affected by who has the power to construct meaning in the world. For critical constructivists, individuals construct meaning in ways that are mediated by their culture and the power relations embedded in it (Mac Naughton forthcoming). Thus, the meanings we construct are often associated with those who have the most power within our culture to articulate and circulate meanings (see, for example, Friere 1970; McCarthy 1979; Mezirow 1981). In other words, children make sense of objects, sounds, movements and smells in and through the power relations of their particular culture, including:

- Relations between genders. The different power that specific boys, men, girls and women exercise in different early childhood programmes affects what meanings children construct. For example, if a girl is in a classroom dominated by traditionally gendered boys, her way of seeing the world as a girl is unlikely to predominate.
- Relations between ethnic and cultural groups. The different power that different ethnic groups exercise in different early childhood programmes affects what meanings children construct. For example, if a child is from an indigenous back-ground is in a classroom dominated by Anglo-Australians, it will be hard for the indigenous child to have his or her ways of understanding the world dominate classroom life.

Karl Marx captured the idea that individuals, culture, meaning and power are intimately connected and inseparable in his famous statement that, 'men make their own history, but not under conditions of their own choosing'. We can paraphrase this statement and say that, 'children make their own meanings, but not under conditions of their own choosing'. Instead, meanings are distorted, limited and silenced by the conditions in which meaning-making takes place.

Critical constructivists would argue that if we want to understand how children make sense of themselves and others and if we want to understand what makes learning possible, we must understand the conditions that limit particular children's sense-making. Borrowing from Bloch (2000: 275), we must understand:

> the power of the power/knowledge relationships that regulate and administer freedom, limiting and defining who is to be included and who to be excluded from participation. While the power/knowledge relations are productive in that they define how we think and act, they have negative effects through the exclusionary understandings we come to take as normal, through the divisions and differentiations we take as truth.

Critical theorists such as the critical constructivists reject the idea that meaning, knowledge and, therefore, learning is a uniquely individual, value-free cognitive pursuit. Instead, they believe that knowledge and thus learning are always social and always embody ethics, values and politics. They are always accomplished within a dynamic of power and the specific conditions that produce that dynamic will inevitably produce much of what is constructed and learned. If we don't look for whose knowledge is being included and excluded in our classrooms we become ignorant of the inequalities and injustices that are produced in our culture and in our ignorance perpetuate them.

The second challenge to constructivists' views is the argument that children's and adults' ways of thinking are equally correct. Scholars such as Burman (1994) and Cannella (1997) believe that developmental approaches to children's thinking imply that logical, adult ways of thinking are superior to those of the child. Sloan Cannella put her concerns in the following statement:

> Child development theories have fostered dominant ideologies and created privilege for those in power. Examples include the establishment of hierarchical stages and the privileging of logical thought.
>
> (Cannella 1997: 63)

The third challenge is the argument that developmental stages in thinking always exist in specific times and cultures. The notion of a universal theory of how we think has been strongly challenged. For example, Viruru and Cannella (2001) offered several different ways in which children in India could be understood. They describe their work as, 'a complex, alternative postcolonial picture, a perspective that challenges the positivist focus on human nature as progressing toward logical reasoning' (p. 163).

Several questions also arise about how cultural differences in thinking occur. For instance, if the stages of progress towards adult ways of thinking are universal, then how can we account for different ways of thinking about the world in different cultures? Is abstract and logical thought the pinnacle of thinking universally? What

cultures who value spiritual and emotional ways of thinking? Does
se cultures have not yet 'grown' fully?
staged, hierarchical ways of thinking about cognition and learning
n which shifts in our understandings as both children and adults are
ound and culturally specific. Indeed, to make sense of, represent and
assess ..... ways of knowing and understanding requires more than just theories
of development. For instance, we might understand, represent and assess a child's
capacity to construct by using theories of architecture, structural engineering or 3D
arts, rather than theories of cognitive development. Similarly, our understandings of
a child's capacity to build relationships with others might be enriched or altered using
anthropological, sociological and feminist theories. These other ways of knowing the
child can offer a richer and more complex picture of how a child is coming to know,
to understand and to live in their world. This doesn't require us to become experts
in anthropology or architecture, but it does entail recognizing the limitations
and problems of basing our decision-making solely on staged-based developmental
theories of the child, such as constructivism (Mac Naughton forthcoming).

Finally, the constructivists' so-called universal theory of cognitive development
privileges those on whose way of thinking the theory is based. For instance, Cannella
and Grieshaber argue that the development of universal theories of thinking by white,
middle class Western men (for example, Piaget) has meant that other ways of thinking
have been devalued and that, 'people of color, women, and minorities in various
contexts have been labeled as deficient, lacking in skills and irrational' (Cannella and
Grieshaber 2001: 179).

Woodhead (1999) discusses the difficulties within universal accounts of child
development at length and highlights how many concepts such as independence,
separation, individual development and autonomy are culturally specific. He draws on
Edwards in his argument:

> For example, in Zinacantan, Mexico . . . The transition from infancy to early
> childhood is not typified by resistant toddlers demanding and asserting control
> over toileting and other self-help skills . . . but instead by watchful, imitative
> children who acquire toilet training and other elements of self-care with a
> minimum of 'fuss'.
>
> (Edwards 1995, in Woodhead 1999: 11)

Similar cultural differences have been noted in several areas of children's development. For instance, there have been differences identified in how children in Spain
and the Netherlands manage conflict (Sanchez Medina *et al.* 2001).

Ideas clarification exercise 3.1 (*from Heather Lawrence*)

1   *Read the following scenario of relationships between educators and children.* What
    did the teacher believe about the baby's development? Did the teachers in
    this scenario draw on a constructivist view of the child? What are the equity
    implications in this scenario for making meaningful relationships between the
    educators and the baby?

A baby was placed on the veranda of a childcare centre. Although the baby cried, the teachers decided that the baby needed to learn to be alone to become independent so the baby was left there for some time.

2 *Review the following summary of relationships between educators and children.* Would you add any additional features to this summary of relationships between educators and children in a constructivist programme at this stage?

Ideas summary 3.2 Summary of relationships between educators and children in a constructivist programme

A programme drawing on constructivist ideas would have the following features:

The educator would:

- observe and facilitate children's learning;
- support and guide the development of new learning;
- provide a creative learning environment;
- see children as active participants in their own learning;
- believe that children learn through doing, especially through play;
- use open-ended materials where there is no right or wrong way to play;
- believe that children can contribute differently at different ages and stages of development to the curriculum;
- focus on intellectual performance as indicators of healthy development and well-being.

The child would:

- develop at an ever-increasing rate that is possible to measure;
- be independent and competent at each stage of development;
- be able to be shaped through interaction with the environment and relationships with adults;
- learn through his or her senses;
- develop through stages and within areas of development which can be compart-mentalized and worked with by teachers;
- be a social being;
- learn in open-ended environments with adults directing and facilitating play so that children have optimal conditions for learning.

Equity reflections:

- staff value individual differences, but may not respond to these in culturally appropriate ways;
- there may be cultural differences in how parents and children understand individual learning and its place in the curriculum.

---

3 *Consider the following questions and what your answers might imply for relationships between adults and children.* To what extent are they consistent with an individual, social or critical constructivist position on learning?

- How can respectful relationships be developed if teachers see the aim of learning as achieving stages determined by a particular world view of development across identified domains? For example, feelings of self-esteem are connected to a sense of feeling good about ourselves, having confidence and independence.

How does it feel for children who come from families where they value decision making on the basis of the greater good of the family? How does it feel for a child to be forced to take up roles the teacher sees as displaying confidence when it would be seen in their own culture as rude and impolite or arrogant to behave in such ways?

- Who decides what independence looks like and in whose interests is it when children become independent?

- How can equitable relationships be formed with children developing at different rates when stages identified are seen by teachers as standards to be reached by a particular age?

4 *Review the ideas of the constructivists* and attempt to complete Reflection sheet 3.1. Use the online and text resources at the end of this chapter to explore their ideas further.

Reflection sheet 3.1 Reviewing the constructivists

Reflection points	To what extent do you agree with this idea?
Reforming through interaction between nature and culture – key ideas.	
Children can learn through active interaction.	
Children need direct experience of the world to learn new ways of thinking.	
Children learn through trial and error. Is nature or nurture more dominant in that interaction?	

Psychodynamics

Key thinkers	Definitions
• Sigmund Freud (1856–1939), Austrian neurologist.	Psyche: the mind (for example, the mind of the child).
• John Bowlby (1907–), British animal behaviour scientist.	Dynamic: a potent and energizing force (for example, a potent and energizing force for developing into adults).
• Erik Erikson (1902–94), German-born developmental theorist working in the USA.	Psycho: relating to the mind (for example, psychodynamic: potent and energizing forces relating to the mind).

The theory in overview

Much writing about how young children learn emphasizes the role of thinking. Psychodynamic theorists look at the place of emotion in learning and explored the extent to which our 'thinking life' and our 'feeling life' are interconnected.

> The achievements of the mind draw upon, and contribute to, a young child's emotional and social development. A baby's delighted laughter, while kicking her legs to make the crib mobile shake, reveals the powerful emotional incentives that drive her to understand, experience and master the world.
>
> (Thompson 2001: 25)

Where have the ideas come from?

The idea that pleasure, desire and emotion are powerful motivators of learning and that they drive our actions and interactions with others is not new. For instance, Sigmund Freud believed that what he called the 'pleasure principle' drives us from birth to satisfy our basic needs and instincts – from our desire for food to our desire for love (Miller 1993). To do this, we engage in a cycle of feeling a need, seeking to meet it and feeling satisfied once it is met (Salkind 1981).

Freud worked in Vienna during the late 1890s and early 1900s building a theory of our psyche and its role in our emotional life. His theory of the psyche was dynamic, structuralist and developmental. This means that he believed that the unconscious and conscious minds (psyche) were a significant force (dynamic) in our personality development, that they were organized through internal, biologically determined structures (frameworks) that moved us from child-like ways of understanding and feeling in the world to adult-like ways of understanding and feeling. He believed that the early years were critical to the formation of our personality and that it developed in stages. We move through stages of attempting to satisfy key biological needs: oral (first year of life), anal (1 to 3 years of age), phallic (3 to 5 years of age), latency (middle childhood) and genital (adolescence).

Our movement from one stage to the other is biologically determined, but we can move from one psycho-sexual stage to the next with 'unfinished business' and with 'remnants' of a previous stage in our current one (Miller 1993: 126). How we resolve our needs in each stage determines how we will feel about ourselves and our relationships with others; and any unresolved needs can haunt a person throughout the rest of their life (Miller 1993). For Freud, development is a troubled process in which maturational forces such as physical and hormonal changes (often unconsciously generated) produce needs that lead to internal conflicts and to external frustrations as we try to meet them. Failure to meet our needs creates a sense of personal inadequacy (Miller 1993). In all of this, emotions directly affect our thinking and, thus, what we learn, under what conditions we can learn and who will learn best.

Other theorists have linked Freud's work more strongly to understandings of young children and their sense of self. Erik Erikson moved away from Freud's focus on the role of inner biological structures in constructing personality and focused instead on the role of society in personality development and in our capacity to build an identity for ourselves. For these reasons, Erikson is often referred to as a psycho-social theorist. Erikson expanded on Freudian theory and emphasized the importance of social interactions in our capacity to resolve a series of eight psycho-social crises that are essential to psychological growth and identity formation. In early childhood, these crises include: trust versus mistrust of others; autonomy versus shame and doubt; initiative versus guilt; and industry versus inferiority. Each stage builds on the previous stage and influences what happens next. As Hendrick (1990: 173) writes of Erikson and his influence on curriculum in early childhood:

> A second fundamental goal of curriculum for the emotional self is encouraging the child to be trustful, independent, and able to reach out and investigate her world. [Erikson] . . . has made a valuable contribution to our understanding of the significance of these attitudes in the emotional life of the child and how to encourage their development.

Anna Freud (1895–1982) was Sigmund Freud's youngest daughter. She drew heavily on her father's work to build her own approach to child psychology and she mapped children's social and emotional development through extensive experience of working with young children from emotionally deprived and socially disadvantaged families. She worked directly in early childhood education when she established the Hampstead War Nursery in London during the Second World War. It fostered children of single-parent families. Her work focused strongly on attachment theory and building sound attachments in emotionally deprived and socially disadvantaged children. She highlighted in her work the importance of children having continuity in relationships with key caregivers to reach a point of emotional self-reliance; and the need for young children to have time to work through their emotional stresses (Singer 1992).

Implications of psychodynamics for early childhood curriculum

The importance of psychodynamic theory for educators was the idea that children needed to be able to work through each of their psychic crises to become emotionally self-reliant and emotionally healthy. For educators, this meant that they could and should play a role in providing environments for young children that help them to successfully resolve each crisis. This meant that educators must:

- help the child's safe separation from home;
- be trustworthy;
- allow the child some independence;
- encourage children's exploration;
- allow for self-expression;
- offer praise for children's accomplishments.

There were several ways in which the early childhood programme could act as a therapeutic space for the child in resolving their emotional crises and thus support their healthy socio-emotional development.

First, it could provide avenues for the safe release of negative emotions by allowing the child to play out their negative emotions and troubles, especially concerning stresses at home. The home corner (or wendy corner) became identified as a key place in which children could do this. For instance, if there was a new baby in the family that a child felt resentful towards, they could express their negative feelings and thus gain mastery over them by playing babies in the home corner (Henniger 1999).

> Teachers need to recognize that emotionally tinged play often deals with the less pleasant aspects of children's daily and fantasy lives (e.g. death, destruction, evil figures such as witches, monsters, and ghosts) . . . Voicing fears and fantasies, trying out alternative strategies in dealing with them, and discovering solutions are steps that children can negotiate in play that will have emotional, as well as cognitive, payoffs.
>
> (Curry and Bergen 1978, in Hendrick 1990: 171)

Art materials were seen as another way in which children could release negative emotions (Henniger 1999). Consider the following rationale for providing art experiences within the early childhood programme from a now classic text on art with the young child:

> To many children painting is a most beneficial emotional release, in my opinion, unsurpassed by any other. This is one reason why we do not set subjects for painting and why we accept what seems an unintelligible mass, or even mess, of colour . . . I have known five- and six-year-olds, when troubled, paint – 'just painting' – for weeks, and have found that doing so was a help for their trouble.
>
> (Durham 1978: 45)

Second, early childhood educators could allow for the child's wish fulfilment in safe ways by allowing the child to engage in free play. In free play, children could imagine and pretend in ways that allowed them to be powerful in the world.

Ideas summary 3.3 explores how you plan for time, materials, space and people if you adhere to a psychodynamic 'reforming through interactions between nature and culture' view of how children learn. As you review this Ideas summary, reflect on which of the planning implications you would feel comfortable with and which would discomfort you.

Ideas summary 3.3 Psychodynamics: implications for planning of 'reforming through interactions between nature and culture'

Key ideas:

- children learn by resolving inner conflicts positively;
- children learn best when they have the opportunity to resolve inner tensions and conflict positively.

Implications for planning:

MATERIALS

- materials will encourage and support children's free play;
- materials that allow children to express themselves freely (such as art materials and dramatic play materials) will be prevalent;
- materials will be open-ended so that children can find their own uses and expressions from them.

TIME

- will be child-centred;
- will allow for long periods of uninterrupted exploration of relationships, feelings and understandings through free play;
- will attempt to follow the child's rhythms, not the adult's.

PEOPLE

The educator's job is to:

- focus on child-centred expressions;
- offer opportunities for children to express themselves as freely as possible;
- act as facilitators of children's free play.

SPACE

- is organized to support self-expression and freedom of movement from one experience to another;
- is organized to allow the educators to act as supports for children, rather than as transmitters of knowledge.

CONTENT

- is directed by children's need for self-expression in particular areas.

Equity reflections

Several interlinked elements of a Freudian approach to identity formation have direct implications for an educator's approach to equity issues – especially to gender equity. These elements are:

- the search for a gender identity is driven by internal psychic forces and tensions that an individual child must resolve positively to achieve a positive gender identity;
- children learn gender through their identification with their parents;
- men and women have distinctly different character traits, and so as children begin to identify with their mother or father they develop gendered character traits;
- children benefit from expressing their emotional efforts and tensions in identifying with their parents in free play.

Identification

Psychodynamics explains gender role development in terms of identification, as Nasper explains:

the route by which the child achieves her/his appropriate sex role identification involves the successful resolution of the Oedipal conflict; with resolution, the child comes to identify with her/his same-sex parent and learns what it means to be an adult of that sex via this identification. The strength of the emotional bond between parent and child promotes the parent as the child's primary model.

(Nasper 1981: 14)

Children learn their gender identity as part of realizing that they have genitals that make them either male or female. Gender identity is equated with genital identity, as Kessler and McKenna explain:

According to Freud, around the age of five, children become aware that they either possess a penis or do not possess a penis. This recognition leads them to develop a particular fantasy involving their genitals (or lack of) and their parents. Out of that fantasy comes a resolution of feeling about the genitals and the parents. This resolution entails identifying with one of the parents and, consequently, internalizing the values of that parent, and eventually exhibiting the same behaviours as the parent

(Kessler and McKenna 1982: 271)

Linked with the need for children to find their own gender identity, Freud believed that men and women had different character traits that were produced in our search for identity. As Battersby explains:

For Freud, female 'character-traits' include showing 'less sense of justice than men', being 'less ready to submit to the exigencies of life', and being 'more often influenced in their judgements by feelings of affection or hostility'.

(Battersby 1998: 227)

When we base our understandings of children's gender development on Freudian theory, then the main role of an educator is to allow opportunities to identify with clear gender role models and to allow children the opportunity to resolve inner emotional conflicts in play. The emphasis in educational programmes based on these ideas would be upon supporting the child's search for a gender identity by:

- ensuring children had clear gender role models;
- allowing the children time and space to 'express, accept and master feelings and fantasies through play' (Crain 1985: 156).

This leads to a non-interference stance towards gender equity that:

- accepts that gender differences are natural;
- provides traditional gender role models for the child;
- allows the child opportunity for free play to experiment with gender roles, express their gender feelings and build their identities.

This stance on gender equity places the adult in a passive role in the development of children's understandings of gender. Structuring the child's identity search and thwarting its emotional expression would be problematic for the child's future development (Faragher and Mac Naughton 1998). This means it makes a reactive stance on equity, rather than a proactive stance to working with gender relationships between children.

Equity alerts
A psychodynamic approach to gender differences ignores the following issues:

- 'Free' play is an impossibility to produce. Most play in early childhood centres is deeply linked to power relations between children and each child's capacity to play 'freely' needs to examined in the light of those power relations. As Mac Naughton (1998a) argued:

   > Playing for power is a remarkably ordinary part of children's daily play. It is this fact that makes children's play dangerous.
   >
   > Play is dangerous because there is so much at stake. It is through play that children construct their understandings of the social world in which they live and learn to value themselves and others (Fleer 1996). Through play children can construct play worlds in which they practice and learn to be fair, to share power equally and with good will and to enjoy social diversity in their daily world (Derman-Sparks 1991; Neugebauer 1992; Kyoung and Lewis 1995). However, through play children can construct play worlds in which they practice and learn to be unfair, to compete for power and to fear the social diversity in their daily world. They can create and experience racism, sexism, homophobia and classism (Derman-Sparks 1991; Creaser and Dau 1995). We know from research in Australia and overseas that children can and do create such inequalities in their play worlds (eg. Alloway 1995; Mac Naughton 1996). They practice what they learn from the adult world and each other about gender, sexuality, violence, love, hate, power, friendship, exclusion and inclusion. Because of this play can be a dangerous place to be for many children.
   >
   > Play can be where others hurt you, call you names, ignore your ideas and exclude you. When girls play with many boys, when children of colour play with white children, when working class children play with middle class children and when children with disabilities play with children without disabilities play can be risky. It can place you at risk of being hurt, being called names, having your ideas ignored or being ignored yourself.

- When children freely express their identity fantasies and emotions, those expressions may be harmful to others. They may be racist or sexist. If this is the case, then non-interference enables racism and sexism to continue. As one early childhood teacher who challenged a non-interference stance on equity said:

   > I made no apologies, really, for doing it [intervening to challenge sexism], because if we were to make apologies about those sorts of issues, then we should be making apologies about everything. In fact, why can't children come and do what they like: throw things at the wall, hit each other, knock

each other out, and why doesn't that continue throughout schooling. I mean we use those rules throughout their whole entire life. In fact the issues relating to racism and sexism are probably more important than issues relating to safety, like running, in some ways, because it's a lot more valuable and effective and it's very unlikely we are going to kill them letting them run fast, but we still encourage that very consistently.

(Mac Naughton 1997: 323)

- Freudian understandings of gender identity have been critiqued heavily for the way in which they reinforce traditional sex role stereotyped relationships and forms of sexuality. As Sayers (1987: 31) noted:

Feminists have generally objected on ideological grounds to Freud's argument that psychological sex differences originate in the child's erotically determined construction of the penis as superior to the clitoris. Instead they have argued that this construction is socially, not biologically determined.

Ideas clarification exercise 3.2

1 *Read the following scenario of relationships between educators and children.* What did the educator believe about the child's development? To what extent did the educators in this scenario draw on a psychodynamic view of the child? What are the equity implications in this scenario for making meaningful relationships between the educators and the child?

Jindi, a 3-year-old child, was angry with having to let another child have a turn on the bike he had been riding. He had been crying and refused to play anywhere else. He just sat and watched the bike being ridden. His carer could see that he wanted to hit out each time the bike passed so redirected him to the clay table and encouraged him to hit and pummel the clay. She left Jindi at the clay table and watched from nearby as he spent time pushing and hitting the clay into a large flat shape. She made a note to remember this for next time Jindi seemed angry.

2 *Review the following statement.* To what extent does it reveal traces of psychodynamic theory in the advice being offered to teachers about helping children's emotional development?

It is not realistic to expect young children to use these materials [art materials] to produce actual pictures of their problems. Nevertheless, the youngster who uses her fingernails to scratch tensely through the finger-painting paper or limits herself to using only the center of the paper is expressing her feelings, just as the child swooping and squishing her way through a fingerpainting is expressing her happiness and lack of constriction. Some of these materials lend themselves particularly well to the sublimated expression of aggression, and some to the relief of more generalized tension.

(Hendrick 1990: 179)

Neuroscience

Key thinkers	Definition
• David Hubel (1926–) and Torsten Wiesel (1924–).	Neuroscience: the scientific study of nerve systems, especially in the brain (for example, the scientific study of nerve systems in the brains of young children).

The theory in overview

Neuroscientists study how our neural (nerve) pathways work. In recent years, significant interest has developed in their work on how neural pathways are formed and reformed in the first years of life. In their work they show that:

- there is an interaction between nature and nurture in how the brain's neural pathways develop;
- the first few years of life is a period of intense brain growth and development;
- early experiences (including nutritional and emotional experiences) stimulate brain activity and can postively and negatively influence how our brain develops its neural pathways;
- how our neural pathways form in these early years can influence later development in areas such as our capacity to learn, control emotions and be disease free (McCain and Mustard 1999; Thompson 1999; National Research Council and Institute of Medicine 2000).

The processes through which these 'effects' on the brain occur are explained as follows:

> The early development of the brain involves both a wiring or connecting of neurons and a pruning or sculpting process. Because the development of different brain functions happens in synergy, the stimulation from sensing systems like vision also affects the wiring or sculpting of neurons concerned with functions of the brain that govern emotional control, arousal and abstract thought.
>
> (McCain and Mustard 1999: 5)

Neuroscientists believe that there are critical periods in the wiring of the connections in the brain and that the majority of these periods occur in the first six years of life. If a critical period is missed through the brain receiving inadequate stimulation, it is difficult to rewire it at a later date. However as Thompson (2001) points out there are remarkably few of these critical periods. The idea of the early years being critical in the growth of the brain has considerable currency at present, as is shown in the following comments from the World Bank Group (2002: 1):

'The influence of early environment on brain development is long lasting . . . Early stress can have a negative impact on brain development'. The key to healthy brain development is stimulation of the right kind at the right time.

Where have the ideas come from?

Neuroscientists David Hubel and Torsten Wiesel gained the Nobel prize for their work on why sight could not be readily restored to children who were born with congenital cataracts and later had them removed (McCain and Mustard 1999). Mandernach (1999: 1) described how Hubel and Wiesel demonstrated the importance of critical periods in the development of the brain from their work on cats in 1970:

> The development of vision in the cat depended on the animal receiving visual stimulation during a 'window of time'. The kitten's eyelids were sewn shut so that no visual stimulation was received for a period of time. When the eyelids were opened, the physical structure of the eye was normal but the cat was 'blind'. The brain cells allocated to vision were non-functional for vision since they had not been used during the window of opportunity. They had either been appropriated for other systems or were lost.

Their work highlighted the importance of early stimulation and experience for how the brain developed and for its capacities to work effectively. Hubel later argued that, 'Early deprivation of social interaction, such as contacts with a mother, may lead to mental disturbances that have their counterparts in actual structural abnormalities in the brain' (Hubel, in McCain and Mustard 1999: 34).

New technologies that have allowed the brain and its activities to be studied in new ways have had a major impact on the field of neuroscience. Catherwood (1999) lists four new methods that have been key to research in neuroscience in recent years, including CAT (computerized axial tomography) scans which make use of tiny X-rays to 'see' brain structures and MRIs (magnetic resonance images) which use the echoes from magnetic waves to 'see' brain structures. This has led to what McCain and Mustard characterized as an 'explosion' of new knowledge about the brain:

> In the last 10–15 years, there has been an explosion of knowledge from neuroscience about the brain and the relationship between development in the early years and learning, behaviour and health risks in the later stages of life.
> (McCain and Mustard 1999: 26)

It is this knowledge that has made its way into developmental psychology and early childhood education through the work of people such as McCain and Mustard. Margaret McCain and J. Fraser Mustard prepared a report for the Ontario government in the late 1990s, it drew in large part on the understandings from within neuroscience to argue that the early years and investment in them was more critical than investment in the later years of schooling. It is a report that has drawn considerable international interest and commentaries such as those by Nash are not uncommon:

> Deprived of a stimulating environment, a child's brain suffers. Researchers at Baylor College of Medicine, for example, have found that children who don't play much or are rarely touched develop brains 20% to 30% smaller than normal for their age. Laboratory animals provide another provocative parallel. Not only do young rats reared in toy-strewn cages exhibit more complex behavior than rats confined to sterile, uninteresting boxes, researchers at the University of Illinois at Urbana-Champaign have found, but the brains of these rats contain as many as 25% more synapses per neuron. Rich experiences, in other words, really do produce rich brains.
>
> (Nash 1997: 1)

The ideas have moved rapidly into websites and magazines geared to parents of young babies. The following extract from the online parent magazine *Baby Talk* by its executive director, Claudia Quigg, is typical:

> Babies who have more sensory experiences are able to develop more brain power. Dr. Frederick Goodwin who is the director of the National Institute of Mental Health participated in some of this research. His conclusion? 'You can't make a 70 IQ person into a 120 IQ person, but you can change their IQ measure in different ways, perhaps as much as 20 points up or down, based on their environment.' In essence, an infant born with a 100 IQ can either become an 80 IQ or a 120 IQ by his fourth birthday, based on the poverty or enrichment of his experience base!
>
> (Quigg)

The 'brain research' as it has become known has also gained considerable attention at a policy level internationally. For instance, in 1997 Bill and Hillary Clinton co-hosted the White House Conference on Early Childhood Development and Learning: What New Research on the Brain Tells Us About Our Youngest Children. It received considerable media coverage and, as Chabris explained, its message was clear:

> This event, widely reported in the media, was designed in part to send an important message to America's parents: a child's experiences and environment during his first three years play a crucial role in determining the course of his later life, directly affecting how his brain will develop and thus his intelligence, his ability to learn, and his lifelong mental health.
>
> (Chabris 1999: 1)

In Australia, several politicians can now be heard citing new knowledge about young children's brains to support a range of policy initiatives (see, for example, Anthony 2002).

Implications of neuroscience for early childhood curriculum

An extensive range of implications for education in the early years has been identified in the literature. Some of those implications are that:

- Brain development and, thus, later cognitive development is helped by a curriculum which encourages young children to be active, to question and to construct their own understandings and meanings (Puckett *et al.* 1999).

- Young children's brains process information best when it is presented in 'wholes' and when children can make sense of it in their own time and in their own way (Puckett *et al.* 1999).

- Positive, nurturing environments are important to healthy brain growth (Catherwood 1999).

- Stressful environments cause us to produce a hormone (cortisol) that can reduce brain cells and neural connections (Dockett 2000).

- Stimulation in the early years is important:

    It is critical in the design of early care environments both in regard to interpersonal and physical dimensions that the young child be offered a context that supports these early capacities but yet does so in a way that allows their optimal use . . . (T)he aim should be to provide the baby with an opportunity to direct her/his own sensory exploration of the environment according to individual preference and competence.

    (Catherwood 1999: 32)

As the influence of neuroscience on how we think about early childhood programmes is relatively recent, there are no clear 'recipes' for educators to follow about how their curriculum should look. It does, however, emphasize the importance of early stimulation and positive, nurturing relationships for healthy growth and development. Thompson put it this way:

Recognizing that the early years are a period of unique opportunity and vulnerability means that the environments of early childhood should be designed so they facilitate, rather than blunt, the remarkable intrinsic push toward growth that is characteristic of every child.

(Thompson 1999: 12)

Ideas summary 3.4 explores how you plan for time, materials, space and people if you adhere to a neuroscience 'reforming through interactions between nature and culture' view of how children learn. As you review this Ideas summary, reflect on which of the planning implications you would feel comfortable with and which would discomfort you.

Ideas summary 3.4 Neuroscience: implications for planning of 'reforming through interactions between nature and culture'

Key ideas:

- children learn through stimulation of neural pathways;
- children learn best when there are non-stressful and positive relationships;
- children learn best when stimulation links with 'critical periods' of brain growth.

Implications for planning:

MATERIALS

- are chosen for their capacity to stimulate the young child's brain activity and development of neural pathways;
- are chosen for their familiarity to infants so as not to overstress them with novel and new sights, smells and sounds (Linke 2000).

TIME

- is planned to keep stress to a minimum;
- is geared towards maximizing brain stimulation during critical periods of brain growth.

PEOPLE

The educator's job is to:

- build warm and positive relationships with children;
- reduce stress in children's daily lives;
- emphasize the development of secure and reliable relationships;
- focus his or her interactions with children on critical periods for their learning.

SPACE

- is planned to keep stress to a minimum;
- is organized to enable the child to receive stimulation of the brain during critical periods of its growth.

CONTENT

- is directed by children's need for neural stimulation.

Equity reflections

While neuroscientists have not written specifically on equity issues, two interlinked ideas about diversity and equity arise from the 'brain research':

- equity of inputs to children can achieve equity of outcomes;
- inadequate early stimulation jeopardizes equal developmental outcomes for children.

Equity in resources

Potentially, these ideas are helpful for arguing for more investment in early childhood services in areas of high need. For instance, the Ontario studies of children's developmental outcomes showed that children from lower socio-economic groups experienced more learning and behavioural difficulties. These results have been used to support the argument for more resources:

> The highest proportion of children who are experiencing at least one serious learning or behavioural difficulty is in the lowest socio-economic group. Step-by-step, up the socio-economic ladder, there is a declining proportion of children who are having difficulties.
>
> (McCain and Mustard 1999: 680)

Equity alerts

Equity arguments based on neuroscience are potentially dangerous, because the neuroscience on which they are based is in contention and because they have the potential to lead to 'giving up' on some children and 'blaming' the brain for behaviours that may be the product of social and political experiences. Specifically:

- It may be problematic to rely on this research to support arguments for investment in areas of high need, given that there is debate about the validity of various neuroscientists' claims:

  > We get from Chugani's important brain-imaging results to a critical period for learning via two assumptions, neither of which is supported by neuroscientific data, and neither of which has even been the object of neuroscientific research. The claim that the period of high brain connectivity is a critical period for learning, far from being a neuroscientific finding about which educators can be confident, is at best neuroscientific speculation.
  >
  > Chugani accurately described the scientific state of affairs in his *Preventive Medicine* review. He believes, along with some educators and early childhood advocates, that there is a biological window of opportunity when learning is easy, efficient, and easily retained. But there is no neuroscientific evidence to support this belief. And where there is no scientific evidence, there is no scientific fact.
  >
  > (Bruer 1999)

- Claims that equity of inputs creates equity of outcomes assume that differences in children's performance in school or their behaviour can simply be accounted for by the early brain stimulation they have received. This idea leads to a stance on equity that has potential concerns within it. On the one hand, it can be used to argue for increased investment in early childhood programmes. On the other hand, the idea can be used to argue that there is no point investing in children and in services for them after the first years of life. It can also lead to people 'giving up' on children if they can be shown to have missed a key window of opportunity for specific learning (see Corrie 2000).

- Blaming the brain for a child's behavioural or learning difficulties can lead to other factors, such as discrimination, being ignored by those who work with young children. A child's learning difficulties may be tied to the fact a child is in a culturally hostile learning environment or with peers who are intolerant. It may be tied to a wider social and political alienation from the processes of learning and schooling that come from living with discrimination and disadvantage from the earliest years of life. Bruer (2002) argued that children's inability at mathematics often links to a lack of particular forms of knowledge, such as mathematical knowledge. This lack of knowledge can be class-based and once children gain the knowledge, they improve their capacity to do mathematics. It was the cultural experience of mathematics, not the lack of specific brain stimulation, that affected children's performance.

- Current enrichment programmes that are being developed to enhance young children's brain functioning are based on 'white middle class values about what is "right" for children, which denies that there are many different pathways to healthy development and many ways for children to achieve the same competencies' (Corrie 2000: 7).

- Relying on neuroscience may undermine the confidence of teachers in their work with young children as they attempt to match their curriculum to a child's 'windows of opportunity' for learning. Failure of children to learn specific skills may then be attributed to educators' failures to do this. Bruer points out:

> Sousa tells of an experienced fifth-grade teacher who was upset when a mother asked the teacher what she was doing to take advantage of her daughter's windows of opportunity before they closed. Unfortunately, according to Sousa, the teacher was unaware of the windows-of-opportunity research. He warns, 'As the public learns more about brain research through the popular press, scenes like this are destined to be repeated, further eroding confidence in teachers and in schools.'
>
> This well-established neuroscientific 'finding' about a sensitive period for learning originated in the popular press and in advocacy documents. It is an instance where neuroscientists have speculated about the implications of their work for education and where educators have uncritically embraced that speculation. Presenting speculation as fact poses a greater threat to the public's confidence in teachers and schools than does Sousa's fifth-grade teacher.
>
> (Bruer 1999)

Ideas clarification exercise 3.3

1   *Read the following story.* What would be problematic about this child's experiences from a neuroscience point of view? What would be problematic from an equity point of view?

> Dorji was born into a very poor family in a remote mountain village in Nepal. As he was an infant, he was strapped to his mother's back all day as she worked in the field, and as a toddler he was cared for by his five-year-old sister in their small hut. There was no running water and hygiene was poor. Food was scarce, the children were malnourished and suffered debilitating illnesses with no medication. Dorji had no access to commercial toys or books, and paper was a rare luxury in the village. When he was five he went to work in the fields to contribute to his family's survival. He left home when he was 10 to work away from the security of his family and his village.
>
> (Corrie 2000: 6)

2 *Now read Corrie's comments on this story.* What issues do they raise for you?

> (H)is deprived upbringing should have resulted in unused synapses in his brain being pruned, meaning that his 'window of opportunity' to learn would be 'lost forever' . . . how do the experts explain the fact that today Dorji is a well-qualified and highly skilled theatre nurse who can converse in four languages. Dorji learnt to read and write when he was a teenager, managed his nursing studies with ease, and now makes an invaluable contribution to the health care of his country in a busy hospital in Kathmandu.
>
> (Corrie 2000: 7)

Further reading and online resources

The reading lists that follow act as a guide to two forms of additional material: reading on the topic related specifically to early childhood, and material of a more difficult level on the same topic.

General child development texts with introductory material

Berk, L. (1994) *Child Development*, 3rd edn. Boston: Allyn and Bacon.

Boulton-Lewis, G. and Catherwood, D. (eds) (1994) *The Early Years: Development, Learning and Teaching*. Melbourne: Australian Council for Educational Research.

Miller, P.H. (1993) *Theories of Developmental Psychology*, 3rd edn. New York: Freeman.

Santrock, J. (1996) *Child Development*. Dubuque, I.A.: Brown and Benchmark Publishers.

Thomas Murray, R. (1992) *Comparing Theories of Child Development*, 3rd edn. California: Wadsworth Publishing.

Constructivism

DeVries, R. and Kohlberg, L. (1987) *Constructivist Early Education: Overview and Comparison with Other Programs*. Washington, D.C.: National Association for the Education of Young Children.

DeVries, R. and Zan, B. (1994) *Moral Classrooms, Moral Children: Creating a Constructivist Atmosphere in Early Education*. New York: Teachers College Press.

Maryland Collaborative for Teacher Preparation. Access to a number of essays on constructivism and its implications for educationalists: http://www.inform.umd.edu/UMS+State/UMD-Projects/MCTP/WWW/Essays.html

Beyond the Individual-Social Antimony in discussions of Piaget and Vygotsky. Online full text essay exploring similarities and differences between Piaget and Vygotsky: http://www.musenet.org/~bkort/constructivism.html

Bruner

Bruner, J. (1985) Models of the learner, *Educational Researcher*, 14(6): 5–8.

Bruner, J. (1986) Play, thought and language, *Quarterly Review of Education*, 16(1): 77–83.

Lambert, B. and Clyde, M. (2000) *Rethinking Early Childhood Theory and Practice*, chap. 4. Sydney: Social Science Press.

New Foundations webpage on Jerome Bruner. A summary of the key aspects of Bruner's educational theories prepared by Nicole Flores: http://www.newfoundations.com/GALLERY/Bruner.html

Piaget

Bringuier, J. (1980) *Conversations with Jean Piaget*. Chicago, MI: University of Chicago Press.

Furth, H. (1970) *Piaget for Teachers*. Washington, D.C.: Prentice Hall.

Piaget, J. and Inhelder, B. (1969) *The Psychology of the Child*. New York: Basic Books.

The Jean Piaget Society. An extensive collection of online resources and information about Piaget and his work via the student page and the links page of the Jean Piaget Society's homepage: http://www.piaget.org//main.html

Vygotsky

Berk, L. and Winsler, A. (1995) *Scaffolding Children's Learning: Vygotsky and Early Childhood Education*. Washington, D.C.: National Association for the Education of Young Children.

Department of Psychology, Massey University has an introduction to Vygotsky's work by Trish Nicoll: http://www.massey.ac.nz/~Alock/virtual/trishvyg.htm

Dockett, S. and Perry, B. (1996) Young children's construction of knowledge, *Australian Journal of Early Childhood*, 21(4): 6–11.

Ebbeck, M. (1996) Children constructing their own knowledge, *International Journal of Early Years Education*, 4(2): 5–27.

Mac Naughton, G. and Williams, G. (1998) *Techniques for Teaching Young Children: Choices in Theory and Practice*, chap. 12. Melbourne: Addison-Wesley Longman.

Vygotsky, L. (1932) *Thought and Language*. Massachusetts: MIT Press.

Vygotsky, L. ([1933] 1978) The role of play in development, in M. Cole, V. John-Steiner, S. Scribner and E. Souberman (eds) *Minds in Society*. Cambridge, M.A.: Harvard University Press.

Vygotsky. An excellent source of resources on Vygotsky's work: http://www.kolar.org/vygotsky/

Neo-Vygotskian theory

Catherwood, D. (1994) Changing views on cognition in early childhood: putting some sacred cows out to pasture, *Australian Journal of Early Childhood*, 19(4): 25–9.

Valsiner, G. (1994) Vygotskian dynamics of development, *Human Development*, 37(6): 366–9.

Piagetian theory

Jean Piaget Society homepage with a number of excellent links: http://www.piaget.org/

Lawrence Kohlberg: http://www.xenodochy.org/ex/lists/moraldev.html

Pschydynamic theory

Erikson, E. (1950) *Childhood and Society*. London: Pelican Books.

Erik Erikson. Online biographies and detailed description of his stage theory: http://elvers.-stjoe.udayton.edu/history.asp/ and http://ship.edu/~ccgboeree/erikson.html

Sigmund Freud. Good online resources from: http://www.pbs.org/wgbh/aso/databank/entres/bhfreu.html

Neuroscience and brain development theories

Catherwood, D. (1999) New views on the young brain: offerings from developmental psychology to early childhood education, *Contemporary Issues in Early Childhood*, 1(1): 23–35.

Corrie, L. (2000) Enrichment programs: low-cost fix for high-risk children? *Every Child*, 6(1): 6–7.

Linke, P. (2000) Infant brain research: what is it and what does it mean? *Every Child*, 6(1): 4–5.

McCain, M. and Mustard, F.J. (1999) *Reversing the Real Brain Drain: Early Years Study Final Report*. Ontario: Publications Ontario.

National Research Council and Institute of Medicine (2000) *From Neurons to Neighbourhoods: The Science of Early Childhood Development*. Washington, D.C.: National Academy Press.

Nummela Caine, R.N. and Caine, G. (1994) *Making Connections: Teaching and the Human Brain*. New York: Addison-Wesley.

Shore, R. (1997) *Rethinking the Brain: New Insights into Early Development*. New York: Families and Work Institute.

Thompson, R. (2001) Development in the first years of life, *The Future of Children*, 11(1): 21–33.

4

Models of the learner:
transforming culture and nature

This chapter introduces you to contemporary thinking about how we can transform culture and nature through our interactions with each other.

Definition

Transforming: changing or altering something into something new (for example, changing or altering how you think and creating something new).

Several broad schools of thought believe we both transform and are transformed by nature and culture and that our capacity to be transformative holds the key to maximizing young children's learning. These schools of thought include:

- social constructionists and postmodernists;
- feminists, especially feminist poststructuralists;
- critical race theorists and postcolonialists.

Social constructionists and postmodernists

Key thinkers	Definitions
Erica Burman	• Construction: something that is built or made. • Social: in relationships with others (for example, ideas or knowledge that are built or made by the child in relationships with others). • Post: after something in time. • Modern: from the Middle Ages until now (for example: after modern times, or after behaviourist or structuralist ways of thinking).

Overview

> Social constructionism demands that the cultural location of developmental knowledge be specified to incorporate researchers as well as the children they study: and that particular attention is paid to the values and power relations implicit in the concepts, design, methods, and language of research.
>
> (Woodhead 1999: 11)

Several key ideas link social constructionist theorists:

- Development of the child is not a fact but a cultural construction. When we describe a child's development we are describing our cultural understandings and biases, not what exists in fact (Dahlberg *et al.* 1999; Woodhead 1999).
- How children develop differs in different places and in different historical times because how we see development is bound by where we are (our culture) and by our time (Burman 1994: Cannella 1997).
- Development itself is a problematic term to apply to children because it produces oppressive practices (Dahlberg *et al.* 1999).
- Children can and do construct their own understandings in, and meanings of, their social world (Davies 1989; Mac Naughton 2000).
- Power suffuses relationships between children and between children and adults (Davies 1989; Mac Naughton 2000).
- Children 'contribute to social resources and production and are not simply a cost and burden' (Dahlberg *et al.* 1999: 49).

Where have the ideas come from?

The social constructionists are a diverse family with a diverse heritage. Their ideas build in part from what is known as the 'new sociology of childhood' (Prout and James 1990), in part from postmodern theorists and in part from poststructuralist and feminist poststructuralist theorists. More recently, postcolonial theorists have also begun to explore images of childhood. As you will see below, these perspectives on the child and childhood intersect with and inform each other.

To understand where these intersecting ideas come from, we need to explore the postmodern ways of understanding the social world that have emerged in many academic disciplines in recent years. This will help to explain the origins of social constructionist ideas.

The term 'postmodern' refers both to an era and to a way of thinking about the world. As a way of thinking about the world, it attempts to subvert modern ways of thinking, so it is called 'post' modern to indicate that it is separate from the modern and succeeds it. Modern ways of thinking are Enlightenment ways of thinking (Chapter 2). They value:

- reason as the means to create a better world;

- scientific ways to explain, predict and thus control the world through building universal truths about how it works.

Postmodernists subvert these ideas by suggesting that:

- reason has brought us not a better world but one in which war, poverty, dislocation and environmental degradation have grown;
- science has given us a particular form of truth that has often been used to benefit dominant groups in societies (see Bertens 1995; Parker 1997);
- it is impossible to discover truths about the world that are fixed at all times and true in all places (Foucault 1978).

Postmodern theory builds from critical theory and interactionism:

> Critical theory is the name given to a poststructural approach when it is used as a basis for designing curriculum (such as that used as the basis for critical literacy and social science curricula). Interactionism is the theory underpinning social and linguistic analysis of classroom discourse, and moves on from constructivism in the sense that learning is perceived as being located more centrally and primarily in the social context.
>
> (McMillan 2001: xii)

New images of the child and of childhood have emerged against the background of these ideas and of those intersections of critical theory and interactionsim. Thus, postmodern subversions of Enlightenment ideas have also subverted developmental, scientific ways of understanding the child as a rational, self-governing individual. Hughes (2001) suggests that both poststructuralists and postmodernists see the world as complex, impossible to map in its entirety and impossible to know. The poststructuralists focus on individuals and the postmodernists focus on society, but they share a view that the world is 'incoherent and discontinuous'. Specifically:

> poststructuralists regard the individual as fundamentally incoherent and discontinuous . . . For poststructuralists, everything and everyone can – and does – shift and change all the time.
>
> (Hughes 2001: 45)

The point for poststructuralist studies of the child is to explore these points of change and shift in the child rather than to try to describe a child at one point in time and see this description as the child. In contrast, postmodernists focus on the shifts and changes within society. Specifically:

> postmodernists regard human societies as fundamentally incoherent and discontinuous. They reject the [modernist] view that each society is at a particular stage of a 'journey' by humanity towards some ill-defined 'goal' or 'endpoint' ['telos'].
>
> (Hughes 2001: 45)

For this reason, 'postmodernists argue that we can only understand the world at a local level, because as we try to generalize our understandings, we rely on "big pictures" or "grand narratives" about humanity's "progress" on its "journey"' (Hughes 2001: 45) that are inaccurate and simplistic.

Postmodernism and poststructuralism are clearly associated with each other – to talk of the individual for a poststructuralist is to talk of society; and to talk of society, for a postmodernist, is to talk of individuals within it. While complex ideas, they are at the heart of understanding what marks out a transforming model of the learner from reforming and conforming models. A transforming model sits within a postmodern view of society and a poststructuralist view of the child, while conforming and reforming models of the learner sit within a modern view of society and often draw on structuralist view of the child (see, for example, the interactionists in Chapter 3).

Ideas summary 4.1 highlights the differences between social constructionists and traditional developmental and modernist theorists (Chapters 2 and 3).

Ideas summary 4.1 A comparision of modern and postmodern (social constructionist) theories of the child and of childhood

The postmodern child – constructing socially	The modern child – developing individually
Differences between children and adults are culturally constructed, not natural.	The child is naturally different to the adult.
Differences between children and adults and between children vary in different places, at different times and according to gender, 'race' and class.	It is possible to develop a set of universal rules or principles about how children develop that holds good for all times and in all cultures, irrespective of their gender, 'race' and class.
We cannot develop true and certain knowledge of the child because of the differences mentioned above. Instead, there are many truths of the child.	Scientific knowledge of the child tells us the truth about their development and what influences it.
'Development' suggests that the child is less 'formed' than the adult.	'Development' explains the process of children naturally moving from less formed ways of being to adult ways of being.
Children can make their own meanings and influence the world.	Children rely on the world for the meanings that they make and are influenced by it.
Relationships between children and adults involve the exercise of power in and through discourse by each side.	Relationships between children and adults involve individual negotiations and choices.
Children contribute to our social 'riches'.	Children are a social cost against which we must weigh the social benefits of investing in them.

We shall now explore these understandings of the socially constructed, postmodern child in more detail. In doing so, we draw on postmodern, poststructuralist and feminist poststructuralist thinkers before turning to explore the specific contributions of feminist poststructuralists and of poststructuralist thinking to understandings of the child.

Differences are cultural constructions, not naturally given

As we saw in Chapter 3, Piaget and Vygotsky looked for theories of language and cognition that can be applied at any place and time. In contrast, poststructuralist theorists believe that no one universal theory of children, of learning, or of human development can explain and predict development across cultures and across time. This is because the process of becoming human is a complex web of interactions between historical, social, linguistic, emotional, communicative, political and cultural dynamics in our particular world:

> We are seen to live in webs of multiple representations of class, race, gender, language and social relations; meanings vary even within one individual. Self-identity is constituted and reconstituted relationally, its boundaries remapped and negotiated.
>
> (Lather 1991: 101)

Despite staged, hierarchical ways of thinking about cognition and learning, in practice our understandings of the world are messy, context-bound and culturally specific. Consequently, it is not possible to develop a universal understanding of, for example, cognition that captures accurately what happens for all children in all places and that fosters fair relationships between children and adults.

There are many truths of the child, not singular certainties

> [We] must begin to critically interrogate knowledge that seductively poses as self-evident truth about child development and appropriate practice . . .

> [W]e must be prepared to forsake the comfort of certainty and accept a less-than-certain orientation to knowledge in the field.
>
> (Alloway 1997: 5)

The social constructionists and postmodernists challenge the idea that we can know anything for certain about the child. They argue instead that we must expect some uncertainty as we try to find new ways to think about and work with and for young children. They argue that there is no such thing as truth about anything – including the child and how they learn – but there are, instead, many truths about the child (see, for example, Davies 1993; Burman 1994; Campbell 1999).

Some 'truths' are more powerful than others because they have institutional backing, not because they are right

To a large extent, the fact that there competing ideas about learning (including those in this book) attests to this idea, which in many ways is not new. However, in addition to arguing that there is more than one way to see something, poststructuralists and postmodernists argue that the existence of many truths is linked to a politics of 'truth' and knowledge. By this they mean that each truth we hold about, for instance, how young children learn, competes to be seen as right and correct – '*the*' truth.

The desire to have or to discover '*the*' truth about how young children learn arises because ideas of what is right and correct give us power to say how others should think and act and how we should think and act. They give us a moral advantage (Mac Naughton 2000). If we know '*the*' truth, then we know the right way to act and we know how it is right, normal and proper for others to act. For instance, we know what normal development looks like in a child and, therefore, we know how to plan appropriate programmes for young children.

The understandings of the child that achieve the position of the '*the*' truth depend on the politics of knowledge of our time and culture (Mac Naughton 2000). If truths of the child are articulated and circulated by those with institutional power, such as professors in esteemed universities, then they are more likely to gain the position of '*the*' truth in Western early childhood textbooks. If those truths also link with political imperatives of the time, then they gain more power from being articulated by politicians and policy makers.

Conversely, if truths of the child are articulated and circulated by a young child in a remote and isolated village in the majority world, they are less likely to gain the position of '*the*' truth in Western early childhood textbooks. The theories that gain the position of '*the*' truth often serve the interests of the powerful and elite groups within a particular society at a particular point in time.

'Developing' is a problematic way of thinking about the child

Scholars such as Burman (1994) and Cannella (1997) believe that developmental approaches that see the child as a 'becoming adult' privilege adults and oppress children. Cannella put her concerns as follows: 'Child development is an imperialist notion that justifies categorising children and diverse cultures as backward, needing help from those who are more advanced' (Cannella 1997: 64). Several theorists (for example, Walkerdine 1988; Silin 1995) have argued that our perspectives on the child have contributed to their oppression and exploitation in different ways, because we are in a process of judging their differences to us as adults as 'inadequacies or weaknesses rather than alternative ways of knowing' (Silin 1995: 49).

Implications of social constructionism for early childhood curriculum

Social constructionism has just begun to influence ways of thinking about early childhood curriculum. The idea that multiple ways of living and being in the world open up possibilities for all of us, including children, to life with greater justice, is increasingly present in international discussions about early childhood curriculum and its purposes.

Consider the following statements made by early childhood professionals in recent years who are beginning to explore what social constructionism means within the curriculum:

- From a 2000s text on early childhood by US, New Zealand and Australian authors: 'Reconceptualist, postmodernist views of the world are not prescriptive, do not claim to be determinism. For early childhood educators the perspectives are tied to diversity, flexibility and critique – to the construction of shifting and reinvented identities that are willing to turn their own worlds upside down to reinvent and increase possibilities with/for those who are younger. We do not engage in a battle for the "right" way to conceptualize understanding. We want to engage in a lifelong struggle to unveil unthought-of possibilities for all of us.' (Cannella and Greishaber 2001: 180)

- From a 2000's early childhood text by US and Australian authors: 'Collabora-tive power models [of early childhood curricula] hold the promise of affording us a view from the mountain top in solidarity with multiple players, toward the dialogic, with the other, with the silenced, toward the personal, toward the feminist, toward our early childhood dreamspace of social justice and equity' (Diaz Soto 2000: 207).

The idea that we can and do transform each other through our interactions creates these views:

- children can construct their meanings in interaction with us;
- children are complex and constructed in and through relations of power, for example, relations of 'race', gender and class power; in turn, they construct relations of power, for example, relations of 'race', gender and class power;
- children offer alternative ways of knowing, not inferior ways of knowing;
- working with those who are younger should expand children's possibilities;
- opening up new possibilities for those who are younger creates social justice and equity.

The social constructionist view of the learner rests on postmodern views of knowledge as non-universal, complex, contradictory and changing (Dahlberg *et al.* 1999). It therefore requires the educator to be open to more than one way to see, be and know something. There is no longer a right or correct way to teach the child; instead, there are many possible answers. The educator's job is to dis-cover these answers with the child, to have her or his own knowledges transformed through the child and vice versa. The educator is not the expert but collaborates with the child to produce knowledge of the world. This, of course, brings its own challenges:

The challenge is to provide a space where new possibilities can be explored and realized through enlarging the reflexive and critical ways of knowing, through construction rather than reproduction of knowledge, through enabling children to work creatively to realize the possibilities and handle anxiety. It can contribute to the emergence of a pluralistic patchwork quilt of co-existing world views and life experiments.

(Dahlberg, Moss and Pence 1999: 56)

It also means that the educator cannot rely on experts for their knowledge of children and child development. Instead, they actively need to build their own pictures of children as learners that capture specific children in specific circumstances at specific times (David 1999). In particular, it means giving up views of the child that may work against the values of those cultures that have been silenced through traditional, Western developmental views of the child:

It might be argued that the individualism and independence that a Piagetian epistemology supports are quintessential mainstream American values. Yet not all societies hold these values in high esteem. When juxtaposed with values espoused by other social groups, we get a broader understanding not only of diversity but of human possibility.

(Lubeck 1996: 158)

Ideas summary 4.2 explores how you plan for time, materials, space and people if you adhere to a social constructionist view of children. Its content represents possibilities and provocations, rather than fixed ideas about how to build curriculum from within this perspective. As you review this Ideas summary, reflect on which of the planning implications you would feel comfortable with and which would discomfort you.

Ideas summary 4.2 Social constructionism: implications for planning of 'transforming nature and culture'

Key ideas:

- children learn in interaction with adults and in and through 'race', gender and class;
- children can enrich and expand our ways of knowing;
- learning can construct new possibilities which must always be critiqued for their power effects.

Implications for planning:

MATERIALS

- will be meaningful to the children and decided in collaboration with children;
- will open up possibilities for diverse ways of being and becoming;
- will allow for critique of the effects of ways of knowing, seeing and being on each other.

TIME

- is organized to allow diverse possibilities to arise and to be explored;
- is organized in collaboration with children.

PEOPLE

The educator's job is to:

- focus on collaborative learning;
- emphasize dialogue and exploring different ways of seeing the world and being in it;
- honour children's perspectives as enriching;
- critique the power effects of different ways of knowing, seeing and being.

SPACE

- is organized to allow diverse possibilities to arise and to be explored;
- is organized in collaboration with children.

CONTENT

- is built collaboratively;
- raises issues of social justice and equity;
- is contextualized, diverse and offers different ways to know, see and be in the world;
- is presented in diverse ways to allow for diverse ways for the child to know, see and be.

Equity reflections

The emphasis on children as active learners and as agents in the world may lead educators to assume that every child is equally capable of constructing the world and acting in it. However, a particular child's social and material circumstances can affect how capable they are to do this. For example, a child who is familiar with more than one way to know, see and be in the world is likely to be more comfortable when they encounter further ways than a child who thinks that there is only one way. Similarly, a child whose parents, peers and others encourage them to see things in different ways and to 'be' in different ways will be more comfortable and more successful in a social constructionist centre than a child whose parents, peers and others disapprove of such 'playing' with different ways of being.

Ironically, the outcome could be very similar to a 'liberal' approach to inequalities, which rests on the belief that if the educator treats all children equally, they create equity between them. A social constructionist who adopts a 'transforming' model of the child may inadvertently and unconsciously assume an equality between children – that all are active agents of their own learning – that masks very real, concrete differences between them.

Even if an educator recognizes those possible equity pitfalls, they must do more than just acknowledge them in their curriculum. Instead, to be consistent with a 'transforming' model of the child, the educator must somehow 'transform' a specific child's disadvantages (for example, relatively limited resources as a result of relatively limited experiences) into a means to transform their circumstances. A way to do this is to use the child's specific circumstances as a major learning resource through critical reflection – as Paulo Freire did with adults in Brazil (see Darder 2002 and Chapter 9).

In addition, by emphasizing children's voices in the curriculum there is a risk that those voices will add meanings to classroom discourses that are problematic for equity. For instance, Van Ausdale and Feagin (1996: 198) described how children's subjectivities and discourses of 'race' intersected in studies of children and racism in the USA:

> Each child in our study possessed connections with family, friends, teachers, and playmates at the center. They were part of even larger social circles and networks – and were thus part of the larger racialized society of which we are all members. How they have managed to create, recreate, and reinvent that racially stratified society in their own discourse and practices is at the center of our analysis. Racism intersects with their lives in a flood of elaborate, blatant, and subtle ways – from the definition of identity and self, to the performance of hurtful practices, to various articulations of dominant group power.

So as children's voices are honoured in the curriculum, it is critical to be watchful for what is being honoured through them.

Ideas clarification exercise 4.1

1   *Read the following scenario of relationships* between educators and children. What did the teacher believe about the child as a learner? Did the teachers in this scenario draw on a social constructionist view of the child? What are the equity implications in this scenario for making meaningful relationships between the educators and the child?

> A teacher has just been to a professional conference in which the experiences of children in Australian detention camps for refugees have been discussed. She learns of their lack of rights and lack of access to education and, with others in the session, she agrees to be an advocate for these children. She decides to talk with the four and five year old children that she is working with to ask them what they know about refugee children in Australian detention camps and to explore their feelings about the issues associated with children in detention camps. She learns that the children have considerable knowledge and in discussion she and the children agree that what is happening to the children is unfair. The children suggest that they write a letter to the 'government' and they dictate a letter to the teacher. It begins, 'To the government, Let them go, it's not fair'. (A copy of this letter can be found at: http://www.edfac.unimelb.edu.au/LED/CEIEC/ in *Newsletter*, April 2002.)

2   *Review the ideas of the social constructionists* and attempt to complete Reflection sheet 4.1. Use the online and text resources at the end of this chapter to explore their ideas further.

Reflection sheet 4.1 Reviewing the ideas of the social constructionists

Reflection points	To what extent do you agree with this idea?
Reforming through interaction between nature and culture – key ideas.	
Children's ways of knowing are as rich and valuable as adult's ways of knowing.	
Children's ways of knowing will always be constructed through 'race', gender and class.	
Children's ways of knowing have power effects.	

Feminist poststructuralists

Key thinkers	Definitions
Valerie Walkerdine Bronwyn Davies	• Structure: fixed and permanent organizer that makes something work (for example, fixed and permanent cognitive organizer that makes thought possible). • Feminist: a person who has a concern with the similarities and differences in how men and women experience power in a given society at a given point in time. • Post: after something (in time or in the order of things) (for example, after structuralist ways of thinking).

The theory in overview

In socialisation theory, the focus is on the process of shaping the individual that is undertaken by others. In poststructuralist theory the focus is on the way each person actively takes up the discourses through which they and others speak/write the world into existence as if they were their own.

(Davies 1993: 11)

What feminist poststructuralists share is a belief that how we learn is through taking up and using discourse and how we do this is linked to our subjectivity and to power. To understand how discourse affects learning and learners we will look briefly at how feminist poststructuralists see the links between discourse, power and subjectivity.

Learning in discourse

Discourse is widely used to refer to talk. However, feminist poststructuralists, as with other poststructuralists, use it in a specialized way. For them, discourse is more than talk. It is:

- the ideas we use to make sense of ourselves and others and the world around us. For instance, the ideas we use to make sense of children's learning are discourses.
- our feelings about the ideas we use to make sense of ourselves, others and the world around us;
- the words and images we use to express our ideas;
- the things that we do to express our ideas and to put them into practice;
- the ways we look at and act on the basis of our ideas.

So, discourse describes the ideas, feelings, words, images, practices, actions and looks that we use to build our social world. It is definitely, for poststructuralists, much more than talk. In relation to young children as learners discourses would describe the ideas, feelings, words, images, practices, actions and looks that we use to build a picture of children as learners. There are many discourses that we use to build our social world, not just one. For instance, we have discourses that we use to build:

- a world in which there are two genders – gender discourses;
- a world in which there are educational settings – educational discourses;
- a world in which there are adults and children - developmental discourses.

A discourse groups together ideas, feelings, words, images, practices, actions and looks around particular areas or domains of our social life and they provide a framework for us to make sense of and act in our social world. They offer us a 'template' for how to think, feel, speak, act, look and be in particular areas of our life. For example, if you are a woman there are a range of templates you can choose from, each of which has ideas, feelings, ways of acting and looking built within it.

When we act in the world as a male or female we are acting within these gender templates or discourses. This means that we will have ideas, feelings, words, images, practices, actions and looks that come together to make us think, feel, act and look in particular ways as a female and a male. As a female, you might emphasize very traditionally feminine ways of looking, thinking, feeling and acting in your social world. Being feminine is more than talking about it; it involves feelings, ideas, actions and ways of looking. You would be said by the feminist poststructuralists to be positioning yourself within discourses of emphasized feminity if you choose traditionally feminine discourses through which to make sense of yourself.

Feminist poststructuralists believe that we learn in and through these templates or discourses – that learning occurs through the ways in which we take up and make our own particular ways of thinking, feeling, looking and acting in the world within these templates. Who we are, and who we believe we can and should be is created in the particular combination of social templates that we put together for ourselves. The process of making discourses our own links to what feminist poststructuralists talk of as our subjectivity. O'Loughlin (2001: 62) described this process: 'Children are continually in the process of becoming. Such becoming necessarily entails performing diverse societal discourses concerned with issues of gender, race, class and so on.'

Learning in discourse and subjectivity

In everyday language, subjectivity is used to refer to a biased or subjective way of seeing the world. Subjectivity also refers to the special ways in which we as individuals think about the world. In this meaning our subjectivity is our ways of seeing ourselves. Feminist poststructuralists believe that we cannot see ourselves or think about ourselves outside of discourse (or outside of the social templates) that exist when we come into the world.

We are born into a world in which discourse exists, because the people in the world into which we are born are constantly speaking them into existence. They are making discourse by acting, speaking, thinking and feeling in particular ways that are consistent with particular social templates.

The social templates for being male and female already exist when we arrive into the world. The social templates for being a child already exist when we arrive in the world. Our work in creating ourselves is to see these templates (discourses) and to choose between them and make our self in ways that are consistent with them – as a child, as a girl or a boy. However, this process is not a simple process of personal choice. It is a process in which the exercise of power makes it more or less likely that some choices will be made and others will not. For instance, even though girls will come into a world in which gender discourses (templates) for being girls and for being boys exist and are available for them, it is more likely that girls will choose from the gender templates that exist for girls than those that exist for boys. Feminist poststructuralists explain this likelihood by talking about the exercise of power in and through discourse.

Learning in discourse and power

At its simplest, power is the ability to make others do things that are to your benefit, even if they resist. As Connell (1987) explains: 'Power sometimes involves the direct use of force, but is always also accompanied by the development of ideas (ideologies) which justify the actions of the powerful.'

Feminist poststructuralists see that some discourses are more powerful than others. Some discourses are more available to us than others, since they have the support of powerful institutions and people within our society and they benefit their ways of thinking, feeling, acting and looking. For instance, some ways of being a girl are more available to young girls than are others. Powerful institutions such as the media and entertainment industries make particular templates for being a girl more desirable than others and more normal than others. They support these templates through the toys that they produce and the adverts for those toys that show girls that it is most desirable to:

- look blonde, Anglo and middle class;
- like Barbies;
- dress in pink.

These ways of being a girl are much more available to girls than other ways of being girls. We become powerful in ourselves when we make ourselves through the most commonly recognized templates or discourses in our society. When we try to make ourselves in ways that disrupt gender templates or challenge the norms within them for how we should look, feel or think, then we are likely to be dismissed for getting it wrong or marginalized for not being normal. For these reasons, feminist poststructuralists, along with other poststructuralists, assert that power exists in discourse (Weedon 1997). For poststructuralists, power is expressed in discourses and exercised through them. Therefore, for the poststructuralist, the social world and how we learn in it is understood through exploring the operation of power in and through discourses.

Learning in discourses and their power effects

Poststructuralists assert that it is particularly important to explore how particular discourses or social templates, through which we can choose to make ourselves, privilege particular interests within particular societies at specific points in their history (Bertens 1995). So feminist poststructuralist analysis of the learner is concerned with the power effects of the discourses through which we choose to make our self (Foucault 1986).

Feminist poststructuralists believe that particular discourses privilege men's and women's interests in different ways at different points in time. Consequently, they look at how power operates in a society and its differential gender effects on boys and girls, men and women. Hence, a key feminist poststructuralist task is to explore and expose the gendered effects of power in all relationships in a given society through analysing discourse (language and practices). As children learn discourses, such as masculinity and femininity, they also learn and become involved in the effects of power in their relationships with each other as boys and girls. A feminist poststructuralist analysis of children's play must therefore attend to the gendered power effects of the discourses in how and what children learn (Mac Naughton forthcoming).

Poststructuralist theorists believe that the values and expectations attached to gender, ethnic, class, ability, age and sexuality positions are central to who we become. Therefore, they say, knowledge of these parts of who we are becoming must be central to how we understand the whole of ourselves and our becoming, because the individual is inseparable from the social – we are one and the same (Cannella 1997; Mac Naughton 2000).

Where have the ideas come from?

Poststructuralism

There are many beginnings to poststructuralist theory, but French social theorist Michel Foucault is a key postmodernist scholar. He has revolutionized much Western

philosophical, social and political thinking – indeed, many claim that he has revolutionized how we understand knowledge itself. Foucault was interested in systems of
social thought and how we come to think in a particular way at a particular point in
time. He argued that modern academic disciplines such as psychology and sociology
have imposed their own desires and needs on how we view the world and given us a
'will to truth', rather than a 'will to knowledge'. Gore explained how Foucault used
these terms: '[Foucault saw] the will to knowledge as the general desire to know, and
the will to truth as the desire to know the difference between truth and falsity in
particular disciplines or discourses' (Gore 1999: 10).

For Foucault, the will to truth is highly problematic because (like other postmodern thinkers) he believed that there is no such thing as truth. He argued that
what we regard as the truth about, for example, child development is subjective,
incomplete, multiple, contradictory *and* politically charged. In contrast, the 'will
to knowledge' is potentially productive, yet dangerous in that all knowledge has an
intimate relationship with power. The 'will to know' draws us to search beyond truth.
Foucault talked of this search as an 'ordeal' (Miller 1993: 280) because it was 'work
done at the limit of ourselves' (Foucault 1982: 47) but if done well, it places us in 'the
position of beginning again' (Foucault 1982: 47). What could and would happen if
professional development in early childhood education were recast to help us work 'at
the limit of ourselves' and to thus begin again revitalized (Mac Naughton 2002)?

Some people might say that the question of whether 'truth' exists is just 'philosophy', but as we have seen, much of our current knowledge of the child has begun
in and through debates by philosophers about the nature of humanity. Foucault
believed that in the modern world, all social institutions survive and thrive through
creating and maintaining 'regimes of truth' about how we should think, act and feel
towards ourselves and others (Gore 1991, 1993). For instance, early childhood
centres survive and thrive through creating and maintaining a regime of 'truths' (or
system of management) about how we should think, act and feel towards ourselves
as early childhood professionals and towards children, parents and colleagues. This
regime (system) defines the normal and desirable ways to think, act and feel in early
childhood institutions. In doing so, it creates and maintains a system of morality
that says what is and isn't a 'good', 'true' way to be an early childhood professional.
For instance, it has been argued that developmentalism – as enacted in developmentally appropriate practice (DAP) – regulates and governs young children,
parents and early childhood staff because it is regarded as a set of facts about the
child. Without these facts, we cannot act appropriately or correctly with children,
understand them or even think about them. In Foucault's terms, we live and work
within a regime of truth called DAP that defines appropriate and inappropriate ways
to raise children and that regulates (controls) how we talk about young children's best
interests.

To show how this regime of truth works, ask yourself:

- Can you know a child or even think about him or her in terms that are *not*
  developmental? What would be the consequences?
- Can you envisage a programme that is *not* developmental – and could you run it?
  What would be the consequences?

Foucault argued that our will for truth – our desire for truths and our need to hold them dear – obstructs learning and impedes change and it is his ideas that have heavily influenced the feminist poststructuralist writings of Bronwyn Davies and Valerie Walkerdine.

The 'feminist' in feminist poststructuralism

Bronwyn Davies studied children's gender development over a number of years. She began her studies using traditional socialization theory to make sense of how children were learning gender. However, she found (Davies 1993: xvii) that many of the children she studied did not seem to learn easily or automatically what was expected of their gender:

> Children were not being pressed into masculinity and femininity as sex role socialisation theory suggested. Rather, in learning to be coherent members of their social worlds they were actively taking up their assigned gender as their own in ways not necessarily compatible with the ways in which teacher and parents were telling them gender should be done.

Davies was concerned initially about the inability of traditional socialization theory to account for children's resistance to adults' attempts to socialize them. She argued that osmosis theories of gendering in which it is assumed we just 'soak up' ideas about gender (see Chapter 1) cannot explain why children are not always socialized as we want them to be. Davies (1988) argued for the rejection of current socialization theory, which she regarded as having little value. It takes no account of the child's active role in socialization and leaves no room for children to reject the dominant ideas or to decide how to deal with adults' sometimes differing and contradictory expectations. Davies also believed that there is evidence that girls do not passively accept female roles, which socialization theory can't explain. Finally, she argued that socialization theory relies heavily on the concept of role, but that role is not the static category the literature often suggests it to be.

Hence, feminist poststucturalists, such as Davies (1988) and Walkerdine and Lucey (1989), argued that an adequate theory of gender development must give credence to the fact that children are actively involved in the construction of their social world. Feminist poststructuralists have focused on individual children's subjective experiences of gendered power, challenging ideas that children's play choices are natural, or simply a result of socialization (Davies 1988).

From this position, Davies has argued that we need to find ways to make visible to children and educators the ways in which gendered power operates in early childhood services and seek ways to create new possibilities through it. This, for Davies, is at the heart of the feminist poststructuralist endeavour: 'Feminist poststructuralist theorizing, in particular, has focused on the possibilities opened up when dominant language practices are made visible and revisable' (Davis 2001: 179).

Given that children enter a pre-existing set of cultural meanings that are constantly reinforced through cultural imagery and cultural practices, some ways of thinking are much more likely than others. Intersecting with this, social structures such as gender, 'race', class and ability prescribe and limit the possibilities for each of us from birth and those of us who delimit our possibilities do so only by challenging the expectations of the structures into which we were born. Social structure refers to the 'underlying regularities, or patterning, in how people behave and in the relationships in which they stand with one another' (Giddens 1991: 19). For instance, it refers to the 'repetitions' (Giddens 1991: 19) in how so many people relate to each other as male and female, the regularity with which we see differences between how people of different socio-economic groups experience the world and behave in it.

These social structures such as gender, class, 'race', ability and age are inescapable from birth. A child who cannot be placed within the structures of gender is a child to be pained about and for. Reflect on what you know happens when a child's gender cannot be determined. Most of us will have seen documentaries of parents in tears and immediate family relations and friends puzzled and pained by the child who cannot be placed immediately into a specific gender. The feminist poststructuralists argue that all of us, including children, construct meanings within these pre-existing social structures and that these structures place limits and expectations on how we should think and act. Why does it matter if a child is a boy or a girl if we are not going to use that knowledge to structure our thinking about how to relate to them and how to construct their daily experiences?

Let's explore how gender structures work by looking at how they have structured some children's play with Barbie. Is it any accident that the boys in the following moment of 'free play' with Barbie construct the meanings with her that they do?

> Tim is pointing to the Olympic Barbie, who is dressed in her tights, and says to another boy: 'Take them off'. One of the boys starts stripping the Olympic Barbie. When it is naked Willie then grabs it and begins to kiss the Olympic Barbie. He then holds her up to Jamie's lips and makes loud kissing sounds. There are lots of giggles between the boys at this. One of the boys then says: 'Boobies, she's got boobies'. This is followed by lots of collective laughter from the boys. Willie then says to the research assistant: 'Heather look at this'. Heather is being invited by Willie to watch Tim press the naked Barbie's head to Jamie's lips. Jamie is being told by Willie to kiss the Barbie.
>
> (Mac Naughton 2000; Research notes)

Can we reasonably believe that these meanings are merely discovered by Tim as a result of individual exploration? Feminist poststructuralists would argue that Tim's meaning construction was not accidental, nor purely individual but fundamentally mediated in and through the social structures into which he was born. Feminists would emphasize that he was born into a culture where gender structures who we are, what we can reasonably do and so how we should be. Tim's meanings are likely to be mediated in and through these social structures. It will not only be gender, but class, 'race', age and ability that will mediate Tim's capacity to construct meaning. Cannella (2000a), working from within postmodern and postcolonialist perspectives, powerfully points to how the adult/child categories and the ageism embedded within these so often privilege adults' meanings and thus ensure that how we see the world is how young children come to see it:

The adult/child dichotomy, and all the power associated with it, has resulted in a group of human beings who are only heard when being 'spoken for' by those who are older. Whether younger human beings are affluent and living in the United States or labeled as destitute and living in a so-called underdeveloped country, they are only allowed to speak through the voices of adults. We hear them through the biological, psychological, sociological, cognitive, or linguistic sciences that we have created.

(Cannella 2000a: 21)

The point of scholarship about meaning construction, whether it is post-modern, postcolonial or poststructuralist feminism, is to explore the effects of our position in the cultural structures we have created on the meanings and possibilities for ourselves that we produce and reproduce. As educators, the point is to explore the effects of cultural and structural positions on how and what children can and do know and learn.

Moreover, the point is to never lose sight of how gender, race, class, and so on mediate learning. Indeed, the point is to ask how this meaning is made possible because of gender, race, class and the position of the child and the teacher within these structures. Without these reminders, it is easy to forget that where, when and into which family we were born fundamentally structures what knowledges we access, what experiences we have and, therefore, what meanings we give to our life. And, for children, what meanings they produce in and through their learning.

The point for each of the feminists (e.g. Davies and Walkerdine) is not just to note this, but to reflect on how this distorts, privileges and silences meanings and to find ways to build teaching and learning relationships that make these distortions, silences and patterns of privilege less likely. For Foucault, as a poststructuralist, it is only once this occurs that we can understand why some meanings are produced and others are silenced and, therefore, begin work to bring the silenced and marginalized meanings to the centre (Foucault 1982; Weedon 1997; Mac Naughton 2000). For postcolonialists, this requires deep attention to what has been 'othered' and to the effects of the diasporic on what possibilities we can construct for ourselves (Ghandi 1998). For feminists, the centring of gender in all analysis of social possibilities, including learning, is essential if we are to avoid the gendered silences and patterns of privilege that have dominated the majority of Western theories of the child (Jipson 1998).

Implications of feminist poststructuralism for early childhood curriculum

Feminist poststructuralists have only recently begun to influence early childhood educators' views of children and learning. Their ideas that power, discourse and subjectivity are inseparable from learning is relatively new in early childhood education. However, they are entering current thinking about children's learning in several ways. Many of these ideas underpin current approaches to gender equity in early childhood. In this section, we will touch on just a few examples of those ideas in action in early childhood programmes and return to them in Chapter 9. Consider the following statements made by early childhood professionals in recent years:

- From two Australian early childhood practitioner-researchers writing about the images of the child used to make sense of play in the construction site: 'Because Sandra's (an early childhood teacher's) intervention did not problematize how power was operating within and through competing discourses to make some ways of being a boy or a girl more desirable, pleasurable and possible, a racist and sexist status quo was continued by the children and by Sandra. The traditional images constructed by developmental observation failed to contest the equity politics of what it was to be a boy or a girl in the construction site and how those politics limited individual participants' (Campbell and Smith 2001: 97).

- From three USA early childhood researchers: 'by examining teaching as the production of discourses, poststructural studies illuminate the range of knowledges and experiences teachers draw on to exercise power in their worlds. Teachers are portrayed as clever thinkers and actors involved in a complicated web of social relationships that create possibilities as well as constraints for curriculum and pedagogy' (Ryan *et al.* 2001: 55).

The specific ways in which feminist poststructuralists understand children as gendered learners, learning in and through discourse, have diverse implications for early childhood curriculum. The following list of implications for early childhood curriculum indicates just some of those that are possible:

- Educators look for discourse and its effects in teaching and learning.

- Educators explore the gender effects of discourse in teaching and learning because they are always present. For instance: 'even when [girls] resist a particular ... position ... [they] cannot escape the implications of femininity. Everything we do signifies compliance or resistance to dominant norms of what it is to be a woman' (Weedon 1997: 8–7).

- Educators attend to emotion and desire in learning. Walkerdine argued that as we focus on learning in young children and how learning occurs, we establish a 'cognitivism' (1999: 13) that ignores the place of emotion and sexuality in children's ways of being and thinking. For instance:

  > The discourse of natural childhood builds upon a model of naturally occurring rationality, itself echoing the idea of childhood as an unsullied and innocent state, free from the interference of adults. The very cognitivism of most models of childhood as they have been incorporated into educational practices, leaves both emotionality and sexuality to one side.
  >
  > (Walkerdine 1999: 13)

- Educators help children to understand the ways in which their possibilities are limited and constrained by gendered discourses by offering them contradictory images, ideas and possibilities for 'doing' their gender.

- Educators seek reciprocity in their relations with children. Reciprocity is a process of negotiating the ends and means of teaching and learning with children. Reciprocal relationships are ones in which there are efforts to have an equal balance within them. Reciprocity has been used by feminist poststructuralist researchers to challenge traditional power relations between researchers and the researched (see Ochsner 2001).

- Educators critically reflect on the relations of power in their classrooms and ask questions such as, 'What relations of power have already been accomplished in our early childhood classrooms between teachers and children and between children and children that distort and silence some meanings and privilege others?', 'What meanings compete in our classrooms for a privileged position?', 'How do these impact on the meanings children construct in our classrooms?', 'How do these impact on the meanings children choose to share or not in our classrooms?'

Equity reflections

Questions of equity and power are core to feminist poststructuralist understandings of the child and how we are becoming. For this reason, if you are drawing on a feminist poststructuralist understanding of the child you are bound to explore issues of equity and power, especially those concerned with gender.

The challenge is to find ways of working with young children that recognize that they are constructing and constructed in discourses that inevitably privilege particular world views and to find ways to help children to resist those discourses that are limiting their possibilities and those of other children.

Ideas clarification exercise 4.2

1 *Read the following short story* in which children had learnt to produce the knowledge that the teachers wanted, while at the same time holding on to what they knew to be right.

> Olivia, a persona doll that I sometimes work with in my research about how young children understand and construct gender, 'race' and class (see Mac Naughton 2001a, b), is given a badge for her birthday that has '5' on it. It is a blue badge. She is so excited by the badge that she wears it to her preschool to show her friends. Her friends laugh at her and say it can't really be her badge because it's blue. At this point in the story we ask the children: 'Do you think that Olivia's friends are right?'. The reply in unison from the eight children listening to the story is, 'No'. Heather asks, 'Why?'. 'Well, girls and boys can wear any colour they like', comes the response, once again in unison. It is clear that the children have been told this regularly by the staff. Heather then asks, 'Why do you think that Olivia's friends said what they did?' The response back was 'Because, well, pink's really for girls and blue is really for boys'.

- To what extent do the power relationships that have already been accomplished between adults and children and within these teachers and children mediate what meanings children construct, and how and when they choose to share them with us?

- Have these children at 4 years of age already learnt to silence some meanings and parrot others?

- To what extent can you ever know what meanings a child can and does construct when power relations are a condition under which meaning is shared?
- To what extent do teacher/child relationships come between what a child might learn or share? How do the power relations embedded in teacher/child relationships mediate what a child in your classroom learns and what meanings they construct with you?
- What meanings compete for power in your classroom?
- What are the effects of this competition on what children learn?

2 *Review the ideas of the feminist poststructuralists* and attempt to complete Reflection sheet 4.2. Use the online and text resources at the end of this chapter to help you to explore further the ideas of the feminist poststructuralists.

Reflection sheet 4.2 Reviewing feminist poststructuralist ideas

Reflection points	**To what extent do you agree with this idea?**
Transforming nature/culture – key ideas.	
Learning cannot escape the effects of gender.	
Educators can constrain children's gender possibilities.	
Learning always occurs in discourse.	

Implications for planning practices

Ideas summary 4.3 explores how you plan for time, materials, space and people if you adhere to the 'transforming nature/culture' view of how children learn. As you review Ideas summary 4.3, reflect on which of the planning implications you would feel comfortable with and which would discomfort you.

Ideas summary 4.3 Feminist poststructuralism: implications for planning of 'transforming nature/culture'

Key ideas:

- children learn in interaction with us and in and through 'race', gender and class;
- children can enrich and expand our gendered ways of knowing;
- learning can construct new gender possibilities which must always be critiqued for their power effects.

Implications for planning:

MATERIALS
- will be meaningful to the children and decided in collaboration with children;

TIME
- is organized to allow diverse possibilities to arise and to be explored;

- will open up possibilities for diverse ways of being and becoming gendered;
- will allow for critique of the effects of ways of gendered knowing, seeing and being on each other.

PEOPLE

The educator's job is to:

- focus on collaborative learning;
- emphasize dialogue and exploration of different gendered ways of knowing, seeing and being in the world;
- critique gendered ways of knowing, seeing and being for their power effects.

CONTENT

- is collaboratively built;
- will raise issues of gender justice and equity;
- will be contextualized, diverse and offer alternative gendered ways of knowing, being and seeing in the world;
- is presented in diverse ways to allow for diverse ways of gendered knowing, being and seeing to be possible for children.

- is organized in collaboration with children.

SPACE

- is organized to allow diverse possibilities to arise and to be explored;
- is organized in collaboration with children.

Further reading and online resources

The reading lists that follow act as a guide to two forms of additional material: reading on the topic related specifically to early childhood, and material of a more difficult level on the same topic.

Postmodern/poststructuralist/postcolonial theories

Alloway, N. (1997) Early childhood education encounters the postmodern: what do we know? What can we count as true? *Australian Journal of Early Childhood*, 22(2): 1–5.

Contemporary Issues in Early Childhood. Full text online journal with many relevant articles drawing on these theories: http://www.triangle.co.uk/ciec/index.htm

A Genealogy of Foucault: http://www.csun.edu/~hfspc002/foucault.home.html

Mac Naughton, G. (1995) A poststructuralist analysis of learning in early childhood settings, in M. Fleer (ed.) *DAPcentrism: Challenging Developmentally Appropriate Practice*. Canberra: Australian Early Childhood Association.

Prawat, R. (1996) Constructivisms, modern and postmodern, *Educational Psychologist*, 31(3–4): 215–25.

Cannella, G. (1997) *Deconstructing Early Childhood Education: Social Justice and Revolution*. New York: Peter Lang Publishers.

Theories of Colonialism and Postcolonialism: http://www.scholars.nus.edu.sg/landow/post/poldiscourse/discourseov.html

Theory, gender and identity: http://www.theory.org.uk/main.htm

Valerie Walkerdine: Beyond Developmentalism http://www.psych.ucalgary.ca/thpsyc/abstracts/abstracts_3.4/Walkerdine.html

The postmodern and social constructionism

Dahlberg, G., Moss, P. and Pence, A. (1999) *Beyond Quality in Early Childhood Education and Care: Postmodern Perspectives*, chap. 3. London: Falmer Press.

De Lair, H. and Erwin, E. (2000) Working perspectives within feminism and early childhood education, *Contemporary Issues in Early Childhood*, 1(2): 153–6.

Lubeck, S. (1996) Deconstructing 'child development knowledge' and 'teacher preparation', *Early Childhood Research Quarterly*, 11: 147–67.

Stott, F. and Bowman, B. (1996) Child development knowledge: a slippery base for practice, *Early Childhood Research Quarterly*, 11: 169–83.

5

Models of the learner: critical reflections

This chapter offers some resources to assist you to critically reflect on the models of the child as a learner that you met in Chapters 2, 3 and 4. First, there are case studies of 'conforming', 'reforming' and 'transforming' models of the learner. Second, the section 'Reflecting on where you are now' assists you to develop your own position statement on the learner. It asks you to consider what your perspective on the learner is and where it sits in relation to the conforming, reforming and transforming positions on the learner that you have met in Chapters 2, 3 and 4. Finally, there is a Gallery of ideas about learners and learning, to assist you in furthering your thinking about learning, learners and the child.

Case studies

> CASE STUDY

A case study of 'conforming' models of the learner: Montessori education

Montessori believed that early childhood educators should conform to nature's patterning of children's learning capacities and not attempt to vary them in any way. We should support and aid nature not, control or force its direction in any way:

> My vision of the future is no longer people taking exams and proceeding then on that certification . . . but of individuals passing from one stage of independence to a higher [one], by means of their own activity through their own effort of will, which constitutes the inner evolution of the individual.
> (From Maria Montessori, *From Childhood to Adolescence*:
> http://www.montessori.edu/maria.html)

Montessori believed that children teach themselves and that they are motivated to learn through 'living and walking about'. Learning comes naturally to children and it is by following nature's cues that children's learning and positive growth can be maximized. She wrote:

> Supposing I said that there was a planet without schools or teachers, study was unknown, and yet the inhabitants – doing nothing but living and walking about – came to know all things, to carry in their minds the whole of learning: would you not think I was romancing? Well, just this, which seems so fanciful as to be nothing but the invention of a fertile imagination, is a reality. It is the child's way of learning. This is the path he follows. He learns everything without knowing he is learning it, and in doing so passes from the unconscious to the conscious, treading always in the paths of joy and love.
>
> (Montessori: http://www.montessori.edu/maria.html)

Montessori argued that learning is an innate characteristic of the child and saw adults as 'servants' to the child's learning through setting up the right environment for learning – much as a servant does for the master. Certainly, the environment needed special attention and children needed adults who knew how to set up the environment with equipment suited to the child's changing ways of learning. However, it was the child who acted on it and who learnt through this action, independently of adults:

> The task of the teacher becomes that of preparing a series of motives of cultural activity, spread over a specially prepared environment, and then refraining from obtrusive interference.
>
> (Montessori, *Education for a New World Adolescence*:
> http://www.montessori.edu/maria.html)

Montessori's ideas show many features of the 'conforming to nature' view of how children learn. Reflection sheet 5.1 can help you to review your understandings of her ideas in particular and the ideas of adherents to the 'conforming to nature' view of how children learn.

Ideas clarification exercise 5.1

Review Montessori's ideas and attempt to complete Reflection sheet 5.1. Use the online and text resources at the end of this chapter to explore her ideas in particular, and those in Chapter 2 to explore the ideas of the Romantics and maturationists in general.

Reflection sheet 5.1 Reviewing Montessori

Conforming to nature – key ideas	Would Montessori agree or disagree with this idea?	To what extent do you agree with this idea?
Observe which stage of becoming adult the child has reached.		
Listen to nature's prompts about what the child needs at each stage.		
Trust and support nature in her task of leading the child towards adulthood.		
Offer nature a helping hand only when necessary.		
Take our cues from the child.		
Adjust our learning environment to the child, not the child to our learning environment.		

CASE STUDY

A case study of 'reforming' models of the learner: the High/Scope programme

The High/Scope programme was created in the USA in the 1960s by David Weikart and others in an attempt to redress the poor academic performance of children from disadvantaged areas in schooling. The programme focuses on improving intellectual performance and creating success in school-valued skills such as literacy and numeracy. It is directly based on the ideas of Piaget and is often known for this reason as a cognitively orientated curriculum. The teaching and learning is based on what is known as a plan–do–review sequence in which children plan what they want to do, often in small, teacher-assisted groups, then implement their plans and finally review what happened as a result.

The 'plan–do–review' learning builds rational thought by helping the 'children learn to place things in categories, to rank things in order [and] to predict consequences' (Weikart and Schweinhart 1987: 253). This process is geared to building children's capacity to think logically in relation to space, time and relationships: 'High/Scope . . . is a method that helps organise the day, frames teacher–child relationships and interaction, encourages use of child development principles' (Morrison 1995: 49).

The curriculum engages children in eight key experiences that centre on (Weikart 1995/96):

- active learning;
- using language;
- experiencing and representing;
- classification;
- seriation;
- number concepts;
- spatial relationships;
- time.

High/Scope's Piagetian heritage is evident in three key ways:

- the curriculum is geared to the child's cognitive development;
- the eight key experience areas relate directly to Piaget's areas of cognition;
- active learning and reflection on that learning links to Piaget's understanding that cognition develops through personal experience in the world (Mac Naughton and Williams 1998).

Ideas clarification exercise 5.2

Review the ideas in High/Scope and attempt to complete Reflection sheet 5.2. Use the online and text resources at the end of this chapter to explore High/Scope ideas in particular and those at the end of Chapter 3 to explore the ideas of the constructivists in general.

Transforming models of the learner: teachers reflecting critically on learning

This section begins with a journal entry from a teacher reflecting critically on the images of the learner that were behind the practices of 'group time' in an Australian early childhood programme. It then invites you to reflect critically on this journal extract and to position the theories of the learner that are apparent in it. The second part of this section explores how a teacher uses action research to transform her teaching and learning and to reflect critically on her own values and practices in how she understands children as learners.

First, read the following journal extract from a South Australian early childhood educator who participated in the Critical Teaching Project (see Jones 2000). Once you have read the journal extract, reflect on it using the following questions:

- How does this educator engage in critical reflection on how children are understood as learners?

Reflection sheet 5.2 Reviewing High/Scope

Reforming through interaction – key ideas	Would High/Scope agree or disagree with this idea?	To what extent do you agree with this idea?
Observe which stage of becoming adult the child has reached.		
Listen to nature's prompts about what the child needs at each stage.		
Trust and support nature in her task of leading the child towards adulthood.		
Offer nature a helping hand only when necessary.		
Take our cues from the child.		
Adjust our learning environment to the child, not the child to our learning environment.		

- Do you have similar ideas or stories you could tell and use to reflect critically on your understandings of children as learners?
- How would you answer the questions at the end of the journal extract?
- Which theorists' ideas of the child as a learner did Bev's ideas link with most closely?

CASE STUDY

Journal extract: Kindergarten Director, Critical Teaching Project

Recently I observed 'group time' at a kindergarten. One teacher, Bev, 'took' group time, calling all children from 'packing away time' to the mat where she stood out in the front with a book, poster and a couple of other props which were to be the focus of the group time. Another teacher, Susannah, sat with the 25 4-year-old children, providing a role model of how to participate in the group experience – quietly whispering to children to 'keep their hands to themselves' and to 'watch what's happening up the front' – and directing children as to where they should sit (particular children were instructed to sit next to her). Another staff member finished the packing away and wiped down the tables ready for lunch.

Of interest to me was Sam, sitting at an activity nearby listening to the group time but continuing his activity (a puzzle he'd been working on for some time). Two or three times, Bev asked Sam to 'finish and come to group time'. After a couple of minutes she indicated to Susannah to bring Sam to the group. The child was brought, under protest, to the group and continued to cry and attempt to leave the group, while Susannah struggled to keep him still and gain his interest – 'Look what Bev's got!' – and Bev struggled to make herself heard above the loud protest. After the session I asked Bev about the group time and on her thoughts on Sam's reaction. Bev replied, quite simply: 'He's very immature for his age, but he's got to learn to sit at group time before he goes off to school'.

This experience has left me with many questions:

- What is our notion of maturity? (To be able to sit still and listen? To get along with the group? To conform to teachers' requests?)
- Can we 'teach' maturity?
- Can we teach a child to develop quicker, become independent quicker? 'Quicker' in relation to what?
- How much does what we see as being 'needed' for school colour the way we see children and the attention we place on 'maturity' and 'readiness'?
- Why are we so reluctant to question what we are doing, and so quick to label a child a 'problem' or 'deficient' in some way?
- What does, and will, this mean for Sam?
- And, why on earth do we 'do' group time? Why do we 'do' it to ourselves? And why do we 'do' it to the children?

Reflecting critically, reflecting equitably: action research for transforming practice

Read the following teaching and learning story written by early childhood educator Sharon Saitta. Once you have read her teaching and learning, reflect on it using the following questions:

- What position on children as learners would Sharon link most closely with?
- What is similar and what is different between her approach to children's learning and your own?
- Which theorists' ideas on children as learners do you think that Sharon would feel most closely allied with?
- Do you have similar ideas or stories you could use to reflect critically on your understandings of children as learners?
- How would you answer the questions at the end of the case study?

CASE STUDY

Sharon Saitta, early childhood teacher, Victoria, Australia

Reflecting back on theories and practices that I have engaged in as an early childhood teacher, before my involvement in several action research projects in recent years, I believe that there have been three major ways in which ways of teaching and my understanding of children's learning have been challenged.

As a mature-age student working full time in childcare I have often had questions about child development theories and how some of those theories and the practices that came from them didn't always seem to suit every child and family that I worked with. It wasn't until I participated in an action research project in 1998 and in subsequent years that I began to feel that there was a valid space from which I was able to question, explore, challenge and critically reflect on theories and practices that I used within the classroom.

The questions about child development theories that continue to surface for me today result from a number of teachers, children, families and critical friends that I have and who I am currently working with. They also have questions of their own and we have shared our questions as part of our journey. Through this network, I have felt safe and yet not always comfortable in questioning, challenging, contradicting and critically reflecting on the various discourses that circulate within my early childhood classroom. Before my involvement in action research, I felt that I was a teacher who operated in a fair and democratic manner, listening to and working with children, parents and teachers in planning and running a programme based on my observations as a teacher and my interpretations of children's interests and ideas. I also tried to incorporate parents' and teachers' knowledge into what I believe constituted a quality early childhood programme.

When beginning with a group of children in Bat Cave (Babies Room), Maureen, the co-teacher, and I engaged in some dialogue around programme planning. One of our questions at the time was, 'How did we know that what we were planning for the children was what they wanted in the programme?' A chance conversation with Helen Ketley from Adelaide, who had been involved in an action research project in which she tried to incorporate children's voices in programme planning, gave us some questions and ideas to explore.

As we moved into Starlight Room with our group we started to engage in conversations (both formal) and informal with parents around the place of children's voices in the programme. We asked:

• Could we design a programme for children under the age of 3 based on what they physically and/or verbally requested?
• How would this link in theory and practice with what teachers, parents and the academy viewed as appropriate resources and play spaces?
• If it didn't work, how would we change it back and would that be fair?

- Were we as teachers ready to share the power and knowledge with children, especially if it didn't fit with our desires?

Over the last two years, this project, with the support and encouragement of parents, children, teachers and critical friends, has led us and continues to lead us to more questions, challenges, dilemmas, changes and excitement in programme planning. For example, having the train set for nearly two years in the room because in each new programme one of the children would request it as their desired resource. Another dilemma emerged for me when a 2-year-old child let me know that I had not set up the doll space in the right way, as it did not look like the one in the other room. She stated to me that she was not going to play with it. She then proceeded to let other children who were listening to the conversation know that it wasn't what they wanted and also shouldn't play with it. This conversation came after me struggling for a week thinking about how I could set up a home corner that Kate requested in a less gendered manner so that I had met both Kate's and my desires within the programme.

As a result of the questions, ideas, changes and critical reflection we were engaging with I believe a shift in our relationships with children, parents and other teachers also emerged, and through conversations both verbal and written in the daily journal. A new understanding and shift of who had valuable knowledge, power and a voice surfaced within the group.

A critical dilemma surfaced for me when reflecting on my practice, I no longer felt like the good teacher who was able to solve issues, have answers for the children's, teachers' and parents' questions and struggles. This led me into many conversations with members of the group, both children and adults, in which we shared our uncertainties and struggles as we deconstructed and reconstructed who we were, our understandings, knowledge, discourses. We learnt that we were not separate identities working in isolation from each other, but rather interactive and interdependent with each other in the social environment of the centre.

Reflecting on these changes and how they have influenced what I believe, say and practice as a person and as a teacher, there were many little narratives (Lyotard) that emerged for me during the project that I now realize play a role in how I teach today. They also play a role in how I continue to question, challenge and, at times, change my theories and practices. I do this as I search for a more fair and equitable environment for all concerned and a community where all voices can be heard, acknowledged and listened to as having valuable knowledge, power, and desires.

One of these stories involves a group of 4–5-year-old girls who challenged the ideas of Meg and myself during a meeting in what we called Spider Room in 1998.

The jewellery meeting
As a way of attempting to open up spaces for children and teachers in the Spider Room to have a voice within the group and work collaboratively, Meg and I introduced group meetings with the children. In this forum, children and teachers

were given the opportunity to raise issues of concern, discuss, debate and decide on appropriate limits. During these discussions, other topics arose where we continued to review, ask questions and then plan.

One such issue emerged during the first half of the year. This centred on a small group of girls in the group who continued to bring in personal items from home to the centre, especially jewellery. The rule that had been set by the group was that all items from home could be shown to friends and then placed in their lockers to ensure that loved items were not lost, broken or inadvertently borrowed by others. We observed that children were using these items as a way of including or excluding children from the groups. The girls in question neatly bypassed this rule by ensuring that they arrived wearing the jewellery as a part of their outfit, which usually consisted of a frilly dress, headband and black patent leather shoes.

Meg and I prepared for the meeting by formulating a plan of action to raise our concerns about items, especially jewellery, still coming into the centre and look for ways that we could encourage the children to cease this practice in a fair and collaborative manner. During the morning we alerted the children to the meeting and gathered as a group before lunch in a circle on the floor in the Spider Room. Meg and I raised our concerns about the impact that items from home, especially the jewellery, were having on the group. For example:

- parents becoming upset if items were lost or broken;
- staff spending valuable time looking for items that had been lost or misplaced;
- children becoming upset if children shared desired items with some children and not others.

When we had finished raising our concerns we asked the group what they thought and how we could solve the issue. At this point Karrin, 5 years old and one of the girls who was wearing the jewellery, spoke up and said: 'So what you're saying, Sharon, is that it's okay for the teachers to wear jewellery but not the children, is that right?' With this statement she looked directly at us and waited for a reply. Meg and I looked at each other and at Karrin with stunned expressions that we could not really hide. At that moment we suddenly realized that Karrin saw what we were saying as unfair practice and had brought us to task over it. We continued to search for an answer, looking at each other and realizing that in fact we were wearing a number of jewellery items ourselves. We had openly discussed and showed them off when children looked at them or questioned us about the origins of them.

We acknowledged Karrin's question as being an important one. We asked the group if they thought it was fair that the teachers were saying that children should not wear jewellery to the centre but it was okay that the teachers did. Karrin and a number of other children all stated that it was unfair and that if teachers were allowed to wear jewellery the children should be allowed too. We then said that if the teachers did not share their jewellery or engage in climbing there were no safety issues involved or problems in losing items. Karrin, Fiona and Rowena replied:

Karrin: Well if the children were allowed to wear jewellery we would not share it.
Fiona: And take it off and put in our lockers if we climb.
Rowena: Yeah!

This reply again showed us how what we said and in fact what we did in practice could be seen as contradictory and unfair through the children's eyes. In an effort to disrupt the power–knowledge relationships between the children and the teachers, we agreed that it was unfair and worked with the children to set up a fairer playing field. New rules were then agreed to by all, that jewellery could be worn, but not shared or worn when climbing. The meeting was closed and we all moved outside.

In discussing the outcomes of the meeting with each other and other teachers over the next few days, we spoke about how stunned we were with Karrin's question and how the children had responded and viewed our practice. At this point in time, I felt that we had resolved the issue and had shifted the power relationships between children and teachers through the decisions made by the group on that day. We thus operated in a more equitable manner for all concerned. But on reflection and with the benefit of hindsight, had we?

The questions I have today are:

- Did I ever acknowledge to the group or myself the courage it took for Karrin to question and challenge the teachers' practice?

- How had other children been silenced in the group, as items apart from jewellery were still expected to remain in lockers?

- Were these items so desirable for the children and their entry to the group that we in fact unconsciously blocked that entry through our practice and desire to hold some power over the group?

- Were our practices and what we actually did contradictory?

- Did we consider class issues? For example, would children ever gain entry into particular groups or themes of play without access to desired commercial products and images?

- Were the meetings forms of surveillance, discipline and normalization?

Ideas clarification exercise 5.3

Review the ideas in the above case studies and attempt to complete Reflection sheet 5.3. Use the online and text resources at the end of Chapter 4 to explore transformative approaches to understanding the learner. At the end of this chapter are text resources that you can use to review additional examples of teachers critically reflecting on their understandings of the learner using ideas from within a transformative approach to the learner.

Reflection sheet 5.3 Reviewing the learner

Transforming each other – key ideas	Which teacher from the above case studies would agree or disagree with this idea?	To what extent do you agree with this idea?
There is no single theory of the learner that applies to all learners.		
Children's learning is connected with their gender, class, culture, ethnicity and geographical location.		
Children are active in constructing their own meanings but these meanings are limited by the discourses they have access to.		
Children are more likely to understand themselves and others through the discourses that are most dominant in their local community.		
Power relations are important in what and how children learn.		
Children's learning is culturally constructed, not developmentally determined.		

Reflecting on where you are now: models of the learner

[we] must begin to critically interrogate knowledge that seductively poses as self-evident truth about child development and appropriate practice . . .

[W]e must be prepared to forsake the comfort of certainty and accept a less-than-certain orientation to knowledge in the field.

(Alloway 1997: 5)

The limits of individual growth are unknown and should not be circumscribed. No person is static, each is ever in the process of becoming. Each person is unique and irrepeatable . . .

(Hansen 2001, in Killoran 2002: 372)

Many ideas about children and childhood offer possibilities to guide relationships and to build learning with young children. This first section of the book has introduced you to the major themes within our attempts to understand children as learners. Against the background of those themes, you are now invited to reflect critically on your views about children, about childhood, about learning and about how early childhood educators should behave with young children. This section of the chapter consists of a set of reflective exercises to help you to create your own position statement about your views. It includes:

- reflection points to help you review your ideas on children's learning;
- a reflection chart on which to summarize your perspectives;
- ideas starters with which to develop your position statement.

Reflection points

- What have you learnt about perspectives on childhood and on children as learners from Chapters 1 to 4?
- What are your 'truths' about how young children learn and develop?
- Which groups of children and adults are most likely to fit your 'truths'?
- Which children and which adults are most likely to benefit in your work with them from the 'truths' of the child that you hold dear?
- To what extent do your 'truths' enable you to think about the effects of gender, 'race', ethnicity, languages, class and ability on who children are becoming? Whose stories of childhood are missing?
- What stories might you build of children as learners if you looked to indigenous peoples, philosophers, artists and political activists, rather than to developmental psychologists?
- What key challenges and possibilities does the chapter leave you with?

Ideas starters

Review the ideas in this chapter and then attempt one or more of the following tasks:

- Create a Questions and I Believe board alone or with colleagues. Use the questions in Reflection sheet 5.1 and invite people to respond with an 'I believe' statement. Use these responses to write a summary for discussion.
- Write a story of a moment when a young child you know learnt something new. Sit for 5 to 10 minutes and write a short story of a time when you watched a young child learning. Reflect on that story and think about what it tells you about learning. What made the child's learning possible?
- Generate some metaphors of learning. Try to find a metaphor that captures how you think learning happens. Then play with and extend the metaphor through words, poems, images and sounds to build a 'picture' of your vision of the child as

Reflection sheet 5.4 Critically reflecting on my theories of how children learn

This links the preceding reflection points with the ones that began this first part of the book.

Reflection questions. Do we learn through:	My 'truths' about how young children learn and develop	Which children and which adults are most likely to 'fit' my 'truths' about the child?	Which children and which adults are most likely to benefit from my 'truths' about the child?	Am I thinking about the effects of gender, 'race', ethnicity, language, class and ability on who children are becoming?
Conforming to nature.				
Conforming to culture.				
Reforming through culture and nature interacting.				
Transforming culture and nature.				
Your other questions about children's learning.				

a learner and as a person who is becoming. As a start, consider the extent to which each of the following metaphors captures your views?

Metaphors for learning	
A child is like . . .	An information processing machine. A blank slate on which the world must be written. A wild animal who needs to be tamed. A seed that needs the right conditions to grow.

- Favourite sayings. Make a list of your favourite sayings about children and how they learn. Whose 'truths' of learning do they privilege?
- Review the Gallery of ideas about learners and education. Which people in the Gallery do you have most in common with? Which people in the gallery do you

have least in common with? What does this suggest about your views of the child as a learner?

Learners and education

In these Ideas galleries about learners and education you will find ideas gathered as follows:

- Ideas from around the world.
- Ideas from the past.

Ideas gallery 5.1 Ideas from around the world

From the Canadian Special Services Committee, Canada:

'The limits of individual growth are unknown and should not be circumscribed. No person is static, each is ever in the process of becoming. Each person is unique and irrepeatable' (Killoran 2002: 372).

From a Kenyan publication on early childhood development:

'Early childhood is seen as a time of freedom and a time when the self-confidence of adulthood is built. The Samburu believe that during the early years the brain develops and the children are therefore responsive to environmental influences. From birth to about six years, the children have little to do except play, listen, imitate, learn and build their language skills' (Lanyasunya and Lesolayia 2001: 10).

From the Swedish Childcare Commission (SOU), 1972:

'[Dialogue pedagogy] starts from the ideas that there should be a continuous dialogue between the child and the adults, on both an inner and outer level, which implies a reciprocal giving and taking of emotions, experiences and knowledge' (Dahlberg et al. 1999: 124).

From an article on indigenous education philosophies in Australia:

'The child is considered perfect at birth and is continually nurtured through food and physical touch. Alienation or separation is considered cruel, equal to deprivation of food or shelter. Touch, smell, the beat of the mother's heart, the sound of family, particularly mother, is considered "food", as necessary as breast milk' (Townsend-Cross 2002: 9).

From John Holt, USA children's rights activist in the 1970s:

' "Giving children time to grow". In one sense, the words mean nothing. How can one person give time to another? We can avoid taking or wasting someone's time, but that's not giving it' (Holt 1972: 112).

From New Zealand:

'Newer approaches to the teacher's role in facilitating children's learning have been influenced by the sociocultural paradigm . . . This view sees learning as social in origin and transferred through the mediation of cultural tools (e.g. language, books, symbols) to the individual where learning is internalised thought' (Hedges 2000: 16–17).

From an article on Japanese early education:

'And to be a decent human being, one must develop one's *kokoro* (heart, center of physical, mental, social, and emotional being). *Kokoro* is an interesting concept because it is at once an individual self-concept (developing personal capacities) and a social self-concept (development empathy, the capacity to relate to others)' (Sato 1993: 122).

Ideas gallery 5.2 Ideas from the past

German social theorist:

- As it is possible to teach anyone anything, education should be for all children.
- The first years are critical to later development.
- Young children learn best through concrete experiences from the real world.
- Educational work is similar to gardening work – the right environment for healthy growth must be created and, for a young child, freedom under close supervision is critical.
- The focus of education should be the individual and their abilities (John Amos Comenuis (1592–1670)).

English philosopher concerned with how learning occurs

'Pray remember, children are not taught by rules, which will be always slipping out of their memories. What you think necessary for them to do, settle in them by an indispensable practice, as often as the occasion returns; and, if be possible, make occasions' (John Locke (1632–1704)) (Locke 1964: 42).

French philosopher with considerable influence on thinking in France and Germany:

- Formal education should not start until 12.
- Young children could learn what they need to from nature and we need to return them to it for their learning.
- The fives senses are how young children learn best.
- Children should self-select their learning experiences.
- Children think differently to adults and thus need to be educated differently to them (Jean-Jacques Rousseau (1712–88)).

Zurich-born educationalist who drew on the work of Rousseau (Johann Pestalozzi (1746–1827)).

- Observation is key to planning appropriate experiences for young children.
- All children, irrespective of background have the capacity to learn.
- Positive and trusting relationships with teachers is at the heart of successful learning for young children.

- Sensory and experiential learning is the natural form of learning for young children.

- Mother love is critical to children's healthy development.

'I wish to wrest education from the outworn order of doddering old teaching hacks as well as from the new-fangled order of cheap, artificial teaching tricks, and entrust it to the eternal powers of nature herself' (quoted in Silber 1965: 134).

Charlotte Perkins Gilman (1860–1935), feminist educational theorist:

'[Infant education should be a] beautiful and delicately adjusted environment . . . in which line and color and sound and touch are all made avenues of easy unconscious learning' (Perkins 1900: 144).

John Dewey (1859–1952), USA educationalist:

'I believe that the psychological and social sides are organically related and that education cannot be regarded as a compromise between the two, or a superimposition of one upon the other' (Cuffaro 1995: 14).

Friedrich Froebel (1782–1852), student of Pestalozzi, who set up the first kindergarten in Germany:

- Play is valuable for young children.

- Bringing children together in a circle (circle time) is a valuable strategy for building group cohesion.

Margaret McMillan (1860–1931), social activist who co-founded with her sister, Rachael, the Open-Air Nursery in London:

- Emotional well-being is as important as physical well-being.

- Parent involvement is important in programmes for young children.

- Outside experiences with open-ended materials facilitate children's healthy development.

- Children's development is assisted when they are encouraged to express themselves through art.

(*Sources*: Singer 1992; Pinar *et al.* 1995; Henniger 1999)

Further reading and online resources

Montessori

American Montessori Society homepage: http://www.amshq.org/indexmain.html
Brewer, J. (1992) *Introduction to Early Childhood Education: Preschool through Primary Grades.* Boston, MA: Allyn and Bacon.
International Montessori Index homepage: http://www.montessori.edu/maria.html
Jackson, P. (1997) The child's delight. Paper presented to the International Montessori Conference: http://www.ilu.uu.se/ilu/montessori/MtheChi.htm
Kramer, R. (1988) *Maria Montessori.* London: Hamish Hamilton Paperback.
Morrison, G. (1995) *Early Childhood Education Today*, 6th edn. New Jersey: Merrill.
Video: Maria Montessori. *Follow the Child*. California: Douglas Clark Associates.

The High/Scope Preschool Curriculum (USA and Singapore)

Bredekamp, S. (1996) 25 years of educating young children: the High/Scope approach to preschool, *Young Children*, 51(4): 57–61.

Hohmann, M. and Weikart, D. (1995) *Educating Young Children: Active Learning Practices for Preschool and Childcare Programs*. Ypsilanti, MI: High/Scope Education Research Foundation.

Weikart, D. (1995/96) High/Scope in action: the milestones, *High/Scope Resource, Special Edition*, 4–6.

Weikart, D. and Schweinart, L. (1987) The High/Scope cognitively orientated curriculum in early childhood, in J. Roopnaarine (ed.) *Approaches to Early Childhood Curriculum*, pp.253–67. Ohio: Merrill Publishing Company.

Note

The following information and resources are available from the High/Scope Educational Research Foundation, 600 North River St., Ypsilanti, MI 48198–2898, USA (Tel: 1 313 4850704):

- *Extensions Newsletter of the High/Scope Curriculum*;
- *High/Scope Resource: A Magazine for Educators*;
- Video: *Setting up the Learning Environment*;
- Video: *High/Scope Curriculum. Its Implementation in Family Childcare Homes*;
- Video: *Supporting Children's Active Learning. Teaching Strategies for Diverse Settings*;
- Video: *The High/Scope Curriculum. The Plan–Do–Review Process*;
- Video: *The High/Scope Curriculum. The Daily Routine*.

Teachers reflecting critically on transforming their visions of children as learners

Campbell, S. and Smith, K. (2001) Equity observation and images of fairness, in S. Grieshaber and G.S. Cannella (eds) *Embracing Identities in Early Childhood Education: Diversity and Possibilities*, pp.89–102. New York: Teachers College Press.

Ketley, H. (2000) Babies: setting their own curriculum, *Every Child*, 6(1): 15.

Robinson, R., Saitta, S. and Smith, K. (2000) Observing babies: the silent community, *Every Child*, 6(1): 17.

Theilheimer, R. and Cahill, B. (2001) A messy closet in the early childhood classroom, in S. Grieshaber and G.S. Cannella (eds) *Embracing Identities in Early Childhood Education: Diversity and Possibilities*, pp.103–13. New York: Teachers College Press.

PART 2

Positions on the early childhood curriculum

6

Reflecting on the early childhood curriculum

This second part of the book explores different positions on the early childhood curriculum. This chapter invites you to explore your own beliefs and ideas about educating young children. Each of the next three chapters (7, 8 and 9) introduces you to a position on the early childhood curriculum categorized according to its views on the role of education in society: 'conforming', 'reforming' or 'transforming'. Each chapter consists of:

- an overview of the position – its philosophy of education and its approach to curriculum;
- a history of the ideas within the position;
- the implications of the position for the early childhood curriculum (i.e. philosophy, goals, planning and assessment);
- equity reflections on the position.

Chapter 10 invites you to reflect critically on your own position on the early childhood curriculum.

Definitions of curriculum are always hotly debated. This book sees curriculum as a politically engaged process in which the educator's intentions and the children's involvement interact to produce the lived curriculum of a specific service. The educator's intentions may be more or less explicit, but they will express a philosophy of education, curriculum goals and approach to the use of time, space, resources and materials and an approach to assessing what is occurring. To this extent, the initial 'look' and 'practice' in curriculum are shaped by the educator's:

- philosophies of education;
- curriculum goals;
- curriculum plans (including scheduling, content, pedagogies and learning resources);
- curriculum assessment.

In what follows you are invited to reflect on your own philosophy and goals, and your approach to curriculum planning and assessment.

Shaping curriculum through philosophy

Philosophies explain why we do what we do. Some people say that matters of philosophy are separate from matters of practice. Decisions about what to do with young children in a particular moment on a particular day are highly practical matters, but they are also deeply philosophical matters. This is because they arise from our ideas about what we believe it is important for young children to know and to experience and how we believe it is best to teach them. As Lovat and Smith explain, educational philosophers are people who have ideas about the goals, practices and intents of education:

> If we have ideas about education, about how it should proceed, about what teachers should do, what shape schools should take, who should control the curriculum and what purposes it should be serving, then we are 'educational philosophers' of some sort.
>
> (Lovat and Smith 1995: 75)

So, ideas about what young children should do on a particular day, how you should shape their day, who should decide what they do and what purposes there should be behind particular activities and experiences they are offered are as much matters of philosophy as they are matters of practice. As such they are matters of personal and professional value, as CETaL (2002: 1) note:

> What one teaches – and who one teaches, and perhaps even how – is a personal expression of professional goals and values. Why does one teach? The question often evokes basic moral values – about an informed citizenry, about self-fulfilment and understanding or about development of the means to achieve one's life goals. The professional teacher reflects on these values, articulates them, makes them explicit and public, possibly justifies them, and uses them as a guide to clarify and develop practice.

They are also matters of broader social and cultural values about what role education should play in society and how that role is best practised. As Bruner (1996: ix–x) reminds us: 'How one conceives of education, we have finally come to recognize, is a function of how one conceives of the culture and its aims, professed or otherwise'.

Critically reflective early childhood professionals are aware of their personal values about the purposes of early childhood education. They also know how their social and cultural contexts connect with their personal values. Such awareness is the core to building a philosophy to guide educational practice because, 'In the absence of a guiding philosophy, the curriculum tends to be a product of ad hoc decisions – typically stemming from a combination of traditional practices and more immediate experiences' (Tanner and Tanner 1975: 63).

Developing your own 'professed' position on the role of early childhood education in society has several additional benefits. It can help you as an educator to:

- prioritize the goals you have for teaching and learning in your setting;
- decide what actions will bring you a sense of personal meaning, purpose and accomplishment in your work with young children;
- choose among competing understandings and interpretations of classroom events;
- develop 'goals, values, and attitudes to strive for' (Merriam 1982: 90–1) that motivate and energize you on a daily basis;
- explore with parents and colleagues what you are trying to achieve in your work with children and why you organize things in the way that you do (Faragher and Mac Naughton 1998);
- enter into discussions with colleagues and provide a basis for an agreed team approach to your work with children (Faragher and Mac Naughton 1998).

To achieve its aim of helping you to develop an explicit position on the role of early childhood education in society, the chapters in Part 2 offer you ideas and processes to increase your awareness of possible roles for early childhood education in society and their equity implications.

Reflecting on where you are

The first step in building a clear philosophical position or statement is to clarify your current ideas and beliefs about what good education for young children means. The following exercises can assist you in this.

Reflection points

- What do I want for children now and in the future?
- What should be the role of early childhood services in society?

Reflection sheet 6.1 My ideas about early childhood education

Reflection questions	Your ideas	Where have your ideas come from?
What do I want for children now and in the future?		
What should be the role of early childhood services in society?		

Ideas clarification exercise 6.1

Developing a curriculum philosophy or a set of philosophical guides for action is complex and challenging, partly because there is no simple consensus about what young children should do or learn in early childhood programmes. Try to complete one or more of the following exercises to clarify your current philosophy of early childhood education.

- *Reflect on why you are involved in early childhood education.* What do you hope to achieve in your work with young children?
- *Talk with four people who come from a different background* to your own about what they think early childhood education does. What is similar and what is different about how they think about early childhood education? To what extent is it similar to your hopes as an early childhood educator?
- *What do you see as the key challenges you face* in building clear philosophical positions on the role of early childhood education in society?

Shaping curriculum through goals

Curriculum goals are our stated intentions in working with young children and they describe the emphasis we will give to particular areas in our curriculum. They can refer to our intentions over several months (long-term goals) or our intentions during several days or weeks (short-term goals). They are generally written down in some form to remind us of what we want to achieve. As writer Alice Walker reminds us, we need to be alert to what we want to achieve in the future if we are going to realize it in practice: 'Keep in mind always the present you are constructing. It should be the future you want' (Walker 1989: 38).

As goals express our intentions, hopes and desires in our work with young children they provide a point of reference for our decisions and actions, helping us to prioritize what we do with young children. Goals can also:

- revitalize your work with young children by offering you a sense of purpose;
- concentrate your efforts and resources by capturing in a few sentences what you see as the most important things to do in your work with young children;
- help you to explore priorities in your service with colleagues and parents by providing you with a basis for conversation about what you believe is important;
- help you to bring your philosophy of early childhood education alive in your work;
- offer a basis from which to drive other key curriculum decisions;
- offer a point for reflection on, and evaluation of, on your work with young children.

Reflecting on where you are

Curriculum goals don't just happen – people must actively build them. The first step in building curriculum goals is to recall your position on the role of early education in society. Use this to reflect on what you think the main emphasis in your curriculum goals will be and how you think you will build curriculum goals.

Reflection points

- What does your position on the role of early education in society suggest you should emphasize in your work with young children?
- What challenges might you face in deciding the emphasis you will give to different skills, knowledges, dispositions and possibilities in your curriculum?

Reflection sheet 6.2 My curriculum goals and my philosophy

Reflection questions	My core position/ideas are	This means I will emphasize the following in my curriculum
What do you believe the role of early education in society should be?		
How do you see the child as a learner?		
What are your hopes and dreams for young children?		
What are your equity and social justice goals?		

Ideas clarification exercise 6.2

Complete one or more of the following exercises to clarify your goals at this point.

- *Reflect on the exercises in Chapter 5.* What curriculum goals are suggested by your position on the role of education in society? Who should decide the goals and what should their content be?
- *Reflect on what your ideal world would look like.* How would people treat each other? How would people act? What would be the strengths and riches of people in that world?
- *Talk in depth with at least one person* from a background different to your own and of a different age to you. What changes would they like to see in the world as it is now?
- *Read an inspirational book or article* on someone who has changed the world. What were their goals for life and/or their goals in making a difference? Some starting points for that reading are offered at the end of the chapter.

Shaping curriculum through plans

Planning designs are the 'nuts and bolts' of putting curriculum into action in an early childhood setting. In designing a curriculum, educators shape their resources (including time, space, people and materials) into a plan or map for their work with children.

Reflecting on where you are

Reflection points

- For what aspects of your day with young children do you believe you need to plan in advance?

- To what extent do you think you need to plan for the use of time, people, space and materials in working with young children?

Reflection sheet 6.3 My curriculum planning ideas

Reflection questions	Your ideas
For what aspects of your day with young children do you believe you need to plan in advance?	
To what extent do you think you need to plan for the use of time, people, space and materials in working with young children?	

Ideas clarification exercise 6.3

Try to complete one or more of the following exercises to help you clarify your ideas about planning for your work with young children.

- *Talk with an experienced early childhood educator.* What aspects of the day does he or she plan in advance? How does he or she plan for the use of time, space, people and materials in his or her daily work with young children?
- *Talk with a person with a background different to your own* who is involved in work with young children. Ask them to comment on whether or not they believe young children should have fixed schedules and routines in their day or whether schedules should be flexible. Ask them to give their reasons. To what extent do you agree with this person?
- *Review an article on Montessori education* or on the High/Scope programmes (Chapter 5). To what extent does its approach to planning fit comfortably with your own?

Shaping curriculum through observation and assessment

To observe something is to look closely at it. More specifically, early childhood educators use the term 'observation' to describe the systematic and structured way that educators look at children (Faragher and Mac Naughton 1998) and assess their learning.

Reflecting on where you are

You are an experienced observer, whether or not you are an experienced early childhood educator. You have observed other people in a variety of ways throughout your life and your knowledge of observation and your skill in performing it will influence how you learn about the children that you work with.

Reflection points

- What place would you give observation of children in your curriculum?
- What do you think are the best ways to study children?
- What issues do you currently face or think you might face in observing children and using that knowledge in your curriculum planning?

Reflection sheet 6.4 My knowledge about observation and assessment

Reflection questions	Your ideas
What place would you give observation of children in your curriculum?	
What do you think are the best ways to study children?	
Would your preferred ways of studying children allow their voices into the curriculum?	
What issues do you currently face or think you might face in this area of your work?	

Ideas clarification exercise 6.4

Try to complete one or more of the following exercises to help you clarify your ideas about the place of observation and of children's voices in the early childhood curriculum:

- *Reflect on your current knowledge of observation:* how could you use observation to help you learn about how a particular child felt about something?
- *Ask an experienced early childhood educator* how he or she uses observation in planning.
- *Watch a video of a young child* and take notes of what you see. What did you learn through taking your notes?

Inspirational readings: people who have worked to change the world

The following websites have extensive lists of bibliographies and short articles on people who have worked to change the world:

- Women's History Site (follow the links to biographies): http://www.womens-history.about.com/mbody.htm
- Afro-American History Site (follow the links to specific people such as Martin Luther King and Malcom X, but also to specific topics where key activists and their work is discussed): http://www.afroamhistory.about.com/
- College Ten: social justice and community page. This page houses images of and links to information on nearly 40 international activists: http://college-ten.ucsc.edu/activists.shtml

7
Curriculum position: conforming to society

Overview

Key thinker	Definition
Ralph Tyler (1949–), USA education-alist.	Conforming: complying with the existing practices, rules, traditions and understandings (for example, education that complies with the existing social practices, rules, traditions and understandings of a given society and, to that extent, governs the individual).

> Teaching is a cultural task and our business is to gear these natural curiosities and interests to the traditional skills which the culture has built up and valued.
>
> (Brearley 1970, in Read *et al.* 1993: 286)

This chapter focuses on how people working within a 'conforming to society' position on early childhood curriculum have answered the question, 'What is early childhood education for?' and, given that, 'How should we build and assess early childhood curriculum?'

A 'conforming to society' position on the role of education in society rests on the belief that education can and should achieve national social goals and that governments define the roles and purposes within education in order to ensure that core national goals and values are maintained in and through education. From this perspective, education can:

- reproduce the skills needed to achieve national economic, social and political goals;
- reproduce the understandings and values that enable society to reproduce itself (Feinberg 1983).

Those ideas are present in weaker or stronger expression in several countries' intentions for their early childhood programmes. Ideas gallery 7.1 lists just some of these expressions.

Ideas gallery 7.1

From Nigeria

'The federal government views pre-primary education (ages 3–5) as the provision of adequate care and supervision; inculcation of social norms; inculcation of the spirit of enquiry and of creativity through active exploration of the environment; play; cooperation; good health habits; and the teaching of numbers, letters, colours, shapes and forms through play.' (Rufai 1996: 31)

From Kenya

'Early childhood is traditionally seen as a stage of life when children slowly learn oral traditions, way of life, and customs. This is the stage when oral traditions are told to the new generation, describing every bit of the past.' (Lanyasunya and Lesolayia 2001: 10)

From Korea

'The primary purpose to educate a child in the traditional society was to make him a person who would provide filial loyalty to parents and ancestors. Currently, the primary purpose in educating a child is to prepare him to adapt to society as an independent and responsible person.' (Lee 1997: 49)

From Australia

'Early childhood development and experiences affect educational outcomes; career prospects; health outcomes; avoiding reliance on welfare, substance misuse and becoming entangled in the criminal justice system.
    These outcomes are significant to all individuals, their families and communities. If we can give our children a better start, we all stand to benefit.' (Anthony 2002: 1)

Where have the ideas come from: a brief history lesson

Social reproduction and utility

Within a 'conforming to society' position on early education's role, the key idea is that it should be useful to society and meet its needs. Early education should prepare the child for the adult world so that the child can adjust and contribute appropriately to that world. Early education can teach the child about their society and about what that society and its educators decide is of most value or use.

Early childhood education's social utility has been linked to two areas. First, it can effectively prepare children for school, thus giving them a 'head start', 'early start' or 'best start' in their schooling. Second, it can prevent crime and deviance in later life. This is illustrated clearly in the following government report:

Because of the long-lasting effects, early investments can have big payoffs. They avert the need for more costly interventions later in life, and so contribute to happier, healthier, and more productive children, adolescents, and adults.

(Report of the Council of Economic Advisors 1997, in Fleer 2002: 2)

Social utility arguments about early childhood education have become remarkably commonplace and significant research resources have been deployed to prove the social worth of early education. Much of this research has emphasized early education's role in preventing deviant behaviour – especially crime. There have been several 'waves' of such research but the general thrust is similar: if we want normal adults who can conform to existing social mores and expectations, then early childhood education can help.

Most recently, research from within neuroscience, known more commonly as the 'brain research' (Lindsey 1998; Joseph 1999; Chapter 3), has been used to demonstrate the importance of the early years in young children's learning and the relevance of this learning for their later life chances. Ideas gallery 7.2 provides a snapshot of some of the present-day international research that highlights the prevalence of social utility arguments in the field.

Ideas gallery 7.2 Why early childhood services matter: some twentieth- and twenty-first-century thinking on the place of cultural transmission in early childhood education.

'Child-initiated programs have long term benefits including improving children's capacity to work independently of adults.' (Weikart 1995/96)

Developmentally appropriate programs in the USA are associated with positive social and academic outcomes for young children (Hoot *et al.* 1999).

Research from the UK indicates that policy expectations about what children should know at key phases in middle schooling influenced what is taught in early childhood programs (Sylva *et al.* 1992; Evans 1996).

'Girls enrolled in early childhood programs are better prepared for school and remain in school longer.' (World Bank Group 2002)

The broad philosophy: cultural transmission

The 'conforming to society' position on curriculum has its roots in cultural transmission theories of education's role in society, which are linked strongly with the rise of the modern industrial state. Kemmis explained:

in the late nineteenth century educational theorising became more specific and more detailed in its prescriptions for teachers and schools as it was harnessed to the needs of the modern industrial state . . . one group of emerging curriculum theories began to take for granted that the role of schooling was to produce a qualified labor force and to achieve the reproduction of society.

(Kemmis 1986: 36)

The best way to ensure that society can reproduce itself is to shape children by deliberately and effectively transmitting desired social values and knowledge to them through their education:

Rather than viewing curriculum as an opportunity to develop mental discipline, as 'windows of the soul', or as organised around the needs, interests, and abilities of the child, curriculum became the assembly line by which economically and socially useful citizens would be produced. Social utility . . . became the sole value by which curriculum would be judged.

(Pinar *et al.* 1995: 95)

The role of scientific thinking and being rational
Scientific thinking – in the form of behaviourist (Chapter 2) understandings of learning – offers educators a ready source of knowledge about how to shape behaviour effectively and efficiently. As will be seen shortly, this knowledge entered the education system through what have become known as technical approaches to curriculum. These approaches offer formulae for teaching and for curriculum design that promise certainty in transmitting knowledge and values to children. Such rationality was believed to be essential to decisions about curriculum, as Giroux explained:

this form of rationality has evolved in a manner parallel to the scientific manage-ment movement of the 1920s, and (that) early founders of the curriculum move-ment such as Bobbitt and Charters warmly embraced the principles of scientific management. The school as factory metaphor has a long and extensive history in the curricula field. Consequently, modes of reasoning, inquiry, and research characteristics of the field have been modelled on assumptions drawn from a model of science and social relations closely tied to the principles of prediction and control.

(Giroux 1988: 12)

Drawing on behaviourist principles of human learning and motivation (Chapter 2) and on scientific management theory, scientific approaches to schooling seemed to offer the hope of building a more modern, efficient and effective workforce. Franklin Bobbitt, a US professor of educational administration in the early 1900s, took a leading role in this development. According to Longstreet and Shane (1993) he was 'in the forefront of the drive to have public education improve its efficiency by following the example of industry and indicating clearly what its "products" were to be' (p.29). He assumed that 'children need to learn how to fit into society and that the schools are the proper socialising agents' (p.31).

Implications of cultural transmission for early childhood curriculum: taking a technical approach

Implicit within cultural transmission theories (and the 'conforming to society' positions on curriculum that they underpin) is a commitment to technical curriculum design and thus clear ideas on the shape and style of early childhood curriculum goals, plans and assessment. They arise directly from a 'conforming to society' model of the child as a learner (Chapter 2).

Technical approaches to curriculum are based on the assumption that the ultimate form of social decision making should be rational (based on reason, not emotion). Rationalists believe that rational decision making is the most effective and efficient form of decision making. It is effective in that you achieve what you want. It is efficient because you take the shortest route towards achieving it.

To be rational, decision making should be:

- goal directed;
- a logical, step by step process of reaching one's goals;
- able to predict its outcomes.

So, rational decision making is a linear, goal directed and incremental process in which you decide (in this order):

- What do I want to achieve?
- What steps do I need to take to get there?
- Which step should I take first?
- How will I know when I have achieved my goal?

Goals

The core educational aim of a cultural transmission philosophy is the adaptation of the individual to society. Within early childhood education, this means developing goals that have direct social utility as defined by the dominant groups within a specific society.

A 'conforming to society' position on early childhood curriculum goals rests on several assumptions drawn from behaviourist thinking about the child, from cultural transmission philosophies of education and from technical approaches to curriculum (discussed above). In overview, these assumptions are that:

- goal development is an unproblematic, essentially technical process;
- goals should have direct social utility;
- goals should be prescribed in advance of meeting the children (generally by government);
- goals should be prescribed for all children.

Pinar (cited in Giroux 1988) suggested that between 85 and 95 per cent of all curricula approach goal development in ways that are closely allied with technical approaches to curriculum.

Smith and Lovat (1990) identified two main approaches to developing goals in a technically orientated curriculum:

- the objectives approach;
- the rational approach.

The objectives approach

In the objectives approach to goal development, you specify your goals before you begin to teach, which assumes that you know what knowledge you wish to pass on to children prior to meeting them. Your goals should be technical, to ensure that children learn the desired skills, knowledge and attitudes. The objectives approach also assumes that there is a logical and obvious relationship between what you intend to teach and your capacity to find the 'best' experience to teach it. This approach to curriculum goals is most closely associated with standardized curriculum, in other words, curriculum in which all children are expected to achieve particular (the same) standards (Scott and Altman 1984: ii).

A behavioural objective is a statement of what behaviour you want the child to exhibit. There are clear rules to follow when writing behavioural objectives. First, they should emphasize the behaviour you want from the child, so they should always start with the phrase, 'For the child to . . .' The second rule is that the required behaviour should be specific and observable, in other words, you must be able to observe it. Finally, you should, if possible, specify by when the behaviour is to be achieved and where it is to be achieved. For example:

- For Sally to use her words to explain her feelings when she is upset by other children;
- For Karia to practise ball-handling skills once each day in the outside play area;
- For Boa to concentrate for at least 5 minutes each day in a pre-reading activity.

The rational approach

The rational approach to developing curriculum goals derives from the work of educationalists such as Hilda Taba, who believed that a curriculum should represent a rationale plan for learning and that curriculum development should itself be rational and orderly. Taba believed 'that there is a logical and universal order to the process of curriculum development [in which teachers can] separate the learning experience from the content of the learning experience' (Smith and Lovat 1990: 86).

Ideas summary 7.1 provides a snapshot of the goal formulation rules within a technically oriented early childhood curriculum. It is based on Davies (1977).

Ideas summary 7.1 A checklist for building conforming early childhood curriculum goals

Example goals

- For the child to do X (the behaviour) in Y (area of knowledge or developmental skill) by Z (when or where).
- For the child to use a wide range of expressive language with their peer group in the next month.

CONTENT

- emphasizes traditional knowledge and skills in areas such as literacy, numeracy and scientific thinking;
- values rationality and observable behaviours;
- specifies time frames.

DON'T

- avoid describing what you will do as a teacher;
- be too general.

LANGUAGE

- states what you want to achieve in terms of outcomes for children;
- states what you want to achieve in terms of observable behaviours.

DO

- specify the behaviour to be achieved by the learner and how the learner will demonstrate this behaviour.

Rational curriculum decision making reflects the influence of scientific management theory on education, where schools are likened to factories (Smith and Lovat 1990). Scientific management theory emerged between 1890 and 1930 from the work of Frederick Taylor and other management theorists, who tried to develop scientific principles that could determine the best way to perform a given work task and the best way to select, train and motivate workers. This theory's focus is on making all aspects of human resource management rational and efficient. The theory has had a significant impact on job design, ensuring that jobs are done as efficiently as possible, taking little account of individual workers' preferences, needs or capabilities. The worker should be matched to the job, not vice versa. As Kuhn and Martinko (1985: 279–80) wrote:

> The major emphasis of this theory was on the development of optimal production procedures through the controlled and systematic study of work methods. Once these optimal methods were developed, adherence to the procedures would be ensured if wages were made contingent upon performance . . . Taylorism has had, and still does have, a profound influence on practices of human resources management. Work simplification, time studies, wage incentive programs, and the assembly line are all direct results of Taylorism . . . As in Taylor's time, these practices are not intended to dehumanize workers or to limit their potential to develop.

Developmental goals in the early childhood curriculum and technical curriculum

Within a technically orientated early childhood curriculum, goals should be:

- specified in advance of meeting the children;
- based either on developmental norms for the child or on a set of skills or knowledge that the child should know;
- written in behavioural terms so that their achievement can be observed and evaluated.

Plans

A 'conforming to society' position on early childhood curriculum links directly with a technical approach to curriculum planning, which consists of deciding objectives, building strategies to achieve them and then assessing the strategies' success. Pedagogies are generally based upon a 'conforming to culture' (behaviourist) model of the child as a learner (Chapter 2). In general, planning is a rational process in which:

- *time* is often segmented and tightly organized, with its use and flow controlled by the educator;
- *people* (educators teach) specific skills and knowledge to children;
- *space* is tightly structured by the educator to ensure that the objectives can be achieved;
- *learning resources* are generally tightly geared towards learning that is associated with specific objectives;
- *knowledge* is generally pre-packaged and organized in ways (for example, themes or subject areas) that make sense to educators.

Shaping the planning process

Planning decisions are generally 'top-down' ways for the educator to answer these questions:

- What do I want to achieve?
- What steps do I need to take to get there?
- Which step should I take first?
- How will I know when I have achieved my goal?

The educator then uses these decisions to map:

- the content of what is to be learnt;
- the use of space and materials;
- the use of time;
- the educator's role in the curriculum.

The educator will plan a set of long-term objectives and each week will include a series of short-term objectives to assist in achieving the long-term ones. This plan will be for the whole group but it will include room for individual objectives for individual children to be achieved. For instance, see Figure 7.1.

Long-term objective for the group:

Date:

Child's name:

Specific objective:

Teaching strategies:

- motivating the child's interest;

- rewards;

- reinforcers;

- materials to be used;

- timing of the experience.

Evaluation:

- What child responses indicated that the objective was/was not achieved?

- Was the objective appropriate for the child's current level of understanding or skill?

- How should I change this experience at subsequent session(s)?

- Were there any unexpected responses or spontaneous learning?

Figure 7.1 Planning for individual children using an objectives-based approach

Shaping the content

Those who take a 'conforming to society' position see curriculum content as either vocationally orientated or neoclassical (Kemmis 1986). Vocationally orientated curriculum emphasizes learning skills and knowledge that will lead to success in the workplace. Reid identifies such an emphasis in the current Australian national education agenda:

> In broad terms, however, both major political parties have constructed the primary role of education as being one of 'value-adding' to students, and supplying the labour market with a ready-made stream of workers who have the requisite job skills and positive attitudes to work.
>
> (Reid 1999: 4)

Neoclassical curriculum emphasizes learning what is considered to be the most valued and significant knowledge of the 'Western' world. For instance: 'Curriculum should consist of permanent studies – grammar, reading, rhetoric, logic, mathematics and the greatest books of the Western world' (Smith and Lovat 1990: 3–4).

Traditional knowledge is the knowledge that has been organized into specific disciplines or fields of inquiry. Often these disciplines or fields of inquiry are used to build school curricula. Jerome Bruner, among others, believes that traditional disciplines or fields of study provide a good basis for curriculum development, because they offer a way for all children to learn what their society considers to be 'intellectually significant' (Spodek and Saracho 1994: 99). This idea has influenced a number of early childhood educators who believe that young children should be introduced to knowledge from key fields of inquiry of the Western world, including:

- science;
- the arts (for example, literature, music, drama, painting and collage);
- mathematics.

Content is generally prepared by the educator and shaped into clear and distinct units or segments for learning. This generally results in content being planned as:

- *units* linking ideas and concepts that the teacher believes the child needs to learn;
- *a calendar curriculum* (Spodek 2002) where content is themed and linked to specific months or times of the year (for example, welcome to the centre, Easter, Spring, Xmas);
- *subjects*, with an emphasis on children learning specific types of knowledge.

Wah (1992) provides an example of how a unit of study can be structured and segmented into specific topics and objectives for the learner (see Figure 7.2).

Singapore

Unit Two: My home and my country

Aim:

· Knowledge of Singapore as an island and a garden city.

Topics:

· This is Singapore Island.

· Here is my home.

· We live in a garden city.

Objectives:

· To point out the location of Singapore Island on a regional map.

· To show the location of one's home on a Singapore map.

· To care for this garden city.

Figure 7.2 Sample of a unit of study

The educator may use curriculum packages and pre-packaged lesson plans which contain detailed descriptions of what is to be achieved and how. For instance, an educator might purchase a commercial curriculum that includes a set of activities and materials that enables them to teach a specific concept such as number, families, people in the community, plants and animals, growth and so on. Or they may purchase a commercial curriculum that is skill-based and focuses on counting skills, memory skills or pre-reading skills. Most of these curriculum packages will have several features in common:

- a detailed list of objectives for the teacher to teach the child the specific knowledge or skill;
- printed materials including worksheets, workbooks, stories and/or posters that can be used by the teacher to teach the specific knowledge or skill;
- clear indicators of behaviours that a child will display to show that they have learnt the knowledge or skill;
- a stepped process for moving children from simple to more complex understandings or skill levels.

For instance, a pre-programmed numeracy skills curriculum could include:

- activities that teach children to count, recognize and recite numbers 1–10;
- card games that teach children to recognize numbers;
- matching numbers and making number sheets;
- number song suggestions.

Examples of pre-programmed curricula can be found on the Internet at http://www.earlychildhood.com/community/act/act_index.asp

Most of the knowledge within pre-packaged curricula is fact-based. In practice, the content in programmes based on behaviourist and scientific education principles often concentrates on cognitive tasks to the exclusion of other areas of development (Weber 1984). It requires the educator to be technically competent in delivering the pre-set curriculum. This technical competence is a sign of educator competence.

Ideas gallery 7.3 provides a snapshot of some examples of the influences of traditional fields of study on how people see the goals of early childhood education.

Ideas gallery 7.3 International expressions of a conforming approach to the content of early childhood curriculum goals: traditional areas of knowledge

From an Australian early childhood journal:

'Mathematics is every bit as important as language development in assisting young children to maximize their potential.' (Hall 1996: 4)

From a USA early childhood textbook:

'Art media offer both child and adult an avenue for the discovery of self and the expression of feeling. Creative expression through the arts, whether in language, music or dance, or the graphic and plastic arts, has an important place in the curriculum.' (Read *et al.* 1993: 328)

From an article about Norwegian early childhood curriculum:

'The plan [Norwegian early childhood curriculum framework] states that all Norwegian preschools should in some way or another experience five subject areas during a year . . . (1) society, religion and ethics; (2) aesthetic subjects; (3) nature, technology, and environment; (4) language, literacy, and communication; and (5) physical activity and health.' (Alvestad and Samuelsson 1999: 3)

From a USA early childhood textbook:

'The processes used to study science are even more important than the content. Early childhood specialists need to promote the same techniques that scientists themselves use in their inquiries.' (Henniger 1999: 365)

Shaping the schedule

The schedule will often follow from behaviourist understandings of the learner:

> The behaviourist approach helps children follow set procedures in physical care activities (e.g. children gather for snacks at a given time; children are seated; snacks are distributed in a predetermined way; and clean up procedures are followed). Staff plan all other activities. Children are encouraged to stay on task and use materials in a specified way. Formal group lessons are often part of the daily plans.
>
> (Decker and Decker 1992: 274)

The main role of the schedule is to ensure that all children conform to a particular programme. To this end, the educator will develop a clear and fixed daily, weekly and annual schedule. (A fixed approach to scheduling is often associated with behaviourist programmes.) The daily schedule will commonly fix when the following occurs:

- outdoor and indoor experiences;
- group and individual times;
- eating, resting and toileting;
- adult-selected and child-selected activities.

For example:

9.00	Greet children and group mat time
9.20	Children to choose indoor activities
10.15	Pack up time
10.20	Bathroom time
10.30	Snack time
10.45	Outdoor activities
11.45	Group time

This means that all children will be inside at the same time, have their snack times together, and so on. The routine is not individualized but fixed to the needs of the educator and the group overall.

The weekly schedule will commonly tie particular events or activities to specific days and be linked to specific learning objectives for individual children. Often the educator will develop weekly plans for achieving specific objectives with specific children. These will be planned in advance and detail what the teacher needs to do to achieve a specific learning objective with a child.

For example:

Date: *My role:*

Child: *Mon*   *Tues*   *Wed*   *Thur*   *Fri*

Objective: Learning experiences and materials:

                Teaching strategies:

                Evaluation – was the objective achieved?

The annual schedule will commonly tie particular themes or areas of content and activities to specific times of the year. For example (for the southern hemisphere):

- January–March: Summer
- April–June: Autumn
- May: Mother's day and families
- July–September: Winter
- September: Father's day
- October–December: Spring – growth of plants and animals
- December: Xmas

The pedagogical relationships

Structuring relationships

The educator is in control of learning and therefore decides what is to be learnt, and the pedagogical relationships will be structured by specific lessons or learning episodes that:

- are educator-directed;
- have a beginning, middle and end;
- seek to achieve specific objectives with specific children.

Structuring space and materials

The educator decides how to use the space and materials. Often, space will be structured to reflect the theme, unit of study or subject areas the educator has chosen. There will be clearly defined areas within the room for specific types of learning and/or skill development. These will have been designed and organized by the educator.

Structuring teaching strategies

The pedagogy will often be based on behaviourist understandings of the learner and use teacher rewards and reinforcement as key motivators of children's learning. Educators will reinforce desirable learning outcomes and attempt to extinguish unacceptable learning and behaviours. For instance:

> An early childhood educator is teaching a group of 4-year-old children about the weather. Her objective is for the children to recognize the symbols for clouds, rain and sunshine that she has made and for them to choose the correct symbol for that day's weather. Jasper, one of the boys in the group, has been tugging at the hair of the child in front throughout the lesson. The teacher decides to ignore this behaviour and to praise the children next to Jasper who are attending to her lesson. She tells the children that those children sitting quietly and listening carefully will be the first children to go outside today and they may choose which equipment they want to use. She knows that Jasper likes a particular bike that is a high status toy that other children are likely to choose first.
>
> (Contributed by Heather Lawrence)

Generally an active behaviour management programme will be in place that draws directly on behaviourist principles. It will use rewards and punishment to control and manage children's behaviour in the classroom. There may be use of 'time out' for children who are not behaving in socially acceptable ways.

Educators will take a lead role in directing children to specific tasks, moving them on to new tasks and deciding when tasks should be completed. This is because behaviourist approaches to teaching and learning rely heavily on 'learning episodes' (Decker and Decker 1992: 275). Learning episodes are seen to be an effective way to teach because:

- teachers do not have to wait for children's interest to teach something;
- teachers can introduce new knowledge and skills to children in an ordered way (Decker and Decker 1992).

The educator may use a bell or specific sound in the room to tell children that a particular activity is finished and it is time to move to the next activity and/or to call them to a group activity.

Observations and assessments

All teachers need to develop skills as observers of children. They learn most about children by studying their behaviour directly. By learning to observe with objectivity, making careful notes, and going over them thoughtfully, a teacher increases her understanding of the meaning behind a child's behaviour.

(Read *et al.* 1993: 71)

Why observe?

In a conforming to society position on early childhood curriculum, assessment expresses the assumption that we can understand children through objectively observing them. The more objective the observer is the more possible it is to reach the truth of the child and what they have learnt or how they are progressing as learners.

Early childhood educators linked educating the child with (empiricist) observations of the child in order to create a more scientific approach to teaching and learning that would professionalize early childhood education and give it greater legitimacy. This happened in the US during the late nineteenth and early twentieth centuries, as Bloch (1992) argued:

> To varying degrees, depending upon the place and the person, there were attempts to use the 'hard' physical sciences, and psychology's definition of science . . . as the model for truth, definitions of valuable knowledge, a way to get factual information about 'normal' child development, as guidance for pedagogy.
>
> (Bloch 1992: 9)

Under the direction of researchers such as Arnold Gesell (Chapter 2), data were generated about children's normal development and the extent to which individual children's development varied from the norm. This produced clear descriptions of normal development in children of different ages that early childhood teacher training and educational texts used 'as an initial planning guide for teachers of young children' (Henniger 1999: 43).

This approach to assessment locks into technical approaches to curriculum in which the educator observes the child for one of three reasons:

- to assess the child's current level of understanding or skill as a basis for planning experiences to match them;
- to assess the child's current level of understanding or skill as a basis for formulating specific objectives for them;
- to assess the child's current level of understanding or skill against predetermined learning outcomes.

How to observe?

Within a conforming to society position on curriculum, assessment of children's learning must be objective and must be able to measure children's progress towards particular objectives, developmental norms or pre-specified learning outcomes. Bentzen typifies this view of how observation should be undertaken in the early childhood curriculum:

> In a very real sense, you will be acting as a scientist when you observe children. You will be doing what every scientist or researcher must do if she is to learn

about the real world ... In your case you will be looking at children, some of whom will be a phenomenon for you to describe, explain, maybe predict and, consequently, understand.

(Bentzen 1985: 7)

The idea that we can know a child and assess his or her learning by objectively observing their behaviour assumes that we can be a disinterested observer of facts who can acquire objective knowledge of a child. This idea has its roots in positivist and empiricist understandings of knowledge:

Empiricists stress that knowledge exists in what they call external reality, or the objective world, and can be found not only in personal experience, but also in a shared culture. The transmission of knowledge, including the standards and rules of the present culture, are considered the mission of institutions of early child-hood education. They often view an early childhood curriculum as content to be learned.

(Yang 2001: 3)

Consider how these features appear in the following description of how to observe children objectively:

The first and most essential step in observation is to look closely and describe as carefully as possible what you see. Objective observation depends on experiencing as completely as possible while suspending judgement. Objectivity means seeing what is actually taking place. It means observing without making value judgements.

(Feeney *et al.* 1983: 110)

Educators often use the following forms of observation to gain objective understandings of a child:

- anecdotal observations;
- time sampling;
- event sampling;
- running records;
- rating scales.

Ideas summary 7.2 briefly describes how to use each of these strategies.

Ideas summary 7.2 Forms of observation

Anecdotal observations

What   Short descriptions or notes of a child's behaviour and actions.

How   Develop an observation sheet or format that allows you to write short descriptive notes about the child. Note the date, time, place, setting and child(ren) involved. Include the child's actual language.

Pros   Quick and simple.

Can be made on the spot with only pencil and paper.

Grouping observations on a child over time allows patterns or trends to be noted.

Cons   Susceptible to observer bias.

May miss key information because they are so brief about what led up to and what followed the note.

Running records

What   Detailed description of a child(ren)'s behaviour and actions over time that tries to capture everything that happens in a specific period of time.

How   Develop an observation sheet or format that allows you to write detailed notes about a child(ren) over a period of up to ten minutes. Note the date, time, place, setting and child(ren) involved. Include the child(ren)'s actual language.

Pros   Can provide a rich and detailed picture of a child and what influences their behaviour on a specific day at a specific point in time.

Cons   Need to set aside time to focus solely on writing a running record and then interpreting it.

Event sampling

What   Taking short observations or notes of what happens around a particular event and what sets off that event.

How   Develop an observation sheet or format that allows you to write down what happens and what triggered it.

Pros   Can help you to understand why a particular event happens – such as a particular child is always present when biting occurs or a particular child is always present when a wonderfully complex block building happens. You can then work on reducing/supporting this event to recur, respectively.

Cons   You can miss important information about a child or group dynamics that do not occur around your targeted event.

Time sampling

What   Taking short observations or notes of what happens every few minutes.

How   Develop an observation sheet or format that allows you to track every few minutes where particular children are and what they are doing.

Pros   Can assist you to see patterns in where children are, how long they are in particular areas and how often.

Cons   You can miss important information about a child or group dynamics that do not occur around your targeted time.

Rating scales

What   A simple tool for rating what a child is doing as you observe them.

How   Develop an observation sheet or format that allows you to rate a child's behaviour on a scale from 1 to 5. You can rate the frequency, the level of skill, the level of support needed to complete an activity, and so on. You can rate negative or positive qualities of a particular skill, disposition or trait.

Pros	Can assist you to capture data quickly about the quality of what a child is doing. For instance, how well or how much support a child needs.
Cons	You can miss details about the context of what is happening that might help you to make judgements about how best to support a child's learning.

The most widely recommended form of observation is anecdotal observation:

> Although teachers use many different types of observation techniques, the anecdotal record may be the most useful in curriculum planning. These brief written notes should include the date and time of the observation, who is observed, what the children were doing, and the time spoken.
>
> (Henniger 1999: 279)

Anecdotal observations are generally very brief and descriptive of the child's behaviour and words. For example: 'Jinda builds a tall building balancing several small blocks upon each other as he does so.' For those who see child study as the key, curriculum planning is a rational and technical process. Educators go through a logical step by step process that starts with observations of children's learning and continues as follows:

- record the observation;
- interpret the observation – generally using developmental theory;
- plan activities or experiences on the basis of the interpretation;
- implement the planned experiences;
- evaluate what happened through observation;
- begin again.

A recent study by the New Zealand Council for Educational Research about educators' assessment tools found that non-formal methods of assessment such as running records and teacher-designed tests and observation formats were used most frequently to assess young children's literacy (Croft 2001: 3).

Ideas gallery 7.4 provides a snapshot of how conforming approaches to child study and assessment of children's learning have appeared in early childhood texts over time and how they linked to curriculum decision making.

Ideas gallery 7.4 Conforming approaches to child study and children's voices in the curriculum

From a 1980s UK early childhood text:

'Making sense of the information from observation, and planning from this, is an area of skill which has to be learned like the skills of making observations.' (Laishley 1983: 12)

From a 1980s US textbook:

'Rather than focusing on children's behaviour in general, this method will help observers to determine specifically where each child stands developmentally in the areas of emotional, social, physical, cognitive, language and creative development.' (Beaty 1986: 3)

From a 1980s Australian text:

'A way must be found to record information about individual children, to ensure that the needs and interests of each child are being taken into account in the program, and that the fit of the program with individual children is being monitored.' (Stonehouse 1988: 18)

From a 1990s US early childhood text:

'As the teacher comes to recognize individual children's developmental and social levels from her observations, she can make plans for such children.' (Beaty 1992: 59)

From an Australian Montessori teacher in 2001:

'Once goals are established, children should then be plotted against these developmental goals according to when they are capable of achieving them.' (Davis 2001: 6)

From an Australian early childhood curriculum policy document in 1996:

'To develop an understanding of individual children staff need to observe children during different activities and record their behaviour and development. All information should be recorded objectively and legibly . . . Learning experiences can be planned by interpreting the observation.' (Preschool and Childcare Branch 1996: 4)

Interpreting observations

Collecting data on children's learning for assessment purposes within a technical curriculum will generally involve particular approaches to making sense of (interpreting) the data that include:

- *Norm-referenced interpretation.* This involves looking at the data collected on individual children to see the extent to which they compare with agreed 'norms' for individual children of their age, stage and so on. In early childhood education these norms are often developmental.

- *Criteria-referenced interpretation.* This involves looking at the data collected on individual children to see the extent to which they meet agreed 'criteria' for performance. In early childhood education these criteria will often concern key areas of learning such as literacy, science, the arts and so on, and they may be developed from nationally or state-mandated curricula.

- *Goal-based interpretation.* This involves looking at the data collected on individual children to see the extent to which they demonstrate achievement of a particular goal. In early childhood education these goals will often concern key areas of learning such as literacy, science, the arts and so on, and they may be developed from nationally or state-mandated curricula or they may be developmental.

- *Theory-based interpretation.* This involves looking at the data collected on individual children to see the extent to which they demonstrate a particular theory of learning or development. In early childhood education this will often be based on developmental theory such as Piaget's stage-based theory of cognition. See, for instance, the report by Clift, Stagnitti and DeMello on a study that compares traditional pen and paper screening tests for school readiness with a standardized Test of Pretend Play (ToPP) that 'assesses the "symbolic" ability of preschoolers in the context of their pretend play' (Clift *et al.* 2000: 22). The ToPP test is based on Piagetian theory and Clift, Stagnitti and DeMello concluded that this standardized ToPP test offers a more developmentally appropriate test of school readiness than traditional screening tests.

Interpreting observations, therefore, involves making decisions about the implications of your data about children. Interpretation is critical to curriculum decision making because in it you use your observations to make judgements about what has been learnt by whom and what might be needed next to support their learning.

A desire for objective measures of children's learning and stages of understanding and development is at the core of a technical approach to curriculum. Consequently, educators who take a technical approach often prefer norm-referenced assessments and checklists (which they often design) over non-standardized tests.

Learning outcomes and assessing children's learning

There has been a strong move in recent years to identify children's learning outcomes at various stages of their preschool and school years. For example, in the mid-1990s, 44 states in the US 'conducted some form of statewide, elementary student testing on a regular basis' (Trepanier-Street *et al.* 2001: 234) using desired learning outcomes; and in Australia, national profiles and curriculum statements identify a set of learning outcomes for children in eight key learning areas. Figure 7.3 shows how learning outcomes link to national statements and profiles.

The national profiles and outcome statements derive from an outcomes-based theory of education which prescribes what children should achieve (outcomes) rather than what educators should teach. In Australia, each state has developed its own version of the national statements and their attendant learning outcomes. Blyth (2002) talks of Australian education being 'awash with outcomes and standards' (p.21) and points to the use of the term outcomes as being 'vague and indiscriminate' (p.21). Within this general move to outcomes-based education (however it is defined), states have explored the links between outcomes in the kindergarten to Year 2 levels and the preschool years and how to use learning outcomes in diagnosing poor learning outcomes and administering remedies. For instance:

- Queensland has a Year 2 diagnostic net to diagnose and remedy children with poor levels of literacy and numeracy (DoE: 1995).
- Western Australia has a First Steps programme to identify and remedy children with early literacy difficulties.

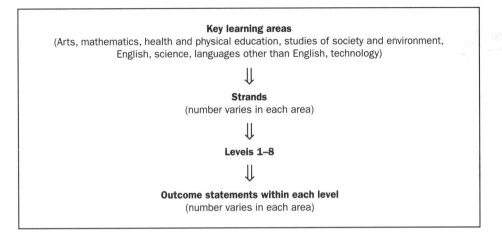

Figure 7.3 Learning outcomes and national profiles and statements

In 1995, the UK School Curriculum and Assessment Authority (SCAA) pre-scribed a set of desirable outcomes for nursery education (children aged 4–5 years) linked to a voucher system of funding nursery education. Parents could use their vouchers to 'purchase' nursery education places and to receive these vouchers, a nursery must demonstrate that it is working towards these desirable outcomes. The extent to which nurseries achieve the desirable outcomes was monitored. The desirable outcomes were organized into six learning areas that linked strongly with the UK's national curriculum framework for schools:

- personal and social development;
- language and literacy;
- mathematics;
- knowledge and understanding of the world;
- physical development;
- creative development.

Each learning area had desirable outcomes in children entering compulsory schooling, linked to Levels 1 and 2 of the national curriculum. Considerable public debate accompanied the move to desirable learning outcomes for nursery education in the UK. Much of the debate centred on using the desirable outcomes to test children entering primary school – the results of which are used later to assess the 'value-added' by a primary school to children's learning outcomes. Anning comments on this in the UK context:

> More research is clearly needed to explore how to link desirable curriculum goals with desirable learning outcomes. What research does show is that early childhood teachers do change what and how they teach when assessment tools make them accountable for what children learn.
>
> (Anning 1998)

More recently (September 2002) the QCA and the Department for Education and Skills released the *Foundation Stage Profile* which details 127 items against which a child's learning and development in the early years can be profiled in the autumn, spring and summer terms. The assessment in the current test phase will normally be made when a child is in reception class.

Items in the profile cover six areas of learning and are 'structured as a set of 13 assessment scales, each of which has 9 points':

- Personal, social and emotional development – dispositions and attitudes, social development and emotional development.

- Communication, language and literacy – language for communication and thinking, linking sounds and letters, reading and writing.

- Mathematical development – includes counting, calculating, shape, space and measures.

- Understanding knowledge of the world.

- Physical development.

- Creative development.

The *Foundation Stage Profile* handbook states that 'A record of children's development across all these areas provides a picture of the whole child at the end of the foundation stage' (QCA and DES 2002: 4).

In New Zealand, the early childhood curriculum has a distinctive set of desirable learning outcomes based on the five strands of the national early childhood curriculum, *Te Whãriki*. Those strands are *Mana Atura* – well-being; *Mana Whenua* – belonging; *Mana Tangata* – contribution; *Mana Reo* – communication; and *Mana Aotûroa* – exploration. The curriculum describes well over 100 learning outcomes that develop from the goals associated with each strand, and links these learning outcomes with the essential skills and learning areas listed in the New Zealand curriculum framework. New Zealand and the UK have different desirable outcomes, but share the principle of linking them to their core curriculum. The New Zealand curriculum is not mandated but its implementation is encouraged through its inclusion in the statements of Desirable Objective and Practices (DOPs). The Education Review Office (ERO) in New Zealand described the relationship between the two in the following way:

> The DOPs contain statements of broad objectives to be achieved by all chartered early childhood services with the aim of providing good quality education and care.
>
> The revised DOPs have been designed to be consistent with *Te Whãriki*. According to the Ministry of Education, it is not possible to include *Te Whãriki* as a direct requirement of the DOPs because of a legal anomaly in the Education Act 1989 which would require all 99 pages of *Te Whãriki* to be printed within the DOPs. Aspects of *Te Whãriki* have therefore been included throughout the revised DOPs.
>
> (ERO 1998: 1)

In summary, early childhood staff in several countries need to monitor an increasing number of specific learning outcomes as part of teaching and learning in their classrooms. Early research from Australia and the UK (see Moyles 1996; Grieshaber 1997) suggests that educators are beginning to buckle under the weight of monitoring learning across so many dimensions. Further, there is considerable debate about what desirable learning outcomes are in the early years:

> If children are generally unhappy then something is wrong. The justification for emphasising such an aspect of care can be made perfectly adequately on humanitarian grounds. Yet there is evidence from China of the positive effects on aspects of development: learning of new concepts proceeds more efficiently when children are in a 'happy' emotional state.
>
> (Meng 1987, in Melhuish 1993: 24)

> The desirable outcomes are goals for learning for children by the time that they enter compulsory education [term after child's fifth birthday]. They emphasise early literacy, numeracy and the development of personal and social skills and contribute to children's knowledge, understanding and skills in other areas. Presented as six areas of learning, they provide a foundation for later achievement.
>
> (SCAA n/d: 1)

> Learning outcomes: knowledge, skills and attitudes. Children develop: an understanding of their own rights and those of others; the ability to recognise discriminatory practices and behaviour and to respond appropriately; some early concepts of the value of appreciating diversity and fairness.
>
> (MoE 1996: 66)

Ideas summary 7.3 Curriculum as conforming to society

Curriculum dimensions	Key ideas	Theoretical links
Philosophy	Early education that prepares the child to conform to society because it: • aims to ensure the status quo remains; • values traditions; • affirms and prepares the child for society as it exists now.	*Key theory families*: Cultural transmission (or instrumentalist, behaviourist, scientific education). *Definitions*: • Cultural: relating to or of one's culture (values, beliefs, ideas, relationships, rituals and roles). • Transmission: transferring or handing on something (for example, transferring or handing on cultural values through early education).
Goals	• emphasize traditional knowledge and/or the knowledge needed for a vocation;	

- decided by those with the power to determine what happens in early childhood education (for example, government-mandated curriculum and/or educators).

Planning	Based on technical approaches, where the process is a rational one in which: - *Time* is often segmented and tightly organized; the educator controls its use and flow. - *People*: educators are used to teach specific skills and knowledge to children. - *Space*: tightly structured by the educator to ensure it links with key objectives. - *Learning resources* are generally closed-ended and may include programmed learning materials. - *Knowledge* is generally prepackaged and organized in ways that make sense to educators (for example, themes and subject areas).	*Key thinker*: - Ralph Tyler, US educationalist. His key text: *Basic Principles of Curriculum and Instruction* (1949). *Other thinkers (influenced by Tyler)*: - Hilda Taba. Key text: *Curriculum Development: Theory and Practice* (1962). - Daniel and Laurel Tanner. Key text: *Curriculum Development: Theory into Practice* (1975, 1980).
Assessment	Educators' observations of the child are the source of curriculum. Observation is used to assess the child's conformity to norms by: - gathering objective facts about the child; - assessing those facts against developmental norms or pre-set objectives; - choosing techniques that aim to provide objective data. Assessment may be against mandated learning outcomes.	*Links with models of the child as a learner*: Behaviourism: the child learns through conforming to culture (Chapter 2). *Key theory II*: Empiricism *Definition*: Empirical: learning about something through the direct experience of our senses (sight, hearing, smell, touch and taste) (for example, learning about a child through watching or listening to them).

Equity reflections

A 'conforming to society' position on early childhood curriculum generates several equity issues. These are examined under the same headings we used to examine the implications of cultural transmission for the early childhood curriculum, in other words, philosophy, goals, plans and observations and assessment.

Philosophy

Conforming to the dominant culture

People disagree about the most valuable and desired knowledge and skills that young children can learn. Multicultural, multiethnic and multifaith societies such as Singapore, New Zealand, Australia, the US and the UK feature diverse and often conflicting values about what early childhood education should achieve. As Hartley (1995: 1) remarked:

> Cultural diversity, including the resurgence of a strong Aboriginal presence and identity, present challenging issues for Australia: what it means to be an Australian; the relationship between national and personal identities; identifying and working in both the cohesive and divisive forces in a multicultural society; and the form and flavour of a future republic.

Among this diversity, who chooses which culture will be transmitted to the child and whose culture the child will conform to? Whose values should a child learn through early education? As Popekwitz says:

> schooling does not just pass on culture: it modifies the content and spirit of culture, and those modifications have unanticipated and unintended consequences. Second, school transmits some, but not all aspects of our cultural heritage; inevitable biases and selection occur which can perpetuate inequalities and injustices.
>
> (Popekiwtz 1987: 11)

Consider the following statements by three Australian early childhood educators who participated in a consultation exercise about early childhood education's core aims. Who would you feel most comfortable having as a colleague?

- I think about our service's role in relation to social justice and equity issues, for example, by providing links for families with professionals and expertise, and looking at a preventative rather than a 'bandaid approach'.
- Linking (Christian) word and deed more closely, with a universal service being a key component.
- Enabling preschool children to enjoy a good solid foundation to their growth as a person and a member of society (Mac Naughton *et al.* 2002).

Conforming to Eurocentric knowledge and power relations

Despite the presence of diverse views in our world, some ideas are more powerful and more prominent than others. For instance, in 'Western' countries such as Australia or the UK, the ideas of the European Enlightenment thinkers are prominent in education and 'Eurocentric' views dominate many early childhood educators' training. 'Eurocentrism' describes the link between particular ways of understanding the world that originated in the European Enlightenment, Europe's colonial expansion and the oppression associated with it. The legacy of that expansion is countries such as Australia, New Zealand and Canada where European ways of thinking are more prominent and powerful than the ways of thinking of the indigenous peoples of those countries (for example, the Koori, Maori and Inuit).

A consequence of Eurocentrism is that a 'conforming to society' position on the early childhood curriculum can mean conforming to the values, beliefs and understandings of the dominant groups within that society and marginalizing the views of indigenous peoples and recent immigrants. As Townsend-Cross (2002: 9) writes of the Australian education system: 'The success of the education system in Australia depends on "abducting" children from their ethnic diversity in order to assimilate them into the [Westernized, Eurocentric] image of contemporary Australians'.

Conformers are people who comply with existing practices, rules, traditions and understandings. Little changes and early childhood educators within a 'conforming' position believe that we should ignore or mask social differences such as class, 'race' and gender. They believe that inequalities arise from talking about and focusing on such differences and that if we regard all children as the same, we will create equity between them. If you think it, it must be true.

Reflection points

- How might your culture, 'race', ethnicity, socio-economic background, history, geographical location and gender influence what you think are the most valuable ideas?

- What forms of diversity can you identify among your colleagues and among the families you work with?

- What opportunities and challenges might this diversity pose to you, given the ideas you value?

Goals

Disempowering educators and learners

> ... the more technical teacher views the instruction act as his primary responsibility. This teacher makes decisions in a much narrower framework – adhering to the text or programmatic guidelines, making only procedural type decisions such as whether to read aloud or silently, when to go over workbook assignments as a group or individually.
>
> (Barbour 1986: 322)

A technical/rational view denies the real character of professionalism where knowledgeable and reflective practitioners make informed, intuitive and commonsense judgements as they engage in their work with the young child. Consideration must be given to contextual variables . . . if we truly act as professionals and advocates for young children.

(Goodfellow 2001: 3)

A technical approach to developing curriculum goals has equity implications both for the educator and for the child as a learner. Each can be deprived of the power to determine what is learnt because:

- Educators are seen as technicians delivering a pre-set curriculum. As such, they have no power to decide broad curriculum goals and their values have no place in the curriculum. 'Behavioural objectives are frequently (left) unspecified in order to avoid acknowledging the value judgments and social influences involved in the modification of behaviour. And again the choice of behavioural objectives is rightfully the clients' (McDonald Ross 1975: 357).
- Children are seen as passive, not active learners. As such, they have no power to decide what they should learn.

Reinforcing stereotypes

A technical approach to developing curriculum goals assumes that knowledge is value free. Questions such as, 'Why this knowledge?' and 'Why not other knowledge?' are displaced by technical questions such as, 'What is the best way to learn this given body of knowledge?' (Giroux 1988: 14).

Consequently, early childhood educators who adopt a technical approach to curriculum risk replicating outmoded social and cultural stereotypes. Siraj-Blatchford (1996) explores this point at length in his examination of Eurocentric approaches to teaching science and technology in the early childhood curriculum. He shows that the ways of understanding the world that are embedded in science and technology are not value free, objective facts but inherently values-based choices. For instance:

Seen from the experience of Third World women, the modes of thinking and action that pass for science and development, respectively, are not universal and humanly inclusive . . . modern science and development are projects of male, Western origin.

(Shiva 1989, in Siraj-Blatchford 1996: 71)

Silin (1988, 1995) has long argued that early childhood educators should be aware of the political nature of the early childhood curriculum and view it 'against the larger societal processes that shape and are shaped by it' (1988: 126). He and others argue that early childhood educators should learn how to reflect on the assumptions and values that they bring to their work with young children and the knowledge that they choose to share or withhold from young children. They should consider how the values of their society's dominant groups influence the philosophy, goals and practices that define and shape their curricula (De Lair and Irwin 2000). A curriculum that responds to these concerns will try to value children with experiences outside of the 'dominant culture' of the early childhood setting, so that these children can build meaningful relationships with others (De Lair and Irwin 2000).

Plans

The following case study presents a series of comments from early childhood educators on different aspects and effects of the 'conforming to society' position on curriculum planning.

CASE STUDY

Our frustrations with objectives-based planning (contributed by Brian Newman, Yarrow Andrew and Denise Rundle):

- Needing to write up activities, however trivial, so that we could put coloured dots on activities that looked like they matched children, and thus link our observations to our plans. However, these 'dots' did nothing except reassure outside observers that 'proper planning' was occurring, and actually seemed to prevent us from planning meaningful experiences for the children.

- Filling in checklists that did not expand our knowledge or understanding but helped prove we were 'covering' all developmental areas.

- Wasting time working out how to write lovely sounding objectives, both long and short term.

- Finding that the *easiest* bits to write were actually the things that were the *least* important, for example completing a 10 piece puzzle and replacing it on the shelf; taking part in a turn-taking game; having a turn in a group game; answering a question in a group. This took time away from the important things, which were hard to think about, and even harder to write about.

- Looking at children in a compartmentalized way (in other words, in developmental areas: physical, cognitive, language, social, emotional), and always looking for what they could *not* achieve. This prevented us from focusing on children's actual skills and how these could be harnessed to improve their time in our care.

- Being unable to include relevant cultural information about children within such a restrictive format. Whether intentionally or not, using a Western cultural model (based on mid-twentieth-century European perspectives) often seemed to leave children who didn't fit within that model (in other words, who were from another culture/language group/alternative social norm) looking inadequate, rather than reflecting the strengths that they did have.

Observations and assessment

Reinforcing biases

A 'conforming to society' position on early childhood curriculum can lead to the educator's views dominating their programme. Educators' observations can merely reinforce what they believe is important, because they focus on what they already think is significant and they interpret it in terms of what they already know. Educators see what they look for. Traditional observation techniques are thought to capture 'real' events, avoiding the observer's selective attention. However, there is considerable debate about the extent to which we can observe a child objectively, as Mac Naughton and Faragher indicate:

> The first stage of observing is looking at what a child is doing. This may seem simple and obvious. However, the process of looking at what a child is doing is extremely complex. There are several different ways of looking at the same event or behaviour. Most of us are familiar with the fact that witnesses to a crime or an accident often have different recollections of what happened or have noticed different aspects of the same event. Observing young children is beset with the same difficulties.
>
> (Faragher and Mac Naughton 1998: 99)

This means that the educator's own values and beliefs about a child can drive what they observe and, therefore, what they plan. However, the educator's biases remain hidden and thus unspoken in a technical approach to curriculum, because they are assumed to be objective. As Elliot reminds us, this can disempower children whose ways of becoming do not fit developmental norms:

> In principle, early childhood educators are committed to fostering children's development of competence and self-esteem whatever their backgrounds. However, by design or omission, policies and practices in early education settings are not always inclusive and may serve to disempower children whose cultural background or life experiences do not resonate with the mainstream.
>
> (Elliot 1999: 8)

McNeil (2002) makes this point more broadly in discussing the use of standardized forms of testing to assess children's learning. She argues that studies of standardized forms of assessment highlight that they have 'masked racial, class, gender, and cultural hegemonies that devalued certain groups while privileging others' (McNeil 2002: 245). In particular they highlight a child's individual achievements against other individual children and in doing so mask the ways in which education disadvantages particular groups of children.

Disempowering children

Traditional approaches to observation and assessment deprive children of the right to be heard. They assume that the disinterested observer can know the child best, because children and others who know and interact with them will inevitably have biased perspectives.

Underestimating children

Traditional approaches to observation and assessment can underestimate what a child is capable of knowing, because all they can tell us about a child concerns the small events and moments in their life that are readily observable by the educator. Thus, these approaches can result in simplistic views of who the child is and who they are becoming. In particular, research has shown that traditional approaches to observation can hide key equity issues. For instance:

- Research in Japan showed that to see bias in children's ethnic and gender understandings, educators need to observe children over time, looking at factors internal and external to the child (Tamaki 2000).
- Research in Australia showed that to see how gender influences children's play and their relationships with each other, educators need to observe boys and girls over time, looking at the power dynamics between them (Mac Naughton 1998).

Within a technical approach to curriculum planning, observations are often based on a 'deficit' view of the child, in which the observer looks for evidence that the child is conforming (or not) to normal developmental patterns, and then offers experiences to remedy any deficits in conformity. Grieshaber (1997) challenged outcomes statements based on developmental continua on two counts:

- The literacy indicators are culturally biased. They have been developed from research on how English-speaking children attain literacy and, therefore, do not necessarily apply to all children.
- The indicators are decided on stage-based notions of children's cognitive development that have been strongly criticized (see Catherwood 1994).

Such challenges are part of a broader critique and reconceptualization of traditional theories of child development and of developmental continua (see Kessler and Swadner 1994; Fleer 1995). Learning outcomes based on traditional theories of development that are being criticized and reconceptualized risk embedding outmoded ideas of teaching and learning within them.

Disempowering educators

A 'conforming to society' position on observation and assessment can disempower educators in two ways. First, the increasing use of standardized tests to assess children's learning directly counters what many teachers believe are appropriate ways to assess young children, discounting the value of their knowledge of the child. In one US study of teachers' assessment: 'teachers reported using and placing much value on various forms of classroom assessment, but not using, and placing little value on, mandated, standardized testing programmes' (Trepanier-Street *et al.* 2001: 240).

Consider the following comments by early childhood educators in Tasmania who participated in a state-wide consultation on curriculum. Their comments highlight their dissatisfaction with outcomes-based assessment:

> Would someone please make up their mind about appropriate learning outcomes for young children – we are tired of being consulted and then not listened to.
> We do have concerns about the over-reliance on outcomes. Teachers spend more time checking to see if outcomes have been reached rather than interacting with the children.

A 'conforming to society' position on observation and assessment can also distance the educator from the child. This is a complex argument, but Lee (2001: 9) introduces it well:

> Adulthood, with all its connotations of stability and completeness has operated as a kind of standard model of a person, which stands ready to be used to measure children's incompleteness. This process of measurement underlies, and acts as a justification for, many distributions of power and authority in society along lines of age and maturity.

Adults can become nervous of interacting with children, because only 'experts' in child development know the right ways to be with children and to help them navigate their way successfully to normal adulthood. Consider the following extract from a US text on curriculum development in early childhood. What does it tell us about what educators need to know if they are to act in children's best interests?

> Teachers also need to understand the theories of John Bowlby (attachment), Abraham Maslow (hierarchy of needs), Howard Gardner (multiple intelligences), Arnold Gesell (gradients of growth), Maria Montessori (maturationist theory), Lev Vygotsky (sociocultural theory), Erik Erikson (psycho-social theory), and Jean Piaget (stages of intellectual development). An understanding of the developmental characteristics of children from infancy through eight years of age allows teachers to successfully prepare materials and activities for young children.
>
> (Henniger 1999: 107)

Silin (1995: 104) argued that such an overemphasis on developmental ways of knowing children creates 'a minefield continually being reseeded with new points of danger' for adults. If adults need to know all these theories of the child before acting wisely for their good and for their success then we must constantly risk acting inappropriately, unsuccessfully and foolishly as we plan for children at particular stages of their development. Silin (1995) pointed to several developmental theories of the child that place the adult 'in danger' of getting it wrong, including attachment theory, cognitive theory and theories of co-construction. To understand Silin's point let's turn to John Bowlby's 1950s theories of attachment and maternal deprivation.

(Henniger (1999) included Bowlby's in the list of theories essential to a successful early childhood programme.)

John Bowlby argued that it is vital that the child attaches to a single prime caregiver (the mother) and that failure to attach or incorrect separation from the mother poses grave risks to the child's future psychological development. Children deprived of mother love were potential criminals. For mothers, fathers and early childhood educators this created questions and fears about whether a child was attaching sufficiently, how moments of material separation should be handled and when. In Bowlby's words:

> There is a very strong case indeed for believing that prolonged separation of a child from its mother (or mother substitute) during the first five years of life stands foremost among the causes of delinquent character development.
>
> (Bowlby 1953, in Singer 1992: 87)

Bowlby's ideas were not new. Johann Pestolozzi writing in Switzerland in the early 1800s believed that mother love was a powerful and unique influence on the child. His student – influential German educator Frederick Froebel (believed to have established the first kindergarten in Germany) – also emphasized the importance of mother love to the child's healthy development.

Bowlby's theories aren't the only ones to warn adults (explicitly and implicitly) about the consequences of their actions with children. The recent 'brain research' (Chapter 3) implicitly warns adults against making children 'vulnerable to harm' (Thompson 2001: 23). Thompson captures four themes from this contemporary research on early brain development that highlight the significance of children's earliest experiences and relationships. In his words:

> A drive to development is inborn, propelling the human infant towards learning and mastery.
>
> The opportunities for growth that enrich the early years also bring with them vulnerability to harm.
>
> The experiences that greet children in their human and physical surroundings can either enhance or inhibit the unfolding of their inborn potential. People (especially parents and other caregivers) are the essence of the infant's environment, and their protection, nurturing, and stimulation shape early development.
>
> (Thompson 2001: 23)

Thompson (2001) invites us to consider the 'harm' that those who are the 'essence' of the infant's world might do. Silin (1995) provokes us to ask, 'If we fear "getting it wrong", how can we connect meaningfully with children? How can we interact with children as friends, collaborators and co-humans if we can never know enough about the child to do so correctly?'

Silin (1995) calls for ways of knowing the child other than through developmental and empiricist theories. Such non-empiricist and non-developmental ways of knowing could draw on literature, the arts and philosophy, rather than on science. In such alternative ways of knowing, Silin sees hope that we might connect with children and build more ethically and morally informed relationships with them.

In summary, the equity concerns from within this approach to curriculum centre on its potential to achieve the following:

- Philosophy: Conforming to the dominant culture; conforming to Eurocentric knowledge and power relations.
- Plans: Frustrating early childhood educators.
- Goals: Disempowering educators and learners; reinforcing stereotypes.
- Observation and assessment: Reinforcing biases; disempowering children; underestimating children; disempowering educators.

Reflecting on your learning

- What have you learnt about building curriculum in early childhood services?
- What key challenges and possibilities does this chapter pose?

Further reading and online resources

Curriculum goals and processes

Lovat, T. and Smith, D. (1995) *Curriculum: Action on Reflection*, chap. 9. Sydney: Social Science Press.

Spodek, B. (1988) *The Early Childhood Professional and the Definition of Knowledge*. ERIC Document ED 293657.

Objectives and planning

Davies, I. (1977) *Objectives in Teaching and Learning: A Perspective*. Maidenhead: McGraw-Hill.

Decker, C. and Decker, J. (1992) *Planning and Administering Early Childhood Programs*, chap. 8, 5th edn. New York: Merrill Publishing Company.

Assessment

Assessment Resource Banks. A number of validated assessment tools are housed at the New Zealand Council for Educational Research's website: http://www.nzcer.org.nz

Dever, M. and Barta, J. (2001) Standardized entrance assessment in kindergarten: a qualitative analysis of the experiences of teachers, administrators, and parents, *Journal of Research in Childhood Education*, 15(2): 220–33.

Fisher, J. (1998) The relationship between planning and assessment, in I. Siraj-Blatchford (ed.) *A Curriculum Development Handbook for Early Childhood Educators*. London: Trentham Books.

Lovat, T. and Smith, D. (1995) *Curriculum: Action on Reflection*, chap. 12. Sydney: Social Science Press.

New Assessment Resources for Early Childhood: http://www.newassessment.org/txt/public/resources/WebLinks/select.cfm

QCA and DES (2002) *Foundation Stage Profile: A Handbook.* See: http://qca.org.uk/ca/foundation/profiles.asp

Examples of pre-programmed plans

- http://www.nps.k12.nj.us/EarlyChildhoodTableII.htm
- http://www.earlychildhood.com/community/act/act_index.asp.

8

Curriculum position: reforming society

Overview

Of the many things young children learn, perhaps the most important is the picture that they develop of who they are and how they fit in the world.

(Novak 1995: 11)

Key thinker	Definitions
John Dewey (1859–1952), USA philosopher and educational theorist.	Reforming: making moderate changes to something (for example, making moderate changes to society).

This chapter examines how people who take a 'reforming society' position on early childhood curriculum answer the questions, 'What is early childhood education for?' and, given that, 'How should we build early childhood curriculum?'

A 'reforming society' position on early childhood curriculum rests on the belief that education can and should produce a rational individual capable of independent thought and self-discipline – often referred to as the 'self-governing' child. The focus is, therefore, child-centred with an emphasis on self-realization, autonomy, individual growth and development, in order to enable each child to achieve their full potential as a self-governing, rational being. Curriculum content should be individualized and linked to each child's specific developmental needs and interests. In summary, adherents to this position believe that education can:

- reform the individual from a dependent and developing child to a self-realized, autonomous, adult, 'free' thinker;
- reform society and its values so that freedom, truth and justice can prevail.

The ideas of a 'reforming society' position on curriculum are present (to greater or lesser extents) in several countries' expressed intentions for early childhood education. Ideas gallery 8.1 presents a selection of these expressions.

Ideas gallery 8.1 International expressions of a reforming approach to the role of early education

From Finland

'it is imperative to remember its [care and education] significance above all to the child. There is a vast need for creativity, fun and love, for respect for the child and for recognition of his or her own unique qualities.' (Honkavaara 1998: 9)

From Lithuania

The aim of education is considered to be 'a personality with wide spread physical, psychological and emotional strengths, completely mature to live in democratic society, creatively talking over and cherishing humanistic values of national and world culture' (Velickaite-Katiniene 1998: 71).

From the USA

'Early childhood curricula must enable children, despite disadvantages, to develop social competence, problem-solving skills, autonomy, adaptability, and a sense of purpose or future to maximise their health development.' (Isenberg and Brown 1987: 38)

From Australia

'An integral aspect of teachers' curriculum work is the ability to observe and interpret the emerging interests and abilities of each child, to note uniqueness and to know how to nurture and enhance that uniqueness. Observations of individual children should provide the foundation for curriculum decision making.' (ACSA 1995: 53)

Where have the ideas come from? A brief history lesson

The philosophy: liberalism and the European Enlightenment

A 'reforming society' position on early curriculum stems from the progressive, child-centred and liberal 'Western' philosophies of early childhood education that have their roots in the European Enlightenment of the seventeenth and eighteenth centuries, also known as the Age of Reason. Chapter 2 introduced you to Enlightenment thinking; here we look more specifically at the Enlightenment's legacy in education.

Briefly, the Enlightenment saw the emergence of new ways to think about the world in social, political and philosophical terms. This ferment of new ideas included new thinking about education and curriculum. German social theorist John Amos Comenuis (1592–1670) and French philosopher Jean-Jacques Rousseau (1712–88) were prominent Enlightenment philosophers whose ideas have influenced our view of early education's role in society. Their ideas were built on by Johann Pestalozzi

(1746–1827) and Friedrich Froebel (1782–1852). Pestalozzi was a Swiss educational reformer who set up an orphanage in Switzerland for neglected and abandoned children who were regarded as incapable of learning. He drew on Rousseau's ideas to achieve considerable success with these children. His key beliefs were:

- observation informs plans for appropriate experiences for young children;
- all children – irrespective of background – have the capacity to learn;
- positive and trusting relationships with teachers are at the heart of learning;
- sensory and experiential learning is natural for young children;
- mother love is critical to children's healthy development (see Singer 1992; Henniger 1999).

Froebel was a student of Pestalozzi and is credited with setting up the first kindergarten in Germany. He believed that play contributes to young children's development and that bringing children together in a circle (circle time or group time) contributed to group cohesion (Pinar *et al.* 1995; Henniger 1999).

Rousseau, Pestalozzi and Froebel each believed that we can reform society by educating the child and each explored how to educate children in ways that achieved social reform. Each believed that the child was born with the potential for good and reason within them (Singer 1992), in contrast to the view that the child is born in sin – a widely held view in Europe at the time of the Enlightenment (and one that Enlightenment philosophers challenged vigorously). Each of these thinkers explored how to allow the potential for good and reason to grow within the child and thus to achieve social reform in their societies. Each emphasized the importance of teaching young children to be self-disciplined and to act rationally rather than emotionally, as Singer explains:

> From the end of the eighteenth century, the idea that power must be based on shared values, general interests and an agreement between individual citizens . . . gained ground. This new view of power presupposed an individual with the self-discipline necessary to maintain the balance between individual and communal interests. The rational human being was the key to a better and more democratic community. Moreover, the general belief was that self-discipline and rationality could be developed by education.
>
> (Singer 1992: 36)

By the end of the eighteenth century, educationalists believed not only that education is the key to 'a better and more democratic community', but also that the earlier education begins, the better. Rousseau's belief in the need for early education is highlighted in the opening of his novel *Emile*, in which he wrote of the speed with which the world 'corrupts' the innocence and good within the child: 'All is good as it leaves the hands of the Author of all things, all degenerates in the hands of men' (Rousseau [1762] 1968: 1). Thus, Rousseau argued that early education should protect the child from 'the hands of men', thus allowing the unfettered unfolding of the natural child. Singer links the keen interest in early childhood education with the view that younger learners are less resistant to teaching and the older the learner, the harder it is to rid them of 'bad habits':

> The basis for this education would have to be laid in the earliest years of child-hood, as what is learnt at a very young age is taken-for-granted and does not call forth resistance. Besides which, at a later age it is very difficult to change the bad habits learnt when very young. In other words: the pedagogue is responsible for bringing the ideal community closer to realization.
>
> (Singer 1992: 36)

Many of these Enlightenment ideas influenced and were developed by education-alists such as Maria Montessori, Margaret McMillan and John Dewey, who, in turn, have influenced contemporary early childhood education. We have seen Maria Montessori's influence in Chapter 5. Margaret McMillan (1860–1931) was a social activist who (with her sister Rachael) founded the Open-Air Nursery in London. She worked with children from low-income areas and developed ideas from this work that influenced the development of early childhood education in the UK significantly. Her work expressed several Enlightenment ideas – especially the importance of the growth of the individual and the notion of the self-realizing child. McMillan emphasized that a child's emotional well-being is as important as their physical well-being, that parent involvement was important in programmes for young children and that outside experiences with open-ended materials facilitate children's healthy development. She also believed that self-expression through the arts contributes to children's development (Singer 1992; Henniger 1999).

Reforming society through independent thinkers: Dewey

John Dewey believed strongly that education could best contribute to society by producing self-governing individuals capable of independent thought and able to question the social world of which they are a part (Dewey 1916). While Dewey did not see education as the major source of social change, he believed that it could play its part in social change by preparing the child to participate in it (Longstreet and Shane 1993). As Glassman (2003: 5) explained: 'Dewey posits that education leads to free inquiry, and free inquiry leads to a richer society, but he lacks a descrip-tion of exactly what a richer society looks like'. Dewey believed that education should arise in and through the everyday events of life, that it should be based on the interests of the child and that the child should be actively involved in their own learning. He is often credited with the saying 'children learn by doing'. Dewey opposed content-driven education, arguing that the child's interests should drive their education:

> When we abandon the attempt to define immaturity by means of fixed com-parison with adult accomplishments, we are compelled to give up thinking of it as denoting lack of desired traits. Abandoning this notion we are also forced to surrender our habit of thinking of instruction as a method of supplying this lack by pouring knowledge into a mental and moral hole which awaits filling.
>
> (Dewey 1916: 51)

Froebel, Pestolozzi, Montessori, McMillan and Dewey arrived at some common conclusions about what education of the young child should achieve and what it should look like. Their ideas, based on Liberalism and European Enlightenment thinking, may sound familiar to you, but they were regarded as radical and controversial at the time:

- play can be a vehicle for young children's learning;
- the young child learns best through their five senses and thus needs the opportunity for active exploration of their natural environment;
- formal education is inappropriate for very young children;
- information gained through careful observation of the child should guide teaching and learning decisions;
- the young child needs to be taught in ways that help them to become self-disciplining and self-regulating.

(Spencer and Krauze 2000)

These ideas link directly with contemporary understandings about developmentally appropriate early childhood education. For example, consider the examples in Ideas gallery 8.2 and the extent to which they show traces of Liberalism and European Enlightenment thinking:

Ideas gallery 8.2 Traces of Liberalism and Enlightenment thinking

From a USA text on early childhood programmes:

'The educational programs we describe not only support, complement, and supplement parental care but also enhance the child's development. They are programs in which children learn as they play and share in their day-to-day experiences with other children, guided by adults who have an understanding of child growth and development of the learning process. These are also programs in which adults learn more about human relationships as they observe and participate.' (Read *et al.* 1993: 3)

From an Australian text on early childhood programmes:

'Curriculum approaches in early childhood must emphasise a stimulating, challenging informal environment where there is a cohesive interrelationship between curriculum processes and the developmental needs of children . . . Play is recognised as a central mode of learning for the young child.' (Ebbeck 1991: 10–11)

From a Pakistani early childhood teacher's handbook:

'The aims of the preschool are to develop the child socially, emotionally and physically . . . and for the teacher to develop the child's ability to appreciate and respect the views, actions and creations of others.' (Parker and Shaikh 1991: 7)

From an article on Jamaican early childhood education:

'The philosophical base for the early education programs in this country is eclectic. Programs draw from theories and practices of many including

> Pestalozzi, Piaget, Froebel, Dewey and Bruner (Ministry of Education 1983). The ECE Unit of the Ministry of Education identifies the intent of programs to be the promotion of physical, social, emotional, cognitive, and creative competence through a child-centred approach geared to the Jamaican situation and experience.' (Morrison and Milner 1997: 52)

Implications of liberalism for early childhood curriculum: taking a practical approach

A 'reforming' philosophical approach to education sits most comfortably with what is described as a practical approach to curriculum, in which resources and pedagogies are selected in and through the process of working with children and on the basis of broad principles and flexible approaches. It links directly with a 'reforming society' model of the child as a learner (Chapter 3).

Goals

The core educational aim of a liberal education is the growth and development of the individual child. Within early childhood education this means maximizing a child's personal growth and development and drawing out the child's inner capacities for self-expression.

The corresponding curriculum goals are developed through an organic process of reflection and interaction with children. The goals are generally holistic (focusing on the whole person, not just the cognitive, physical or emotional person), no time is prescribed for their achievement and no specific outcomes are predicted in advance of meeting the children. Goals generally are derived from two sources:

- broad guiding principles to ensure that they are morally wise goals and for the good of the child;
- practical judgements in action to ensure that wise decisions are taken as educators attempt to enact their goals in practice with children.

Broad guiding principles

The broad guiding principle is that goals should always be for the good of the child, as Grundy explains:

> The practical curriculum is not, however, a contentless curriculum: it is a curriculum in which the content is never taken-for-granted. Content must always be justified in terms of moral criteria relating to 'the good', not simply justified cognitively.
>
> (Grundy 1987: 76)

You can develop goals from any knowledge-base in your society about young children's capacities as learners and about what knowledge your society values most highly. An adherent to practical curriculum should think about why it might be 'good' or 'bad' to have certain knowledge included in their curriculum. For example, our considerable knowledge about young children's development indicates that they can categorize colour, texture, sound and shape in the first few years of life. This knowledge could lead an educator to have as their objective: 'to enable young children to practise their capacity to categorize'. In a technical approach to curriculum, the educator would then select experiences that would achieve this objective. However, a practical approach to curriculum would lead the educator to ask, 'Is this objective morally wise?' – more specifically, 'Will this objective contribute to the good of the child?'

Consider the following scenario. An early childhood art curriculum book includes this objective: 'For the child to begin to explore and learn to name different textures'. The book lists many materials that could be used in achieving this objective, including rice and silk. An educator who takes a technical approach to curriculum would try to think of interesting ways to introduce these textured materials to children and try to find creative ways to give them appropriate language with which to describe them. However, an educator who takes a practical approach to curriculum would think in very different terms, asking whether learning about textures is good for the child? Is it a wise decision, given the other things a child could be learning? Specifically:

- Should children play with food (for example, rice)? What does this teach children about the value of food?
- Silk is produced by oppressed and underpaid labour in countries such as Thailand and is consumed by wealthy people in countries such as Australia. Should we introduce silk to children as a special and interesting material? Should we focus on its texture when the morally significant issue is the oppressed labour that produced it?

Within a practical curriculum, what is to be learnt and how it is to be learnt is an issue of morals and the 'good' of the child. Hence, a reforming approach to early childhood curriculum goals assumes that questions of values are core to the teaching process and that goals are a practical engagement with values: 'By contrast with the technical view, education, curriculum and teaching may be considered as practical. Considered from this perspective, education is essentially a process or an activity' (Carr and Kemmis 1986: 36).

Practical curriculum goals are generally written as broad statements of intent such as:

- Developing the mind, developing the verbal skills, cultivating the intelligence (Chinese Welfare Institute Nursery brochure – no date, 6, 8, 11).
- Providing opportunities for practising self-help skills and expressing the self through a variety of art media (Decker and Decker 1992).

Ideas summary 8.1 provides a snapshot of the goal formulation guides within a practically orientated early childhood curriculum.

Ideas summary 8.1 A checklist for building reforming early childhood curriculum goals

Example goals for 4–5-year-old children

- To provide the children with a variety of ideas and experiences that help them to understand what friendship means.
- For children to use scientific methods to explore their environment.
- For children to use words to express their feelings.

CONTENT
- emphasizes educational processes rather than knowledge;
- values moral reasoning;
- gives no specific timeframes but plans for learning experiences or episodes (Decker and Decker 1992);
- ensures that child choice is evident.

LANGUAGE
- State what you want to achieve in a set of broad guiding statements.

DON'T
- Assume that pre-specified objectives or goals are appropriate for the children you work with.

DO – IF DEVELOPMENTALLY BASED
- Observe the child's developmental level and/or interests.
- Decide goals that will help the child to either consolidate their developmental skills or to extend them, asking what is for the developmental good of the child.

DO – IF PRACTICAL REASONING IS IMPORTANT
- Explore the moral wisdom in your goals and debate whose good they promote. Specifically, do they promote the child's developmental good?

Ideas gallery 8.3 provides some examples of how a reforming approach to early childhood curriculum goals is evident in several international expressions of what early childhood curriculum should achieve.

Ideas gallery 8.3 International expressions of a reforming approach to early childhood curriculum goals

From a USA teacher writing of how she and her co-teacher responded to the death of a pet rabbit in the classroom:

'It would have been impossible (one might say presumptuous) for the teachers to anticipate the children's needs and to orchestrate the morning's activities as effectively as the children did themselves. Had the teachers taken charge much of this rich experience would have been lost. Instead the teachers took dictation, read stories, answered questions, and offered emotional support for those who needed it.' (Sandstrom 1999: 13)

From an Australian text on working with young children:

'The Creative Perception process explores how we view children and their living environment. It focuses on children and encourages carers to use their intuition, feeling and reason, collectively and individually to form a vision of growing children. With a vision in mind, carers design an environment for children. The process is about design rather than planning and is a result of inspiration as well as rational thinking.' (Broinowski 1997: 85)

From the Centre for Early Childhood Development, South Africa:

'A learner centred approach is adopted in the early years . . . by . . . :

- an enriched, play- and activity-based curriculum which emphasises continuity with the home and community and recognises the values of the children's own knowledge and experiences;

- educators in the early years developing a pedagogy based on an interactive approach to learning.'

(Atmore 1998: 296)

From a USA text on working with young children:

'Curriculum goals are broad learning outcomes that identify the key results anticipated from the educational process . . . In a developmentally appropriate program for young children, the curriculum goals should include all aspects of child development.' (Henniger 1999: 280)

Practical judgements in action

Adherents to a practical approach to curriculum believe that curriculum is so complex and unpredictable that it can't be reduced to a series of objectives or goals. For example, consider the following scenario:

> You are working in a centre that has an active motor development programme and a technical approach to curriculum development, in which educators use their knowledge of child development norms to decide what children can and should be doing. You have agreed that the children need to practise their ability to balance and you know from research on child development that children's ability to balance is related to their literacy. You set up a set of balancing boards in the outside area and you encourage all the children to use them. During the day you face a series of dilemmas about if and how to intervene in the activity:

- All of the boys want to use the balancing boards, but none of the girls. What do you do? Is this important? How much encouragement should you give? Should you formalize who has a turn?

- One child has a physical disability that makes it difficult to balance. If you insist that all the children should 'have a go', what are you saying to this child?

- One child gets angry with another child's success and pushes them off. What do you do and say?

- How important is it anyway for the children to succeed at balancing?

In this scenario, an apparently simple objective creates several dilemmas for educators who seek to achieve it. What will it mean to specific children to be involved or not? What will they learn from your reactions in a range of situations? Adherents of a practical approach to curriculum argue that such dilemmas are just part of a normal teaching day and demonstrate that curriculum is a complex process in which your understandings of children's behaviours is at the heart of what you say and do and don't say and do. This complexity led Stenhouse to raise the following question about the content and development of curriculum goals: 'Can there be principles for the selection of content other than the principle that it should contribute to the achievement of an objective?' (Stenhouse 1975, in Smith and Lovat 1990: 96).

Joseph Schwab, in the US, attempted to answer those questions especially, in his 1970 paper: *The Practical: A Language for the Curriculum*. Carr and Kemmis describe it as follows:

> In the paper, Schwab distinguished between the 'theoretic' approach [and] the practical. He argues that the theoretical approach fragments curriculum as a field and as practice, that it leads to confusion and contradiction, and that it does not help the practitioner in the real work of making wise choices about what to do next . . . It is an image remarkably close to Aristotle's view of the wise man choosing the right course of action in the political context of the Greek state.
>
> (Carr and Kemmis 1986: 17)

These sorts of judgements occur through educators using practical reasoning in which we are 'cracking open' (Smith and Lovat 1990: 99) inner meanings. Practical reasoning involves making wise judgements in situations where the ends and means are open to question. It 'is required when people must decide on a wise and proper course of action to take when confronted with complex social situations which must be "lived through" ' (Kemmis 1986: 52). For instance, when educators confront teaching dilemmas they ask, 'how can we interpret the meaning and significance of human works' (Brown and Lyman 1978, in Kemmis 1986). For instance, how can we interpret the meaning and significance of this particular interaction with a child or of this particular curriculum goal?

For Carr and Kemmis (1986: 30–1) this form of reflection about our curriculum goals and actions is at the heart of practical curriculum. For them practical curriculum is about 'morally defensible decisions about practice [and] sound practical judgements . . . that are realized not by teaching but in and through teaching.' In a practical early childhood curriculum, goals are based on this form of practical reasoning, developed through 'wisdom in action' and emphasize the processes of education rather than its products. Curriculum goals don't describe what you want to achieve but state your intentions, developed by evaluating the comparative wisdom of various options.

Developmental goals in the early childhood curriculum and practical curriculum

Major traces of practical approaches to curriculum in early childhood curriculum lie in some developmental approaches, which have been the most widespread in early childhood education (Anning 1998; Yang 2001). Developmentally appropriate curriculum is associated with maturationism (Chapter 2) and with progressive child-centred education. It emphasizes the process of learning and the development of the individual, rather than the acquisition of pre-specified knowledge and skills. Curriculum goals therefore build from the educator's practical reasoning about the child's development. The educator seeks to 'crack open' what is happening developmentally for the child and to choose goals that are for the developmental good of the child. Adherents to developmental approaches to curriculum typically base their curriculum on:

> an in-depth understanding of child development and [often refer to learning] as developmentally appropriate practice. Rather than focus first on what is to be learned, in a developmentally appropriate classroom, the teacher begins by working hard to understand the developmental abilities of his class and then make decisions about what should be taught.
>
> (Henniger 1999: 80)

Plans

In a 'reforming' position on early childhood curriculum, curriculum design is organic (changing) and responsive to daily happenings, and so preparing and shaping a curriculum is an essentially practical task. In general:

- *time* is used flexibly and its use and flow are responsive to individual children's needs;
- *people*: educators guide children's self-expression and self-governance;
- *space* is tightly or loosely structured by the educator in response to children's changing needs and interests;
- *learning resources* are generally open-ended and chosen to reflect children's current interests;
- *knowledge* is developed in and through children's changing interests.

Shaping the planning process

Planning is generally based on a 'bottom-up' approach, in which educators' decisions respond to children's changing needs and interests. Thus, educators try to answer these questions:

- What are the children's current interests and needs?
- What do I need to do to extend their interests and needs?
- Which step should I take first?

The educator uses their answers to those questions to plan:

- possible content;
- the use of space and materials;

- the use of time;
- their own role.

This plan is more than a simple 'box-like' timetable consisting of simple, linear relationships between content, space and materials, time and the educator. Instead, the plan tries to map the complex interrelationships between different parts of the planning process; and it would grow and develop in response to children's changing needs. Some plans may take the form of a journal reflecting the educator's changing thinking over time. Other plans may look more like webs than timetables.

Shaping the content

Curriculum content emerges in and through the children's needs and interests and it is generally seen holistically, rather than as units or areas of study. Thus, content is developed through experiential learning based on children's interests and is based on practical reasoning that looks for wisdom in action and attempts to take content decisions. Content is based on 'wise practice', which Goodfellow (2001: 5) described as follows:

> Wise practice incorporates the making of ethical and philosophical choices and value judgements. Wise practices are framed within the understanding that making sense of the world occurs through relationships. Wise practices require wisdom.

Goodfellow (2001) drew on the work of practical curriculum theorists such as Schwab and argues that wisdom builds from moral and ethical reflection. Such reflection requires the educator to build content by:

- Maximizing the desirable consequences in choosing specific content and minimizing the undesirable ones (Kemmis 1986: 52).
- Steering a course through competing values about what content should be and not relying on narrow mastery of a few techniques or on narrow conceptions of the ends and values involved (Kemmis 1986: 53).

Questions that can assist in the process of deciding on content include:

- What rules usually guide action in this situation?
- Where do those rules originate?
- Are they the best rules for this situation?
- How relevant are these rules to this situation?
- How could I act in this situation?
- Which way to act is the most morally wise?
- Who should benefit from my actions?
- Who will benefit from them?

Hendrick (1990: 40–1) lists some questions that educators must answer to take wise content planning decisions based on young children's interests. The list includes:

- How appropriate is the idea for the children in the group?
- How feasible is the idea?
- Are activities reasonably consistent with each other?
- Can this topic be used to provide curriculum that develops all five of the children's senses?
- Does the curriculum take the needs of individual children into consideration?
- Does the list include anything that can be used to promote a multi-ethnic or non-sexist approach?

A practical approach to curriculum content in early childhood education is generally expressed as one of the following approaches to content:

- An emergent curriculum in which the children's needs and interests drive curriculum goals, content and processes. Carlina Rinaldi describes the process of planning an emergent curriculum:

    the teachers lay out general educational objectives, but do not formulate the specific goals for each project or each activity in advance. They formulate instead hypotheses of what could happened on the basis of their knowledge of the children and of previous experiences. Along with these hypotheses they formulate objectives that are flexible and adapted to the needs and interests of the children.

    (Rinaldi 1993: 102)

- An integrated curriculum in which 'learning experiences emerge from "real life" situations without reference to subjects' (Thornley and Graham 2001: 32). Educators who use this approach to develop content may create an initial concept map showing how a child's or group of children's interests might provoke further learning. Figure 8.1 shows an example of such a map.

- A project-based curriculum in which children's needs and interests drive in-depth work on areas or topics of interest (see, for example, Tinworth 1997). Tinworth suggested that retrospective records of how a project or interest developed, how the educator supported children's interests, and how the children responded can inform the planning process. Here, planning becomes a process of documenting what happened and collecting samples of children's work in order to critically reflect on what needs to happen next.

Shaping the schedule

The daily schedule is likely to be flexible about when the following events occur:

- outdoor and indoor experiences;
- group and individual times;

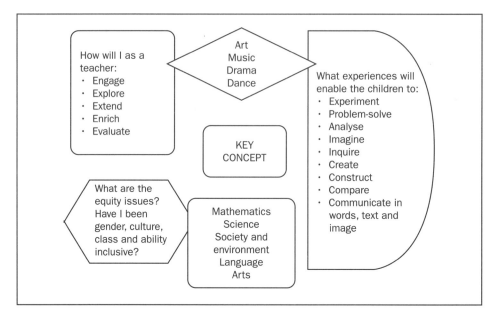

Figure 8.1 Intregrated planning

- eating, resting and toileting;
- adult-selected and child-selected activities.

For example, a daily schedule may involve free movement between indoor and outdoor times; group times in response to children's requests; and eating, resting and toileting times based on children's timetables rather than on those of the adults. The emphasis will be on child-selected activities and directions. Similarly, the annual schedule is likely to be flexible and to evolve over the year as children's interests evolve.

The pedagogical relationships

Structuring relationships

The child is in control of their learning and therefore decides what is to be learnt and the pedagogical relationships will be loosely structured to ensure that learning is:

- child-centred;
- holistic; and
- for the good of the individual child.

However, the educator does have a role in deciding what is for the 'good' of the child and for the larger 'moral' good. Jones captures this in her discussion on selecting topics based on children's interests:

Are all topics equally valuable? No. Here, adult judgement enters in. A good topic is one of interest to the adult as well as to the children, and the adult knows enough about it (or is willing to learn about it) to introduce more ideas and correct children's misconceptions. It doesn't promote bias, violence, or commercial exploitation.

(Jones 1999: 16)

Structuring space and materials

Children's interests determine the use of space and materials. Space will probably be structured to reflect children's current interests and needs, with core areas to support them. Space and materials may be 'themed' into learning centres that give children considerable choice and control over how they use the materials and how their learning progresses.

For example, consider the following description of how space and materials followed children's interests in an early childhood classroom in the UK:

> The role of the teacher throughout is to support what the children themselves are keen to learn and interested in approaching. Some of this support is provided long before they arrive in the form of material preparation, eg. the circular paper for the 'painters', the science equipment for the stimulus area, the materials for the pretend/imaginative area. She has also prepared back-up materials in the form of duplicated sheets, directed play suggestions with particular materials, and selected games pertinent to the topic which children can choose from the 'I don't know what to do box'.
>
> (Moyles 1989: 96–7)

Structuring teaching strategies

The pedagogy will be child-centred and probably it will reflect developmental and constructivist thinking (Chapter 3). The educator will act as a guide and resource for children's learning but the children's needs and interests drive the direction and content of learning. The educator will choose teaching and learning strategies that help to build a curriculum that is for the 'good' of the individual child by:

- encouraging children to research and make sense of their world with more competent others (including early childhood educators);
- respecting children's thinking and understanding;
- encouraging children to collaborate and to negotiate meanings;
- using children's knowledge as a basis for planning;
- supporting social interaction as a key factor in children's learning (Watson 1997).

A 'reforming' educator values a 'pedagogy of listening' (Rinaldi 1999, in Goodfellow 2001: 3). In Goodfellow's description of this 'pedagogy of listening', note the importance of finding children's meanings through interacting with them:

listening requires staff to exhibit reciprocity and mutual respect in their relationships with children. What is critical within these communicative processes is the ability to apply all of one's senses in relationships with children and in gaining insight into the children's theorising.

(Goodfellow 2001: 3)

A 'pedagogy of listening' requires educators to make themselves readily available to children and to document their understandings as a basis for further interaction with them. In this way, the educator can be influenced by the child as they plan their curriculum. Clark (2000) presented a way to listen to children that consists of the following elements:

- the assumption that the child is expert in their own lives;
- the use of different methods to 'hear' children's different languages (for example, movement, sound, image);
- reflection by children and educators on the meanings of what is said.

A pedagogy of listening also means being influenced by the child and what is heard through listening. Consider how Rinaldi and Gomez see the effects of listening on the educator:

We reinvent and re-educate ourselves along with the children. Not only does our knowledge organize theirs, but also the children's ways of being and dealing with reality likewise influences what we know, feel, and do.

(Rinaldi 1993: 111)

In partnership, listening to and learning from one another, [teachers] participate in breaking the literal and metaphorical silences that characterize the experiences of so many people diverse in race, gender, ethnicity, social class, and language background in our country.

(Gomez 1992: 184)

Educator-directed lessons are rare. Instead, children are given opportunities to ask questions, make comments and reflect on their understandings (Hughes 2002). Children will take the lead in directing the direction and flow of learning with support from the educator. This is because developmental approaches and constructivist approaches to teaching and learning rely heavily on children's inner cognitive, emotional and physical unfolding to structure appropriate learning.

Observations and assessments

An integral aspect of teachers' curriculum work is the ability to observe and interpret the emerging interests and abilities of each child, to note uniqueness and to know how to nurture and enhance that uniqueness. Observations of individual children should provide the foundation for curriculum decision making.

(ACSA 1995: 53)

Why observe?

In a practical approach, much of the curriculum is planned as events happen and as children's understandings emerge and so early childhood educators often refer to it as an emergent curriculum. In emergent curriculum, knowledge of the child and their perspectives on the world are seen as central to curriculum decision making.

This approach to knowing the child assumes that knowledge 'develops from active relationships between the child and his problem situations' (Yang 2001: 3) and through curriculum based on 'a shared and equitable state of justice between teacher and child' (Yang 2001: 3). The approach grows from the liberal progressive ideas of John Dewey and others who took a reforming position on the role of education in society and on the child as a learner (Chapter 2).

How to observe?

Knowledge of the child and their perspectives on the world are central to an emergent curriculum and while traditional techniques of observing children may offer some insight into the child and may suggest what is for the developmental good of the child, by themselves they are not sufficient. Instead it is important to find ways of gaining children's insights. This approach to observation is linked to an interpretivist understanding of knowledge. Hughes (2001: 35) explains:

> For interpretivists, the social world is not just 'out there' waiting to be interpreted, but 'in here' or 'in us' – it *is* our interpretations. Interpretivists argue that rather than simply *perceiving* our particular social and material circumstances, each person continually makes sense of them within a cultural framework of socially constructed and shared meanings; and that our interpretations of the world influence our behaviour in it.

The idea that we can know a child by observing them and bringing their meanings to the fore sits firmly within this interpretivist tradition, because it assumes that:

- observation alone can't enable us to know the child;
- to understand a child's actions, we must understand how they 'see' the world;
- the child can have meaningful knowledge about himself or herself.

The following description of building a developmentally relevant curriculum with young children shows those interpretivist views on observing children and seeking their perspectives:

> An educator from the USA is talking about using ideas of emergent curriculum for Reggio Emilia . . . It has been difficult for many of them [teachers] to learn how to plan for possibilities, hypothesize directions for projects, express general goals, and plan ways to provoke and sustain children's interest. They recognize that it is important to study the ideas expressed in children's words, drawings, and play. They know that this will help them learn how to scaffold further learning,

but the process of interpreting dialogue and hypothesising possible lines of a project is often both strange and unfamiliar.

(ERIC/EECE 1995: 1)

Techniques that illuminate children's perspectives include:

- journal writing;
- videoing/audio-taping;
- learning stories;
- narratives – recording and studying conversations, emerging understandings as well as observations;
- collecting artefacts – especially using children's drawing and other representations and dialogue to access their understandings (Hughes 2002).

Ideas summary 8.2 briefly introduces each of these techniques.

Ideas summary 8.2 Techniques for illuminating children's perspectives

Journal writing

What   Detailed descriptions of a child or children's behaviour and actions over time. It tries to capture everything that happens in a specific period of time.

How   Develop an observation sheet or format that allows you to write detailed notes about a child or children over a period of up to ten minutes. Note the date, time, place, setting and child(ren) involved. Include the child(ren)'s language.

Pros   Can provide a rich and detailed picture of a child and what influences their behaviour on a specific day at a specific point in time.

Cons   Requires time to focus solely on writing a running record and then interpreting it.

Videoing/audiotaping

What   Use of video or audio equipment to capture all that a child says or does in a specific period of time or in a specific area.

How   Set up the equipment in an area or near a child and decide what you will focus on, for how long and why. The child should always be aware of what and when you are recording.

Pros   Frees the early childhood educator as the equipment does the observing; allows educators to revisit information and reinterpret it; can provide a rich and detailed picture of a child and what influences their behaviour on a specific day at a specific point in time.

Cons   Expensive; time consuming to transcribe and re-view.

Learning stories

What   Structured narrative documentation based on critical incidents of children's learning from within a strength-based approach to children (see Carr 2001).

How   Uses the framework of *Te Whāriki* to provide a structure for documenting learning from children's questions about belonging, well-being, exploration, communication and contribution, and capturing critical incidents to weave stories of children's learning over time.

Pros   Brings multiple perspectives to bear over time to an ongoing reflection on children's learning; allows a rich and diverse source of information to be gathered; allows the child to actively contribute to what is being documented and how.

Cons   May be considered time consuming by some.

Narratives

What   A story of how a child or a group of children have come to understand something. It is generally built from the data gained from other observation techniques, such as transcripts and written records.

How   Collate a series of observations, conversations and comments about a specific issue, theme or project. Then try to build a story (narrative) from them that includes time, place, plot and the scene or context (Pinar *et al.* 1995).

Pros   Can provide a rich and complex understanding of how events and contexts shape children's learning and understandings; can include children's interpretations of events and children's voices in the observation and assessment of their learning; retelling a story can help educators to understand events in new ways.

Cons   Can be time consuming.

Collecting artefacts

What   An artefact is something that is made. For example, a child's drawing, painting or collage.

How   With their permission, collect children's drawings, paintings, photos of their play or other constructions. Name and date each and give some sense of context. You may also wish to add children's words and comments to the artefact. Involving children in deciding which of their artefacts should be collected may help to you understand their learning and ideas.

Pros   Can provide a rich archive of children's changing interests, capacities and approaches to making meaning in their world.

Cons   Can be bulky to store and difficult to categorize.

A reforming approach to observation and assessment rests on the belief that educators need not just objective observational data about the child but also the child's own perspectives. The more that the educator highlights the child's perspectives on and constructions of the world, the more likely they are to know the child in meaningful ways. This approach gives the child a voice in the curriculum. For instance, there is growing international interest in the work of the pre-primary schools of the Reggio Emilia region of Italy. There, children's questions, interests and ideas are used as a basis for curriculum building (see Fleet and Patterson 1998). Hughes drew on ideas that have flowed from Reggio Emilia when she wrote this of the place and techniques of observation in her curriculum:

Observations of children's and teachers' actions can shed light on how we establish our curriculum, for example. In addition, we can learn how to transform our teaching principles into daily practices. Transcripts, children's work, tapes, or written notes can offer a context for teachers as they communicate and find ways to plan experiences that evolve from children's interests, questions, or theories. The study of observations also can be a powerful context in which teachers exchange views about child development and the interpretation of children's actions and words.

(Hughes 2002: 135)

Those ideas about how to observe and assess in early childhood curriculum are present to greater or lesser extents in many recent early childhood curriculum documents and texts. These texts emphasize the educator working with the child to gain insights into their development and using those insights to build curriculum. Ideas gallery 8.4 presents just some of these expressions.

Ideas gallery 8.4 Bringing children's voices forward

From Japan, talking about approaches to work with children with disabilities:

'The teacher does not merely observe the child's behaviour objectively according to the ethic of positivism, but tries to discover its meaning from the child's point of view and responds according to what the teacher understands.' (Tsumori 1998: 79)

From New Zealand, a researcher seeking alternative ways of assessing consistent with Te Whāriki:

'The documentation [of learning stories] had become integral to the wider process whereby practitioners got to know the children, planned for their learning, and established a learning community with shared values. Children were included as active participants, and the documenting also provided feedback for families about their children's well-being and learning.' (Carr 2001: 157)

A USA teacher inspired by approaches to child study within Reggio Emilia:

'For both children and teachers, observation plays a critical role in the development of a meaningful curriculum. Careful study of children's classroom behaviour provides teachers with the information to plan connected learning experiences that build on children's interests and allow for continued inquiry . . . In the process, teachers become "researchers" with children.' (Hughes 2002: 134)

From some US teachers:

'Children can awaken in us an understanding of what it means to be inventive, engaged, delighted, and determined to rearrange the world. If we listen to and watch them closely, they will teach us to be more observant, inquisitive, and responsive in our overall work and overall lives.' (Curtis and Carter 2000: xii)

Interpreting observations

Adherents of a practical approach to early childhood curriculum interpret their observations of individual children's learning to make morally wise curriculum judgements in action. They interpret children's understandings and meanings as a basis for further curriculum work using these techniques:

- *Intention-based interpretation.* This involves looking at the extent to which a particular goal has been achieved. Often in early childhood education these goals will focus on key areas of learning such as literacy, science, the arts and so on, and they may be developed from nationally or state-mandated curricula, or they may be developmental.
- *Theory-based interpretation.* This involves looking at the extent to which the data demonstrate a particular theory of learning or development.

Ideas summary 8.3

Curriculum dimensions	Key ideas	Theoretical links
Philosophy	Early education develops the child to reform society because it: • aims to reform the status quo; • values individual and independent thought; • develops the child to reform society.	*Key theory*: Progressive, child-centred education. *Key theory families*: • humanist education; • progressive education; • liberal education; • child-centred education.
Goals	• emphasize producing the self-governing child; • decided by reference to the developing child (for example, the experts in child development and/or educators with children).	*Definitions*: • Progressive: moving forward (for example, education that allows the individual to flourish and has wide currency). • Liberal: favours moderate social changes and individual freedoms (for example, education that favours moderate social changes and the growth of the individual).
Planning	Based on practical and child-centred, developmental approaches, where the process is an organic one in which: • *Time* is flexible and organized for long periods of play and dialogue.	*Key thinker*: • John Dewey (1859–1952), US philosopher and educational theorist. His key texts: *Essays in Experimental Logic* (1917) and *Democracy and Education* (1916).

- *People*: educators are to guide children's learning, facilitate it and often use a pedagogy of listening.
- *Space*: loosely structured to allow for children's emergent interests to be appropriately responded to.
- *Learning resources* are generally open-ended and varied.
- *Knowledge* is built in holistic ways, in ways that make sense to the child.

Other thinkers (influenced by Dewey):

- Harold Rugg and Ann Shumaker: *The Child Centred School* (1928);
- Patty Smith Hill (1868–1946), a kindergarten teacher and professor. Founded the laboratory nursery school at Columbia University Teachers College, USA. Founded what is now the National Association for the Education of Young Children.

Assessment   Educator's observations and dialogue with the child are the source of the curriculum.
Observation is used to facilitate the self-governing child by:

- gathering developmental knowledge of the child;
- assessing that knowledge through specific developmental theories;
- choosing techniques that capture the child's development and perspectives over time.

Assessment is based on the 'good' for the self-governing individual child.

Links with models of the child as a learner:

Constructivism;
Psychodynamics – the child learns through interaction between culture and nature (Chapter 3).

Key theory of knowledge:

Interpretivism

Definition:

Interpret: bringing out meanings and understandings about something (for example, bringing out meanings and understandings about the self-governing child).

Equity reflections

There are several equity issues that arise when using a reforming approach to curriculum that we now explore in turn.

Philosophy

Reinforcing conservative cultural values

Writers such as Bernard Spodek have argued that a developmental curriculum with its focus on the development of the individual child denies the implicit social and moral agenda that is the curriculum content (Spodek 1987, 1988). Spodek (1988) argued that there has been a confusion within developmentally appropriate practice (DAP) between curriculum content and teaching method which has embedded dominant social ideologies within the curriculum. DAP prescribes how to teach, not what to teach and it provides very little guidance about how to take decisions about appropriate curriculum content.

A developmental or child-centred curriculum can reinforce conservative social ideas and knowledge, because educators often act as the cultural 'gatekeepers' of what children should know. Anning makes this point in relation to early childhood education in the UK:

> it is important to remember that so-called 'child-centred' education espoused by early childhood educators in the UK has often been an idealised, teacherly version of what interests and motivates young children. Before the advent of a National Curriculum, topics upon which the content of the curriculum was based regularly included such themes as Animals in Spring, The Royal Family or People Who Help Us. They rarely reflected the real, consuming interests of many young children – bikes, football, pop music, fashion, TV soap operas, commercially successful toys like Barbie dolls or My Little Ponies, computer games or guns.
>
> (Anning 1998: 305)

Goals

Privileging culturally narrow and/or ethnocentric individualistic goals

Much developmental knowledge of the child is ethnocentrically narrow, so a developmental approach may result in curriculum goals that are culturally narrow. New (1994b) presented cross cultural research findings on child development to show that the knowledge upon which child development is based is associated primarily with white, middle class America. Holmes (1992) reinforces this point. He believes that many developmentally appropriate early childhood programmes have failed to serve the needs and aspirations of indigenous peoples in Australia, the United States and New Zealand. This is because the knowledge and ideas of the majority culture in those countries drives what the child learns in so-called developmentally appropriate programmes. Holmes called for culturally appropriate early childhood education for indigenous peoples, with these goals:

> (1) acknowledging the validity of cultural knowledge and ways of learning; (2) enhancing self-esteem, cultural pride, identity, and self-concept; (3) enhancing educational outcomes, including maintenance of the people's native language; (4) educating for self-determination; and (5) furthering bicultural and multicultural understanding.
>
> (Holmes 1992)

Culturally relevant goals are essential in today's fractured and complex world, as Dermon-Sparks suggests:

> In a society in which institutional structures create and maintain sexism, racism, and handicappism, it is not sufficient to be non-biased (and also highly unlikely), nor is it sufficient to be an observer. It is necessary for each individual to actively

intervene, to challenge and counter the personal and institutional behaviours that perpetuate oppression.

(Derman-Sparks and the Anti-Bias Task Force 1989: 3)

Plans

Masking social interests and relationships

Child-centred education assumes that the individual child's growth and development is a natural, individually determined process that should be allowed full expression. This requires early child educators to 'know the child' and to 'facilitate the child's development' through this knowledge (Mac Naughton 1995). The educator faces a moral imperative to enable the individual to express themselves fully with judicious but minimal intervention (see, for example, Bredekamp 1987; Beaty 1992; Mallory and New 1994; Arthur *et al.* 1996). In a child-centred, practical approach to curriculum planning, the individual educator's curriculum decisions are linked with their developmental observation and assessment of the individual child.

The late 1980s and 1990s saw a growing body of feminist argument that educators' adherence to individualism in child-centred curriculum works against equitable pedagogical practices. Feminists such as Valerie Walkerdine argued that the child-centred pedagogies at the heart of early childhood education are based on an ethics of individualism and on the 'dream of democratic harmony' (Walkerdine 1992: 22). Individualism arises in two ways. First, only the individual educator can know the individual children within his or her centre, so only the individual educator can plan for each child's learning. This means that it is the individual educator's values and ideals that drive how the child is seen and what is planned for the child. These values may be conservative and work against progressive social change (see Mac Naughton 2000).

Second, the focus on the individual child can mask the way in which the social relationships and dynamics produced through gender, ethnicity and class influence a child's becoming. Masking these influences also masks the inequalities and injustices that they create in our social relationships and dynamics. Mac Naughton (2000) shows how this can happen in her study of Australian early childhood educators working for gender equity. She explains how Anne (one such educator) focused on the individual child and, therefore, missed the influence of gender on children's relationships:

When Anne privileged the developmentalist gaze, as she had when she joined the group, it hid gender differences in children's play choices and cloaked the construction of gendered power relations between children, thus enabling them to continue. This was because the object of Anne's 'developmental' gaze was the individual, gender-neutral child, not the gendered child constructing gendering with others. This meant that she did not see and, thus, could not challenge sexism between the children. As a result, boys were able to exercise power over girls in areas such as block play; and patriarchal gender relations between the children were maintained.

(Mac Naughton 2000: 75–6)

Some educators who take a reforming position on the role of early childhood education believe that we need to change our practices to make them more equitable. After all, a reforming position on early childhood curriculum is meant to create a more democratic society. However, since a 'reforming' position focuses on individual's needs and interest, many educators who adopt this position only raise issues of equity when children do. This can silence equity issues or it can mean that only the interests of the most confident and powerful children in the group are recognized.

Observation and assessment

Privileging the voices and meanings of the powerful

The idea that children's perspectives are central to our understanding of them is highly democratic and, at first sight, seems to promise equity in relations between educators and children. However, Mac Naughton and Williams (1998) point to some key issues concerning gender and 'race' that may undermine the potential for equity:

> Young boys' tendencies towards violent social problem-solving strategies have implications for staff encouraging children to co-construct knowledge with each other and with staff. Firstly, in mixed-gender groups girls may feel inhibited in expressing, sharing and negotiating meanings with boys. When girls fear that a difference of opinion may be resolved physically rather than verbally they become silent or move away from the conflict (Mac Naughton, 1997). Girls' meanings may be silenced or marginalised as a result. This turns co-construction of meaning into male-only meaning construction. Staff can guard against this by allowing girls to work in girl-only groups or by actively seeking and supporting girls' meaning-making in mixed-gender groups ... Children's 'racial' identity can influence their desire to co-construct meaning with others. To contribute to group meaning-making children need to have positive self-esteem and a belief that their contributions will be taken seriously by others (Hill 1994). Children who have experienced racism may have poor self-esteem and believe that their contributions will be dismissed or ignored by the group (Dermon-Sparks *et al.* 1989). Children who have to negotiate their sense of self within two cultural groups are particularly vulnerable to low self-esteem because '... they assume that they cannot be successful in either society' (Ramsey 1987: 117). Two aspects of co-construction support the development of positive self-esteem for these children. Children are more likely to develop positive self-esteem when they can construct meanings rather than learn facts and when adults show interest in their ideas.
>
> (Mac Naughton and Williams 1998: 183)

Mac Naughton (2000) has argued that countering these possibilities requires educators to 'see' the politics of young children's daily lives. (We examine some ways to do this in the next chapter.) For example, educators can change the 'gazes' through which they 'read' children. Mac Naughton suggests that combining a multiracial feminist 'theoretical lens' with a feminist poststructuralist 'theoretical lens' produces an anti-bias 'gaze' that enables educators to:

- Look for links between children's gender, 'race', class, ability and sexuality and see how these influence children's willingness to share their perspectives with others.
- Research children's experiences of power and how it affects their choice of whether, when and how to share their perspectives with others.
- Reflect on how their own gender, 'race', class, ability and sexuality influence the possibilities and ideas that children choose to share with them.

In summary the equity concerns from within this approach to curriculum centre on its potential to achieve the following:

- *Philosophy*: reinforcing conservative cultural values.
- *Goals*: privileging culturally narrow and/or ethnocentric individualistic goals.
- *Plans*: masking social interests and relationships.
- *Observation and assessment*: privileging the voices and meanings of the powerful.

Reflecting on your learning

- What have you learnt about building curriculum in early childhood services?
- What key challenges and possibilities does the chapter pose?

Further reading and online resources

Curriculum goals and processes

Goodfellow, J. (2001) Wise practice: the need to move beyond best practice in early childhood education, *Australian Journal of Early Childhood*, 26(1): 1–6.

Lovat, T. and Smith, D. (1995) *Curriculum: Action on Reflection*, chap. 10. Sydney: Social Science Press.

Rinaldi, C. (1993) The emergent curriculum and social constructivism: an interview with Lella Gandini, in C. Edwards, L. Gandini and G. Foreman (eds) *The Hundred Languages of Children: The Reggio Emilia Approach to Early Childhood Education*, pp.101–11. Norwood, N.J.: Ablex Publishing Corporation.

Schwab, J. (1970) *The Practical: A Language for Curriculum*. Washington, D.C.: National Education Association.

Planning, emergent curriculum and project-based curriculum

American School Foundation of Guadalajara, A.C. What is emergent curriculum? Text plus images that provide examples of how to build an emergent curriculum: http://earlychild-hood.asfg.mx/emercurr.html

Dizes, D. and Dorl, J. (1999) Your mop is my guitar: emergent curriculum in our classroom, *Young Children*, 54(4): 14–16.

London Children's Connection. Text plus images: http://lcc.on.ca/emergent_curric-ulum_program.html

Nimmo, J. (2002) Nurturing the spirit to teach: commitment, community and emergent curriculum, *Australian Journal of Early Childhood*, 28(2): 8–12.

Sloan, M. (1999) All kinds of projects for your classroom, *Young Children*, 54(4): 17–20.

Observation and assessment

Carr, M. (2001) *Assessment in Early Childhood Settings: Learning Stories*. London: Paul Chapman Publishing.

Video: *Assessing Children's Learning in Early Childhood Settings*. Wellington: New Zealand Council for Educational Research.

9

Curriculum position: transforming society

Overview

Teachers whose curriculum intentions are transformative and whose interests are emancipatory struggle to create environments that are enabling, democratic and just.

(Jungck and Marshall 1992: 100)

Key thinker	Definition
Paulo Freire (1921–97), Brazilian social activist, educational theorist, educator.	Transforming: fundamentally changing the existing practices, rules, traditions and understandings (for example, education whose goals arise from the desire to transform existing social practices, rules, traditions and understandings of a given society to achieve greater social justice and equity).

This chapter examines how people working within a transforming society approach to early childhood curriculum have answered the question, 'What is early childhood education for?' and, given that, 'How should we build early childhood curriculum?' A 'transforming society' position rests on the belief that educators can work with children and their families to create a better world. In this position, education can (Giroux 1990):

- transform the individual into a morally, intellectually and politically engaged actor;

- transform society and its values to extend the possibilities for justice in public life.

Within this position, early education equips children with the knowledge they require to recognize and confront injustice and to resist oppressive ways of becoming. Thus, 'transforming' educators prioritize 'a particular ethico-political attitude or ideological stance that one constructs in order to confront and engage the world critically and challenge power relations' (Sleeter and McClaren 1995: 7).

Those ideas from within a transforming society philosophy of education are present to greater or lesser extents in various groups' intentions for their early childhood programmes. Ideas gallery 9.1 presents just some of those groups' intentions.

Ideas gallery 9.1 International examples of a 'transforming society' position on early childhood curriculum

From a Pakistani women's newsletter with a feature on early education:

'Education – or simply learning – has a lot to do with facilitating change. And the popular education method [critical education] makes it possible.' (*Shuba* 1991/92: 9)

From the Minister of State for the Department of Justice, Equality and Law Reform, Dublin, Ireland:

'it is obvious that this is the time to concentrate efforts to rectify the situation by developing an anti-prejudice curriculum, which enables all children to develop positive attitudes so that they can accept, learn and appreciate differences of race, culture, language, disability and gender.' (Wallance 1998: 7)

From Carol Bellamy, Executive Director, United Nations Children's Fund:

'While gender biases and inequalities are deeply rooted in cultural traditions, ECD [Early Childhood Development] offers a beginning for correcting gender inequities and improving women's lives.' (Bellamy 2001: 5)

From the Goals of the Early Years Trainers Anti-Racist Network, UK (Membership leaflet 2001):

'We believe educators should encourage students and practitioners to understand how racism operates throughout British society and to motivate and empower people to challenge it.'

Where have the ideas come from?

Social activism and social reconstructionism

The idea of transforming society through early education arises from the work of several social theorists and social activists:

> While critical pedagogy draws inspiration from liberation struggles in Latin America and elsewhere and invokes the examples of individuals such as Farabundo Marti, Cear Augusto Sandino, Rosa Luxemburg, and Che Guevara, it is most often associated with Brazilian educator Paulo Freire.
>
> (Sleeter and McClaren 1995: 14)

These theorists and activists were linked with groups such as the Frankfurt School of Cultural Theorists, USA social reconstructionists, UK critical sociologists and Latin American educational activists, feminists and black activists. Each of these groups has, in its way, contributed to ideas about how education might transform society, and educationalists have drawn on those ideas to build what is called critical educational theory. Critical educational theory rests on these assumptions about education (Carr and Kemmis 1986; Sleeter and McClaren 1995; Darder 2002):

- education is historically located;
- education is a social activity with social consequences, so it concerns not just individuals but social outcomes;
- education is a political activity affecting the life chances of people involved in it;
- education is fundamentally problematic.

Critical educational theory as a form of social activism

Critical education theory sees educators as 'cultural workers' (Darder 2002: 171) who can be actively involved in the transformation of their society to a more just society by challenging discrimination and its effects on learners and by opening up multiple possibilities for learners. Educators face a choice. They can choose to be actively involved in transformation of inequalities in their work or implicitly involved in reproducing inequalities:

> As teachers we are cultural workers, whether we are aware of it or not. If teachers don't question the culture and values being promoted in the classroom, we socialize our students to accept the inequalities of our society along lines of race, class, gender, and ability.
>
> (Darder 2002: 171)

Critical educational theory thus focuses on challenging the socio-political and economic structures that prevent the creation of a wiser and more just society (Carr and Kemmis 1986). These include socio-political structures such as 'race', class, gender and ability, and the effects of globalization and capitalism on these structures. For this reason, critical educators are concerned with discrimination, oppression, marginalization; their diminishing effects on our possibilities of becoming; and the role that critical knowledge can play in challenging them.

Brazilian critical educationalist Paulo Freire drew on these ideas to develop what he called a 'problem-posing' approach to education. In this approach, the educator encourages adults living with oppression to reflect critically on their everyday problems and issues and on how to challenge the structures and processes that oppress them. Freire believed that education should enable people to 'participate in the practice of freedom . . . and discover how to participate in the transformation of their world' (Freire 1970: 16). He argued that such education is meaningful only if it confronts people's real, day to day problems and provides them with the intellectual and political tools to solve these problems and thereby transform their lives. More

recently, Giroux has described critical education as: 'attentive to developing a democratic public philosophy that respects the notion of difference as part of a common
struggle to extend the quality of public life' (Giroux 1990: 33).

Freire worked particularly on developing an approach to adult literacy education
that held within it the possibilities of freedom and emancipation:

> For Freire, the purposes of education are to enlighten the masses about the
> inequities that their social order has inflicted upon them and to empower them to
> acquire their freedom. Whatever is learned is a function of these purposes. Thus,
> reading is taught not to prepare people for a job or for the sake of coming to
> know great literature, but so that they may become aware of the oppression that
> characterises their lives.
>
> (Longstreet and Shane 1993: 66–7)

Freire's work has had much to say to educators around the world about the place of
education in challenging injustice and opening up possibilities for people. McClaren
(2002: 250) characterized his work as being concerned with 'practicing a politics of
diversity and self-affirmation – in short, a cultural politics – not as an end in itself but
in relation to a larger politics of liberation and social justice'.

However, like the constructivists (Chapter 3), critical educators do not form a
homogeneous whole. Instead, the critical education 'family' has several 'branches'
that pursue particular issues and interests and challenge all educators to do the same.
We will examine two branches of the critical education 'family': feminist educational
theories and critical race theory (sometimes called critical multiculturalism).

Feminists and social reconstructionism

Feminist educational theorists have argued – in different ways – that education can
help to transform oppressive gender relations and to broaden children's gender
possibilities. For example, liberal feminists often draw on social learning theory
(Chapter 2) to explore how modelling non-sexist ways of being can encourage
children to break free of traditional sex-role stereotypes. These feminists emphasize
the importance of providing non-sexist materials and of encouraging children to
explore all aspects of the curriculum. In early childhood education, this means
ensuring that both boys and girls:

- play in construction areas and dramatic play areas;
- engage in physical challenges;
- take on caring roles;
- encounter songs and stories in which girls can do anything and boys can be gentle
  and caring.

Liberal feminist ideas were prominent in educational thinking in the 1970s and
1980s. More recently, two other groups of feminist theorists have explored education's role in transforming oppressive gender relations: cultural feminists and feminist

poststructuralists. Cultural feminists draw on Carol Gilligan's exploration of gender issues in moral reasoning (1982) and on Nel Noddings's framework for education that centres on domains of caring and is based on an ethic of care (Noddings 1992). Noddings explores how children's education can be linked to social justice through focusing on building a culture of caring – for the self, for others, for the environment and for non-human creatures. The 'feminine' pedagogues regard education as the: 'crucible for our coming to understand ourselves, others and the possibilities life holds for us' (Witherell and Noddings 1991: 10).

Lisa Goldstein, a USA early childhood scholar, draws heavily on Noddings to propose a curriculum based on love. She describes Noddings's views on curriculum thus:

> Noddings further suggests that the standard curriculum of secondary schooling be abandoned and replaced by 'domains or centers of caring' (1992: 47). Academic subjects would no longer be segregated into disciplines and taught in isolation . . . children will learn about caring for the self, for others (both in their inner circle and for strangers and distant others), for animals, plants and the earth, for human-made world and for the world of ideas.
>
> (Goldstein 1997: 29)

Goldstein calls on early childhood educators to teach with love and, by doing so, to create transformative relationships:

> Teaching with love is also a way to bring young children under the umbrella of feminism, thus furthering its transformative agenda. We have nothing to lose by teaching with love. And we – and the children we teach – have everything to gain.
>
> (Goldstein 1997: 168)

These cultural feminists (sometimes known as feminine pedagogues) differ markedly from critical pedagogues, as Rivera and Poplin (1995: 224) explain: 'The critical pedagogists are concerned with the justice side of moral reasoning while the feminine pedagogists are more concerned with the care voice of moral reasoning'.

The cultural feminists also stand in marked contrast to feminist poststructuralists – another group of feminists that has influenced recent debates about early childhood curriculum. Feminist poststructuralists are diverse in their interests but share a concern with the ways that discourses (our language, our ideas and how we understand and feel about who we are) make some ways of being gendered more likely and more possible than others. (These ideas were discussed in detail in Chapter 4.) These feminists examine how interconnections between power, discourse and subjectivity (our ways of thinking about our self/selves) reduce our sense of who we can be. They believe that education should deconstruct (take apart) gender discourses and reconstruct them in new ways that create more equitable, just and diverse possibilities for everyone. Consequently, they believe that educators should (Alloway 1995; Mac Naughton 2001c):

- encourage children to question their own and others' gender norms;
- explore ways of being that challenge gender norms, especially the idea that there is just one way to be a girl and one way to be a boy;
- expand children's capacity to reflect critically on the effects of gender on their choices of who to become;
- support children who attempt to blur and cross the gender boundaries.

Critical anti-racists and critical multiculturalism

Another branch of the critical pedagogy 'family tree' is critical race theory and critical multiculturalism. In overview, educators working from within this perspective challenge the racism in the curriculum, privilege the knowledge and perspectives of people of colour, and emphasize the importance of using culturally relevant pedagogies that respect children of colour as competent learners and that help them to transform their communities (Collins 1990). To do this they (Sleeter and Grant 1999):

- recognize, respect and celebrate cultural diversity;
- challenge the effects of institutional racism on specific groups in a given society;
- practice democratic relationships;
- analyse how inequality affects specific children and groups of children;
- develop social action skills;
- seek links between different forms of discrimination.

Critical multicultural education differs from multicultural education as follows:

[Critical multicultural education] deals more directly than the other approaches with oppression and structural inequality based on race, social class, gender, and disability . . . [It] prepares future citizens to reconstruct society so that it better serves the interests of all groups of people and especially those who are of colour, poor, female, gay, lesbian, transexual, disabled or any combination of these. The approach is visionary.

(Sleeter and Grant 1999: 189)

The work of the critical race theorists emerged during the civil rights movement in the USA in the 1970s. Writers such as Derrick Bell and Alan Freeman were concerned with the erosion of civil rights in the 1970s for black Americans and how racism framed the lives of black Americans (Tate 1996).

Each of these critical perspectives on education emphasize the need for educators to be involved in socially reconstructing the world through education. Educators are placed in a position of leadership for progressive social change. That not all educators will choose to take this position is clear. However, Freire believed that when educators abdicate this position their students are diminished:

Freire exposed how even well-meaning teachers, through their lack of critical moral leadership, actually participate in disabling the hearts, minds and bodies of their students – an act that disconnects students from the personal and social motivation required to transform their world and themselves.

(Darder 2002: 35)

Implications of social reconstructionism for early childhood curriculum: taking a critical approach

Social reconstructionism is a 'transforming' philosophy of education that is associated with:

- a 'transforming' model of the child as both a product of social construction and a site at which social construction happens;
- a critical, 'transforming' approach to early childhood curriculum.

Educators who hold a 'transforming' philosophy of education believe that education can:

- transform the possibilities for individuals and the groups of which they are a part;
- transform society to create greater social justice and equity.

Consequently, they see their tasks as:

- attempting to change ideas, practices, stories and emotions that oppress people and produce inequality;
- promoting equality of opportunity and participation in education for all;
- opening up possibilities for all children;
- helping children to recognize and deal with what's fair and unfair in their world;
- creating a living democracy in the early childhood programme;
- building social action skills in children.

How they do this will be linked to the specific social and political contexts in which they work and thus the early childhood educator is required to be critically reflective on how best to achieve their tasks with the specific group of children that they are working with. As Freire argued: 'The progressive educator must always be moving out on his or her own, continually reinventing me and reinventing what it means to be democratic in his or her own specific cultural and historical context' (Freire 1997, in Darder 2002: v).

Goals

Within a 'transforming' position, early childhood curriculum goals should contribute to the creation of a more just and wise society that offers diverse possibilities for who we can become. This requires educators to analyse critically their current goals and to be open to developing goals that include the voices of the oppressed, silenced or marginalized. This means choosing goals that:

- link with specific children's experiences and issues;
- explore alternative ways to see issues and to think about them;
- give children respectful power in their world.

Early childhood educators who adopt a 'transforming' position see that curriculum goals are always political (Carr and Kemmis 1986) whether or not educators acknowledge this. The point in taking a 'transforming' position is to consciously set the politics of your goals so that they contribute to a more socially just and wise society – now and in the future. This would include setting goals that build subordinate groups' skills and knowledge and enable them to change their power relations with the dominant groups in their society (Rivera and Poplin 1995). Such change-orientated goals need to work on several fronts simultaneously:

- enabling children to analyse critically their daily lives to highlight the ways that they contribute to or experience oppression;
- enabling children to think about their daily lives in new ways that challenge the dominant stories or narratives about what subordinate groups can accomplish;
- creating change through such critical analysis and new narratives about the world.

Some people may argue that these goals are 'too adult' or 'too complex' for work with young children. The words of two early childhood critical educators offer ways to reflect on those arguments:

In my teaching, I have found that children who come from families who are struggling to survive economically, culturally, and politically can benefit from teaching practices that are rooted in critical theory because these children already have an awareness that all is not just in their world.

(Goldstein 2002: 179)

One of the most powerful lessons that I have learned is that even young children are able to reflect on issues that impact on their identity and their lives. The world of children is governed by the same values and beliefs that govern the world of adults.

(Segura-Mora 2002: 176)

A 'transforming' approach to curriculum (like a 'practical' approach – Chapter 8) assumes that educators can build meaningful curriculum goals by reflecting critically on their teaching. However, critical educators argue that individuals' critical reflections may be constrained by a series of political and social conditions. For instance, an individual's own class, 'race', gender and ability may limit their capacity to reflect critically on the ways in which their own biases are influencing their choice of curriculum goals. Or, an individual's access to ways of seeing and understanding the world other than their own may restrict their ability to develop goals that are transforming for particular groups of children. Consider the following comment:

> I knew through my personal experiences as a student, teacher, female, and working class Chicano from a non-traditional family, that young students, like older students, were also silenced and coerced into blind obedience . . . Many of these children eventually disappeared from the classroom, weeded out in a process so insidious that even the most well-intentioned teachers did not (and do not) recognize their pivotal role in this economic and social maintenance of the status quo.
>
> (Goldstein 2002: 178)

Ideas summary 9.1 Building transforming goals in early childhood curriculum

Example goals

Broad statements of intent and commitments that highlight equity and social justice (for example, from the University of Ghent daycare centre, Belgium: 'In our day-care centre, we consider it our duty to educate the children to be without prejudice, in an atmosphere of trust, tolerance and openness' (Vandenbroeck 1999: 162)).

CONTENT
- emphasizes non-traditional knowledge and the skills needed to create social change;
- seeks new forms of knowledge;
- emphasizes equity and social justice, especially around issues of 'race', gender, class and ethnicity;
- explores diverse possibilities for children's becoming.

DON'T
- ignore the interests and perspectives of groups experiencing discrimination and oppression;
- restrict new ways of becoming for children.

LANGUAGE
- Always use non-sexist, non-racist, non-disablist and non-classist language in formulating goals.

DO
- reflect critically on the equity implications and possibilities of your goals. For example, ask yourself if and how your goals will promote greater equity and social justice in relation to gender, 'race', ethnicity, culture, language, ability and class;
- include the perspectives and interests of groups experiencing discrimination and oppression.

The 'anti-bias' approach to early childhood curriculum is a major expression of critical educational theorists' ideas. Louise Derman-Sparks and the Anti-Bias Curriculum Task Force first coined the term 'anti-bias education' in the USA, to describe a transforming approach to early childhood curriculum that emphasizes equity and social justice; and that aims to empower all children and to challenge discrimination and oppression. 'Anti-bias' curriculum goals are (see Dau 2001):

- to build self-esteem and pride in all children;
- to enable children to feel comfortable with diversity;
- to enable children to recognize what is fair and not fair in their daily lives;
- to give young children the skills needed to counteract unfairness.

From these specific goals can be built an anti-bias approach to gender, 'race', ethnicity, disability and class. For instance, a sample of curriculum goals for an anti-bias approach to disability that flow from these broad goals include (Derman-Sparks *et al.* 1989: 40):

- To provide an inclusive educational environment in which all children can succeed.
- To enable children with disabilities to develop autonomy, independence, competency, confidence and pride.
- To provide all children with accurate, developmentally appropriate information about their own and others' disabilities and to foster understanding that a person with a disability is different in one respect but similar in many others.
- To enable all children to develop the ability to interact knowledgeably, comfortably and fairly with people who have various disabilities.
- To teach children with disabilities how to handle and challenge name-calling, stereotypical attitudes and physical barriers.
- To teach non-disabled children how to resist and challenge stereotyping, name-calling and physical barriers directed against people with disabilities.

Derman-Sparks (1998: 22) describes how the anti-bias curriculum began:

The term 'anti-bias' has a similar meaning to 'education without prejudice'. We chose it because we wanted to say that this work requires a very active stance in relationship to challenging racism, sexism and all other forms of systematic oppression . . . We also need to look at the power relationships that interfere with the possibility of true diversity – the institutional structures and beliefs that systematically result in less resources, power and status for large numbers of people because of their racial and ethnic group membership, their gender, their class, their sexual orientation.

In the UK this approach to early education has often been called anti-discriminatory practice (see Brown 1998).

Those ideas link directly with several 'transforming' approaches to work with young children including anti-racist and anti-sexist education. Ideas gallery 9.2

presents some examples of these 'transforming' approaches. Use it to consider how these perspectives link to the anti-bias curriculum and to 'transforming' approaches to education in general.

Ideas gallery 9.2 International expressions of a 'transforming' approach to early childhood curriculum goals

From a discussion of the 1980 National Congress of Buruku people in Japan:

'Dowa educare should be defined as useful educare for liberating the Buruku people from discrimination . . . the congress were to re-confirm the need for human rights educare and emphasise that educare and the educator should learn the reality of discrimination.' (Tamaki 2000: 3)

From research in Spain:

An educational approach based on the respect and value of cultural diversity, aimed at all members of society as a whole that proposes a model of action that is both formal and informal, holistic and integrated, and which shapes all aspects of the educational process in order to achieve equal opportunities and results, overcome racism in its various shapes and forms, and obtains intercultural communication and skill.' (Aguado 1996, in Aguado and Jimenez Frias 1999: 125)

From an Australian text on early childhood curriculum:

'This edition continues the theme of the first edition, and every reason still exists for us to "confront bias, eliminate discrimination and encourage all people, both children and adults, to feel confident, competent and comfortable in dealing with diversity" '. (Dau 2001: xx)

From an Irish report on early childhood education, care and training:

'Anti-bias education embraces an educational philosophy as well as specific techniques and content. It is value based: differences are good, oppressive ideas and behaviours are not . . . It asks teachers and children to confront troublesome issues rather than cover them up. An anti-bias approach is integral to all aspects of daily life in early years settings.' (Murray and O'Doherty 2001: 62)

Plans

A 'transforming society' position on early childhood curriculum links directly with a critical approach to curriculum planning which is organic and driven through critical reflection on action. Pedagogies are generally based upon a 'transforming through interaction' (social constructionist and/or postmodern) model of the child as a learner (Chapter 3). In general the curriculum plans will show these characteristics:

- *Time* is used flexibly in response to individual children's needs.
- *People*: educators collaborate with children towards more just and equitable learning.

- *Space*: educators structure space loosely in response to individual children's changing needs and interests, and are alert to any equity implication of that space.
- *Learning resources* are examined for any equity implications.
- *Knowledge* is developed in and through children's changing interests and questions and educators always examine any equity implications.

Shaping the planning process

Plans will be organic (changing) responses to daily happenings and will be prepared through action research (Lovat and Smith 1995). In action research, educators reflect, plan, act, gather data on actions and their implications, review and replan in a series of cycles driven by critical reflection. These cycles will often involve colleagues and children as collaborators in the planning process and as 'critical friends' in the reflection process. For example, see Figure 9.1.

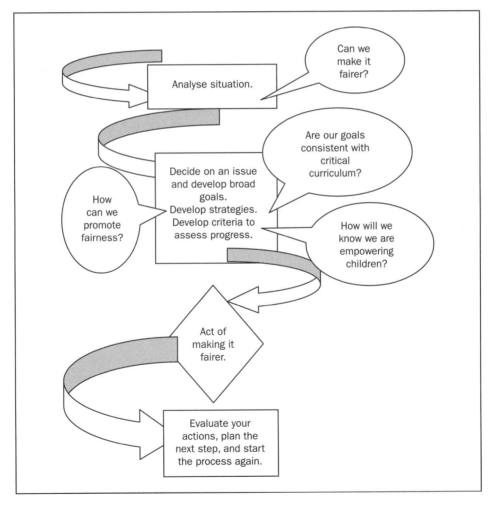

Figure 9.1 Action research planning cycle

The planning process based on this cycle follows a pattern something like this:

- Analyse situation – observe what issues are current in your centre. What aspects of children's ideas or relationships suggest that work needs doing to reduce discrimination in their ideas or relationships? What resources need reviewing to make your centre's resources more useful in anti-bias work?
- Decide on one issue you will work on.
- Develop some broad goals. What will you and the children achieve/work towards?
- Check the goals are consistent with the goals and principles of critical curriculum. How are your goals consistent with an 'anti-bias' approach? Modify if necessary.
- Develop strategies to achieve your goals. How will you achieve your goals? Are your strategies empowering for children and staff? In what ways?
- Develop criteria to judge whether you have achieved your goals. What will you need to see, do, hear to help you know you have achieved goals?
- Do it.
- Evaluate your actions using your criteria.
- Plan the next stage. Start the process all over again.

Educators who adopt this approach to curriculum planning don't design a set of techniques to 'drive' learners towards expected outcomes (as in a technical approach to curriculum – Chapter 7). Instead they plan to direct learning in ways that are spontaneous, flexible and sensitive to 'the subtle changes and responses of other participants in the enterprise' (Carr and Kemmis 1986: 37). In particular, they are alert to the effects of their curriculum on particular groups of children and who might be silenced or marginalized through their intentions as educators.

For this reason, a critical approach to curriculum planning also highlights children's voices and educators draw on children's knowledge in their planning. To do this educators:

- encourage children to research and make sense of their world;
- recognize the influence of gender, 'race', class, disability and sexuality on what educators see and share and how they share;
- seek multiple sources of knowledge about the child and use them to plan curriculum;
- test multiple 'lenses' through which to 'see' the child and 'hear' their voice;
- test multiple 'techniques' to 'see' discourse in action;
- engage in critical dialogue with children about what they regard as fair and unfair.

Thus, in this approach much of the educator's curriculum is planned through reflecting critically on what he or she has learnt by using different 'lenses' and adopting different perspectives on the child. Curriculum plans imply that the child is a learner who is active and knowing, but who always and inevitably acts and knows within specific discourses (frameworks for making sense of the world).

Shaping the content

From the perspective of critical educational theory, critical race theory and feminist theory, decisions about what children can and should learn rest on several interrelated principles:

- knowledge is socially constructed and problematic;
- meaningful content is generated in interaction with students/children;
- meaningful content helps children to transform their world.

Knowledge is socially constructed and problematic

Knowledge is problematic because it is socially constructed to serve the needs and interests of particular groups of people – all knowledge comes from culture and is, therefore, culturally limited and culturally bound. For these reasons, critical educators should engage critically with knowledge, rather than focus on its consumption. Critical educators believe that each of us can contribute to greater social justice and emancipation by building critical knowledge. To explain this point, Smith and Lovat (1990) draw on the ideas of German social theorist Jürgen Habermas who is associated with the Frankfurt School of Social Theory:

> Self-reflective, or critical knowledge, would then cause us to ask whether the information we have received is reliable, whether we are in a position to learn or not to learn through it, or whether we might not be controlled somehow by the forces of propaganda which surround us: this is helping to satisfy our interest to be free.

> For Habermas, it is only when we have reached [critical knowledge] that we are guaranteed true knowledge because true knowledge demands that we be free . . . The information which comes from any subject can become a means of bondage, rather than emancipation, a way of oppressing people or keeping them in straitjackets.
>
> (Smith and Lovat 1990: 69–70)

Critical educators see all knowledge as value-based. Sleeter and McClaren put this forcefully: 'All pedagogical efforts are infiltrated with value judgements and crosshatched by vectors of power serving particular interests in the name of certain regimes of truth' (Sleeter and McClaren 1995: 18). Against that background, critical educators seek to build curriculum by 'knowing from the inside' (Smith and Lovat 1990) and by developing knowledge that is critical and reflective. As part of that process, they challenge taken-for-granted assumptions about what early childhood curriculum content should look like, asking, 'Whose knowledge is in my curriculum and whose knowledge should be in my curriculum?'

For example, educators working within a critical race perspective would focus on identifying and challenging silences, inaccuracies, and stereotypes about people of colour and their perspectives in the curriculum content. They would look for the ways in which the content of what young children learn through stories, songs, images and other classroom texts might be racially stereotyped and racially inaccurate and avoid using such texts. They would also look for the ways in which curriculum texts rely solely on the perspectives of dominant white groups within a particular society. This is because critical race theorists see 'the official school curriculum as a culturally specific artifact designed to maintain a White supremacist master script' (Ladson-Billings 1999: 21).

Critical educators therefore build curriculum content by questioning what they are doing and why, reflecting critically on the values in their curriculum and looking for any unintended bias in their work with young children. Kerry Jones and Ruth Mules (2001) are early childhood educators who take an 'anti-bias' approach to early childhood curriculum. They challenge other early childhood educators to ask the following questions about their curriculum and its content:

> What other hidden messages are children receiving from the curriculum? What do I think is important for children to learn and understand? Why? How does the curriculum allow for culturally diverse ways of learning? How does the curriculum encourage critical thinking in young children? How often do I ask children questions about diversity and bias as a basis for curriculum development?
>
> (Jones and Mules 2001: 197)

Critical educators need to look carefully at how values construct the teaching and learning relationships, processes and products. What follows is an extract from the journal of an early childhood educator in South Australia, who participated in a project known as the Critical Teaching Project (funded by the South Australia Department of Education). It illustrates how she approaches the process of building critical knowledge into her curriculum:

> Critical teaching is about not just reflecting on practice, but through that, uncovering what it reveals about what we think and believe . . . and an opportunity to find out exactly who we are doing things for and why, and to change and adapt if you need. I know as an educator one of the main things I've got out of it is changing, and being able to change and knowing that you can. Whereas before, I went along thinking I had to do things because that's the way they were done, that's the way I was taught at Uni. And so you do them. But now I know that I can question, and I can change if I need to . . . it's quite a liberating experience. If anything I've felt that I've actually got more out of my work because I'm looking at what I'm doing, the way I'm doing it. I've changed some things, and I've felt that I've got a tool that I can use with other things . . . even things outside of work, outside of education.
>
> (Mac Naughton *et al.* 2000: 21)

Meaningful content is generated in interaction with children

In critically reflecting on the knowledge content of their curriculum critical educators will seek to develop content that builds from what children know, honours their cultural experience and knowledge and extends children's capacity to be active in their own learning. In this approach, curriculum is not 'unplanned'. Instead, the educator seeks to ground curriculum in children's lived experiences, interests and concerns and to reflect critically on the consequences – for themselves and for the children. Nimmo (2002: 10) links planning and reflection as follows:

> Grounding our curriculum in the dynamic intersection of children's questions and our own passions and skills involves planning and reflection. This curriculum is not pre-planned or received from outside experts, rather it emerges from an intimate knowledge of the particular children and community.

Ways of doing this with young children are described by Castillo (2002: 155–6):

- having daily 'sharing circles' for children to voice their ideas and concerns on a specific subject;
- writing journals with children on specific issues and ideas they have;
- drawing pictures with children about things that are hard or not fair;
- creating stories with children about hard or difficult issues in their lives.

Meaningful content helps children to transform their world

In a critical/'transforming' approach to early childhood curriculum, educators ensure that the content is transformative for the specific children with whom they're working. For example, children from socially, culturally and economically privileged groups should learn how to 'work towards the production of a less unjust society' (Thompson 1999: 41) and to build positive attitudes towards diversity. Similarly, children from socially, culturally and economically subordinate groups should gain the 'primary goods' (Thompson 1999: 41) that give them social, cultural and economic privileges. These might include critical literacy and numeracy skills. This knowledge should not be merely 'transferred' to children. Critical educators should always teach content that enables children to think and to act. As Freire put it – 'One teaches how to think through teaching content' (Freire 1993, in Darder 2002: 139).

In the following statement, principles for planning and organizing content within a critical multicultural curriculum Sleeter and Grant (1999) highlight the importance of helping children to gain knowledge that helps them to critically reflect on and act to transform their world:

> Organize content around current social issues involving racism, classism, sexism, handicappism; organize concepts around experiences and perspectives of several different . . . groups; use students' life experiences as starting point for analyzing

oppression; teach critical thinking skills, analysis of alternative viewpoints, teach social action skills, empowerment skills.

(Sleeter and Grant 1999: 189)

Shaping the schedule

Critical curriculum requires that children have opportunities to explore multiple understandings and possibilities for themselves and others. In turn, this requires a flexible curriculum schedule, to allow for diverse possibilities to emerge and for children to explore those possibilities individually and in groups. Educators can plan a schedule loosely before they meet the children but will re-evaluate and alter it as required throughout the day. Lovat and Smith (1995: 156) explain:

> Feedback from students, by using questions, or from observation, is a very important indicator as to the necessity to change. If students show a great deal of interest in something, teachers will often spend more time on that and less time on something else.

Educators will be sensitive to diversity within learners and will attempt to acknowledge it in how they schedule activities in the curriculum. Pease-Windy Boy (1995) indicated how the use of time within traditional USA classrooms can work against the interests of Crow American Indian students:

> For some students, this time factoring knocks them out or pushes them out forever. American Indian students have frequently been damaged by time-based learning, and the tribal colleges have attempted to relieve the connections to time.

(Pease-Windy Boy 1995: 405)

The pedagogical relationships

Structuring relationships

The educator is working to construct equitable and democratic relationships with the children (see, for example, Sleeter and Grant 1999). This means that what is to be learnt and the relationships will be structured through:

- dialogue between educators and children. In Freire's terms dialogue 'represents a powerful and transformative political process of interaction between people' (Darder 2002: 103);
- acknowledgement of individual children's specific cultural interests and learning styles;
- critical reflection that enables future learning to be planned collaboratively between educators and children, creating culturally safe spaces;
- building teaching and learning relationships that are fair, inclusive of all children and anti-biased through posing problems with children and identifying ways forward.

Building meaningful and respectful relationships with children will be a core part of the educator's role. For instance, early childhood educators who draw on 'feminine' pedagogues such as Nel Noddings (1992) and Lisa Goldstein (1997) place teaching relationships at the core of their curriculum. They place an ethic of care at the centre of all their relationships and they build their curriculum by creating caring communities with children. Sleeter and Grant (1999) also place relationships at the centre of their work on critical multicultural curriculum. For Freire, collaborative dialogue is at the core of respectful and transformative relationships (Darder 2002).

Structuring space and materials

Critical educators critically reflect on how they can use space and materials to further children's critical reflection in their world and their capacity to act to transform injustices in it. To do this they need to structure space and materials in ways that enable children to explore their own and others' diverse ways of understanding and being in the world. Answering some questions should assist critical educators to choose materials that 'reflect social action themes, culture diversity, student interests' (Sleeter and Grant 1999: 189) and that reflect the curriculum's goals and intents:

- Do the everyday objects we use reflect the languages and cultures of the children within this group?
- Do we have everyday objects from diverse cultures?
- Do the materials respect and celebrate cultural and racial diversity?
- Do the materials challenge traditional sex-role stereotypes and understandings?
- To what extent do the materials support and respect diverse abilities and ways of being?

Critical educators will also need to work to create equal access and opportunity through the use of space and materials in their work with young children. The following questions can assist educators to critically reflect on access and opportunity for participation in their learning spaces and materials (Mac Naughton and Williams 1998):

- Can children of differing physical abilities move around the space easily?
- Can children of differing physical abilities participate in a range of activities?
- Can children of differing abilities and ages easily see and touch display areas?
- Can all children in the group – irrespective of their cultural background – recognize their own cultures in the materials and staff they encounter?

Many critical educators will use materials about controversial issues and material from popular culture to critically engage children in reflection on their world.

Structuring teaching strategies

The pedagogy will be based on transformative understandings of the child as a learner and it will emphasize collaborative, dialogic and empowerment pedagogies.

Collaborative dialogic pedagogies focus on bringing children's ideas and perspectives to the fore. They centre on finding ways of sharing meanings and ideas (dialogue) between children and between children and educators. If the dialogue is genuinely inclusive of all children it will highlight their 'similar, different and contradictory views of the world' (Darder 2002: 105). However, dialogue and seeing multiple perspectives on the world is not seen as an end in itself. The point of dialogue within transformative curriculum is to 'forge collective social action in the interest of an emancipatory political vision' (Darder 2002: 105). It is necessary to the process of seeing what is fair and unfair, challenging unfairness and finding new possibilities for being and thinking and acting that offer dignity to all children. Hence, educators will attempt to use dialogue with children to build their capacity to reflect critically on and act in the world. Educators can do this in several ways.

First, by teaching children how to deconstruct different ways to understand the world. A critical approach to curriculum assumes that people develop knowledge as they negotiate their way in the world and that, therefore, children can know and understand something without the educator knowing it. For example, as an author I can't know how you understand what I'm writing and if and how you will use it unless I talk with you about it. From that perspective, an educator's job is not to impart knowledge, but to ensure that children learn knowledge that empowers them and that children can evaluate what they learn. (See Mac Naughton and Williams 1998; Darder 2002.)

Second, by speculating with children about what might happen if we did things differently. For instance, critical early childhood educators choose what to do in interaction with children and, as they do so, they continuously explore the political and social consequences of their curriculum content, as Rivera and Poplin (1995: 223) explain:

> Critical pedagogy seeks to draw out student voices and put these voices in dialogue with others in a never ending cycle of meaning making characterized by reflection/action/reflection/new action and so forth.

In this process educators can invite children to think about how they rethink or reorganize what they do to make it fairer and more equitable. Those are challenging tasks for educators, as Bronwyn Davies (a key feminist poststructuralist writer) has noted:

> Children do not accept what adults tell them as having application to every aspect of their lives ... It is not possible for children simply and straightforwardly to accept the world as it is told to them, not least because the difference between the 'real' and the 'ideal' world is often quite marked in adult–child discourse.
>
> (Davies 1989: 6)

For instance, inviting children to rethink or reorganize gender relations to make them fairer contains many challenges and potential points of resistance. Young children who do want to explore non-traditional gender relations by blurring and crossing the gender boundaries may have their peers taunt them, reject them or try to make them be more like they are – normally gendered children. Mac Naughton (2001) suggests that educators may need an active risk-minimization plan for these children. Such a plan involves the educator:

- being alert to the gendered power dynamics in the group;
- discussing with children their feelings about crossing the gender boundaries;
- being honest with children about both the advantages and the disadvantages of being different;
- promoting as heroines and heroes people who cross the gender boundaries;
- discussing with children different people's ideas about gender;
- showing children that 'it's OK' to have contradictory ways of being at times.

Third, by asking how we know things and what the consequences are of thinking about people unfairly or treating them unfairly. For instance, educators will support children to recognize the real inequities in their classroom and to challenge them through their own and others' actions, as Rossato indicates:

> Critical pedagogical approaches can help students to construct an engaging knowledge based on their background experiences as a self-empowerment tool . . . This means building schools as sites for historical, critical, and transformative action . . . In this process, critical educators emphasize how social identities are constructed within unequal relations of power within the schools.
>
> (Rossato 2001: 373)

In early childhood education anti-bias curriculum principles offer a source of ready knowledge about how to do this. Young children can understand what is fair or not fair in their daily world. Early childhood educators can help children to talk about what they know about fairness and unfairness and use this knowledge from their own experiences to talk about how to change what is not fair (Derman-Sparks et al. 1989; Brown 1998). Stories, discussion groups and informal conversations can help young children to think about what to do when someone is unfair to them, their friends and people that they don't know well. They can learn how to take action to transform what is unfair in their lives with each other.

Fourth, by engaging children in the process of praxis in project-based, collaborative learning groups. Paulo Freire's method of praxis is a process using theory to guide action and using action to build theory. Theory and action inform and reform each other as new theory builds through action and reflection and new actions are taken based on reflection and theory. As Grundy puts it, praxis means that curriculum is made: 'through an active process in which planning, acting and evaluation are all reciprocally related and integrated into the process' (Grundy 1987: 115). Children can be taught how to plan, act and evaluate with each other in collaborative project-based work. Such projects centre on collaborative dialogue in which the goal is:

bringing participants' focus on critical engagement of similar, differing, and contradictory views in order to understand the world together and forge collective social action in the interest of an emancipatory political vision.

(Darder 2002: 105)

The process in these projects if they are praxis-based will be one in which children and educators exchange ideas and meanings about a particular issue or idea. They then go through a process in which they 'reflect, critique, affirm, challenge, act, and ultimately transform [their] collective understanding of the world' (Darder 2002: 82).

Observations and assessment

Why observe?
Through our observations and assessment practices, we can see the biases in our relationships with children and we can see possibilities for collaborating with children to transform injustices in our world. To do this we must be able to see more than one view of the child and our relationships with the child. The idea that it is not possible to see without bias and that there are many ways to 'see' the child has its roots in several theories of knowledge, including critical and feminist views of knowledge. It also links with poststructuralist views of knowledge, which Hughes (2001: 47–8) introduces as follows:

> Poststructuralists seek to understand the dynamics of relationships between knowledge/meaning, power and identity . . . [They] reject the idea that we can *ever* be certain about the world because its complexity and dynamism defy encapsulation, categorization and closure. Seeking certainty about the world is as futile as trying to hold a river in your hand – its dynamism precludes its capture and whatever you capture is no longer dynamic. Thus, our understandings of the world can only ever be provisional – it is unattainable because it is ephemeral.

Poststructuralist educators are interested in how language influences and structures children's understandings of the world. They observe children to discover how the discourses expressed in their language facilitate some ways of being and preclude others. They then revisit their observations to explore whether and how the curriculum reduces or increases children's possibilities to explore and learn (see, for example, Campbell and Smith 2001). These educators often use audiotape or video-tape to capture their observations (perhaps transcribing them) so that they can revisit their observations to explore the different ways that children and educators learn and make meaning.

How to observe?
A 'transforming' approach to observation and assessment rests on the belief that it is not possible to gain objective observational data about the child. This is because observation is always skewed by the observer's biases and by the particular 'lens' through which the observer 'sees' the child and the child's perspectives. Building

meaningful and equitable curriculum with young children starts by a recognizing one's biases and using 'lenses' that negate those biases in favour of ways of seeing that promote social justice and equity. Campbell and Smith suggest ways to do this:

> Teachers and researchers will need to explore ways of viewing children and classrooms from multiple perspectives. Examples could involve paired observations and discussions, the use of multiple theoretical discourses to understand events, and the exploration of diverse perspectives on equity and fairness in classroom activities.
>
> (Campbell and Smith 2001: 99)

Poststructuralist early childhood educators believe that we can never capture 'the truth' about a child and that power relations influence what we can see and know about the child. These ideas about observing children are expressed in the case study in Chapter 10 by Kylie Smith, and in her following statement:

> As we work to reconceptualise the knowledge generated through observation in our early childhood curriculum we are revealing the multiplicity of parent's ideas and understandings about their child which have been silenced and marginalised by our traditional approaches to observation. The emergence of non-traditional views such as Feng Shui is important. It offers us the opportunity to change relationship between parents and professionals by allowing us as staff to see normally subjugated non-developmental knowledge of the child as valid.
>
> (Smith 2001: 12)

Such an approach to observation grows from an anti-bias perspective on early education and from critical pedagogy. It assumes that we can only ever have partial knowledge of the child and that to create socially just and equitable relationships with children requires educators to seek multiple perspectives on the child, including their own, and to attend to issues of power in those relationships.

Educators can use various observational techniques to collaborate with children in building knowledge of the world and their understandings of it. Those techniques include journalling, narratives and collecting artefacts (Chapter 8); but these need to be generated in collaboration with each, mindful of whose voices are being represented and whose are being silenced and marginalized, and accompanied by detailed critical analysis of what is being learnt. Core questions for analysis of what is learnt through observing children would include, 'In whose interests is the knowledge being generated and how is it being used to help us transform injustices and open up multiple possibilities for children?'

Interpreting observations

Educators practising critical pedagogy interpret observations by exploring:

- the equity dynamics within a specific group of children;
- the equity implications of what is being seen;

- the multiple ways of seeing what has been found;
- the possibilities for transformational action through what has been learnt.

For instance they might:

- Note the equity dynamics, such as relationships between children of different genders, cultures, abilities, ethnicities and language groups. Who is playing with whom and how?
- Assess the significance of the equity dynamics by asking who they benefit and disadvantage. Do all children engage equally in learning? Are specific groups of children silenced or marginalized within the group? Do children limit their involvement in activities because of other children's treatment of them? Are some children (and some types of children) more powerful than others? When does this happen?
- Seek colleagues and children's interpretations of what they have seen.
- Identify how discrimination affects specific children in the group and then plan to take action against it.

The following critical analysis table (Table 9.1) offers one format that educators can use to help them interpret their observations.

Critical interpretation of observations will draw on transforming positions on the learner and thus from theories of the child influenced by social constructionism, feminist theory and critical race theory.

Ideas gallery 9.3 presents some snapshots of 'transforming' approaches to observation and assessment.

Table 9.1 Critical analysis table

Steps in critical analysis of observations	Comments
<ul><li>What meanings of words or concepts are key to my understandings of this issue or this child?</li><li>Are there other ways of understanding what these words mean?</li><li>What meanings are 'othered' – marginalized or silenced?</li><li>How do these meanings lead to taken-for-granted assumptions about this child or this incident?</li><li>How do my meanings limit what I consider possible for myself and others?</li><li>Who benefits from my specific taken-for-granted assumptions on this observation or incident?</li><li>How might I act given this knowledge to create greater justice and/or open up more possibilities for the children involved?</li></ul>	

Ideas gallery 9.3 'Transforming society' approaches to observations and assessment

'Educators need to be ready to stretch their knowledge and understanding, to be observant, and to have proactive strategies for listening to the voices of families outside their experience.' (Nimmo 2002: 10)

'We are increasingly seeking the parents' theories of the child, recognising and engaging with meanings of culture, race, class, gender and sexuality for parents and for children and opening ourselves up to multiple views of the child. In doing so, parents are being recognised as important partners in producing knowledge of the child through observation.' (Smith 2000: 14)

'Observations should be used to evaluate not only the developmental appropriateness of planned experiences but also the possible gender biases. Such evaluation enables staff to plan an anti-bias curriculum suited to children's needs, abilities and interests, and the particular gender politics of the group.' (Mac Naughton 2001: 53)

'By thinking about how each child accessed and invested in competing ways of being a boy or a girl (or subject positions) – and how these subject positions limited and made possible what each child could think, say, and do – we began to create a different story about how power operated to make it possible to be included in play.' (Campbell and Smith 2001: 96)

Learning outcomes and assessing children's learning

Critical educators will have a prime interest in using assessment to generate more meaningful transformative curriculum with children. Their assessment will look at how critical knowledge of the child and of learning in their programmes can assist them take their curriculum decisions. To achieve this within the context of a critically informed curriculum they need to search for information that will help them think about:

- The social construction of knowledge. How are children constructing understandings and how is the social context and their gender, race, class, ability, power, and so on influencing the knowledge that is being constructed.

- What are the effects of the curriculum for specific children and specific groups of children.

- How do children's answers/knowledge intersect with the teacher's knowledge/ intentions.

The case study in Chapter 10 offers you an opportunity to see how one early childhood educator is attempting these processes. The following questions are offered as 'critical friends' to help you reflect on the equity effects of your work with young children and on the possibilities for democracy in your curriculum:

- Do my curriculum goals recognize and respect diversity?
- Do my curriculum goals recognize the concerns and interests of the children and their families?
- Do my curriculum plans respond to children's different needs?
- Do my curriculum plans recognize and respect diversity?
- Whose ideas are most prominent in the content of my curriculum?
- Does the content of my curriculum include diverse cultures and languages?
- How does the content of my curriculum help children to think critically about their social relationships and social worlds with each other?
- How does the content of my curriculum encourage children to explore different ways to be a girl and to be a boy?
- How can I bring silent or marginalized voices into the centre of my curriculum?
- What gendered ways of being dominate my curriculum?
- Whose interests do they serve?
- Are my relationships with children democratic?

Ideas summary 9.2 Curriculum as transforming society

Curriculum dimensions	Key ideas	Theoretical links
Philosophy	Early education that works with the child to transform society because it: • aims to challenge discrimination in the status quo; • values emancipation and social justice.	*Key theory*: Anti-bias education *Key theory families – radical education*: • Social reconstructionist education • Critical education • Feminist(s) education *Definition*: Radical: favours deep social changes in the interests of all, but especially groups who experience discrimination (for example, education that favours deep social changes in the interests of all, especially those who experience discrimination).
Goals	• based on working with the child to transform society; • seeking to produce social activists;	*Key thinker* Paulo Freire (1921–77). His key texts: *Pedagogy of the Oppressed* (1972) and *The Politics of Education* (1985).

	• informed by social and political analysis.	*Other thinkers (influenced by Freire):* • Peter McClaren • Henri Giroux
Planning	• organic; • based on cyclical action research of planning, doing and critically reflecting.	*Key theories* • critical curriculum theories; • feminist curriculum theories; • critical multicultural theories. *Definition:* Critical: questioning and being sceptical (for example, questioning and being sceptical of the status quo and existing power relations between specific groups).
Assessment	Learning how the child is becoming and transforming by: • gathering information about the social and political dynamics in the group and their effects; • assessing how and by whom power is exercised, with what effects; • choosing techniques that allow language and practice to be analysed and revisited over time.	*Links with positions on the child as a learner:* • feminist poststructuralism; • social constructionism; • critical race theory.

Equity reflections

A 'transforming' approach to early childhood curriculum generates several equity issues. These are examined under the same headings we used to explore the implications of social activism and social reconstructionism for the curriculum.

Philosophy and goals

Mandated curricula can marginalize critical pedagogues
Williams argued that the critical issue in any approach to equality is different groups' power in a particular society and gently parodied the white majority in Australia as follows:

> We happily agree of course with the general principle of equal rights. But, with a
> nervous glance over our shoulder, we feel uneasy or downright hostile towards
> any proposals that might remove our cushion of unfair advantages. What? Special
> rights for blacks/tribals/women/Maoris/Aboriginals/Indians/Catholics? We're
> in favour of equal opportunities, but not preferential treatment. That wouldn't
> be fair. But fairness is a relative concept. It means nothing when two groups are
> already grossly unequal.
>
> (Williams 1983: 9)

Williams described how a society's dominant majority maintain inequalities that
benefit them and maintain their dominance. Many educators who take a 'transforming society' position on early childhood education assume that some groups in
society are treated unfairly. They believe that a human rights, anti-bias and/or anti-
discriminatory approach to equity is required to change the power relationships and
the attitudes and practices towards differences in a society. These educators see the
aim of education as identifying and challenging all forms of discrimination. However,
these educators can often find themselves in an untenable position in education
systems where other priorities demand that they as educators focus on test results and
academic performance. It is not that the system is directly against anti-discriminatory
approaches to work with the young child, but that its demands make this work
increasingly difficult: 'A most powerful way of indoctrinating pupils is by so
organising their studies that certain kinds of reflections . . . are off the agenda' (White
1989, in McGuinn 2002: 136). When an educator's base philosophy clashes in this
way with system-wide demands, it becomes difficult for the educator to be reflective
about their work and they can experience marginalization and disillusionment
(McGuinn 2002).

Plans

Time for critical reflection is not structured into educator's days

A transforming approach to education implies no hard and fast way to plan
curriculum, although it emphasizes reflecting on the extent to which each element of
planning and implementing your curriculum is consistent with your curriculum
intent. Johnson and Reid argue that genuine democracy is at the heart of this
approach:

> The central question for curriculum decision-making, therefore, is how to
> establish processes of curriculum debates which are genuinely democratic,
> that is, which do not marginalise particular voices. Indeed, given the importance
> of education to the making of a civilised society, this is a question fundamental to
> the operation of our democratic system.
>
> (Johnson and Reid 1999: xi)

Curriculum debate can be difficult to achieve among the daily demands of
teaching and learning, as Goldstein shares:

As a teacher who worked to imbue my practice with critical pedagogical principles, I struggled with the daily, practical issues of running a classroom. Keeping
attendance, assembling portfolios, passing out lunch tickets, remembering
rain-day and block schedules, sitting through faculty meetings, and finding time
for a bathroom break . . . Seldom do I find the time to reflect, discuss, question,
and share ideas about my practice with my co-workers.

(Goldstein 2002: 177)

For critical educators this lack of opportunity to reflect critically with others places
particular strains and challenges on their efforts to plan in ways that are consistent
with the principles of critical pedagogy. It also makes it extremely difficult to be
critically reflective on what occurs with children. What Sleeter and McClaren (1995)
describe as naming what has been silent or not visible is a key issue for critical
educators and is crucial to creating democracy and, therefore, equity within a programme. Among lack of time for critical reflection and debate, how can educators
name racism and sexism in relationships and curriculum processes? How can they
ensure that children who experience racism and/or sexism feel safe within this process
of naming? How can they make them feel safe as they talk about what they experience
because of their gender, 'race' or culture? It is also not unusual for educators in this
position to find 'opportunities for speculation, discussions, sustained exploration have
to be abandoned in favour for more "transmissive" modes of teaching and learning'
(McGuinn 2002: 136).

Observations and assessment

System-wide demands for formal assessment and reporting on children
can undermine children's rights and democracy in the classroom

Adherents to a 'transforming' approach to observation and assessment in the curriculum consciously attempt to use 'lenses' (ways of seeing) in observing children that
offer diverse understandings, including the children's. We examined some different
'lenses' in Chapter 3, and they are explored in Kylie Smith's case study in Chapter 10.
Here we will discuss how critical educators can use principles governing ethical
research with children to assess children more equitably by involving children as equal
partners in the process.

Educators can begin to involve children in equitable assessment of their learning
by introducing these practices:

- Offer children a 'credible and meaningful explanation' of your intentions in
  observing and assessing them and offer them a 'real and legitimate opportunity to
  say that they do not want to take part' (WHO 1994: 353).
- Offer each child the right to refuse at any point to be observed and assessed.
- Devise observation and assessment methods that prioritize 'freedom of choice'
  (Evans and Fuller 1996). For instance, observe and assess children only when
  they come voluntarily and knowingly into your view.

- Ensure that you ask children appropriate and acceptable questions. For instance, ensure that your questions acknowledge their emotional and social maturity and their family and cultural background (Dwivedi 1996).

- End any observation or other data collection exercise in which a child shows any distress or discomfort.

- Conclude your observations and assessments by debriefing, reassuring, thanking or praising the children, or by doing whatever seems appropriate to sustain the children's self-esteem and power as you observe and assess them.

However, these principles can be difficult for an educator to enact when there are system-wide demands for assessment and reporting on children's progress. As McGuinn explained: 'It seems that we live increasingly in an educational environment in which only that which can be measured is regarded as important' (McGuinn 2002: 137).

In summary, the equity concerns from within this approach to curriculum centre on the system within which critical educators work and how it can produce the following:

- *Philosophy*: mandated curricula can reinforce traditional power relations rather than transform them.

- *Goals*: mandated curricula can marginalize the work of critical pedagogues.

- *Plans*: time for critical reflection is not structured into educator's days.

- *Observation and assessment*: system-wide demands for formal assessment and reporting on children can undermine children's rights and democracy in the classroom.

Reflecting on your learning

- What have you learnt about perspectives on the role of early childhood education in society?

- What are the key challenges and possibilities that the chapter leaves you with?

Further reading and online resources

Anti-bias curriculum

Dau, E. (ed.) (2001) *The Anti-Bias Approach in Early Childhood*. Frenchs Forrest, N.S.W.: Pearson Education.

Derman-Sparks, L. and The Anti-Bias Task Force (1989) *The Anti-Bias Curriculum*. Washington, D.C.: National Association for the Education of Young Children.

Jones, K. and Mules, R. (2001) Developing critical thinking and activism, in E. Dau (ed.) *The Anti-Bias Approach in Early Childhood*, (pp. 192–209). Frenchs Forrest, N.S.W.: Pearson Education.

CD-ROM. Mac Naughton, G., Campbell, S., Smith, K. and Lawrence, H. (2002) *Equity Adventures in Early Childhood*. Melbourne: Centre for Equity and Innovation in Early Childhood, The University of Melbourne. http://www.edfac.unimelb.edu.au/LED/ CEIEC/

Email address of a childcare centre in the US with anti-bias philosophy: cshrc@stuaf.umass.edu

Video: *Anti-Bias Curriculum*. Oroles from: Pacific Oaks College, Extension Services, 714 West California Bvd., Pasadensa, CA91105.

Video: *Fair Play: Anti-Bias in Action. A Training Kit* (1997). Sydney: Lady Gowrie Children's Centre.

Equity and diversity. Great list of resources: http://www.ali.apple.com/naeyc/06.shtml

Institute of Anti-bias Education Study Guide, which describes the aims of anti-bias education. Full text reading: http://www.adl.org/tools_teachers/tip_antibias_ed.html

Journal on projects that foster equity, respect and understanding: http://www.splcenter.org/ teachingtolerance/tt-index.html

Practical resources for implementing social justice and anti-bias curriculum with young children: http://californiatomorrow.org/

Critical curriculum and empowerment

Freire, P. (1972) *Pedagogy of the Oppressed*, M. Bergman Ramos trans., Middlesex: Penguin Books.

Freire, P. (1985) *The Politics of Education: Culture, Power and Liberation*, D. Macedo trans., Massachusetts: Bergin Garvey Publishers.

Grundy, S. (1987) *Curriculum: Product or Praxis*. London: Falmer Press.

Thompson, P. (1999) How doing justice got boxed in, in B. Johnson and A. Reid (eds) *Contesting the Curriculum*, pp. 24–42. Sydney: Social Science Press.

Feminist theories in early childhood

Goldstein, L. (1997) *Teaching with Love: A Feminist Approach to Early Childhood Education*. New York: Peter Lang Publishing.

Hauser, M. and Jipson, J. (eds) (1998) *Intersections, Feminisms/Early Childhoods*. New York: Peter Lang Publishers.

International perspectives

Butterworth, D. and Candy, J. (1998) Quality early childhood practice for young Aboriginal children, *Australian Journal of Early Childhood*, 23 (2): 20–6.

Commission for Racial Equality (1995) *From Cradle to School: A Practical Guide to Racial Equality in Early Childhood Education and Care*, pp. 22–31. London: Commission for Racial Equality.

Gallas, K. (1997) *Sometimes I Can Be Anything: Power, Gender, and Identity in a Primary Classroom*. New York: Teachers College Press.

Kirmani, M. and Frieman, B. (1997) Diversity in classrooms: teaching kindness through folk tales, *International Journal of Early Childhood*, 29(2): 39–43.

Miller Marsh, M. (1992) Implementing anti-bias curriculum in the kindergarten classroom, in S. Kessler and B. Blue Swadner (eds) *Reconceptualizing the Early Childhood Curriculum: Beginning the Dialogue*, pp.267–87. New York: Teachers College Press.

Ritchie, J. (1996) The bicultural imperative within the New Zealand draft curriculum guidelines for early childhood education, '*Te Whāriki*', *Australian Journal of Early Childhood*, 21(3): 28–32.

Soek-Hoon, S. (1994) Educating young children in a diverse society. Paper presented at the 8th Annual Conference of the Educational Research Association, 24–6 November, Singapore.

Key thinkers in critical and postmodern theories

University of Columbia. The School of Education Critical Theory page has extensive links to key thinkers in this area: http://www.cudenver.edu/-mryder/itc_data/postmodern.html#habermas

10

Curriculum positions: critical reflections

This chapter offers you a number of specific resources through which to reflect critically on the differing views of how to approach curriculum planning that you met in Chapters 7, 8 and 9. It uses case studies and Reflections sheets to support you to build your own approach to curriculum planning. Ideas galleries about planning and curriculum goals are provided at the end of the chapter to assist you in furthering your thinking about curriculum in early childhood.

Case studies on curriculum planning

Read the following case studies written by a group of early childhood educators who have been reflecting critically on their approaches to planning. It explores the links between values, philosophies, approaches to the child as a learner and planning decisions. Once you have read the journal extract, reflect on it using the following questions:

- How do these educators engage in critical reflection on how children are understood as learners?
- Do you have similar ideas or stories you could tell and use to reflect critically on your own approaches to curriculum planning?
- Which theorists' ideas of curriculum planning did Yarrow and Denise most closely link with?

CASE STUDY

Rethinking planning (Yarrow Andrew, Brian Newman and Denise Rundle)

Why rethink planning?
A 4-year-old boy holds a pencil in a palmar grasp. The same child also uses physical aggression to resolve differences with other children in the group.

Should we plan for the child to adjust his grip or to skill him to use non-violent methods to resolve conflict? Traditional models of planning see both these as needs of equal significance.

We have been meeting to discuss planning for two years now and have found our discussions have inspired and supported us to think beyond traditional approaches to planning in early childhood services. We work in different settings – childcare, kindergarten and teaching in Tertiary and Further Education (TAFE) – but share a strong commitment to equity principles and children's rights.

Philosophies

These meetings came about through a shared frustration with the planning models that are usually used. From our first discussions, it emerged that our disquiet came from feelings that traditional planning often seemed to contradict our teaching philosophies – the reasons why we work in early childhood. Some of these beliefs were:

- *Seeing the child as a whole.* Piagetian ideas, which form the basis of much Australian early childhood programming, are reflective of European values from the middle of last century. They look at children in sections and rarely build on their skills and interests. Planning happens within separate developmental areas – physical, cognitive, social and emotional, measuring the child individually against 'norms'. This results in a deficit model of the child, focused on what they cannot achieve and what they are not, rather than on who they are and what they can do. We wanted planning that respected children as unique, capable individuals, living and learning within complex environments.

- *Seeing the child in his or her social, cultural and political context.* A developmental framework ignores the social, cultural and political contexts that children live within. In particular it short changes children who are not growing up in middle class, Anglo, nuclear families. All these factors have a strong influence on how children learn and grow, the ways they see themselves and the values and beliefs they hold.

- *Seeing early childhood programmes as dynamic and interactive.* We felt that what is documented in traditional planning formats is rarely the real learning that takes place. These methods fail to capture the complex dynamic processes happening in our rooms every day. This is really our programme – the interaction between children, staff, the environment and families.

The constraints of external monitoring systems such as accreditation and regulations often lead to us planning to meet these rules rather than to reflect the complex learning environments we build with the children, families and communities we work in.

A written plan, prepared a week in advance, often does not reflect what actually takes place and inhibits the flexibility we believe is important. We agreed that much of the most important learning that happens is often not what we have planned. It more often comes from the children's spontaneous questions, comments or play, and we wanted processes that recognized the importance of this aspect of our work, and integrated children's experiences into our planning. We wanted planning to be about children's experiences and not just about the activities provided for them.

We wanted to explore ways that we could make planning more meaningful, more reflective of children's experiences and learning, and more equitable for the children. It also needed to be manageable within the constraints of our time for planning.

Values

From these discussions of philosophy we moved on to explore the values behind our programmes. These are what underpin the ways in which we work with the children. Consciously or unconsciously, what we do reflects our own aspirations for the children we work with. We talked about what we wanted the children to learn from their time in our programmes, and produced long lists of ideas.

These values focused on both the ways in which children approach the world, and the ways they relate to other people. These were the skills and attitudes we believe equip children to build a better world. Fundamental to these values is a commitment to human rights and social justice.

The New Zealand early childhood curriculum, *Te Whāriki*, particularly inspired us because of the way in which it conceptualizes our work. *Te Whāriki* has both principles and strands woven together to create something greater and more complex. Its principles (empowerment, holistic development, family and community, and relationships) interweave with its strands (well-being, belonging, contribution, communication and exploration) to create a whole within a context. The language it uses also conveys a warmth and humanity not found in so many more functional statements about what is expected of early childhood services. This provided us with a starting point to see beyond the frustrations we felt with traditional planning.

We have been exploring ways to make our key values a visible part of our planning and to document children's learning from this perspective. We also want to explore how we can make these bigger questions the subject of debate and negotiation with children, colleagues and families, to create shared values within our communities.

Our philosophical beliefs and values form the basis of our planning for children and we wanted to use these as our planning tools. Below are Denise and Yarrow's accounts of how they've been working to put some of the ideas that emerged from our discussions into their practice.

Denise and Yarrow's experiences – putting ideas into practice

Through working together on planning issues, many of our ideas about the problems and possibilities of planning have become intertwined. Nonetheless, to an outside observer, what we do still looks different because our approaches inevitably reflect not only the communities we work in, but also our own ways of working and our values. As a result of our discussions, we both went to our various centres (for Denise, a culturally diverse sessional kindergarten in inner-city Melbourne; for Yarrow, a multifunctional childcare centre servicing a diverse population in rural Victoria) and tried to put some of our ideas into practice.

CASE STUDY

Denise's story

As a starting point, I have identified four fundamental values of my programme, which represent my philosophy and my understandings of the interests of the community in which I work. The overall programme and the plans for individual children relate back to these fundamental values.

I am trying to see the child as a whole person and not worrying so much about each developmental area. Instead I am looking at their skills, interests, dispositions and needs. This takes me away from a narrow view that limits seeing the child as a positive whole – in this culturally diverse centre it helps me to reflect better that child's culture, first language and home experiences.

I have become clearer that it is not the *content* of the activities the programme offers that is important but the *way* they are offered, how adults and peers interact within them and how this interaction is experienced by the children, making them *experiences* rather than *activities*.

The way I am planning now allows me to focus on what children are really learning, as well as supporting individual staff to input directly as and when they can with the children. This method helps acknowledge that teaching strategies, routines and rules are a vital part of the learning environment – part of what underpins all that happens.

I now write the overall plan so it includes staff timetables, routines, the location of experiences, our objectives, with space for possible groups and modifications. Groups and modifications are written onto the plan as part of the evaluation process.

Individual children have plans written for them, with objectives, strategies and experiences relating back to the underlying values of the programme. One experience in the overall programme may meet several children's plans due to our teaching strategies.

For example, one of the *underlying values* of my programme is for children to understand that their actions have an effect on others and take responsibility for these consequences.

To achieve this children need to have the following *skills* or *dispositions*: empathy, communication and self-belief.

To develop or enhance these skills or dispositions, *long-term objectives* can be identified that lead children to develop or practice: cooperation, problem solving, concentration, conflict resolution, impulse control, resilience, understanding and acceptance of difference.

Plans for an individual child will reflect this objective, as too will parts of the overall programme. It might be that the overall plan has an objective that relates to this underlying value and three of the children do too, but the identified skills or dispositions will be different. The experiences offered will be across the programme but the way they are implemented with each child will depend on the objectives we are focusing on.

How I would like it to work

- A basic programme would be planned based on our knowledge of where children are and where we would like them to be going, reflecting staff interests and strengths, and involving all staff.

- The plan would be written on an (electronic) whiteboard that could be added to during the day/week by staff, children and parents, including modifications, additions and evaluations by all or any parties. This could then be printed from the whiteboard and would be our documentation.

- Staff would maintain records on children from observations, overviews, individual plans and information from meetings with parents.

- We would give more time to the quality of relationships, spending more time with children and reducing surveillance of them.

- There would be ongoing evaluation and modification of the planning process involving all the participants in the centre.

CASE STUDY

Yarrow's story

Changing the way we do things at my centre began with a centre-wide inquiry about what our real values are, rather than just the few things that have made it into policy documents over the years! This has meant long discussions at staff meetings, and soon we will open this process up to parents for them to give their comment.

From this has come our aims for the children, although ideas about how best to achieve these aims will differ from staff member to staff member. This will be due to the different ages of children they are working with and how they interpret the centre-wide document.

In my own planning work I attempt to take into account the values of critical curriculum, which tries to include all participants in the early childhood service in the curriculum process. I want to use methods that increase the involvement of other staff, the children and their parents. Partly this is pragmatic, because I have to acknowledge that some of the best things we have experienced together in the room, in my time at the centre, have been the product of a child's suggestion, and not of my skills as a teacher.

So how does this all come together?

The observations of children, when written down, are designed to reflect as much as possible the verbal discussions we have as staff about those children. These draw on two separate elements – our knowledge of that child (from all sources) and our values – and they seek to combine those two forms of knowledge into ideas that together will form a plan of action for that child.

The planning of activities in early childhood settings can never be something that happens once and for all in a planning time, once a week or once a fortnight. Any plan, however well designed, will need altering once we see how the children respond to the activities outlined. And, whether this is as simple a response as doing more of the most popular activities or removing one that holds no interest, a good plan will be able to reflect that in some way.

A planning board that allows frequent activities to be stuck on or removed with velcro tabs is a method I am experimenting with to reflect the moment by moment and day by day changes in the programme. This also helps to include, in formal processes, those activities generated by staff who do not ordinarily participate in the planning process, including any relief staff.

A daily journal outlining some of the most compelling activities in the day is one method I use to document spontaneous activities and activities that *actually happen*, rather than being *in the plan*.

I also try to have a calendar of upcoming events that parents receive as part of a newsletter. While it is impossible to predict what the children will be interested in so far in advance, this does enable excursions, or other events that require planning or coordination, to be scheduled. It also gives parents a different way to see the sorts of things that are happening in our programme and some chance to participate in them, or perhaps challenge or question them.

As someone who job shares, the evaluation of what has happened in the room usually takes place at a weekly meeting. As we are always discussing what has gone on during the week and how we could develop or improve it, we are trying to tape all of those discussions as a record of our evaluative process.

Something that I see as an important part of the children's lives is for them to learn to solve their own problems. One of the ways we do this together is to have a circle time where we bring to the group problems we have had during the day in negotiating or getting along with others. For me this is a time when the children are participating actively in the programme by finding solutions to their own or each other's dilemmas. I have found that concrete questions work best in this situation, such as, 'Has anyone else been in this situation? What did you do?'

While this is a summary of the things that happen in my room that might fit under the heading of planning, I am always on the lookout for other ways of adding to this process, which will fit in with what is already happening.

Our conclusions: continuing the journey
It is vital that we, as early childhood practitioners, validate what we are doing ourselves and argue strongly for the ways we want to plan. We are being asked to document a complex and ever-changing phenomenon. This is a difficult task. It is far easier to relate to children in complex and challenging ways than it is to write about it. Traditional, more basic, programming seems to provide an inadequate response to the challenge of this task.

New approaches to planning give the opportunity to be less of a 'top–down' approach and instead can acknowledge that in early childhood, we *all* (staff, children and families) have the opportunity to learn from each other.

With traditional planning, if a child suggests an activity they would like to do, the response tends to be more about whether it 'fits in with the weekly plan', than whether it is a valid suggestion or not. We believe that in this situation our question to ourselves should be, 'Why can't we do this now?' Sometimes there may be a good reason for why not, but more often we should do the work of asking, 'What might this child be wanting to learn, or be able to learn, through this activity?' With an even wider focus, we might want to ask, 'How can we make this request a vital part of the life of our whole community?'

Similarly, we often encounter parents with ideas very different from our own. Much of what they want for their children conflicts with the values we have as teachers or as an organization. In any meaningful planning system we will be actively seeking ways to acknowledge those parents' desires for their child, but in ways that harmonize with our existing programme.

We have found that many people in early childhood education are frustrated by current models of planning and are searching for ways to use the little time they have to plan in more productive and meaningful ways. Our small group has provided productive support for moving away from traditional planning, with our discussions focusing on the dynamics of good early childhood planning. These discussions have given us the opportunity to think critically about and to reflect together on how to make our early childhood programmes more exciting, culturally relevant and reflective of the real lives of young children. The effort of finding the time has been very worthwhile. Ongoing meetings also seem a far more effective way of changing practice, than simply attending one-off inservice sessions.

This process has reinforced that there is no one definitive way of programming. If our programme is dependent on our philosophy and the values of the community in which we work, then we need to find the best way to reflect this. Planning is a tool that should enable us to do our job well and it therefore needs to be a useful tool.

Most importantly, a planning system that works is a revitalizing force, a way of engaging with the children in a different way and a way of exploring new directions in our teaching. It is a way of asking ourselves difficult questions and setting ourselves new challenges.

Reflecting on where you are now: the role of early childhood education in society

Which approach is the best one is a value decision that the individual educator must make . . . One cannot choose not to choose, because to accept the status quo is also to make a choice.

(Sleeter and Grant 1999: 224)

Governments, as well as international institutions, must be held accountable for their leadership in putting the rights and well-being of children above all other concerns. And those that fail to do so must also be held accountable.

(Bellamy 2001: 4)

Having clarified 'where you are' and 'where you could go' in relation to your positions on the role of early childhood education in society, the third step is to reflect critically on these ideas and their implications for your work for equity. It is clear that conforming, reforming and transforming positions on the role of early childhood education have equity implications.

Against this background you are now invited to reflect critically on your position on the role of early childhood education in society you share:

- Are there any particular thinkers whose core ideas about the role of early childhood education in society you share?
- With which thinkers did you share fewest core ideas about the possible roles for early childhood education in society?
- To what extent is your current philosophy on the role of early childhood education linked with a conforming, reforming or transforming position?
- Whose interests does your position benefit?

Reflection sheet 10.1 links these questions with the ones with which we began this chapter to help you to reflect critically on your position on the role of early childhood services in society.

Reflection sheet 10.1 Critically reflecting on the role of the early childhood services in society

Reflection questions	My initial ideas	Thinkers whose ideas I share
What do I want for children now and in the future?		
What should be the role of early childhood services in society?		
Is my position conforming, reforming or transforming?		
Equity implications – whose interests does my position benefit?		

Some simple starting points to building a philosophy position statement

Review the ideas in the chapters in Part 2 and then attempt one or more of the following tasks to help you to 'get started' on developing your philosophy positions:

- *Create a 'Questions' and 'I believe' board.* You can do this alone or with colleagues. Generate a set of questions that you would like addressed in your individual, centre or staff group's philosophy position statement. People can then be invited to make an 'I believe' statement in response to the question. These can then be used to write a summary for discussion.

- *Write a story of a time you taught well.* Sit for five to ten minutes and write a short story of a time when you taught well. Reflect on that story and what it is in the story that makes you think it was good teaching. What does this say about what you believe good teaching with young children looks like? How should you be as a teacher and what does learning look like with young children?

- *Generate a metaphor.* Try to find a metaphor that captures how you and/or your team see your work with young children. Then play with and extend the metaphor through words, poems, images and sounds to build a 'picture' of what your philosophy is.

- *Favourite sayings.* Make a list of your favourite sayings on what early childhood education can accomplish. What do they tell you about your philosophy of teaching and what it says about children as learners and you as an educator?

- *Read the statements in Ideas gallery 10.1 about the role of early childhood education in society.* Once you have read the statements reflect on them using the following questions: what position on the role of early childhood education in society is implied in each statement? What is similar and what is different between these position statements and the key ideas within your own position statement? Which theorists' ideas on the role of early childhood education in society would each statement most closely link with?

Ideas gallery 10.1 The role of early childhood education in society

From Germany:

'However the emergent role profile [of early childhood educators] represents an extension of traditional educational perspectives. It is linked to a wider vision of early childhood centres as forums for community networking and as institutions of social, educational and cultural significance.' (Oberheumer and Coleberg-Schrader 1999: 255)

From an international non-profit organization, OSI, based in New York:

'The Open Society Institute (OSI) funds the Step by Step Program, with the belief that educating the youngest members of society in a way that encourages individualism, choice, initiative, and appreciation of differences can lead to a new generation of democratic citizens' (The programme operates in 26 countries across Europe, the Caribbean and South Africa.) (Ford and Coughlin 1999: 32)

From Brazil:

'Critical pedagogical approaches can help students to construct an engaging knowledge based on their background experiences as a self-empowerment

> tool . . . This means building schools as sites for historical, critical, and transformative action . . . In this process, critical educators emphasize how social identities are constructed within unequal relations of power within the schools.' (Rossato 2001: 373)
>
> *From the USA:*
>
> 'schools paradoxically teach Amercians to believe in democratic participation, but also in allegiance to a culture and social structure defined primarily by Anglo-Saxon men of at least moderate wealth . . . schools have historically functioned to suppress cultural diversity, often marginalizing, disrespecting, rendering invisible, or aiming to "civilize" particular groups of students.' (Sleeter and Grant 1999: 116)

At this point you may want to review your initial beliefs and values about early childhood education and its place, purpose and practices.

Reflecting on where you are now: your curriculum goals

> The curriculum is a life course where education is understood as the construction and reconstruction of experience.
>
> (Beattie 1997: 9)

> The future of our children lies in leaders and the choices that leaders make.
> (Graca Machel and Nelson Mandela, Global Movement for Children)

You have met different views on how curriculum goals should be formed for the early childhood curriculum and different perspectives on what curriculum goals should look like in early childhood education. Against the background of these ideas you are invited to reflect critically on your views on the nature and content of curriculum goals for young children.

Reflection points

- What have you learnt about curriculum goals and equity in early childhood settings?
- Where will your curriculum goals come from?
- How have you attended to social diversity and equity in establishing your goals in relation to gender, 'race', ethnicity, languages, class and ability?

Reflection sheet 10.2 links these questions with the ones that we began this chapter with to help you to reflect critically on your curriculum goals.

Reflection sheet 10.2 Critically reflecting on curriculum goals in early childhood services

Reflection questions	My initial ideas	Thinkers whose ideas I share
Where will my curriculum goals come from?		

What will be the core curriculum goals that I will use to plan my curriculum?

Is my position conforming, reforming or transforming?

Equity implications – whose interests does my position benefit?

Ideas clarification exercise 10.1 Some simple starts to building meaningful curriculum goals

- *Brainstorming and mapping goals.* Make a list of the words and ideas that capture the core things that you believe children should learn in an early childhood programme. Once you have your list look for the connections between them and try to generate some broad statements about your core curriculum goals.
- *Review the curriculum goal statements* in Ideas gallery 10.2. Which goals most closely reflect those that you believe to be core to work with young children?

Ideas gallery 10.2 Curriculum goals for young children

From the USA, 1912, feminist educator Charlotte Perkins Gilman:

'Judgement [was] the crucial [ingredients] of citizenship in fostering respect for others, in developing critical thinking skills, and in guarding against "the habit of acting without understandings, and also of understanding without acting".' (in De Simone 1995: 2)

From an article on Japanese early education:

'And to be a decent human being, one must develop one's *kokoro* (heart, center of physical, mental, social, and emotional being). *Kokoro* is an interesting concept because it is at once an individual self-concept (developing personal capacities) and a social self-concept (development empathy, the capacity to relate to others).' (Sato 1993: 122)

From a German researcher:

'Every child should know that he can make his home, his town, his country a better place for his being in it.' (Elschenbroich 1999: 262)

From the European Commission Network on Childcare:

'Target 14: All services should positively assert the value of diversity and make provision for both children and adults which acknowledges and supports diversity of language, ethnicity, religion, gender and disability, and challenging stereotypes.' (Vandenbroeck 1999: 244)

Reflection point

Are there any changes you would like to make to your initial goal statements in the introduction to Part 2?

Reflection sheet 10.3 Changes to my initial goal statements

Reflection questions	My initial ideas	My core position is	Changes
What do you believe the role of early education in society should be?			
How do you see the child as a learner?			
What are your equity and social justice goals?			
What are your hopes and dreams for young children?			
What would you emphasize in your curriculum goals?			

Reflecting on where you are now: approaches to curriculum planning

The tradition of apprenticeship characterizes the curriculum in Pistoria's municipal preschools, with an emphasis, for example on needlework and sewing in one preschool and carpentry in another. These diverse emphases were not selected because of children's initiatives, rather, they represent areas of expertise and passionate pursuit among some of the adults in the school and neighbourhood settings. The explicit goal, in this case, is to create opportunities for children to work with and learn from the adults as a means of connecting them to each other and to the larger community.

(New 1999: 4)

Reflection points

• Are you most comfortable with a technical, practical or critical approach to curriculum?

• Talk with an experienced early childhood educator about his or her approach to curriculum planning. What elements of this approach are technical? Is there any evidence of practical or critical approaches to planning?

Reflection sheet 10.4 links these questions with the ones with which we began this chapter to help you to reflect critically on your position on the role of early childhood services in society.

Reflection sheet 10.4 Critically reflecting on the role of the early childhood services in society

Reflection questions	My initial ideas	Thinkers whose ideas I share
How should I structure children's learning?		
Where should curriculum content come from?		
Is my position conforming, reforming or transforming?		
Equity implications – whose interests does my position benefit?		

Ideas clarification exercise 10.2 Some simple starting points to building an approach to curriculum planning

Review the ideas in the chapters in Part II and then attempt one or more of the following tasks to help you to 'get started' on developing your approach to curriculum planning.

- *Review the planning formats in the Ideas gallery at the end of this chapter.* Try to classify them into technical, practical and critical approaches to planning format. Which planning format do you think you would be most comfortable using and why? Which format sits most comfortably with your philosophy positions on the child as a learner and on the role of early childhood education in society?
- *Generate some curriculum metaphors.* Try to find some metaphors that capture approaches to curriculum planning that you have seen. Add these metaphors to reflection sheet 10.5. What are the pros and cons you see in each of these approaches to planning?

Reflection sheet 10.5 Metaphors for curriculum

Metaphors for curriculum planning	Pros	Cons
The Egg Carton curriculum which emphasizes the gimmicky art and craft (Stonehouse 1988).		
The Acceleration curriculum which emphasizes hurrying the child to the next skill level (Stonehouse 1988).		
The Fill in the Blanks curriculum which emphasizes listing activities for the sake of filling in the daily boxes of what to do when (Stonehouse 1988).		
The Calendar curriculum (Spodek 2002).		

Ideas clarification exercise 10.3

1   *Review the case studies that opened this chapter.* How did the values and philosophy of each of the teachers affect their approach to curriculum planning? What do you see as the pros and cons of the different approaches to curriculum planning taken by Denise and Yarrrow?

2   *Review the statements below in Ideas gallery 10.3* about how and what young children should be learning. Which approaches to pedagogy most closely reflect your own? What does this suggest about which approach to curriculum planning you feel most comfortable with?

Ideas gallery 10.3 How and what should young children be learning?

From a USA teacher and author:

'I try to stand aside and allow [the children] to speak for themselves. It is not easy to wait and listen.' (Paley 1986: xv)

From the Swedish Childcare Commission:

'[Dialogue pedagogy] starts from the idea that there should be a continuous dialogue between the child and the adults, on both an inner and outer level, which implies a reciprocal giving and taking of emotions, experiences and knowledge.' (SOU 1972 in Dahlberg *et al.* 1999: 124)

From a Botswanian parent:

'I want my child to be taught by a someone with a good heart towards me and my child.' (le Roux 2002: 69)

From a Kenyan publication on early childhood development:

'Early childhood is seen as a time of freedom and a time when the self-confidence of adulthood is built. The Samburu believe that during the early years the brain develops and the children are therefore responsive to environmental influences. From birth to about six years, the children have little to do except play, listen, imitate, learn and build their language skills.' (Lanyasunya and Lesolayia 2001: 10)

From an Indigenous Australian:

'Our Aboriginal way has taught us to be still and wait. We do not hurry things up. We let them follow their natural course – like the season. We don't mind waiting because we want things to be done with care.' (Fleer and Williams-Kennedy 2001a)

From Maria Montessori, Italian educational theorist:

'My vision of the future is no longer people taking exams and proceeding then on that certification . . . but of individuals passing from one stage of independence to a higher [one] by means of their own activity through their own effort of will, which constitutes the inner evolution of the individual.' (Montessori, 1973)

Case studies on observation and assessment

Read the following case study written by early childhood educator Kylie Smith. Once you have read her case study reflect on it using the following questions:

- What position on child study and children's voices in the curriculum would Kylie most closely ally herself with?
- What is similar and what is different between her approach to child study, and children's voices in the early childhood curriculum and your own?
- Which theorists' ideas on child study and children's voices in the early childhood curriculum do you think that Kylie would be most comfortable working with?

CASE STUDY

Rethinking knowing and observing children by Kylie Smith

In 1999 I began an action research project with children, parents and teachers in an inner urban long day care service to look at how, who and why we observe in the early childhood setting. One of the moments that started us questioning how we viewed the child occurred in February 1999 in the Spider Room (3–5-year-olds' room). We were audio and videoing children at play while Gemma, a teacher in the room, and I were taking written observations.

The Book Corner
Isabel, Malcolm and Bridie were in the book corner sitting on the cushions looking at a photo album. They had been in the area for about 10 minutes quietly looking at the pictures and talking among themselves. Donald entered the area and walked in front of them and then lay down on the cushions behind them.

Donald: Excuse me I need room. [Stretches out on the cushions behind]
Bridie: Ooowww!
Isabel: All right guys! Move, move, move, move!
 [Isabel stretches her arms out and pushes the children back. Her right hand connects with Bridie's ear]
Isabel: Oh Aaww now cos this is how people get hurt!
Donald: Well I'm swimming.
Bridie: Donald . . . hurt . . . my . . . ear.
 [Isabel reaches over to Donald and holds onto his arm and explains]
Isabel: Ow . . . that hurt.
 [Donald pushes Isabel away. Isabel reaches over and grabs Donald by the arm and bites him on the hand]
Malcolm: I'll get him!
 [As he says this he has his finger pointing to Donald. Malcolm stops looks at the camera and then looks away and pokes Donald in the leg with his finger]

Isabel: Malcolm get him!
          [Malcolm continues to poke Donald in the leg and Bridie starts tapping him on the leg with her hand]
          [Onya, who is working with a group of children on the other side of the room, calls out]
Onya: No Bel how about you just turn around and look at the photo album.
Donald: Errr Errr Errr.
          [Onya enters the book corner]
Onya: And Malcolm this really doesn't have much to do with you.
          [Onya takes Donald by the hand and helps him to stand up and move off the cushions]
Onya: Let's go and find a book to look at Donald. You haven't got a book on the cushions. Let's choose a book.

All four children look at each other and Onya, but no one says anything about the poking, tapping or the bite. Isabel remains on the cushions looking at the photo album and the other children sit with Onya and listen to her read a story away from the cushion area just on the edge of the book corner.

At the time of the observation Gemma and I did not see Isabel bite Donald. It was not until I had reviewed the video footage and I saw what had happened. I felt sick about the bite and how in my observation I had not seen what had happened for Donald. I went to speak with Donald about what had happened to him but he didn't want to talk about it, telling me that it was lunchtime and that he had washed his hands and was going to the table for lunch. Gemma, Onya and I met to look at that video and reflect on how using traditional observational approaches becomes problematic. Currently the observer is constructed as a detached, rational and objective person and the child is understood as a fixed and unitary individual who is knowable through a predetermined set of expectations and norms (Cannella 1997; Dahlberg *et al.* 1999). These traditional constructions of observation and the observer assume there is one 'true' and objective way of seeing and assessing the child. The observer is limited by the views he or she may use to authorize her understanding of the child, which means other possible views are silenced.

Donald had been at the centre full time from the age of 3 months and was now 3 years 6 months. I thought that I 'knew' Donald through my observations and the relationship that I had developed with him and his family right from when he was in the babies' room. I had learnt through undergraduate and postgraduate courses, accreditation documents, curriculum and policy documents, and early childhood textbooks that observational theory assisted the early childhood professional to obtain knowledge about who a child is, which was essential for a quality early childhood education. I had used my observations as a base for the development of the Spider Room programme. But what Meg, Onya and I began to question was how developmental observation reinforces, normalizes and categorizes children in a unitary way. Foucault believed concepts such as observation could be substantiated as 'true' through continual reinforcement and positioning of people in appropriate ways. From this perspective, developmental observation acts as a form of disciplinary power. The child is placed under surveillance, is regulated and normalized using techniques of measurement, classification, categorization and assessment. This raises important questions about the effects for children, parents and early childhood professionals of how traditional developmental observation forms a discourse, which limits and potentializes the ways each child is understood. Some of these questions include:

- How do the universal categories of traditional observation silence the child?
- Do we know what the different discourses in operation are in our early childhood classrooms?
- Why did Donald avoid further conversations around what happened for him in the book corner?
- How are children included or excluded in play and why?
- What do children have to do or give up to be part of the social discourse?
- How do we create a community where children can have a voice that is not constituted within a narrow frame, which operates to privilege, validate and/or marginalize particular groups?

Tell me what you like about fighting games?
As we work to reconceptualize the knowledge generated through observation in our early childhood curriculum we are revealing the multiplicity of children's, parents' and early childhood professionals' ideas and understandings about the child and themselves which have been silenced and marginalized by our traditional approaches to observation. Recognizing the observer and the observation as subjective also entangles the early childhood professional in reflections about who he or she is and how his or her gender, culture, class, race, sexuality and lived experiences intersect to frame his or her view of the child. Recognizing the subjective qualities of observation makes any singular, final truth about the child problematic.

However, in the uncertain spaces created there are new possibilities for observations based on multiple views to be recognized as valid and important, and new relationships between parents, children and professionals to be constructed. Reconceptualizing the relationships between parents, children and professionals also involves recognizing and engaging with the complex historical and political meanings of culture, race, class, gender and sexuality within the social context. We have tried to do this by challenging the current discourses in early childhood based on developmental psychology and use postmodern theory to open up multiple views of what it is to be a teacher, a parent and a child. We have begun to do this by reflecting as early childhood professionals on who we are and disclosing to parents, children and colleagues that our understandings of ourselves – our culture, class, race, gender and sexuality – influence what we say and how we practise.

When we use a discourse where parents' and children's history, culture and race arc important and the 'good teacher' isn't positioned as knowing everything, then knowledge/power relations may shift to open up space for different dialogue between parents, children and teachers. This space began to emerge in the research. Twelve months after The Book Corner observation, Gemma, Onya and I had been working with the children in Spider Room and with parents, asking how children can have a voice in the programme. One of the ways that we have begun to do this is by asking the children to talk about their ideas and understandings. In doing this we have listened and documented their conversations so that they can share their knowledge with parents, other children and professionals in the centre, rather than teaching them what we see as appropriate understandings and actions. An example of this was when I spoke to Donald in February 2000. I had been frustrated with some of the fighting games that had been happening in Spider Room, so I asked Donald to tell me what he liked about fighting games.

Kylie: We were talking about fighting games and you were telling me about how you see fighting games at the movies.
Donald: At the cinema.
Kylie: At the cinema, that's right.
Donald: I went with my cousin at the cinema and then I went to my cousin's house and then he had a c.d.
Kylie: Can you tell me are there fighting games at the centre?
Donald: [shakes his head no]
Kylie: No! There are no fighting games at the centre? So you never fight here?
Donald: [shakes his head no]
Kylie: What about the other children here, do they play fighting games?
Donald: [shakes his head yes]
Kylie: They do?
Donald: My cousins play fighting.
Kylie: Do they? What do they do when they play fighting?
Donald: They play the punching game. The punching fighting.
Kylie: They play the punching fighting do they?
Donald: [shakes his head yes]
Kylie: And what about here at the centre? Do the other children play fighting games?
Donald: [shakes his head yes]
Kylie: What sort of games do they play?
Donald: They play hid and seek games.
Kylie: Yep.
Donald: Hid and seek games fighting.
Kylie: OK, so what do you do? Do you play hid and seek and then what do you do?
Donald: Fight.
Kylie: And then you fight?
Donald: [shakes his head yes]
Kylie: And what do you do . . . what sort of games do you play? What sort of um who do you become when you become the fighting person?
Donald: Malcolm.

Kylie: You become Malcolm?
Donald: [shakes his head yes]
Kylie: Does Malcolm do fighting?
Donald: [shakes his head yes]
Kylie: He does. Who else does fighting?
Donald: Isabel.
Kylie: Isabel does fighting?
Donald: [shakes his head yes]

In talking about his understandings and desires in fighting games Donald was able to begin to reflect and talk about issues of fighting and raise his understandings of Isabel and Malcolm in fighting and exclusion.

To move from a traditional approach of observation to a postmodern approach requires a theoretical shift in how the observer is understood. In the process of reflecting on my relationship with Donald I see how much has changed in how I see Donald and how I see myself as an observer. I acknowledge that I am selective, partial and contradictory, and that I construct what I see from within the social, political and historical context in which I am seen. Questions that I am currently reflecting on include:

- How often have I assessed children through my observations in unfair and unjust ways, which has further marginalized them within the social discourses in operation in the early childhood classroom?

- In who's best interest is it to observe from a traditional perspective?

- How might technology like video and audiotaping support my ability to go back and revisit what I have observed?

- How might technology like video and audiotaping support children and parents to have a voice in observation?

Ideas clarification exercise 10.4 Reflecting on where you are now: observation and assessment

At this point, review your initial ideas about child study and assessment in the early childhood curriculum and then use the following exercises to explore your own approaches to child study and assessment:

- What do you see now as the main reasons for knowing and observing children in early childhood settings?
- What will be the main intent behind your assessment of children in the curriculum?
- What do you now see as the key issues that you need to attend to in your study of children as an educator?
- What have you learnt about child study and assessment in the early childhood curriculum?
- How will you study the children?
- Who will benefit from your approach to assessment?

- How will you attend to social diversity and equity in relation to gender, 'race', ethnicity, languages, class and ability in your study with the child and assessment of children's learning?

Reflection sheet 10.6 Critically reflecting on my approach to child study and assessment

Reflection questions	Your ideas in summary
What place do you see observation of children having in your curriculum?	
Would this allow children's voices to be heard in the curriculum?	
What do you think are the best ways to assess children?	

Ideas clarification exercise 10.5 Some simple starting points to child study and assessment in your curriculum

1 *Review the Ideas gallery at the end of this chapter.* Use two different traditional techniques for observation to observe a group of children on a videotape. What were the pros and cons you experienced as you used them? Rewatch the videotape and use a non-traditional observation method. What was different about the information you collected?

2 *Find an observation buddy.* Link up with one other early childhood educator to observe a segment of children's play. Each person should choose to look at the children through a different theoretical lens. Compare notes at the end of this process. What was similar and what was different about the information you collected?

3 *Practise seeing group dynamics.* The following experience can be used to practise seeing gender dynamics. First read the observation and then work through the questions following it. The observation details play between several 4-year-old children in the Home Corner area of a childcare centre.

> *Just tidying*
> Two boys (James and Fred) enter the Home Corner speaking very loudly and moving all around the space where three girls (Annette, Eeling and Gretta) are setting the table for a party. The girls ignore their presence and the boys leave after a few seconds.
> Thirty seconds later, the boys re-enter. James throws material from the table on the floor and leaves, followed by Fred. Gretta goes to the adult (Trish) for help.
> Thirty seconds later the boys re-enter, approaching the table and shouting. Each knocks objects from the table one at a time. Annette

sits quietly at the table playing with her rings on her fingers while the toys are being knocked to the floor. The other girls have left the Home Corner.

Annette looks at an adult nearby and says, 'The boys just knocked it over', to which the adult asks, 'Do you feel happy about that?'. Annette replies, 'No' and is asked what she will do about it. She says, 'Do it all over'.

During this exchange, the boys left the Home Corner and the girls returned. Within seconds of the girls' return to the table the boys re-enter and shout at the girls, 'Throw it in the air'. In response all the girls leave.

James starts singing a Ninja turtle song and he is joined by Fred and Barry who start rough and tumble play on the floor in the centre of the Home Corner. Within seconds the boys have begun a hide and seek game in which they move all around the Home Corner space.

As the adult (Trish) moves into the Home Corner, the boys leave and the girls re-enter. The adult comments, 'The Home Corner is very untidy now. What will happen about that?'. Annette replies, 'We'll tidy it up . . .' and she moves off and starts tidying the Home Corner. Later, Annette is heard to comment that, 'Mummies pick things up, even children at school, make drinks, make coffee. They don't do painting, they help daddy' and, 'Daddies eat fruit and biscuits and drinks, they don't tidy at all'.

Reflecting on how your positions link with early childhood policy

Curriculum models currently receiving consistent international attention (and acclaim) each have a set of assumption models on what young children should be learning and how content should be built. Some models and how they view content are detailed in Ideas gallery 10.4.

Ideas gallery 10.4 Some sample models and content in early childhood curricula

High/Scope model:

Cognitive skill-based programme based on 58 key experiences grouped into active learning, language, experiencing and representing, classification, seriation, number, spatial relations and time.

No specific content but sits comfortably with an emphasis on numeracy and literacy. However, the emphasis in on children constructing the curriculum content (Hohmann *et al.* 1979).

Reggio Emilia:

Content is driven by the children's interests. This leads to indepth project-based work that could cover content across diverse subject areas. Curriculum content is integrated into these projects.

Anti-bias curriculum in the USA and Australia:

Content is not specified in subject areas. However, one aspect of the content-based curriculum is children learning about equity and social diversity in relation to gender, 'race', class, sexuality and disability (Derman-Sparks *et al.* 1989; Creaser and Dau 1995).

Te Whāriki, *New Zealand:*

Focus is on a holistic, emergent approach to curriculum. The content emerges from children's interests which are tracked and assessed through the key principles of empowerment, holistic development, family and community and relationships.

Leeway for flexibility in local content is seen as important in meeting the needs of culturally diverse groups, including the Maori, within New Zealand (see MoE 1996).

The four 'e's: experience, extension, expression and evaluation, USA:

A means of selecting and organizing the 3–8 curriculum based on constructivist theories of learning. Experiences with materials and people are expressed through construction, texts and the arts, extended via expressive arts and evaluated via interviews, observation and work samples. Content is built from children's interests (see van Scoy 1995).

Reflection point

What policies impact on your approach to curriculum and the curriculum content you deliever in early childhood settings?

Ideas clarification exercise 10.6

Complete one or more of the following exercises to clarify the position(s) taken on the role of early childhood education within those documents:

1 *Review a curriculum policy document* that you are familiar with. What view of early childhood education is explicit or implicit within this document?

2 *Review the Ideas galleries in this chapter.* Whose view of the role of early childhood education do you feel most comfortable with? To what extent is this view expressed in the policy documents that guide your curriculum work?

The curriculum in early childhood settings

In these final Ideas galleries, about curriculum in early childhood settings, you will find ideas gathered as follows:

- goals for children's learning;
- ideas for planning formats;

- ideas for evaluating teaching and learning;
- observation and assessment ideas.

Ideas gallery 10.5 Goals for children's learning

UK:

'children should learn about civil, political, social and human rights and how various forms of injustice, inequality and discrimination, including sexism and racism are violated . . . So, it is surely developmentally appropriate to encourage, support, and extend children's understanding and help them to develop strategies and confidence to deal with unfair situations and to realise that they can bring about change.' (Brown 1998: 89)

Australia:

'Children's services are communities of learners that exist in the interest of children's well-being and learning . . . Healthy communities are characterised by:

- commitment to a common purpose
- fostering of positive, productive, constructive relationships
- recognition of unity through diversity
- respect for the rights of each individual.' (Office of Childcare, NSW Department of Community Services, 2002: 14)

USA:

'children will need to be confronted with ideas and experiences which challenge the simplistic and violent political themes in their play. Without this challenge, they can easily remain stuck with the militaristic thinking promoted by media and toys.' (Carlsson Paige and Levin 1990: 115)

New Zealand:

'The cognitive and intellectual development of children before they enter school is critical to their future educational achievement. Literacy and numeracy are essential to progress at school and children's ability to acquire these skills is influenced by the nature of their early childhood experiences.' (ERO 1998: 4)

Nigeria:

'We need to value our children and provide opportunities for their full development in an environment that reflects and respects their individual identity, culture and heritage.' (Objisanya 2001: 129)

Denmark:

- 'to care for the child and to support its appropriate social and general abilities;
- to offer the child possibilities of experiences and activities, aiming at stimulating its imagination, creativity and linguistic development;

- to give possibilities for participation in decision-making and joining responsibility in order to develop its autonomy and abilities to participate in binding social communities;
- to promote children's understanding of cultural values and interaction with nature.' (Brostrom 2001: 152–3)

New Zealand, **Te Whāriki:**

'This curriculum is founded on the following aspirations for children: to grow up as competent and confident learners and communicators, healthy in mind, body, and spirit, secure in their sense of belonging and in the knowledge that they make a valued contribution to society.' (MoE 1996: 9)

From China:

Based on the physiological and psychological characteristics of young children, the nursery and kindergarten integrate children's care with education and make scientific arrangements for the children's daily life. The vivid and lively games are used to give children enlightening education and physical training in order to cultivate their ability of observation, imagination and expression. (China Welfare Institute 2001: 6)

Ideas gallery 10.6 Planning formats

Using an action research cycle

- What do I know currently about the children?
- What do I intend to work on with them?
- What happened as a result?
- Who benefited?
- Who was silenced or marginalized?
- Who gained?
- How many different ways are there to understand what has happened?

Planning group experiences

NAME OF EXPERIENCE:

REASON: Why this learning experience? In what ways have your child observations influenced your choice? What are possible learning opportunities for children in relation to knowledge, skills and attitudes? How might this learning experience contribute to your professional development? How might it contribute to the teacher's programme? What ethical considerations have you made?

Write a brief statement summarizing your reasons.

ORGANIZATION and PREPARATION
(time, space, people, materials):

TEACHING STRATEGIES:

What you might do to provide maximum learning opportunities for the children. What you will say to children, or do, to:

- invite participation;
- settle the children;
- maintain the children's involvement;
- logically sequence the experience;
- conclude the experience;
- move children to another experience;
- respond to the children's interests;
- extend the children's interests.

REFLECTIVE EVALUATION:

Consider the child responses which indicated the appropriateness of the planned experience:

- Any *unexpected* or *spontaneous* learning?
- How might this experience develop further?
- How could you facilitate this?
- Would you make any changes in a subsequent implementation of this experience?
- What approach to curriculum is reflected in your planning choices?

Planning for individual children – format 1

Child's name:

My teaching and learning intentions:

Reason:

Teaching strategies:

Reflective evaluation:

Planning for individual children – format 2

Activity:	**Child:**	**Date:**

Why this activity?

Things I need to remember	Materials	Intentions/goals for children's learning	Teaching strategies

Evaluation – my reflections and where to next?			Children's responses

Planning for individual children – format 3

Child:

Date:

Aim	Rationale	Learning experiences	Strategies

Evaluation	Ways to extend

Ideas gallery 10.7 Questions for evaluating teaching and learning

Children's participation and learning

- What child responses made me feel that my objective was/was not achieved?
- How might I change/develop this experience at subsequent session(s)?
- Were there any unexpected responses or spontaneous learning?
- How appropriate was this experience for this child?
- How appropriate was this experience for my objective?

Respectful interactions with babies (Based on Linke and Fleer 2002):

- How did I respond to the baby's messages?
- How did I build positive relationships with the baby through my responses?
- Did I turn-take in my interactions with the baby?
- Did I help the baby to feel she/he could have an impact on their world?
- Did I show respect for the baby's needs and feelings at all times?

Creating stress-free environments for children (Based on Lawrence 2000):

- How did I encourage laughter and singing in everyday interactions with children?
- How did I allow children to hear the sounds of nature and/or busy and happy human voices?
- How did I enable children to be involved in caring for our environment?
- How did I honour children's efforts to achieve things?
- How did I allow children some control over their learning?
- How did I allow children time for play?

Effects of gender on learning and teaching:

What information do I have about gender dynamics between the children in this instance? For example, what information do I have about how children's play choices, use of space and use of time are influenced by gender?

What are the 'gender politics' evident in my classroom? For instance:

- Who uses the area and when?
- How often is it boys only, and which boys? What roles do they take on, how do they play and use materials?
- How often is it girls only, and which girls? What roles do they take on, how do they play and use materials?
- How often is it both boys and girls? When this is the case, what roles are each playing?
- Where are the adults when these things are happening?

Ideas gallery 10.8 Observation and assessment ideas

Journalling

Journalling involves describing what happened over time in specific instances. There are samples from a journal:

Questions for your journal:

- What were my intentions?
- What happened for specific children as a result of what I did?
- Who benefited from my actions and words?
- Who seemed silenced or marginalized?
- What were the effects of what I did for equity in this instance?
- Who else should I talk to or read to make sense of this?
- What seems the best way forward given this?
- What questions am I left with?

Using a critical friend to help you in your observations:

Ask someone to be your critical friend and to watch your interactions with children in general or around specific parts of your work with children. Offer them some questions to focus their observations of your work or your joint evaluation of it afterwards.

Considering children in your observation of them (Based on Campbell and Smith 2001):

- How do I give children a voice in the observation process?
- How do I consider and document the silences of children?
- How do my biases enter into my interactions with children?

Considering social relationships (Based on DoE 2002):

- How did I develop positive social relationships between all the learners?
- How did I build a sense of community and group identity?
- How did I plan for purposeful interactions with children?

Considering the culture of learning (Based on DoE 2002):

- How did I challenge children to learn new things?
- How did I show a passion for learning?
- How did I model curiosity and persistence?
- How did I acknowledge children's individual styles and differences?
- How did I negotiate with the children?

Considering the emotional climate (Based on Lawrence 2000; DoE 2002):

- How did I ensure children felt emotionally safe at all times?
- How did I attend to children's emotions in what I did?
- How did I celebrate and acknowledge children's successes?

Using time sampling: observing gender dynamics and friendship patterns

Area/setting of observation:

Date:

Children present:

Time begun:

Time ended:

Time sampling group dynamics: friendship patterns

Time (select time interval):	Play area:	Children present (initials):	Gender balance:	Type of play (solitary, co-op, parallel, etc.):
9.00am				
9.15am				
etc.				

Using child conversations: evaluating friendship patterns in the classroom

Child's name:	Which children will you invite to your birthday party?	Who do you like to sit next to on the mat? Or at the snack table?	Who would you like to share this toy with?	Comments. Cultural and gender balance in friendship choices

Further reading and online resources

Building a philosophy statement

Articulating Your Philosophy of Teaching. CETal website containing useful practical advice and links to examples of teaching philosophies: http://www.utep.edu/cetal/portfoli/ writetps.htm

Briggs, N., Renck Jalongo, M. and Brown, L. (1997) Working with families of young children: our history and our future goals, in J. Isenberg and M. Renck Jalongo (eds) *Major Trends and Issues in Early Childhood Education: Challenges, Controversies and Insights*. New York: Teachers College Press.

Goffin, S. (1994) *Curriculum Models and Early Childhood Education: Appraising the Relationship*, chap. 8. Boston, MA: Merrill.

Planning and assessing early childhood curriculum

http://www.members.tripod.com/upkins/education.html. Within this page, you will find a very helpful list of Internet sites dedicated to educators and those aspiring to be educators. You can find sites for electronic magazines, teacher bulletin boards, the USA national and state education boards, along with a plethora of other useful sites that are especially geared toward early childhood education majors. This site leads in many directions and is an excellent resource.

Bertram, T. and Pascal, C. (2002) Assessing what matters in the early years, in J. Fisher (ed.) *The Foundations of Learning*, pp.87–102. Buckingham: Open University Press.

David, T. (2001) Curriculum in the early years, in G. Pugh (ed.) *Contemporary Issues in the Early Years*, 3rd edn. London: Paul Chapman Publishing.

Hurst, V. (1997) *Planning for Early Learning*, 2nd edn. London: Paul Chapman Publishing.

Hutchin, V. (1999) *Right From the Start: Effective Planning and Assessment in the Early Years*. London: Hodder & Stoughton.

Seefeldt, C. and Barbour, N. (1998) *Early Childhood Education: An Introduction*, 4th edn. Columbus, OH: Merrill.

Siraj-Blatchford, I. (1996) *Learning Technology, Science and Social Justice: An Integrated Approach for 3–13 Year Olds*. London: Education Now.

Siraj-Blatchford, I. (ed.) (1998) *A Curriculum Development Handbook for Early Childhood Educators*. London: Trentham Books.

Spodek, B. and Saracho, O. (1994) *Right from the Start: Teaching Children Ages Three to Eight*. Boston, MA: Allyn and Bacon.

van Scoy, I. (1995) Trading the three R's for the four E's: transforming curriculum, *Childhood Education*, 72(1): 19–23.

Early childhood pedagogies

David, T. (1999) *Teaching Young Children*. London: Paul Chapman Publishing.

Mac Naughton, G. and Williams, G. (1998) *Techniques for Teaching Young Children: Choices in Theory and Practice*. Melbourne: Addison Wesley Longman.

Malaguzzi, L. (1998) History, ideas and basic philosophy: an interview with Lella Gandini, in C.P. Edwards, L. Gandini and G. Forman (eds) *The Hundred Languages of Children: The Reggio Emilia Approach – Advanced Reflections*. Norwood: Ablex Publishing.

Scott, W. (2002) Making meaningful connections in early learning, in J. Fisher (ed.) *The Foundations of Learning*, pp.74–86. Buckingham: Open University Press.

Critical reflections on curriculum planning in early childhood settings

Fleet, A. and Patterson, C. (1998) Beyond the boxes: planning for real knowledge and live children, *Australian Journal of Early Childhood*, 23(4): 31–5.

Mac Naughton, G. (2000) *Rethinking Gender in Early Childhood Education*. Sydney: Allen & Unwin.

Page, J.M. (2000) *Reframing the Early Childhood Curriculum. Educational Imperatives for the Future*. London: RoutledgeFalmer.

Silin, J. (1995) *Sex, Death and the Education of Children: Our Passion For Ignorance in the Age of AIDS*. New York: Teachers College Press.

Contemporary early childhood curriculum policy and online documents

Issues in curriculum policy

Elschenbroich, D. (1999) A childhood free of knowledge? Reflections on German educational policy for the early years, *International Journal of Early Years Education*, 7(3): 259–65.

Moyles, J. (1996) Nationally prescribed curricula and early childhood education: The English experience and Australian comparisons – identifying the rhetoric and the reality! *Australian Journal of Early Childhood*, 21(1): 27–31.

Many governments have developed guidelines for staff working with young children that establish broad goals for the children. Some of these are called curriculum documents, others are statements of values and principles. Some of the key government documents that are available online in the English language are:

Australia

South Australia: *Foundation Areas of Learning: Learning about Aboriginal Children and their Culture: Curriculum Guidelines*, Department of Education, Training and Employment.

Victoria: *Babies, Toddlers and Two Year Olds; Preschool Quality Assessment Checklist*, Office of the Family.

Queensland: *Preschool Curriculum Guidelines*, Department of Education.

New South Wales: *Curriculum Framework for Children's Services: The Practice of Relationships. Essential Provisions for Children's Services*. New South Wales Department of Community Services, Office of Childcare (2002).

Western Australia: *Children's Services Manual, Children's Services Resource File*, Childcare Services Board; *Curriculum Framework K-Year 12*, Department of Education.

Australian Capital Territory: *Early Childhood Education: Our Shared Understandings*, Department of Education and Training and Children's Youth Services Bureau.

Northern Territory: *Assessment in the Early Years of School; An Integrated Curriculum Approach to Teaching in the Early Years; Strengthening the Early Years: Improving Outcomes*, Department of Education.

Australian government websites for accessing the most recent curriculum documents

Commonweath government: Department of Family and Community Services: http://www.facs.gov.au/childcare/

Human Services: Community Care, Victoria: http://www.dhs.vic.gov.au/commcare

National Childcare Accreditation Council (NCAC): http://www.ncac.gov.au

Qld State Government Childcare: http://www.families.qld.gov.au/childcare/

Department of Community Services NSW: http://www.community.nsw.gov.au/progpub.htm

Tasmanian Department of Education: http://www.doe.tased.edu.au/

Western Australia Department for Community Development: http://www.fcs.wa.gov.au/

New Zealand

Ministry of Education (1996) *Te Whāriki: Early Childhood Curriculum*. New Zealand: Ministry of Education: http://www.minedu.govt.nz/

United Kingdom

United Kingdom: *Investing in Our Future. Curriculum Guidance for the Foundation Stage*. London: Department for Education and Employment and the Qualifications and Curriculum Authority. Issued May 2000. Ref. QCA/00/587: http://www.qca.org.uk

PART 3

Curriculum contexts

11

Reflecting on contexts

With Patrick Hughes, Heather Lawrence, Sheralyn Campbell and Jane Page

This third and final part of the book explores different ways to think about the contexts within which you work. It examines curriculum contexts in relation to:

- parents and communities;
- being professionals.

Those two contexts have their own chapters (12 and 13) that introduce you to contrasting ways of understanding the context within one of three positions on relationships:

- conforming relationships;
- reforming relationships;
- transforming relationships.

In this introductory chapter you are invited to explore your own beliefs and ideas about how the contexts of curriculum work in early childhood should influence your work. The final chapter in this section (Chapter 14) asks you to reflect critically on your own position on building relationships and what will inform how you approach relationships in early childhood programmes. It supports you in this task by including:

- curriculum relationship case studies;
- reflection tasks on where you are now and where to go next;
- an Ideas gallery and practices on how to approach different relationships.

Working in early childhood programmes involves working with young children, their parent(s) and guardian(s), possibly their sisters and/or brothers, often their extended family and at times their family's friends. It also involves working with colleagues and within a larger professional network. Approaching these relationships in ways that create and sustain a sense of well-being for all involved is both enriching and challenging. Having a strong sense of what you want those relationships to look and feel like provides a sound basis for building constructive and positive relationships with all those people who will form part of your work life.

In what follows you are asked to reflect on what your current views are about the nature of relationships that you wish to build with:

- children, parents and local communities; and
- the profession and yourself as a professional.

Reflecting on children's contexts: parents and communities

Relationships with young children are at the heart of the early childhood curriculum. How you imagine and practise those relationships is core to all that you do as an early childhood educator. For instance, how you design and practise early childhood curriculum directly affects your behaviour and relationships with children. However, your behaviour and relationships will also be affected by what young children bring to the curriculum and how you respond to the contexts of their lives. In this introductory chapter you will be invited to reflect on what children might bring to the curriculum, and then we will move to exploring how you might attend to those contexts through how you work with children's families and their local community.

Children's relationships with each other and with adults are being formed and reformed in an ever-changing world in which children's lives are affected by the way our societies are constructed. Some of those factors that touch children's lives can strengthen them for now and for the future. Some of those factors have the potential to undermine children's well-being now and in the future.

Children's well-being can be strengthened when they are with early childhood educators who (Dockett 2000; Lawrence 2000; Linke and Fleer 2002):

- develop trusting and respectful relationships with them and their families;
- develop relationships that make children feel safe and secure;
- promote children's inner strength and sense of self-worth and value;
- recognize and honour children's diversity in gender, abilities, culture and class;
- provide nurturing environments that are warm, responsive and validating for the infant and young child;
- allow time and space and materials for children to feel relaxed and happy.

Consider the following:

Each child will be known by name and have a place that will be his or hers. Adults familiar with the development of young children will create learning environments that connect to the known worlds of the children. Young children can explore, become familiar with their own ability to make an impact on their environment, and reach beyond what they know into what is yet unknown. In this process, they sense the respect due them as members of a group of children and as a unique individual. They also develop respect for others. There are an adequate number of adults to see them, hear them, understanding both their non-verbal and verbal languages, and plan meaningful activities. Such adults believe that each child can contribute to a classroom community.

(Myers 2002: 3)

Children's well-being can be particularly diminished and undermined when stress is part of their daily lives. For some children the daily stress of their lives involves the wait for food and shelter. For other children the daily stress of their lives comes from a day packed with experiences to promote their learning, to keep them busy and to help them get 'ahead' before they can walk (Hyson 1991). For many children this produces chronic tiredness.

Other stresses that increasing numbers of children face and that may diminish and undermine their well-being include:

- facing the fear of and/or memories of war;
- experiencing violence in families;
- losing loved family members;
- long hours away from parents who are working in stressful and increasingly demanding jobs;
- living with HIV/AIDS;
- living without running water;
- experiencing the effects of unemployment and parental depression;
- living without support networks;
- sharing the care of adults, toys and space with large groups of children from infancy;
- watching fearful images on television.

Some child stresses come from the changing nature of many Westernized contemporary societies in which materialism, competition and the pursuit of personal freedom have changed how we relate to children and to each other.

How early childhood educators respond to children's daily stresses and how they form relationships with young children, their families and their local communities is core to children's health and well-being, now and in their futures. For instance, how early childhood educators build their relationships with young children and their families can give children the gift of strength to face the challenges of their current and future worlds, or take that possibility away from them. The extent to which children are connected to their families and their local communities through what happens in an early childhood setting is critical in determining which of those pathways is followed.

In policies concerning early childhood services, early childhood educators have been expected to (Hughes and Mac Naughton 2000):

- work in partnership with families to build relevant and responsive programmes;
- create links with their local communities so that their strengths, values and issues are reflected in early childhood programmes;
- be advocates for children in association with parents and with the local community.

Like any form of community, a community in an early childhood setting doesn't just happen – people must actively build it. However, building positive connections with parents in early childhood services is widely regarded as problematic in countries as diverse as Greece (Laloumi-Vidali 1996); Australia (Ebbeck and Glover 1998); the UK (Moore and Klass 1995); the USA (Rescorla 1991); Taiwan (Liu and Chien 1998); Switzerland (Unteregger-Mattenberger 1995); and Japan (Huira 1996). Staff often report that their relationships with parents are strained and meaningless (Kasting 1994; Elliott 1998). Staff struggle to know best how to communicate with parents (Wright-Sexton 1996), and are often anxious about it (Studer 1993/94) to the point where they are often reluctant to even talk to parents (Huira 1996). Staff may regard parents as an important source of information about children (Rosenthal and Young Sawyers 1996), but in many early childhood settings, staff–parent conversations are brief and infrequent and only half of them involve the exchange of meaningful and useful information (Endsley *et al.* 1993).

Researchers have suggested various reasons for these difficulties in staff–parent relationships, including inadequate staff training in staff–parent communication (Laloumi-Vidali 1997) and cultural differences between staff and parents (Gonzalez-Mena 1992; Espinosa 1995; Coleman and Churchill 1997; Ebbeck and Glover 1998). However, many of the difficulties stem from disagreements between staff and parents about the nature and purpose of early childhood education (Hyson 1991; Rescorla 1991). Parents often value early academic work more than teachers do and they often question the educational relevance of self-directed, play-based programmes (Stipik *et al.* 1994; Unteregger-Mattenberger 1995; Liu and Chien 1998). In contrast, early childhood staff claim that their expert, professional knowledge about children equips them to know what's best for children, and they believe that parents need to learn this expert knowledge in order to help their child(ren) to learn (Gelfer 1991; Stipek *et al.* 1994; Moore and Klass 1995; Laloumi-Vidali 1996).

Early childhood staff deploy their expert knowledge not as individuals but as members of one social institution – the early childhood profession – and as employees of another – the early childhood centre. Each social institution reaffirms and re-inforces the expert knowledge of each individual (trained and qualified) staff member, making it hard for a 'non-expert' like a parent to challenge staff views. Nonetheless, parents do challenge staff expertise, arguing that as parents they know more about their child(ren) than anyone else can. Thus, although staff and parents may disagree about what's best for children, each side argues its case in the same way: 'I have specialist knowledge to which you *must* defer'. Each side links knowledge with power – 'My specialist knowledge means that I can tell you what to do' – and these knowledge–power links are at the heart of much of their disagreement about the nature and purpose of early childhood education and, therefore, about the nature and purpose of parent involvement.

Disagreements between staff and parents about what's best for young children are generally expressed indirectly, rather than in direct conflict. For example, a parent who disagrees with how centre staff care for their child may not directly challenge staff. Instead he or she won't involve himself or herself in the life of the centre, leading staff to label the parent 'uninterested' or 'difficult to communicate with'. Similarly, centres rarely disagree openly with parents about how children should spend their time. Indeed, a centre may well enthusiastically invite parents to become involved in their children's care and education – but strictly on the centre's terms. The effects of these tensions on young children can be considerable and they can create disconnection for the child from their family and their local communities.

Reflecting on where you are now

In what follows you are asked to reflect on how you see relationships with parents in your work with young children.

Reflection points

What are your hopes for your relationships with parents? More specifically, in your ideal early childhood centre:

- How and why would staff and parents communicate with each other?
- What principles would guide relationships between staff and parents?
- What goals would guide staff's and parents' behaviour towards each other?
- What do you mean by 'community'?
- What do you think people in early childhood services mean by 'community'?
- Do you believe that an early childhood centre should have any particular sorts of links with its community? On what do you base your belief?
- Do your beliefs about a centre's relationships with parents link with your beliefs about a centre's relationships with its community?

Ideas clarification exercise 11.1

1   Try to complete one or more of the following exercises to clarify your current philosophy of early childhood education:
   - *Reflect on what parents might know* about young children that you don't. What knowledge might they offer you to help you in your curriculum work?
   - *What would your ideal relationship with parents look like?*
   - *Talk with four people who come from a different background* to your own about what role they believe that parents should play in young children's education. What is similar and what is different about how they think about early childhood education? To what extent is it similar to your hopes as an early childhood educator?

2   Complete the following reflection sheet (*Reflection sheet 11.1*).

Reflection sheet 11.1 allows you to summarize your thinking:

Reflection sheet 11.1 My ideas about parents in early childhood services

Reflection questions	Your ideas
Do you believe that parental involvement is important to early childhood services?	
If you do, what do you believe are the goals of parent involvement in early childhood services?	
What should the role of parents be in early childhood services?	
What do you know about whether/how parent involvement appears in current policies concerning early childhood services?	
What challenges do you currently face or think you might face in involving parents in an early childhood centre?	

Reflecting on being professional

Becoming an early childhood professional is an exciting, complicated and never-ending journey of discovery into the ways that theories, practices and people come together in the daily world of early childhood education. Building meaningful relationships with children, their families and their local communities is part of that journey. Building a sense of who you want to be as a professional in the lives of children and their communities is also part of that journey. It should not come as a surprise at this point in this book to learn that there is more than one way to think about being professional.

Words that have been used to characterize an early childhood professional include:

- early childhood educator (for example, Nimmo 2002);
- early childhood teacher (for example, Katz 1995);
- early childhood pedagogue (for example, Dahlberg *et al.* 1999);
- early childhood practitioner (for example, Carr 1998).

Broadly, all of these words describe a person who:

- has specialized knowledge that enables him or her to work with children aged between birth and 8 years of age;

- belongs to a body of people or 'profession' who share a common purpose, standards and ethics in their work.

More specifically, a profession has a distinct body of knowledge that is characterized by (Katz 1995):

- research, theory and practice;
- deep understandings that go beyond basic comprehension, commonly held beliefs, or hearsay;
- lengthy preparation and study in formal educational organizations;
- shared interests, standards and a code of ethics.

Reflecting on where you are now

In what follows, you are asked to reflect on how you see relationships with the early childhood profession and your own knowledge as a professional in order for you to think about who you want to be as a professional.

Reflection points

- What does being a professional mean to you?
- Who are the key stakeholders in your early childhood community?
- What are the key fields of specialized knowledge and policy frameworks that apply to your early childhood community?
- What are the ethical standards of your profession?

Ideas clarification exercise 11.2

1   Try to complete one or more of the following exercises to clarify your current philosophy of early childhood education:

- *Visit the website* of an early childhood association or professional group. What does this website tell you about what it means to be an early childhood professional?

- *Talk with two people who come from a different background* to your own about what they think the ideal early childhood professional should know about children, curriculum and families. What is similar and what is different about how they think about early childhood education? To what extent is it similar to your hopes as an early childhood educator?

- *Talk with three other people* who have chosen to work in early childhood education. What are their reasons for working with young children? What ideals do they have about how early childhood professionals should behave with children, families and in the wider community?

2   Complete the following reflection sheet (11.2).

Reflection sheet 11.2 My ideas about being professional in early childhood services

Reflection questions	Your ideas
What does the ideal early childhood professional never do?	
What does the ideal early childhood professional know?	
Who are the key stakeholders in my early childhood community?	
What are the ethical standards of my profession?	

12

Curriculum contexts: parents and communities

With Patrick Hughes

The models of the child and positions on curriculum that you encountered in Parts 1 and 2 of this book aren't just 'theories' divorced from day to day events in 'the real world' of an early childhood centre. Instead, they enable us to see those day to day events in general terms that connect them to other events in other centres in other places at other times. Thus, models of the child don't interact with positions on curriculum in the abstract or in a vacuum, but in specific places and at specific times – as specific early childhood educators care for specific children in a specific centre. Indeed, the models and positions only come alive in the day to day material and social circumstances of a specific centre – anywhere else, they really are just 'theories'.

A centre's specific, day to day material and social contexts can distinguish it from other centres. Its material circumstances are its physical structure and the resources it uses in its day to day work; its social contexts are its relationships with parents and with other people in its neighbourhood. This chapter introduces you to a diversity of ways to think about the roles of parents and others in early childhood education and it encourages you to reflect on your own beliefs, attitudes and values concerning parent involvement as a context for curriculum. It introduces you to ways of thinking about parents' and communities' relationships with the early childhood curriculum and how to use communication to build those relationships. The chapter examines some different ways to think about and describe a centre's relationships with parents and others under three headings:

- Conforming to the knowledge–power relationships. The centre teaches parents and others the right way to care for and educate young children.
- Reforming the knowledge–power relationships. The centre involves parents and others in caring for and educating young children – but on the centre's terms.
- Transforming the knowledge–power relationships. The centre collaborates with children, parents and others to change the relationships between them.

Definitions

- Communication: creating shared meanings and understandings.
- Community: an association – of individuals, of groups, of organizations, or of all three.
- Community involvement: the nature of the association between one element and the rest.
- Community building: activities that aim to improve the quality (and perhaps the size) of that association.

Conforming to knowledge–power links in relationships between educators and parents: parents don't know, communities volunteer

Overview

In this approach to knowledge–power relationships between educators and parents, educators are professional experts about how young children learn and, therefore, how they should be educated. In this approach, the educator is the teacher and the parent is the learner, which assumes two things about the relationship between them:

1 Educators should teach parents the appropriate ways to teach their children and to support their learning, because parents consistently seem to prefer inappropriate (generally, highly structured) education (see, for example, Rescorla 1991; Stipek *et al.* 1994; Hughes and Mac Naughton 2000, 2001). In particular, educators should be 'teaching parents how to observe and understand their child's development' (Hirschey 1999: 270). The belief is that parents will learn how to behave appropriately with their children once they know what the educator knows. For instance, Popham (1998: 70) suggested that explaining the problems of subjecting children to standardized testing can alter parents' expectations:

> If parents understand the nature of standardized achievement tests and what their historic function has been, those parents should be less likely to appraise a school's quality, or a teacher's skill, on the basis of standardized test scores.

2 Educators should teach parents about children's development so that they understand the difference between appropriate and inappropriate educational practices. For example:

> It is important for parents to understand the damage they can do to their children by forcing them to grow up too quickly. Parents are usually well intentioned when pushing children to grow up. Information about the hurried child syndrome and its side effects needs to be shared with parents to make them aware that even though they mean well, they may be hurting their children. It is the responsibility of the teachers and teacher educators to emphasize the various aspects of this problem and to share their concerns about the child from the perspectives of the teacher.
>
> (Moore and Klass 1995: 35)

This assumption of the 'right' knowledge potentially leads early childhood educators to disregard parents' knowledge of their individual children. Once parents gain the appropriate knowledge of the child – in other words, the educators' developmental knowledge – then they can relate to the child appropriately and, in doing so, conform to educators' expectations of them. This is because when eductors regard their developmental knowledge of the child as scientific, they can dismiss parents' anecdotal knowledge as non-scientific, as Hughes and Mac Naughton (2000) wrote:

> Professional knowledge of the child is 'developmental' (scientific), objective, norm-referenced and applicable to all children. In contrast ('in binary opposition'), parental knowledge of the child is anecdotal, subjective, ad hoc, individualized and applicable only to specific children. In much early childhood literature concerning parent involvement, parental knowledge is 'other' than professional knowledge in that it is inadequate, misguided or just plain wrong!
>
> (p. 243)

Some writers regard parents' knowledge as wrong because it is based on 'false expectations' (Unteregger-Mattenberger 1995: 59); others see it as educationally inappropriate because it lacks or ignores developmental knowledge of the child (see, for example, Gelfer 1991; Moore and Klass 1995). Ideas gallery 12.1 exemplifies these views.

Ideas gallery 12.1 Views on parental knowledge as a context for curriculum

From USA and UK researchers:

'Parents have gone so far as to "hot house" their children like tomatoes forced to grow out of season in an artificial environment' (Sigal 1987). In many cases, according to Sigal, children have been forced to 'perform without consideration of biological and psychological characteristics'. (Moore and Klass 1995: 31)

From UK researchers:

'Mothers with more knowledge of child development, from books, courses or training, have been observed to be more affectionate, talkative, playful and responsive, to impose fewer restrictions, to do more teaching, and to stimulate the children at more appropriate levels.' (Clarke-Stewart 1982: 94)

This approach to educator–parent relationships within the contexts of curriculum rests on the following links between knowledge and power:

- parents conform to educators' expectations;
- educators' views draw on 'conforming' models of the learner and positions on curriculum;
- educators promote traditional knowledge–power links in which they are experts and parents are non-experts.

'Conforming' views of educator–parent relationships often appear as volunteering. In many early childhood centres, parent involvement takes the form of the voluntary committee of management that run the centres, with officers elected annually at a general meeting open to all users of the centre. Voluntary work is central to much of the writing on education and community – indeed, volunteering and community building often appear synonymous.

Where have the ideas come from?

These ideas that parents need to learn how to be with their children have a long history:

- Frederich Froebel believed strongly in connecting the school with the home. A key feature of his approach to education of the young child was the mothers meeting, where educators and parents (generally mothers, clearly) discussed the child's development.
- In the late 1800s, kindergarten teachers in the USA taught the children in the morning and visited their homes in the afternoon (Decker and Decker 1992). This practice was commonplace in the USA and in Australia in the 1960s and 1970s, when kindergarten teachers were expected to spend a substantial portion of their non-contact time with children (two afternoons a week) visiting homes to educate parents.

Hepworth Berger (1995: 53) wrote of the beginnings of the 1800s parent education programmes in the USA as follows:

> Pestalozzi's and Froebel's belief that parents are integral components of education influenced the educational roles of parents. A climate for change, the possibility of the perfectability of man, and reverence for motherhood prevailed. Thus, the time was ripe for the parent education movement to begin.

Parent involvement was a required part of the Head Start early childhood programmes in the USA that began in the 1960s. Parent involvement was regarded as essential to successful developmental outcomes for young children, but as Decker and Decker (1992: 362) suggest, it was also seen to benefit parents by helping them to become 'more effective with their children and within families' and to 'learn their importance in their children's education and how to help schools maximize educational benefits'.

Similar developments occurred in the UK. In 1967, the Plowden Report 'concluded that part-time nursery education for children over 2 was good for children and parents' (Clarke-Stewart 1982: 44). In the 1980s, local authorities began to develop family centres rather than day nurseries, because there was a strong belief at the time that child and mother needed to be educated in appropriate ways to respond to each other. As day nurseries were for the child only, a new form of institution in which the parent (generally the mother) was involved was necessary. New and David (1985: 257) explained: 'Family centres are no longer expected to replace the mother for part of the day; their function is to provide an educational setting for child and mother, where they can both learn different ways of responding to people and to each other.'

In Australia, the Lady Gowrie Child Centres articulated clearly a 'conforming' approach to parent involvement (Brennan 1994). These demonstration childcare and development centres were established in each state in the 1940s to research normal child development and to teach parents living in poverty in the inner cities how to rear their children and how to live as normal (two parent) families. As Brennan explained: 'The staff pointed out to families ways in which they failed to live up to this ideal and attempted to "educate" them about the "proper" ways children should be reared' (Brennan 1994: 43).

This work influenced preschool development throughout Australia. By the 1960s, the dissemination of Piaget's work created growing interest in children's cognitive development. Preschools in low income areas were increasingly seen as places that could 'compensate for deficits' (Mellor 1990: 180) in children's home environments, and new parent training programmes taught parents how to maximize their children's intellectual development.

More recently, there has been ambivalence about the role of parent involvement in early childhood centres. Consider Singer's (1992) description of relations between early childhood educators and parents in the USA Head Start projects:

> On the one hand, the participation of parents in the Head Start Project was felt to be important for strengthening their involvement. On the other hand, developmental psychologists attached little value to the views of incompetent parents/ mothers, who were judged to be in need of guidance from the 'expert staff'.
>
> (Singer 1992: 115)

Early childhood educators aren't alone in dismissing parents' knowledge as inadequate. Consider the following introduction to a booklet produced for parents by the South Australia state government and based on the South Australia early childhood curriculum. The booklet advises parents how to use everyday events to support their children's learning, thus assuming that parents don't know about this already:

> This booklet looks at children's learning and ways parents, family and other adults in their lives help children to learn . . . It is based on Foundation Areas of Learning, a curriculum framework used by early childhood educators to plan for children's learning and development. It suggests just a few of the ways that children's learning can be supported through everyday interactions with families and others.
>
> (DETE 1998: 3)

Parents in the UK and the USA also face pressure to use their daily interactions with their children to educate them appropriately. Writing of the beginnings of these pressures in the 1980s, Scarr and Dunn (1982: 161) concluded that they rested on 'two misleading assumptions – that "instructing" babies early on will give them some advantage, and that professionals know how parents should educate their children. This first is not only misleading but puts unwarranted pressure on parents'.

Implications for early childhood practices

Parents' perceived lack of appropriate knowledge of the child has two clear implications for early childhood educators – the experts in child development. First, educators' communications with parents should emphasize their specialist knowledge, expertise and qualifications, to prevent parents from questioning their expertise. Second, educators need to communicate clearly what they know to parents so that parents can know more about their child and, therefore, interact with them appropriately. Typically, communication with parents will take the form of imparting to them information about, for example, child development in general and/or what is happening in a centre. The techniques and tools for imparting this information include newsletters, bulletin boards, information evenings and parent–staff meetings. More recently, early childhood educators have also used new communications technologies such as email and the Internet to inform parents about children's learning and development (see, for example, Hughes and Mac Naughton 1999; Yonetani *et al.* 2001).

Ideas gallery 12.2 gives examples of this 'conforming' approach to relationships between educators, parents and parental knowledge.

Ideas gallery 12.2 Relationships between the knowledge of educators and parents

From a USA textbook:

'Many parents also benefit from opportunities to learn more about children in a general way, and for this reason, parenting meetings are an additional helpful service offered by many preschools . . . thereby providing splendid opportunities to develop an informed population of parents.' (Hendrick 1990: 391)

From a US textbook:

'It is helpful to offer training sessions for parents where techniques and suggestions for working positively with the child are discussed . . . Methods of teaching that provide for observation, demonstration, and role playing prove useful. Parents, like children, learn best through active participation.' (Hepworth Berger 1995: 285)

From a US textbook:

'Maximum returns in the area of parent–staff communication require the use of various information channels: conferences, home visits, and written communication.' (Decker and Decker 1992: 365)

From a UK textbook:

'Inviting new parents into the nursery or reception class to participate in children's activities, is an excellent way of encouraging parents to see the value in play.' (Moyles 1989: 162)

Equity reflections

When early childhood educators subordinate parents' knowledge to their own, they create hierarchical relationships with parents that make it hard to communicate with them equitably, especially with parents whose ways of behaving with children they regard as inappropriate. 'Conforming' approaches to educator–parent relationships generally mean educators teaching parents who are working class and from culturally diverse backgrounds to conform to white, middle class norms of child rearing. This has two adverse consequences. First, it can often produce conflicts between diverse cultures' traditional knowledge of the child and Western, 'expert' knowledge (Liou and Price 2001).

Second, the close links between educators' 'expert' knowledge and middle class values and behaviours is likely to privilege middle class parents over others. For example, Singer (1992) shows that early childhood educators value (developmental) knowledge of the child that directly expresses middle class values about parenting: 'According to Schachter (1979), mothers with a higher level of education spontaneously follow the theories of Dewey and Piaget. They behave like teachers in a child-centred nursery school' (Singer 1992: 120). No surprise, then, that working class parents from minority ethnic groups have been the consistent targets of parent education programmes, which have sought to teach them 'the facts' about child development and 'appropriate' ways to behave with children. For example, Singer (1992) tracks how the Head Start programmes in the USA sought to train working class mothers to behave 'appropriately' with their children. Much of this training derives from research linking child outcomes with the parenting styles in their early years. It just so happens that much of this research emphasized the value of middle class parenting styles for child outcomes. Cannella summarizes the late 1970s research that came to this conclusion:

> Ghetto individuals were considered to be lacking in operative intelligence because of the lack of appropriate early experience. For example, ghetto black children were considered to have stunted mental growth because their parents transmitted an ideology of despair to them.
>
> (Cannella 1997: 76)

Against this background of class-biased research, it is not surprising that some parents resist becoming 'involved' in their child's education and/or resist white, middle class ways of behaving with their children. However, such parents risk being regarded as socially maladjusted:

> Perseverance, patience, and true interest in the parent are the most important factors involved in overcoming parent reticence . . . In every situation parents may refuse to be involved. Some may have serious social adjustment problems and need professional help in that area.
>
> (Hepworth Berger 1995: 283)

However, Walkderine and Lucey (1989) show how working class mothers in the

UK resisted middle class ways of behaving with their children, not because they were socially maladjusted, but because they chose to value their own ways of behaving with children. Further, Ramsey (1987) argued that parents who live in poor housing on low incomes may actively choose to be highly directive with their children to protect them from social and physical harm in their local communities. (However, recent research in the US found that age, not class, was a key influence on educators' and parents' beliefs about developmentally appropriate education. See Ernest 2001.)

A 'conforming' approach to relationships with parents and communities clearly benefits educators and middle class parents. Educators' belief that they know the scientifically based truth about children removes any doubts and uncertainties they may feel in unfamiliar situations and removes any need to consult with parents about their programmes. This potentially creates absolute professional autonomy, because parents lack the scientific knowledge required to hold educators to account for their practices and educators can use their status as 'professionals' to defend their autonomy (Foot *et al.* 2002: 7).

Creating inaction through knowing too much, yet knowing too little

The promise of the extensive developmental research on children was that scientific child rearing – based on collecting and analysing scientific data – can 'make' people (Singer 1992: 6). However, despite the existence of large amounts of such scientific (developmental) research data, many educators and parents are more uncertain than ever about how to act with children. Denick's (1989, in Lee 2001) comments on this issue remain as pertinent today as they were over ten years ago:

> Modern parents know a lot about children and child development as compared with previous generations. Still, many of them simply feel at a loss at what to do. They listen eagerly to the advice of experts, but soon discover they often change their minds and prove themselves to be unreliable . . . Nobody can give hard and fast advice, the know-how changes just as quickly as the development itself. Uncertainty is chronic.

So, is it the case that the more we know about children, the less we know how to be with them? If it is, then how do we negotiate through the contradictory views and visions of the child that keep emerging as our knowledge base grows? Some writers say that the answer is to improve our capacity to find the right way to understand the child – in other words, we need more sophisticated research techniques. To a large extent, Frede (1995) takes this the position. She recognizes how difficult it is to decide which curriculum produces the best developmental outcomes for young children:

> Comparing the curricula on the same outcome measures may disguise differences in their full effects on children. Another source of difficulty is that children's development is quite complicated: it is influenced by many environmental factors, and children shape their environments through their own actions . . . The complexity of children's development and the multiple

factors that influence it make simple cause and effect relationships difficult to establish. Indeed, children with certain characteristics and family background may benefit more from one type of program while others may benefit more from another.

(Frede 1995: 116)

Frede (1995: 128) calls for 'more finely tuned studies' into how curriculum can meet individual children's needs, and more studies to 'replicate' and 'extend' previous findings on early education's long-term outcomes to convince policy makers to fund particular types of programmes. If researchers continue to produce diverse answers to the question of how we can maximize young children's life possibilities, how can we decide which answers to privilege? Not from more developmental research, clearly, since this for many is the cause of their dilemma. Instead, the answers could come from moral and philosophical discussions about who benefits from our work with young children and how we can build a better world with them.

Dominance of ethnocentric knowledge

Most of the extensive research and scholarly thinking about the child that is available in the English language comes from 'Western' countries – especially the USA, Australia, the UK, Canada and New Zealand. These English language textbooks about early childhood education present knowledge and understandings about the child that originate from a very limited range of cultures and concerns.

Helping the state to abdicate its responsibilities to young children

The state is a major beneficiary of a 'conforming' approach to educator–parent relationships based on hierarchical knowledge–power relationships between them. If parents accept that their 'ignorance' about developmentally appropriate practice excludes them from their children's education, they are encouraged to become 'involved' in financing and running their child's centre on a voluntary basis. This eases the pressure on the state to provide early childhood services that are appropriately funded and managed. Using the rhetoric of 'community control of services', the state can then abdicate its responsibilities to young children.

Equating 'involvement' and 'voluntary work' not only undermines the state's responsibility to young children, it also creates class-based divisions between parents associated with their ability to do voluntary work. Poor, working class people may have less control over their hours of work, may work 'unsocial' hours and may end their working day more tired physically than wealthier professionals who are, therefore, more able to attend committee meetings, fund raising events, and so on. Hughes and Mac Naughton (2000: 256) question whether equitable involvement is possible in such circumstances:

How can staff wishing to promote parent involvement . . . accommodate such diverse working patterns? Nor can we assume that all parents who can become involved will be equally comfortable with early childhood educators' specialist, technical language. How can staff wishing to promote parent involvement eschew forms of communication with parents that are condescending and patronizing in favour of those that are inclusive and respectful? Equitable staff–parent relationships rest on how staff answer these questions.

Voluntary committees manage finances, staff and resources, which requires skills and experiences that are more accessible to professionals than to working class people. Fell cites Weston to highlight these issues:

> [A] management structure which is dependent on committees elected from the cohort of current parents . . . 'creates a lack of continuity, isolation from other services, varying levels of expertise and commitment and difficulty for both staff and parents in dealing with staff matters (Weston, 1994, p.8).
>
> (Fell 1999: 6–7)

Indeed, Fell (1999: 6) is highly critical of the equation between voluntary work and community:

> There is no long-term future for volunteer committees managing preschools. Contrary to the belief that voluntary service empowers communities (Osborne and Gaebler, 1992, pp. 66–70), it exhausts them and diverts them from focusing on the educational needs of their children rather than on the financial needs of the service. This form of funding and financial management is one of system maintenance at best.

Press (1999: 23) has argued that successive Australian governments have fostered a shift from early childhood services based on volunteers to purely commercial services, which changes parents' role in the centres from citizen to consumer: 'While the notion of citizenship confers the notion of rights and obligations, the obligation of a consumer extends little beyond paying for a product'. However, while someone whose child attends a particular centre may be an active citizen in another part of their life, they may prefer to just 'consume' the centre's service, rather than participate in running it. We can't be actively involved as citizens in every institution in our lives. Further, such democratic involvement can't just ignore or dismiss the roles and responsibilities of government, as Smith (1997: 8) argues:

> Typically, the resources of even well-funded coalitions and partnerships are inadequate to address the enormity of need in disadvantaged areas . . . Voluntarism and civic participation through community-based programs such as coalitions and partnerships hinge upon government action. Comprehensive community initiatives have proliferated through government support and financing, and more indirectly, by fostering a positive climate for voluntary activity at the local level through leadership and responsiveness to citizen concerns.

Reforming the knowledge–power links in relationships between educators and parents: parents as collaborators in communities of learners

Overview

In a 'reforming' approach to knowledge–power relationships between educators and parents, educators collaborate with individual parents to produce the 'self-governing child' (Chapter 2). Parents' particular knowledge of their child(ren) can be a resource for educators, because it can complement their own, more general knowledge (Gelfer 1991; Kelly 1995). Ideas gallery 12.3 presents examples of this view.

Ideas gallery 12.3 Seeing parents as collaborators

'Parent–teacher communications can . . . assist teachers by providing information helpful in addressing students' individual needs, interests, capabilities, backgrounds and learning styles.' (Gelfer 1991: 164)

'The teacher needs to learn about the child from the parents. The parent needs to share with the teacher information about the child, the child's needs, and what the parent's expectations are for the child as the child enters the group. The teacher needs also to know more about the parent's point of view, for parent and teacher must work together for the good of the child.' (Read et al. 1993: 206)

'Understanding, support, and interest will usually encourage the parent to take that first step toward collaborating with the teacher for the good of the child.' (Hepworth Berger 1995: 283)

In this approach, educators and parents reinforce and reform each other's knowledge. Educators learn about a child from its parents and parents learn about educators' expectations of the child. Each uses their reformed knowledge of the child to 'work for the good' of the individual, self-governing child in a collaborative, mutually supportive project. This approach underpinned the development of kindergartens in Victoria, Australia. During the 1940s, the Victorian state government began to fund preschools as educational rather than philanthropic programmes. Each preschool was required to establish a management committee in which parents played a key role as volunteers (O' Toole 1999). This 'reforming' approach was also the hope in the growth of nursery education in the UK: 'The greatest hope for schools to grow as community resources, in which parents and teachers can be identified as joint contributors to the development of children, lies in the nursery movement' (Poulton and James 1975: 79). Early childhood educators in a centre that adopts a 'reforming' approach to knowledge–power relationships see the children and parents who attend the centre as a community of learners. For such 'reforming' educators, 'community involvement' means that their centre not only cares for and educates children – it also teaches parents to support that care and education. Thus, 'community building' means increasing the number of people in the centre's community of learners, and/or improving the learning within it, and/or involving parents more directly in children's learning.

Where have the ideas come from?

This 'reforming' approach to parent involvement reflects the view that children's education is improved when their parents are involved in it. Hepworth Berger (1995) highlights the evolution of this idea in the USA:

- The late 1950s: the launch of Sputnik by the USSR caused increased concern in the US about children's intellectual development.
- The 1960s and 1970s: Piaget's ideas of cognitive development were used in the Head Start early childhood programs in the USA. The programs aimed to give children a 'head start', increasing their chances of success at school and they increasingly emphasized the importance of family involvement in children's learning.
- The 1990s: increasing efforts to involve families in children's learning with much international research concerning the effects.

Similar patterns have been seen in the UK (Scarr and Dunn 1982) and in Australia (Brennan 1994). The 1990s research consolidated the idea that parent involvement supports children's learning. It showed that parent involvement:

- positively influences children's cognitive and social development (see, for example, Endsley et al. 1993; Studer 1993/94; Laloumi-Vidali 1997);
- improves children's educational outcomes, especially literacy (Baker et al. 1996; Cooter et al. 1999; Bryant et al. 2000);
- increases parents' ability to support children's development by increasing their understanding of appropriate educational practices (see, for example, Gelfer 1991);
- improves parents' commitment to schooling (Izzo et al. 1999);
- contributes to national development by improving children's educational outcomes, especially literacy (Cone 1993; Hannon 1995; Cairney 1997);
- benefits business by creating a more literate and, therefore, a more productive workforce (PFIE 1997).

More recent research highlights the importance of educators moving from advising parents to supporting them as they raise their children, and of educators recognizing that parents are 'active, thinking agents, not passive recipients' (Liou and Price 2001: 3).

Implications for early childhood practices

A 'reforming' approach to the knowledge–power relationships between educators and parents can create tensions for educators. Parent involvement clearly benefits children's learning and many early childhood texts and reports emphasize the value of parent involvement as a resource for educators. Ideas gallery 12.4 presents several examples of this view.

Ideas gallery 12.4 Parents as a benefit to children's learning

From a UK text:

'It appears so far that the emphasis is on what teachers can do for parents and other interested adults and, in a sense, this has to be so. School is traditionally the teacher's territory and if parents are really to understand its processes as many wish to do, then they must in some way enter at least into its ethos. This is not to say that teachers should not equally value the home milieu.' (Moyles 1989: 163)

From Russia (reported in a UK newsletter):

'Parents involved become an important resource in the process. They significantly support the creation of the material and spiritual educationally "preparable" environment by participating in action games with the children . . . This gives harmony to the environment and integrity to the community.' (Kritskaya 1996: 13)

From an Australian text:

'The role of the professional, in meeting parents' expectations on one hand and providing guidance on another is complex. The teacher and other professionals must meet parents beyond the half way mark . . . Mutual understanding, respect and support are vital for both parents and teachers.' (Ebbeck 1991: 181)

From a USA journal:

'While teachers and parents may meet for a variety of reasons, the overriding goal should be for the teacher to "join" with as many families as possible. Joining means "letting the family know" that the teacher "understands them and is working with and for them".' (Rosenthal and Young Sawyers 1996: 195)

However, tension arises because there is always the danger that parents will behave in educationally and developmentally 'inappropriate' ways. Educators tend to resolve that tension by inviting and encouraging parents to become involved in their children's care and education through activities such as:

- raising money;
- helping with snack times;
- serving on the management committee;
- assisting with excursions;
- distributing newsletters;
- sharing a special skill or interest with the children.

Such forms of parent involvement are very beneficial to an early childhood centre and can be essential to a centre that is under-funded. However, none of them involves parents as partners, advocates and decision makers in an early childhood curriculum (Wright Sexton 1996) and none of them features educators as co-learners with parents. Instead, each form of parent involvement restricts them to non-educational areas and can subordinate parents to educators' expertise in curriculum decisions.

Equity reflections

In a centre that regards itself as part of a community of learners, the knowledge–power relations between parents and educators are liberal and ambiguous. On the one hand, the centre can have a genuine desire to reform the knowledge–power links in educator–parent relationships by recognizing that parents may have specific skills and experiences that educators lack and that can be valuable resources for a centre. On the other hand, the centre may continue to reinforce those knowledge–power links by excluding parents from curriculum decisions and implementation – the domain of the professional, expert educator. Such a centre 'reforms' those knowledge–power links, in that it involves parents in decision making – but on terms that subordinate them to educators' expertise in curriculum decisions.

In such circumstances, parent involvement is shaped largely by the educator and is 'inevitably harnessed to, and shaped by, institutional policy' (Foot *et al.* 2002: 7). Educators invite parents to become involved on the assumption that parents' knowledge of the child supplements their own expert knowledge, rather than being a necessary component of it. When parents' knowledge is seen as merely supplementary, educators can – and do – ignore it without compromising their professional standards. For instance, a Greek study found that only 25 per cent of educators wished to work collaboratively with parents (Laloumi-Vidali 1997), and a Japanese study found staff reluctant even to talk with parents (Huira 1996).

Parents' subordination to educator expertise runs through a standard (USA) textbook on parental involvement:

> If parents and teachers work together and communication is ongoing, *the parents can help teachers* in their role of classroom manager. If the expectations of the teacher are for children to be responsible and learn and *if the expectations of the parent are for the same,* consistency between the two can be very helpful.
>
> (Berger 1995: 131, emphasis added)

The book lists the sorts of activities that encourage parent involvement, many of which exclude parents from curriculum design and implementation. For example:

- 'Back-to-school nights'. 'Teachers often complain that the *parents who need to come to learn* about the educational program are the very ones who do not come' (p.135, emphasis added).
- 'Parent education groups'. 'Parents become real resources for the school through parent education meetings, which *teach them* to become effective tutors and school volunteers' (p.136, emphasis added).

- 'School projects'. 'Enlist parent help if you plan to add to the playground or build a reading loft in your classroom . . . Many fathers find this the most comfortable way to contribute to the school' (p.138).

The Pen Green Centre in Corby, UK, is a community of learners that seeks to involve parents in all aspects of its programme. In its 17 years, the centre has involved more than 6000 local parents and Whalley *et al.* (2001) argue that the centre's success in two government-funded programmes – Sure Start and Start Right – stemmed from its emphasis on involving parents from the beginning in designing projects:

> A particular feature of the Corby Sure Start program was that large numbers of parents were involved in conceptualizing the local targets and programmes of work. The Start Right report made it clear that the key issue for early childhood educators . . . was to develop a strong relationship with parents as the child's first and enduring educators. The role of early childhood settings was to support parents.
>
> (Whalley *et al.* 2001: 7, 9)

Under the guise of creating collaboration between parents and educators, educators can invoke a 'right to know' what happens to a child at home. In Australia, this right to know is embodied in the funding and regulation of early childhood services. In particular, it underpins the requirement to involve parents as a pre-requisite for accreditation under the federal government's Quality Improvement and Accreditation (QIAS) (NCAC 2001).

Paradoxically, this institutionalized imperative to seek parental knowledge of the child disinclines many educators and parents to create parent involvement. First, the demand that educators should acknowledge the value of parental knowledge of the child undermines their status as experts and professionals, because it 'says' that parents' subjective, personal and emotional understandings of their child(ren) are as valuable as educators' scientific, objective and norm-referenced knowledge of child(ren) in general. Consequently, the more credence they give to parents' knowledge, the more they undermine the 'expert' status of their own knowledge on which they base their claim to be professionals. Second, to investigate how parents raise their children at home, educators scrutinize those homes and subject them to their 'expert' judgement. Any 'inappropriate' child-raising practices render the household liable to further scrutiny by state agencies such as social services and child welfare (Donzelot 1979) – hardly an incentive to become 'involved' in these terms.

Transforming the knowledge–power links in relationships between educators and parents: creating learning communities

Overview

A 'transforming' approach to relationships between educators and parents promotes democratic citizenship by inviting parents and others to form policies, manage resources and evaluate services; and by devolving decisions about what and how children should learn.

Educators who adopt this position seek to create equitable and inclusive relation-ships with parents by challenging the knowledge–power links that currently underpin them. Specifically, they challenge the assumption that there is a fixed and final body of knowledge about children that professionals possess and parents lack, attempting instead to collaborate with parents and others to transform the existing knowledge of the child. This involves these educators in actively renegotiating the politics of knowledge that infuse their relationships with parents and others by shifting the con-tent of their communication away from non-negotiable facts about children and towards negotiable knowledge about them.

Hughes and Mac Naughton (2002) highlighted some practices for educators that are associated with this position on the knowledge–power links in their relationships with parents and others:

- giving parents a real voice without feeling that this directly threatens their pro-fessional identity;

- negotiating shared meanings and understandings about who the child is and how he or she should be treated – these negotiations should benefit both sides equally and should eschew exclusive claims to 'truth';

- ensuring that they have sufficient time to negotiate with parents face to face and in ways that rest on and continually recreate shared understandings of the child.

However, if educators are to perform those practices successfully, they need to create professional identities that aren't threatened by parents questioning or challenging their knowledge of the child. Instead of relying on the sorts of non-negotiable 'truths' about who the child is and should be that inform current pro-fessional practice and identity, educators need to recognize the existence of different (perhaps competing) knowledges of the child – knowledges that are negotiable precisely because several co-exist. Finally, such educators need the time and space to negotiate and recreate understandings of the child with parents and others. Each of these preconditions for substantive parent involvement requires staff to see themselves not as experts marshalling the (scientific) facts about the child, but as collaborators with parents and the wider community in the task of building shared understandings of who the child is and what the child is capable of.

A growing number of people in early childhood services are attempting to create these sorts of collaborative relationships with parents. One especially well publicized example is the preprimary programmes of Reggio Emilia in Italy, where community-based management of early childhood programmes has grown significantly:

> It now encompasses, in both its organizational and educational form, all the pro-cesses of participation, democracy, collective responsibility, problem-solving and decision-making – processes all integral to an educational institution. Com-munity-based management embodies the theoretical and practical synthesis of the interrelationships forged between children, families, service providers, and society at large.
>
> (Spaggari 1993: 93)

In broad terms, this consititutes what is called a learning community, in other words, an association of individuals, groups and organizations that evolves or develops as a whole through learning, rather as a living organism does. Fidler (1995: 4) defines a learning community more specifically in terms of the relationships within it:

> A group of colleagues who come together in a spirit of mutual respect, authenticity, learning and shared responsibility to continually explore and articulate an expanding awareness and base of knowledge. The process of [a] learning community includes inquiring about each other's assumptions and biases, experimenting, risking and openly assessing the results.

The Pen Green Centre in the UK shows that there can be considerable slippage between a community of learners and a learning community – not least because the more learners there are in a community, the more it becomes a community that is learning. Jilk (1999: 2–3) distinguishes the two types of community thus:

> A community of learners . . . is a community that is a good place to live, work and play, and where everyone is engaged in lifelong learning . . . A learning community . . . is continually expanding its capacity to create its future; the community itself is a learner; and it is a community that responds to needs much faster than others.

Where have the ideas come from?

There are diverse roots to the idea of a learning community in which democratic communication can transform knowledge–power links between educators, parents and others. One root is the work of Jürgen Habermas, a German critical theorist associated with the Frankfurt School of Critical Theory (Chapter 1). Habermas believes that we can create democratic and just relationships with each other if we infuse our personal, social and cultural relationships with what he called 'ideal speech' (Habermas 1979: 144).

Ideal speech is a genuinely open discourse of 'truth', 'freedom' and 'justice', free of 'distortions' such as ideology, custom, habit, tradition or coercion. For instance, ideal speech about the child between educators and parents would be genuinely open, free from the distortions, habits and traditions associated with the structured inequalities between staff and parents. Those 'distortions' derive from professional knowledge and ideologies of caring based on gender and class. Habermas's work offers the hope that creating genuinely open dialogue between educators and parents can lead to greater equity and freedom for each group. Habermas believes that 'ordinary' conversation already features the preconditions of ideal speech: 'Everyday communication makes possible a kind of understanding that is based on claims to validity and thus furnishes the only real alternative to exerting influence on one another in more or less coercive ways' (Habermas 1990: 19). Thus, we can use ordinary conversation to challenge the ways in which bureaucratic relationships (including those between educators and parents) oppress and silence people.

Government programmes increasingly bureaucratize and regulate educators' relationships with parents. For example, New Zealand's Early Childhood Development department published a brochure advertising the Parents As First Teachers (PAFT) programme that included these statements:

> PAFT is based on the philosophy that parents are their children's first and most important teachers, and offers support and guidance to parents in this role . . . Trained Parent Educators will provide regular home visits to share information, practical ideas, and give guidance as your child grows and develops.

Other roots of the idea that parents have a right to be involved in building democratic communities and in the education of their young children include the social activist movements – especially the women's movements – in those countries. The demand for community-based, community-owned and community-run services for young children has been a recurring theme in countries such as the UK and Australia over many years. These demands imply that parents have clear rights to participate actively in decision making about their young children's care and education because they know about their children and because such active participation represents democratic relationships in action (see New and David 1985; Brennan and O'Donnell 1986). New and David (1985: 257) state that community nurseries in the UK differ from local authority nurseries on several counts, but in particular their partnership approach to work with parents, in which parents are considered equal partners in the enterprise of building programmes for young children.

Implications for early childhood practices

In an early childhood centre that sees itself as part of a learning community, parent involvement is at the core of children's learning and of the centre's life, rather than just layered onto them. The centre encourages and enables its learning community to decide what they learn, how they learn, how they evaluate what they learn and so on, and it does so by inviting members of its community to decide its policies, manage its resources and evaluate its services. For such a centre, 'community involvement' describes the extent of such devolved decision making, and 'community building' means increasing the community's capacity to employ those devolved decision making powers successfully. Indeed, community involvement and community building become synonymous and as they grow, the centre becomes an organic part of its community and an expression of its community's character, hopes and dreams:

> Practicing democracy also has implications for how teachers interact with the communities they serve. A teacher or a school committed to democracy makes a point of involving parents in deciding on the goals and educational practices of the school.
>
> (Sleeter and Grant 1999: 202)

A learning community relies on communication between educators, parents and others that creates shared meanings, rather than merely transmitting information.

Effective communication recognizes that different people may understand 'facts' about, for example, children in different ways and so communication between two people is effective when each one acknowledges the other's way of understanding those facts. Thus, effective communication between staff and parents entails more than speaking clearly and writing simply in order to 'get the message across'. Instead, it entails creating 'interpretive communities' (Fish 1979) of educators, parents and others who share a particular view of the child and whose communication expresses that shared view, thus continuously recreating their relationship:

> Understood in this way, working with parents does not mean pedagogues giving to parents uncontextualized and unproblematized information about what they (the pedagogues) are doing, nor 'educating' parents in 'good' practice by transmitting a simplified version of a technology of child development and child rearing. Rather it means both parents and pedagogues (and others) entering into a reflective and analytic relationship involving deepening understandings and the possibility of making judgements about pedagogical work.
>
> (Dahlberg *et al.* 1999: 77)

The early childhood profession is an interpretive community defined by its view of the child. Unlike most interpretive communities, however, the early childhood profession expresses its view of the world and of the child formally in a written code of professional ethics and conduct that clearly states the behaviour, values and responsibilities it expects of its members.

Creating an interpretive community can be a discomforting task. When we share and compare our understandings of the world with someone else (a colleague or a parent), we implicitly hold our sense of ourselves up to scrutiny because each of us defines ourselves in terms of the way we understand the world and our place in it: 'I am this sort of person because I see the world in this way'. If the other person understands the world differently from us, we lack the 'common ground' from which to make sense of each other. In contrast, if the other person shares our views of the world, then they confirm our identity, we confirm theirs, and on the resulting 'common ground' we can begin to build an interpretive community.

Ideas gallery 12.5 presents some attempts to create such interpretive communities.

Ideas gallery 12.5 Creating interpretive communities with parents

From a study with indigenous families on their views on education:

'This study foregrounds the voice of Indigenous people through positioning them as knowledgeable about their children. The questions (about research videos of children learning) (What can everyone see? What can only the family see? What can we no longer see?) were powerful in encouraging families to look more deeply than simply at what the children were doing, but to move toward an analysis of cultural content and context.' (Fleer and Williams-Kennedy 2001: 53)

From a Kenyan case study:

'[Parents] now participate in the production of materials. For example, in curriculum development, a participatory approach is used . . . Trainers meet parents and community members individually or in groups to collect folklore materials (stories, riddles, poems, games, plays) which are later edited and reproduced. This methodology has encouraged the tapping of available human and physical resources and enhanced the development of confidence and a sense of achievement and satisfaction in the parents and local communities because they feel that they have made contributions to their children's learning.' (Bernard van Leer Foundation 1994: 9)

From a USA text:

'Once a program opens itself up to dialogue with parents, there is almost a loop that develops between school and the home. The school environment becomes sort of a laboratory for teachers to work on ideas they can share with parents. The parents also become resources that the teachers can utilize. There isn't this sort of estranged relationship between the two.' (Chang *et al.* 2000: 158)

From Blue Sage Community Partners, in the USA:

'The broader community must understand that there is not one right and true way and that many perspectives are desirable and necessary for survival and growth. We must all realize that the only thing stopping us from providing young Indian children with the essential things they need to grow and learn so that they can assume their rightful place in our world is ourselves.' (Rinehart 2000: 142)

Equity reflections

Parents and staff can create 'common ground' between them if they share a commitment to challenging unequal power relations between them and to valuing each other's specific contribution to children's care and education (Filp 1998: 350). If parents understand their rights and responsibilities within a programme, they can be confident that their needs will be met appropriately and that their concerns will receive professional and ethical responses. The following principles and practices (built from the literature on parent–staff relations) can encourage parent involvement in policy and programme decisions.

Creating opportunities for regular dialogue with parents

Educators who wish to change their relationships with parents could start by drawing on these suggestions by parents to researchers about how to encourage good communication (see Mac Naughton *et al.* 1986; Balcombe and Tansey 1996):

- actively encourage parents to spend as much time in the centre with their children as they wish;
- keep informal conversations positive, open and friendly;

- recognize that particular individuals' general shyness and a lack of confidence may prevent them from discussing their issues and concerns;

- ensure that when parents bring their child to the centre and collect them, there is regularly time for informal staff–parent communication, but remember that parents may have little time to discuss their child's moods, foods and behaviour;

- remember that parents can talk more easily to staff at the end of the day if their child has been involved in a quiet activity and is relaxed;

- raise any concerns with a parent at a special time, away from the daily bustle;

- don't expect parents to feel confident in formal meetings if they have little or no experience of such meetings and of the procedures used in meetings, and encourage parents to participate by introducing parents to each other, providing refreshments and supplementing formal 'business' meetings with informal 'socials';

- remember that parents enjoy being able to discuss issues of concern with each other.

Being goal orientated in your communication with parents

Effective communication with parents doesn't just happen. It needs to be actively created and it needs to be more explicitly goal orientated than on some other occasions. A general question to ask yourself about your communication goals is: How do my goals for my communication with parents connect with my views about links between the centre and children's homes? The following questions will help you to make your communication with parents more goal orientated:

- What are my communication goals on this particular occasion?

- Can I offer this parent any information that would make my goals clear to them?

- What questions should I ask this parent to get the information I need from them and to offer them the support I intend?

- Is this way of communicating with parents the best way to achieve my goals?

Practising 'anti-biased' communication with parents

Finding 'common ground' among people with diverse world views can be tricky, because those with the most power will often use it to ensure that their views prevail. To counter this, staff can draw on the principles of anti-bias education (see, for example, Derman-Sparks et al. 1989) to help them to communicate equitably with parents (Hughes and Mac Naughton 1999):

- offer all parents equal access to you and time with you;

- provide all parents with the same basic information about the centre and encourage them to share information with you;

- ensure that all parents know about any current and planned opportunities to become involved in the centre, including attending meetings;

- ensure that all parents are able to participate in meetings and that the meeting space is physically accessible to people with disabilities;
- be aware that parents from a culture different to yours may not feel comfortable about disclosing personal family information;
- check your own reactions to parents for possible stereotypes;
- avoid discriminatory language at all times and use inclusive terms for family members such as 'parent' or 'guardian' rather than 'father' or 'mother'.

Table 12.1 presents these ideas as an equity 'checklist'.

Table 12.1 An anti-bias approach to communicating with parents

Initial interviews with parents
- Provide all parents with the same basic information about the centre.
- Spend equal time with all parents.
- Arrange an interpreter if parents speak a different language to your own.
- Use inclusive terms for family members such as 'parent' or 'guardian' rather than 'father' or 'mother'.
- Be aware that parents from a culture different to yours may feel uncomfortable about disclosing personal family information.

Daily communication with parents
- Offer all parents equal access to you.
- Encourage all parents to share information with you.
- Ensure all parents know about any current and planned opportunities to become involved in the centre.
- Ensure that bilingual support is available for parents who do not speak the main language spoken in the centre.
- Check your own reactions to parents for possible stereotypes.

Written communication with parents
- Avoid discriminatory language at all times.
- Challenge stereotypes, including the view that the 'normal' household consists of male and female partners with the female bearing the main responsibility for the care of children.
- Provide translations of all written material for parents who do not read in the centre's main language.
- Ensure that all your marketing material maintains high ethical standards.

Meetings with parents
- Ensure all parents have information about meetings being held.
- Ensure that bilingual support is available for parents who do not speak the main language spoken in the centre.
- Check that all parents are able to participate in meetings.
- Ensure that the meeting space is physically accessible to people with disabilities.

Record keeping
- Do not write anything down about a parent and/or family that you would feel uncomfortable about a court seeing.

Practising respectful cross-cultural communication

Early childhood educators can forge strong partnerships with parents from different cultures when there is a shared commitment to regular, face to face communication that acknowledges each other's cultural perspectives. To encourage such communication, educators should reserve judgement about parenting styles and about parents' hopes for their children. Instead, they should encourage parents to be proud of their ethnic and 'racial' heritage and to share stories about their culture, its development and its struggles. Hewitt and Maloney (2000: 91) offer a good example of this approach in their comments about Malaysian parents' perceptions of preschool education:

> Many of the research studies reviewed [in this article] concluded by suggesting that where parents' perceptions were not consistent with the position espoused by developmental theory or educational psychology, the parents should be 'educated' regarding appropriate practice in early childhood education. But the very notion of educating parents with a view to making their perceptions more congruent with current theory is denying the possibility that there exists more than one interpretation or dimension of 'appropriateness' . . . Perhaps the concern, therefore, should lie not with parental perceptions but with the manner in which the field defines the notion of 'appropriate' perceptions . . . What we must come to accept is that all tasks and accomplishments are not equally valid in all cultural settings.

Educators should maintain contact, create opportunities for dialogue and seek to resolve conflicts through negotiation and compromise with parents and others. More specifically, they should ensure that bilingual support is available to parents who do not speak the main language spoken in the centre; and they should learn about cultures different to their own (Gonzalez-Mena 1992; Espinosa 1995; Swick et al. 1995).

Acknowledging parents' knowledge of their children

All parents know about their children and they can be dispirited and frustrated if early childhood educators silence or ignore this knowledge. Conversations with parents need to start from the recognition that parents' daily experience of their child can generate strong views about how their child should be educated and cared for. While this may seem obvious, educators can be unwilling to acknowledge some parents' particular expertise. Recognizing parents' specialist knowledge and encouraging them to share it requires educators to accept that there are many different ways to care for children, to explain their specialist terminology and to avoid jargon.

Stereotypes and cultural assumptions can undermine equitable communication and shared understandings of the child when educators and parents are from different cultural and 'racial' groups (Blue Swadner 2000). In these circumstances, educators can seek and acknowledge parents' knowledge of the children by sharing life stories, discussing diversity and critically reflecting. Educators have used these strategies to create alliances with parents in Head Start programmes (Chang et al. 2000) and in

Australian early childhood programmes (Smith 2001). Siraj-Blatchford and Clarke (2000: 96–7) suggest that educators need various types of knowledge to work successfully with families from diverse cultural and language backgrounds:

- family history;
- religious beliefs and practices;
- children's everyday experiences at home;
- language practices;
- parents' theories about learning;
- parents' views on schooling and early education;
- community events and contacts;
- areas of expertise.

Reflecting critically on 'race' and ethnicity in your relationships with parents and others

Most educators in early childhood services in Australia will work with parents from diverse cultural backgrounds. In these circumstances, educators and parents can forge strong cross-cultural partnerships when each side is committed to understanding the other's perspectives. Such partnerships can best be achieved through regular, face to face communication, in which educators (Hughes and Mac Naughton 2000, based on Gonzalez-Mena 1992; Espinosa 1995; Swick *et al.* 1995):

- reserve judgement about parenting styles and about parents' hopes for their children;
- maintain contact and create opportunities for dialogue;
- resolve conflicts through negotiation and compromise;
- offer bilingual support to parents;
- learn about cultures different to their own;
- support parents in their efforts to feel pride in their ethnic and 'racial' heritage and in their parenting;
- encourage parents to contribute to multicultural programmes for all children;
- encourage parents to share stories with the group about their culture, its development and its struggles;
- work with parents in small groups on specific projects such as cultural celebrations in the centre, developing anti-bias policies and advocating equity within the wider community.

Reflecting critically on disability in your relationships with parents and others

Many parents of children with disabilities find it difficult to establish positive relationships with their child's centre. These parents often experience and express a range of feelings, from denial and anger through to grief, shame and guilt. Further, their daily experience of their child's disability often gives them expertise and strong views about their child's care and education, but educators are often unwilling to acknowledge their expertise and views, dismissing them as 'more of a nuisance than a resource' (Gargiulo and Graves 1991: 176).

Educators can create positive relationships with parents of children with dis-abilities by trying to understand how such parents feel about their child(ren). Educa-tors should expect these parents to express a wide range of feelings and should deal with them positively by (Gargiulo and Graves 1991):

- trying to empathize with parents;
- informing parents about what is offered to their child;
- accepting that there are different ways to educate and care for a child with a disability;
- listening to and acting on parents' views about how best to care for their child;
- avoiding jargon about a child's disability and learning to explain their specialist terminology.

Key ideas summary

Three views dominate the recent research literature on 'community': community as agencies, communities of learners; and learning communities. Each view implies a particular approach to community involvement, to community building and to com-munication with parents. Each view also represents an approach to the links between knowledge and power – specifically, between expert, scientific (developmental) know-ledge about young children, and the power to have it accepted as the truth – 'conform-ing' to those links, 'reforming' them and 'transforming' them.

Ideas summary 12.1 summarizes those views on community and shows how a centre's approach to those knowledge–power links relates to its view of community, community involvement and community building. The various distinctions in the table aren't watertight demarcations – they are predominant tendencies in a centre's attitudes, policies and practices.

Ideas summary 12.1 Relationships between knowledge interests and community

Knowledge interests	Community	Community involvement	Community building
CONFORMING to knowledge–power links:	• A community is an association of agencies. • The centre is one agency among the several that make up its community.	• Providing a service to the community.	• Forming or strengthening links with other agencies.

REFORMING knowledge–power links:	• A community of learners is an association of individuals who are learning together. • The centre is the hub of a community of learners: i.e. the parents and children who attend it.	• Caring for and educating the children; and educating their parents about how best to do so.	• Improving the learning in it and/or by encouraging more parents to join it.
TRANSFORMING knowledge–power links:	• A learning community is an association of individuals, groups and organizations that develops or evolves as a whole through learning.	• Promoting democratic citizenship by inviting parents and others to form its policies, manage its resources and evaluate its services, and by devolving decisions about what and how to learn.	• Participating in a broad-based movement for changes through learning, for example, by devolving more decisions about what and how to learn.

Reflecting on your learning

• What have you learnt about building equitable communities in early childhood services?

• What key challenges and possibilities does the chapter pose?

Further reading and online resources

Bridge, H. (2001) Increasing parental involvement in the preschool curriculum: what an action research case study revealed, *International Journal of Early Years Education*, 9(1): 5–22.

Centre for Equity and Innovation in Early Childhood. A website that regularly updates links on working with parents (follow links to project resources): http://www.edfac.unimelb.edu.au/LED/CEIEC/

Diffily, D. and Morrison, K. (eds) (1996) *Family Friendly Communication for Early Childhood Programs*. Washington, D.C.: National Association for the Education of Young Children.

Henry, M. (1996) *Young Children, Parents and Professionals: Enhancing the Links*. London: Routledge.

National Parent Information Network. A website for parents and those who work with them: http://npin.org

Spaggari, S. (1993) The community–teacher partnership in the governance of the schools, in C. Edwards, L. Gandini and G. Forman (eds), *The Hundred Languages of Children: The Reggio Emilia Approach to Early Childhood Education*, pp. 91–100. Norwood, N.J.: Ablex Publishing Corporation.

UK Parents. A website for parents: http://www.ukparents.co.uk

Working with culturally diverse parents

Chang, H., Muckleroy, A., Pulido-Tobiassen, D. and Dowell, C. (2000) Redefining childcare and early education in a diverse society: dialogue and reflection, in L. Diaz Soto (ed.) *The Politics of Early Childhood Education*, pp. 143–64. New York: Peter Lang Publishers.

Liu, K. and Chien, C. (1998) Project approach and parent involvement in Taiwan, *Childhood Education*, 74(4): 213–19.

Lopez, A. (1995) Creation is ongoing: developing a relationship with non-English speaking parents, *Childcare Information Exchange*, 107: 56–9.

Siraj-Blatchford, I. and Clarke, P. (2000) *Supporting Identity, Diversity and Language in the Early Years*, chap. 5. Buckingham: Open University Press.

Critical reflections on parental involvement

Blue Swadner, B. (2000) 'At risk' or 'at promise'? From deficit constructions of the 'other childhood' to possibilities for authentic alliances with children and families, in L. Diaz Soto (ed.) *The Politics of Early Childhood Education*, pp. 117–34. New York: Peter Lang Publishers.

Hughes, P. and Mac Naughton, G. (2000) Consensus, dissensus or community: the politics of parent involvement in early childhood education, *Contemporary Issues in Early Childhood*, 1(3): 241–58.

Hughes, P. and Mac Naughton, G. (2001) Building equitable staff–parent communication in early childhood settings: an Australian case study, *Early Childhood Research and Practice*, 3(2): 241–58.

Video

Contrasting Perspectives. Magna Systems. Available from www.marcom.com.au A video that explores the different perspectives of parents and early childhood staff on a variety of issues.

13

Curriculum contexts: becoming an early childhood professional

With Sheralyn Campbell and Jane Page

> All professional practice is based on knowledge. That knowledge ranges from the general, such as knowledge about contemporary Australian culture or child development, to local knowledge of a particular community, through to particular knowledge about the families and children who participate in the service. Using the totality of this knowledge as a base, professionals make thoughtful provision for children, reflect on their own experiences and evaluate constructively.
>
> (NSW Department of Community Services 2002: 39)

> The goal is for teachers to support the learning and development of all children. To achieve this goal, teachers need to know children well and use everything they know about each child – including that individual's learning styles, interests and preferences, personality and temperament, skills and talents, challenges and difficulties.
>
> (Bredekamp and Copple 1997: 40)

In each country, a range of specialized fields of knowledge about children and families have been valued for some time as a way of creating developmentally and individually appropriate teaching and learning. This specialized learning and developmental knowledge underpins many legislative documents, government policies, professional standards, codes of practice and curriculum documents. Traditionally, this knowledge has stressed the importance of viewing children within wider developmental norms and planning for individual variations of physical, emotional, social and cognitive growth against these norms. Observations of children's developmental status would be recorded and analysed as a means of ensuring that the learning experiences set up in a programme are responsive to the wide range of individual differences that exist within a group of children.

One of the challenges that you face as an early childhood professional is to decide on how to put your knowledges into practice. What are your intentions and aspirations for working with children and families as an early childhood professional?

- Do you want to belong to a profession that works to conform to a particular body of specialized knowledge and practise this knowledge in the same way with all communities?
- Do you want to belong to a profession that works to reform how a particular body of specialized knowledge is practised with different communities?
- Do you want to belong to a profession that works to transform how a particular body of knowledge is understood and practised with different communities?

The beliefs that you hold about what it means to be an early childhood professional will guide your journey into working with children and families in your community. In this chapter we explore the specialist knowledge and practice that the profession is required to conform to as a background to reflecting on what a transformative approach to being professional might look like.

Conforming to specialized knowledge and practices as a professional

The key ideas in overview

Early childhood professionals are often required to translate social policy into practice in their community. There are many dimensions to the social policy that early childhood professionals need to conform to. These may include:

- legislation and regulations enacted by governments to ensure the care and protection of young children and families;
- standards and ethics widely held by early childhood professionals in your country and early childhood curriculum documents;
- accountability systems that regulate the quality of services to young children and families.

The nexus between social policy and early childhood practice means that you must become familiar with the legislation, standards and ethics that will guide how you begin the process of understanding and practising quality teaching and learning in an early childhood community.

Legislation and regulations

Documents such as regulations will vary between countries and states and will provide early childhood professionals and employers with the legislative frame-works for understanding what constitutes minimum standards within early childhood educational programmes. Regulations detail expectations around a number of practical issues such as child/staff ratios, record keeping procedures and health and safety standards and procedures. Regulations bring with them levels of accountability and set basic standards. They also need to be complemented with documents that are concerned with what constitutes quality practice in early childhood settings.

Quality assurance

The Quality Improvement and Accreditation System (QIAS) is a means of setting higher standards of accountability in Australian early childhood services. The federal government seeks to achieve this goal by linking financial support to families using early childhood services directly to the participation of early childhood services in their national quality assurance system. While there are different quality assurance systems for family day care services and for childcare services in Australia, they were both designed to: 'provide children in centre based childcare throughout Australia with high quality care that best promotes their learning and development in the vital early years' (NCAC 2001: 3). The national quality assurance system for family day care and childcare services both defines standards of practice and provides opportunities for Australian children, families and early childhood professionals to work for improvement in these standards. For example, in childcare services there is a five stage process of quality improvement and accreditation completed every two and a half years.

1   The childcare centre registers with the National Childcare Accreditation Council (NCAC).

2   The childcare centre undertakes and submits a self-study report about the quality of their practices in each of ten key elements:

- relationships with children;
- respect for children;
- partnerships with families;
- staff interactions;
- planning and evaluation;
- learning and development;
- protective care;
- health;
- safety;
- managing to support quality.

The childcare centre also identifies a process for continuing improvements in practice for each area.

3   The NCAC sends a trained peer to validate the quality of the practices being used in the childcare centre and to collect surveys completed by parents, staff and the director about the quality of practices being used in the childcare centre.

4   The NCAC moderators assess the quality of the centre's practice using information provided in the self-study report, the validator's report and the surveys completed by parents, staff and the director.

5   The NCAC makes a decision about whether the childcare service should be accredited.

A key premise underlying the Quality Improvement and Accreditation System is that it brings early childhood professionals and parents together to discuss what constitutes a quality programme for children. The following quotations from staff and parents at a Melbourne metropolitan early childhood centre highlight the value of this process for all involved:

> Quality assurance gives us the opportunity to look at our centre from an objective viewpoint and evaluate our day to day practice. Together with parents, we can ensure that we are providing children with the best early childhood service. As a team, it presents the perfect forum for discussion, brainstorming ideas and working together to implement new approaches and therefore continue to meet the needs of kindergarten children.
>
> (Staff comment)

> The input from the accreditation subcommittee [made up of parents representing each group within the centre] is invaluable. They are able to complement ideas from staff, add new insights and together with feedback from all families ensure that we have a cohesive approach to best practice in our centre.
>
> (Staff comment)

> Being a participant in the accreditation process has helped me to appreciate what is involved in teaching young children. It is far more complex than I initially thought.
>
> (Parent comment)

> I can now see what skills are involved in creating a learning environment for young children. Hearing from staff what is involved has enabled me to see what is happening in the program more easily. Early childhood staff are very skilled teachers.
>
> (Parent comment)

Much of the current thinking about quality assurance and best practice in early childhood services stresses the importance of setting up processes to ensure that partnerships between professionals and parents can occur in early childhood curriculum and service development.

Quality assurance across the world
There are many ways in which partnerships between parents and professionals can be realized. For many, the importance of partnerships is embedded in a strong philosophical base which is then translated into practice. The Reggio Emilia programmes in Italy, for example, are built on the belief that the foundation of quality teaching and learning lies in the ability to create a community of inquiry within early childhood settings where children, families and early childhood professionals actively negotiate knowledge and meaning.

> We think of a school for young children as an integral living organism, as a place of shared lives and relationships among many adults and very many

children. We think of school as a sort of construction in motion, continuously adjusting itself.

(Malaguzzi 1998: 62)

Te Whāriki, the nationally mandated early childhood curriculum in New Zealand, is also founded on the importance of reciprocal partnerships between family, early childhood professionals and the wider community.

The Pen Green Centre in Corby, one of 29 Early Excellence Centres in the UK, places a strong emphasis on the importance of including parents in devising and designing projects: 'large numbers of parents were involved in conceptualising the local targets and programmes of work . . . the key issue for early childhood educators . . . was to build a strong relationship with parents as the child's first and enduring educators' (Whalley *et al.* 2001: 7, 9).

The Head Start programmes in the USA have sought to investigate, more broadly, the conditions required to set up greater collaborative linkages for professionals in early childhood services. The Investigating Partnerships in Early Childhood Education (I-PIECE) project identified different levels of collaboration that can be used as models that include fiscal integration, administrative integration and curriculum integration (Sandfort and Coleman Selden 2001).

The United Nations Convention on the Rights of the Child (1990)

The United Nations Convention on the Rights of the Child (see Cantwell 1995) offers an additional framework against which we can define and assess our professional obligations towards children. The significance of the convention is that it placed children's rights, for the first time, on a legally binding international level and that it granted children the same range of rights enjoyed by adults. Ratification of the convention places states under a legal and moral obligation to offer the administrative, legislative, judicial and other means to advance the cause of implementing the rights outlined in the convention. As Australia is a signatory to the convention, these obligations extend to early childhood professionals in terms of our philosophy and practice. As such, it is important that we become conversant with the document and examine ways in which we can acknowledge the key articles of the Convention in our practice.

There are several articles that relate to our obligations as curriculum designers. Article 29 of the Convention, for example, outlines the aims of education as being directed towards the development of the child's personality and abilities, preparation of the child for a responsible life, and development of respect for his or her parents, for human rights, for the natural environment and for his or her own cultural and social identity and values and those of others. In addition, the Convention calls for the *best interests of the child* to be a primary consideration in all measures concerning him or her (Article 3), *the child's right to express opinions* in all matters affecting him or her (Article 12), *the child's right to be protected from discrimination* (Article 2) and *rights of children from minority communities and indigenous populations* to enjoy their own culture, practise their religion and use their own language in community with others of their group (Article 30).

Against this background, the key principles underlying the Convention challenge us to reflect on a number of issues concerning our practice with young children. These include:

- How do we assist young children to understand their rights within our programmes?
- How do we acknowledge and celebrate the differing knowledge and skills brought by children and families into our programmes?
- How do we ensure that we are treating all children equitably in our programmes?
- How do we evaluate whether children are being discriminated against in our programmes?
- How do we incorporate children's voices into our programmes?
- To what extent do we offer children genuine opportunities to make decisions in our programmes?
- How do we evaluate whether the best interests of children are being addressed in our programmes?
- To what extent are we concerned with laying foundations for the long-term growth and development of the children attending our programmes?
- What values, skills and outlooks do we seek to instil in young children for the future?

Questions of this kind assist us, as early childhood professionals, to begin to reconsider what it means to offer responsive programmes for the children and families in our early childhood communities. The Convention further encourages us to view children as active agents in the early childhood setting, with specific needs and rights that should be addressed in and through our practice. In this way, it helps us to recognize the political nature of teaching and to rethink how we view children and make decisions about them in our programmes.

Mandatory reporting

In addition to assessing our roles and responsibilities as teachers, the Convention calls us to play a role in protecting children's fundamental rights. Article 34 of the Convention, for example, stresses the importance of *protecting children from sexual exploitation and abuse* and of taking all appropriate measures to protect children from unlawful sexual activity or exploitation in prostitution or pornography. In many countries, this principle is further enshrined in legislative frameworks. These frameworks commonly list early childhood professionals as professionals who should be mandated by law to report any suspected cases of child abuse. Early childhood professionals possess a specialized knowledge of child development and have a special relationship of trust with young children and are thus in an important position to make such judgements. Indeed, for these very reasons one could argue that, whether early childhood professionals are mandated by law or not, they would still have a moral obligation to report suspected abuse. Despite this, a number of practical factors such as lack of training and experience in this area often make it difficult for teaching professionals to feel confident in relation to fulfilling these obligations (McCallum 2001). It is thus important to understand what is required in relation to reporting suspected child abuse.

In order to form a reasonable belief that a child has been abused, early childhood professionals are required to:

- identify and distinguish between different forms of abuse and neglect;
- know the physical and behavioural indicators of different forms of abuse;
- distinguish between concerning and unconcerning behaviours in young children.

Professional judgements will also be required for knowing how to respond should a young child tell you that he or she has been abused. Knowledge of the legislative frameworks and the processes through which to take a suspected case will assist you to make decisions about how best to respond in such a situation. An understanding of the broader service system that is set up to protect children from abuse will also be vital to ensure that children and families are being offered the best support possible. If professionals do not feel confident in this area, it is important to undertake further educational training to assist them to feel more confident in understanding their responsibilities in reporting suspected child abuse.

As professionals, it is thus important to understand the key premises underlying social policy documents. Collectively, they offer us multiple perspectives on the nature of young children and teaching. These new viewpoints will assist us to redefine and refine our beliefs and values.

Standards, ethics and early childhood curriculum documents

Documents such as the Australian *Early Childhood Association Code of Ethics* (1991) and New Zealand's early childhood curriculum *Te Whāriki* (MoE 1996) further assist us in this task by weaving together culturally specific knowledge, principles, intentions and outcomes for early childhood education in each country. In so doing, they highlight additional considerations that early childhood professionals can bring to their programmes.

The Australian *Early Childhood Association Code of Ethics* (1991: 3) is a set of statements that express the core values underpinning the work of early childhood professionals in relation to children, families, colleagues, community and society, and oneself as a professional. It has been formulated in consultation with practitioners, as a guide for early childhood professionals to use for critical reflection, professional behaviour and, when necessary, the resolution of ethical dilemmas. It particularly stresses a commitment to:

- 'viewing the well-being of the individual child as having fundamental importance';
- 'acknowledging the uniqueness of each person';
- 'considering the needs of the child in the context of the family and culture as the family has a major influence on the young child';
- 'taking into account the critical impact of self esteem on an individual's development';

- 'basing practice on sound knowledge, research and theories while at the same time recognizing the limitations and uncertainties of these';
- 'working to fulfil the right of all children and their families to services of high quality'.

As such, it stresses the importance of viewing the child from multiple perspectives and of assessing one's practical knowledge and understandings against a range of critical frameworks.

The New Zealand early childhood curriculum document *Te Whãriki* (MoE 1996) offers additional insights into these issues. It was borne out of a bicultural imperative to ensure that both Maori and 'Western' philosophies informed early childhood practice and thus highlights the political nature of teaching through the priorities that we place on the values that inform our programmes and the day to day decisions that we make (Ritchie 1996: 28). The *Te Whãriki* vision outlines the key experiences of early childhood programmes as ones which are humanly, nationally, culturally, developmentally, individually and educationally appropriate (Ritchie 1996: 30). It is through these broader experiences, it is argued, that children will begin to feel that they are valued contributors to the early childhood community:

> The curriculum is founded on the following aspirations for children: to grow up as competent and confident learners and communicators, healthy in mind, body and spirit, secure in their sense of belonging and in the knowledge that they make a valued contribution to society.
>
> (MoE 1996: 9)

Intertwined with these experiences are (MoE 1996: 14): 'four broad principles . . .

Empowerment	*Whakaman*
Holistic development	*Kotahitanga*
Family and Community	*Whãnau Tangata*
Relationships	*Ngã Hononga'*

By stressing these experiences and principles, *Te Whãriki* highlights the broad range of issues children and families bring with them into our programmes and the challenges those place on early childhood professionals in their work.

Equity reflections

Standards, codes and legislation can reinforce dominant cultural values

> Each society has its regime of truth, its 'general politics' of truth – that is, the types of discourse it accepts and makes function as true; the mechanisms and instances that enable one to distinguish true and false statements; the means by which each is sanctioned; the techniques and procedures accorded value in the

acquisition of truth; the status of those who are charged with saying what counts as true.

(Foucault 1997: 131)

There is a growing argument about the effects of documents that set out broad standards for practice. This argument has emerged in part from the work of post-modern thinkers. Two such people were Michel Foucault (1926–84) and François Lyotard. French philosophers Foucault and Lyotard raised concerns about how some forms of specialized knowledge become 'regimes of truth' (Foucault) and 'grand narratives' (Lyotard) that sometimes work against social justice by excluding, rather than including, different ways of understanding and living in the world. Specifically, their concerns were about how only some groups of people are able to exercise power and experience privilege when certain meanings count as 'true' and 'right'. In different ways, Foucault's and Lyotard's concerns are linked to the history of social and cultural colonization of the knowledges, languages, values and traditions of minority groups by majority groups.

For example, Australia has a history which includes the removal of Aboriginal children from their families by government agencies who were concerned with the welfare of these children. The repercussions for these children and families continue today. As the Australian Indigenous singer Archie Roach says of his own experiences:

Said to us: Come take our hand,
Sent us off to Mission land,
Taught us to read, to write and pray,
Then they took the children away,
The children away.
Snatched them from their mother's breast,
Said it was for the best,
Took them away;
The Welfare and the policeman said:
You've got to understand,
We'll give them what you can't give,
Teach them how to really live.
Teach them how to live, they said;
Humiliated them instead.

(Roach, cited in Rintoul 1993: 172)

Stories like these caution against creating a 'one size fits all' set of standards that either:

- perpetuates and elevates the cultural and social biases of a majority group; or
- marginalizes the knowledge, languages, values and traditions of minority groups.

The history of colonization across the world raises many challenges for your practice of professionalism in the diversity of your community. New Zealand has recognized this and gone some way to addressing how early childhood curriculum, quality standards and legislation represent narrow definitions of what professional practice looks like. Their bi-cultural early childhood curriculum document, *Te Whāriki* (MoE 1996) acknowledges the cultural location of two groups: Maori and Pakeha. However, there always remain questions about how other minority groups in New Zealand are acknowledged by this curriculum document, and about the ethics of majority groups defining professional practice in a 'one size fits all' set of standards.

Some international researchers and practitioners are also questioning the roles of early childhood professionals in creating quality learning programmes for children. In Sweden, for example, researchers and teachers highlight the importance of professionals 'passing between the language of one's professional community (theories and practical wisdom) and one's personal passions, emotions, intuitions and experiences' (Dahlberg *et al.* 1999: 154). Reflecting on where you can go involves looking at the social policy frameworks for your practice, the challenges that face your community and how your knowledge helps you to understand and respond to these challenges.

Specialized knowledge and codes of practices can't always answer how we ensure 'wise' and just practices

You may begin to find that when you take social justice seriously you are faced with many situations that are not easily answered by your specialized knowledge. For example, one teacher from a rural childcare centre in Australia shared an episode from her journal that highlights how action for equity cannot always be legislated for:

CASE STUDY

Being part of a small rural community means that many of our families are related, are neighbours, or are friends. In a crisis the whole community seems to pull together to help. In my group of children we nurture this sense of community by constantly working towards fair, respectful and inclusive practices with each other. These are principles that are also part of how the quality of our programme is assessed in the National Quality Improvement and Accreditation System. However, recently I was confronted by two girls who used racist remarks to exclude another girl from play. These were girls who had lived and worked together for over a year, and I thought we knew each other well.

Two girls were seated on a seesaw. As I watched I could see the pleasure that they were sharing. Their laughter echoed across the playground as they went up and down. A Koori[1] girl joined them and sat in the middle seat. One of the girls immediately shouted at her to 'Get Off!'. The Koori girl sat very still, but made no move to leave. The two girls who had played with such pleasure then used a range of threats and strategies to force her to leave. Despite the ways that I tried to help them to play together, they insisted 'We don't like people with black skin' and refused to let her join them. When I challenged them and stated that their words and actions were unacceptable, they ran off leaving the Koori girl sitting alone on the seesaw.

Our Australian Early Childhood Code of Ethics, our NSW State Regulations, our Quality Improvement and Accreditation System, and our new Curriculum all said that as a teacher I had an obligation to ensure the dignity and rights of each child. But I was faced with an incident of racism that was not fixed by my actions, and one that has serious implications for every child and family in our community.

For this teacher, despite the professional knowledge that she had to draw upon and the documents that she used to frame what and how she should teach, there were still children like the Koori girl on the seesaw who sat at the margins of learning. Working as a teacher means facing issues in learning and relationships that do not depend simply on the teacher's knowledge of the child, or on legislation, policies, standards and codes of practice, but also on the politics that operate for and between children. These politics may involve how each person practises the meanings of gender, wealth, 'race', culture, sexuality and age. Studying how these meanings are implicated in what is happening for and between children, and listening to children's voices is an important way of working against unfairness in learning and relationships. These issues are important to children. As Kaarin (aged 4, born in central Asia) confided to her teacher, Leyla, when she was excluded from play with the Barbie dolls (Campbell 2001: 224):

Leyla: How do you feel when Diana and Bella won't let you be their friend?
Kaarin: I just feel dizzy and sad.

Part of reflecting on who you will be as a professional involves looking for and asking questions about social justice, and about how some people in your community are located on the margins of life. It is these margins and the specific life of your community that Michel Foucault and François Lyotard recognized as exciting opportunities for change.

In summary, the equity risks from working solely within this approach to being professional centre on the following:

- standards, codes and legislation can reinforce dominant cultural values;
- specialized knowledge and codes of practices can't always answer how we ensure 'wise' and just practices.

Transforming approaches to being professional

A profession predicated on, and constrained by, gendered, apolitical, and narrow theoretical constructs is unlikely to attract and retain a 'critical mass' of early childhood educators with the personal-professional agency to achieve greater community recognition of and commitment to the early years.

(Sumison 2002: 13)

The ideas in overview

Beliefs and understandings about how and what children learn, and how best children learn will always remain central to early childhood professionals' work. Furthermore, these values will not remain static, but rather, will change over time as early childhood professionals gain new perspectives from their engagement with young children and families. Karen Gallas's words, for example, illustrate new levels of excitement and challenge for her as she gained experience as an early childhood professional. Her experience highlights how the early childhood professional can use a commitment to social justice to engage with, rethink and change the 'distinct body of knowledge' shared by her profession:

> When I entered the classroom as a novice teacher . . . I was sure that my work would create new worlds of possibility for children . . . [A]s the years progressed, my concept of 'teaching well' altered and good teaching became more than believing that I was covering important curricula and that children were mastering subject matter. The social and political began to loom large as driving concerns. Children's desires for affiliation, their need to play and create new worlds, pressed in. Issues of power and entitlement, of alienation and failure, of silent or silenced complicated the process.
>
> (Gallas 1998: 1–2)

This professional's reflections indicate that she understands and uses her specialized knowledge, interests and practices of teaching with political intent. She sees the process of teaching and learning as inseparable from how issues of social justice are addressed in the classroom. In her teaching she has created a new way of being a professional and another dimension of specialized knowledge for her profession by treating seriously the issues facing children. This raises an important question that every teacher must face when they begin the process of defining what it means to be a professional in early childhood: 'What specialized knowledge is essential to quality teaching and learning?' 'The challenge . . . for us all is to explore the potential of alternative knowledges critically so that we might be able to create new versions of early childhood teaching and learning' (Ryan and Oschner 1999: 19).

There are many ways from within a transformative approach to professionalism that you might begin the process of blurring the boundaries of what you know, believe and want for children and families in your community. Each requires a serious commitment to theory, practice and professionalism, and an 'ethic of care' that acknowledges the risks and dangers of change for each person.

- An early childhood professional is *strategic and reflective* because he or she uses specialized knowledges as the basis for actions, and questions the effects of specialized knowledges in action.
- An early childhood professional works with others in the learning context to build a *critical community*. This is a place where each person's history, knowledges and social and cultural identities are valued, validated and included.

- An early childhood professional *practises socially just teaching and learning* 'in process'. This means reading, questioning, researching and reflecting on who is advantaged and disadvantaged by how teaching and learning occurs in each early childhood setting, and acting to create changes that work for social justice.

Implications for being professional

There are a number of specific implications that flow from a transformative approach to being professional. We will now canvass each one in turn.

Advocacy

The political nature of teaching can also be realized through early childhood professionals acting as advocates for young children. An advocate is someone who pleads the cause of another. Early childhood professionals are in a strong position to advance children's needs and rights within the wider community as they have a specialized knowledge of child growth and development and work at the interface with young children. For these reasons, they can act as a conduit for children's concerns and needs to be aired in contexts that many children and their families would not normally have access to, for example, legislators, government departments, and politicians. They are also in a strong position to promote these causes successfully by framing issues in terms of their relevance to children's short- and long-term development. In this way, they can help to influence public attitudes towards young children and the resources that will be allocated to them.

Advocacy requires early childhood professionals to step outside the safety of the early childhood setting to advance issues concerning young children. It further requires that we highlight the broader issues that impact on children's growth and development and the concerns that children and families bring with them into early childhood settings to a wider audience.

Networking with early childhood organizations

As an early childhood professional, it is important to find others who will help to sustain you in your work for equity with young children and families. There are many professional early childhood organizations across the world that you can draw on to add to the frameworks that you use in creating and reflecting on your teaching and learning. For example, European teachers who are involved with the organization Diversity in Early Childhood Education and Training (DECET) are committed to (www.decet.org/common_goals_en.html):

- nurturing each child's construction of a knowledgeable, confident self-concept and group identity;
- promoting each child's comfortable, empathetic interaction with people from diverse backgrounds;
- fostering each child's critical thinking about bias;
- cultivating each child's ability to stand up for himself or herself and for others in the face of bias.

Reflecting with families and children

> Professionalism is a double-edged sword that (1) could lead to a strengthening of position and increased respect, but (2) has more often resulted in increased domination by those in power.
>
> (Cannella 1997: 137)

The importance of early childhood professionals including families as 'partners' or 'collaborators' in their work, as we have noted, is a key tenet of many early childhood best practice programmes. However, the family's knowledge of the child has often been used to supplement the professional's 'specialized knowledge' rather than becoming the point from which the early childhood professional critically reflects on what is happening for the child (see Smith 2000; Campbell and Smith 2001). In addition, children have often remained the 'silent partners' in their education. Their voices have rarely been used to reflect on and critique early childhood theory and practice. More recently, however, researchers (for example, Hughes and Mac Naughton 1999, 2002; Mac Naughton and Smith 2001) are beginning to see the nexus between what is understood as 'professional knowledges' and 'family or child knowledges' as a site where innovation and change can occur in ways that challenge and disrupt early childhood theory and practices. In particular, these researchers are interested in changing whose voices are used to understand and respond to what is happening in the early childhood classroom.

There are some practical ways that you might use the children and families in your community to reflect on, challenge and change how you understand and practise as an early childhood professional. You might:

- include a question in the newsletter for families about an incident from the classroom that has troubled you and ask them to help you to decide what to do;
- use a persona doll story to present an incident to children, families and others and listen to the different issues that it raises for each person;
- use a journal to reflect on or share your dilemmas, questions and reflections about what is happening for and between children;
- use creative or expressive arts to represent and provoke a range of perspectives about a question or issue.

Professionalism as an 'ethics of care'

> [The early childhood professional:]
>
> - is at the forefront of the struggle for social justice and increased opportunity;
> - is a celebrator of diversity;
> - is unfaltering in attempts to hear and value (rather than construct) the multiple voices of those who are younger;
> - is a critical activist.
>
> (Cannella 2000b: 218)

Redefining the early childhood professional as a critical activist is a political act that involves making a commitment to socially just teaching and learning. However, there are many risks and dangers for the critical activist in planning a journey that takes you towards to the margins of your community. These include:

- creating dissent between families, children and teachers;
- censorship from other professionals;
- marginalizing or silencing views that are different to yours;
- losing your way or your impetus.

Careful thinking and planning with others will help you to meet the risks and dangers of critical activism and to celebrate the rewards of changes. What you need is a process that will help you to begin your journey, to make changes along the way to your understandings and practices, and to sustain your commitment to working for social justice.

Action research as a process of creating a professional activist for young children and families

> making the familiar seem strange.
>
> (Anderson and Herr 1999: 15)

Deciding where and how to begin your journey towards being a transformative professional is at times overwhelming. One way forward is to use established processes that help you to work with others for change in your community. Action research is one process that invites you as an early childhood professional on a journey with others to define and redefine theory, practice and professionalism in your early childhood classroom. For many early childhood professionals, action research is a way of looking again at the moments that are familiar or taken-for-granted and thinking about these moments differently. It is a systematic process of:

- locating an issue that troubles you as a teacher in your classroom;
- attempting to understand it theoretically, practically, and institutionally;
- taking action with others to transform inequities and injustices in how theory, practice and institutions play out for you, your children and your families.

Action research can help you and your community to unpack and reshape what is happening in your classroom, and then to share your work with other professionals and communities.

There are four cycles in action research that can be used to look at a specific moment, event or issue in your classroom. These are:

- reconnaissance;
- planning;

- acting; and
- reflecting critically.

Reconnaissance involves framing a question about what is happening in your community. It means you begin to ask questions and gather details about the broad issue that you have identified and how it has been understood by you and others. Your reconnaissance enables you to use the information that you gather to look a little more closely at what is problematic, troubling or exciting about this issue for your community.

When you have gathered sufficient information to refine your understanding of what is happening, you begin strategically to *plan for change*. These plans involve careful and considered discussion within your community about what changes are desirable, how these changes might be accomplished and what risks might be involved for people in the community in making a change.

Translating your plans into *actions* is often more challenging than you expect. You may find there are many unexpected outcomes of your change, and many issues that arise for individual people in your community that mean you will need to reconsider what you are doing. This is one reason why it is important to *document* what happens when you implement your change. Another reason for documenting your actions and their effects is to enable you to theorize and share your journey with others who might want to make changes in their community.

As you look at the data you collect about how the change has impacted on your community, you will find that you are inevitably involved in *critically reflecting* on what has happened and asking new questions about what has happened. This is an important step for rethinking what you and your community will do next. Ultimately, action research enables you to begin to unpack how theory, practice, people and institutions construct and are constructed by a 'regime of truth' that makes some changes possible for some people and not for others. If you are a professional who is committed to transforming early childhood education, this will continually bring you back to thinking about what the 'regime of truth' means to your work for social justice.

Issues you might use to begin a journey into action research with others
An early childhood professional shared one of the issues that troubled her.

CASE STUDY

Scientist, feminist or girlfriend

I had been sitting for some time with Kaarin (4 years) at the science table. She had shown a sustained interest in exploring and experimenting with a range of materials. However, her rich descriptions of mixing oil and water were interrupted when Mick (5 years) joined us at the science table and sat between us. For Kaarin, Mick's 'male' presence became a potential threat to being able to play with other girls like Fiona (4 years) later in the day:

Kaarin: I can't sit next to him because when Fiona comes she will think he's my boyfriend.
Sheralyn: No, I think she will think he's talking to me.
Kaarin: No! She always thinks that. [She picked up her chair and moved firstly to the far end of the table, but then quickly left to use the glass threading beads.]

I felt that the ways Kaarin understood and practised her gender and hetero-sexuality were limiting who she could play with, when and ultimately what forms of knowledge she could access. Instead of being a scientist or feminist, Kaarin potentially became Mick's girlfriend. While there were many aspects of this situation that I didn't understand and many dangers for Mick, Kaarin and myself in raising issues of gender and sexuality, I wanted to create opportunities for all children to play together at the science table. For me, this meant disrupting how gender and sexuality were operating for Kaarin and for Mick. Action research offered ways of:

- looking more broadly at what was happening in this and in other moments of learning for Mick, Kaarin and the other children;
- talking with others about how they saw gender and sexuality operating in our early childhood classroom and in other early childhood classrooms;
- finding out what researchers and theory said about how gender and sexuality are part of children's learning and relationships;
- looking at how broad social policy and specific early childhood service policies and practices were part of how gender and sexuality was constituted within the classroom;
- using this information to plan, document and reflect on a change that might create more socially just learning for Kaarin, Mick and others.

These are some possibilities for how I could use action research to explore this moment between Kaarin, Mick, myself and others.

Reconnaissance
This might involve:

- talking with Kaarin and Mick and other children, teachers and families about when girls and boys can sit together, what they can do together, what they can't do together;
- reading current research studies and literature about how gender and sexualities insert themselves into children's learning choices;
- asking questions about how policies in the early childhood service, QIAS, and government legislation talk about gender and sexualities;
- reflecting on how my own gendered and sexual intentions, practices and beliefs generate the questions that I have, and the ways in which Kaarin and Mick interacted.

Planning a change
This might involve:

- using a persona doll to replay and rewrite what happened between Mick, Kaarin, myself and others at the science table;
- grouping Fiona, Kaarin and Mick to work together at the science table with my support;
- placing bead threading and science at the same table;
- reflecting on the dangers and risks of change for Kaarin, for Mick, for Fiona and for myself.

Acting and documenting
This might involve:

- tapes of conversations between children, families, my colleagues and myself;
- written observations of what happened when I implemented changes;
- keeping a journal about these changes;
- video- or audio-taping moments in the classroom where the children, families and myself were involved in these changes;
- collecting and recording children's stories, dramatic play and storylines, and drawings;
- mapping continuities and changes in who is playing with whom, when, where and how.

Critically reflecting on the data of what happened
This might involve asking:

- How did our understandings, feelings, words and actions change or remain the same as a result of the changes?
- Who was advantaged and disadvantaged by what happened?
- What were the dangers, risks and opportunities for each person?
- What questions do you have about what happened from these reflections?

Equity reflections

Seeking multiple sources of knowledge and perspectives is ongoing
The international early childhood community in more recent times has drawn on a broad range of theories such as postmodernism, postcolonialism, futures studies and feminism to inform current thinking on children and how best to support their growth and development (Silin 1995; Cannella 1997; De Lair and Irwin 2000; Page 2000; Hughes and Mac Naughton 2001; Lubeck 2001; Mac Naughton, in Dau 2001; Moss 2001). You have met some of these theories in Parts 1 and 2. These theories have

served to highlight the multiple perspectives that can be employed in order to understand how children develop and learn, and how best to design curricula and teach in order to support and extend children (Lubeck 2001).

These perspectives have also highlighted the need for professionals to view the early childhood curriculum beyond the confines of a particular service and 'against the larger societal processes that shape and are shaped by it' (Silin 1995: 126). When you as a professional begin to address the broader social and political realities that inform and shape your values and practice, you will begin to assess your roles and responsibilities in working with young children and their families against a wider range of frameworks.

Further reading and online resources

Critical reflections on professionalism

Penn, H. (2000) Is working with young children a good job? in H. Penn (ed.) *Early Childhood Services: Theory Policy and Practice*, pp. 115–30. Buckingham: Open University Press.

Ryan, S. and Oschner, M. (1999) Traditional practices, new possibilities: transforming dominant images of early childhood teachers, *Australian Journal of Early Childhood*, 24(4): 14–20.

Sumison, J. (2002) Revisiting the challenge of staff recruitment and retention in children's services, *Australian Journal of Early Childhood*, 27(1): 8–13.

General professional resources and organizations

Association for Childhood Education International (ACEI): http://www.udel.edu/bateman/acei/

Convention on the Rights of the Child, Unesco: http:///www.Unicef.org/crc

Early childhood organizations online

Pacific region
Pacific Early Childhood Education Research Association: http://www.hept.himeji-tech.ac.jp/~ashida/PECERA/

Australia
Australian Early Childhood Association: http://www.aeca.org.au
Australian Federation of Childcare Associations (AFCCA): http://www.afcca.com.au
Australian Infant Child Adolescent Mental Health Association: http://www.aicafmha.net.au
Commonwealth Childcare Advisory Council: http://www.ccac.gov.au/
Creche and Kindergarten Association of Queensland: http://www.candk.org

North America
National Association for the Education of Young Children (NAEYC): http://www.naeyc.org

Canada
Canadian Association for Young Children: http://www.cayc.ca/

UK
British Assocation of Early Childhood Education: http://www.early-education.org.uk/

Singapore
Assocation for Early Childhood Educators Singapore: http://www.aeces.org/

New Zealand
New Zealand Childcare Assocation: http://www.nzchildcare.ac.nz/

Note
1   Koori is the preferred name for Australian South Coast Aboriginal groups.

14

Curriculum contexts: critical reflections

With Diana Hetherich, Patrick Hughes,
Jane Page and Sheralyn Campbell

This chapter offers you a number of specific resources through which to reflect critically on the differing views on how to approach the contexts of your work as a professional with children, their families and the wider community that you met in Chapters 11, 12 and 13. It uses a case study, Clarification exercises, Ideas summaries and Reflection sheets to support you to build your own approach to contextualizing your work with children, parents and yourself as a professional. The Reflection sheet about relationships in the early childhood setting provided at the end of the chapter is to assist you in furthering your thinking about relationships in early childhood.

Contextualizing the curriculum: futures education

Early childhood educators believe that the knowledge, skills and outlooks we impart to children will assist them to make the transition to school and later to the broader social contexts within which they will engage, as the following quotes from practitioners attest (from some unpublished research):

> Skills children acquire in early childhood form the basis of learning and attitudes to learning which influence the rest of their formal education.

> We are hopefully preparing children for life: their self-esteem, their ability to fit into community and school life and to cope with day to day living.

> We need to prepare children and help them to gain the skills necessary to be a part of society and to help them develop and grow personally.

> You are providing them with every opportunity for growth and [the] ability to cope positively in the world.

Professionals can work towards this goal within their understandings of child growth and development. If we wish to understand the full complexity of this task, however, we also need to look beyond the traditional frameworks often employed in our teaching. For example, research on youth attitudes on the future can help us to appreciate the broader social, economic, cultural and political issues that inform children's ideas and understandings about themselves and the world from a very young age (Page 2000). Take, for example, the following quotation:

> There will be more street fighting, more colour gangs, bigger gangs, more street deaths. Life will be three times more dangerous than now . . . Hoping that it won't happen but it will . . . People –such as pollies, big nobs –live in rose-coloured worlds and won't change. They won't take notice of kids.
>
> (Ann, in Hutchinson 1996: 75)

Considering the pessimism that frames this kind of comment can help us to appreciate the importance of our roles as early childhood professionals in counteracting this negativity by fostering the development of positive values, attitudes and knowledge in the early childhood years.

Further to this, the discipline of futures studies provides additional frameworks that assist us to define more clearly the specific attitudes, thinking abilities and outlooks that will help children to deal with the complexities of modern life now and in the future. These frameworks address issues such as the nature of change, the relationship between the past, present and future, the importance of developing foresight, critical thinking skills and an ability to interpret symbols.

Reflection points

- How do the contemporary contexts of children's lives offer challenges for your work as an early childhood educator?
- How do the contemporary contexts of children's lives offer you possibilities for enriching your work as an early childhood educator?
- Can developmental knowledge of the child help you in the challenges you face?
- What other knowledge might help you enrich your work with young children?

Rethinking curriculum and its contexts

Read the following case study. An early childhood educator, Diana Hetherich, who has been reflecting critically on her approach to working with children, their families and their wider community has written the case study. It explores the links between the educator's reflection on her knowledge, her relationships with parents and her relationships with children in her centre. Once you have read the case study, reflect on it using the following questions:

- How does this educator engage in critical reflection on how parents are understood as contributors to her curriculum?
- How does this educator attempt to bring the wider community into her curriculum?

- Do you have similar ideas or stories you could tell and use to reflect critically on your own approaches to working with communities?

- What are the challenges faced by this educator in continuing her journey in building learning communities as part of her curriculum?

- Which theorists' ideas of relationships with children, parents, the wider community and herself as a professional do you see traces of in her case study?

CASE STUDY

Bringing diversity into the curriculum community

(*Diana Hetherich, early childhood educator, Victoria, Australia*)

> After a good night sleep the boys woke up at 6.00am. I found Morgan feeding Ngurung chocolate custard and milk. They watched ABC shows then switched to watch *Pokemon*. Morgan fed Ngurung some baby cereal and burbed [sic] him. He should have a full belly for the morning. We dressed him. Then we all left for kinder. It was a great pleasure having Ngurung in our home. We hope he continues to enjoy his visits and have a lot to report home. He was an excellent baby and Morgan was an excellent carer. At least I know Morgan has been paying attention to his Mother when looking after his sister and getting a few tips on caring for babies.
>
> (*Ngurung*, Book 1 (2000))

Each year in my centre we have an additional member enter the kindergarten group. We don't know who it will be or what form it will take from year to year, or even what will result from their entry into the group. In 2000, I used dolls as a way of teaching children about another culture, one that was unfamiliar to both myself and them. I was spurred on to try this from my participation in a research project about reconceptualizing the inclusion of Indigenous culture in the early childhood curriculum. Each participant was encouraged to challenge their beliefs and understandings about Indigenous Australians and to consider how they might include this new knowledge in reconceptualizing their curriculum.

Why this pathway?
There were many contributing factors which led me to use dolls as a teaching tool, not the least of which was the experience in 1999 of sending home a mouse puppet as part of a whole group socialization activity. This idea did not just appear to me fully formed – it came to me from a number of different sources that arrived together in a productive mix at one time. What happened was that the many converging influences came together when I decided to trial the dolls. One critical experience, early in my teaching career, was attending a professional development workshop which was strongly critical of the 'Tourist Approach' (Bredekamp and Copple 1997: 131) for teaching children about other cultures. Much of my early teaching experience was in centres with largely monocultural groups of children and parents with similar socio-economic

backgrounds. I did not have much confidence in myself and my knowledge of other cultures, so when I saw and heard that the 'Tourist Approach' was not a good way to teach children, I simply avoided programming for cultural inclusivity, at all, for many years! When teaching interstate, I found myself working for a bureaucracy with differing expectations and a completely different emphasis to what I had been familiar with. I also found myself in a centre with a large population from NESB (a Non-English Speaking Background), which included children from Indigenous families. Ignoring the cultural backgrounds of these children and families was no longer possible and I was challenged to develop a program that was culturally appropriate and inclusive. I believe that I did try to achieve this with some measure of success, however, the program was not inclusive of the perspectives of Indigenous Australians. During this time, I attended another professional development session where the concept of persona dolls was presented.

> Persona dolls have been used within the anti-racist curriculum to expose children to social, cultural and/or physical diversity. The dolls have a 'story' that provides them with their own unique identity or 'persona'. They are used in conjunction with storytelling to explore equity issues with children and promote joint problem-solving of equity issues the dolls may face.
>
> (Mac Naughton and Davis 2001: 84)

Around the same time, a colleague passed on some photocopied material from the UK which promoted literacy development in school aged children through the taking home of a teddy bear, complete with case, personal belongings and a diary for children to record information about the visit. It looked interesting, but I was unsure as to how I could do this kind of activity. It seemed to be developmentally inappropriate given that it is known that children 'show difficulty sharing . . . but begin to understand turntaking . . . in small groups' (Bredekamp and Copple 1997: 117). As well, I knew that they could not write in the book and their drawings would be mostly made up of scribble – they would have to rely on an older person to do this for them and then it would not be their work anymore leading to 'feelings of inadequacy and stress' (Bredekamp and Copple 1997: 104) which would be detrimental to the children. Also, a common view is that their concentration span is limited and they would quickly lose interest in such a long-term project – the novelty would wear off (New 1994b). How wrong I was!

I put this information aside, with no intention of doing anything with it, but the ideas remained in my thoughts, especially those about new ways of teaching. One day I found myself in a puppet shop with fantastic puppets. Not being confident in using puppets, I had no intention of purchasing one until the shop owner convinced me that children respond really well to a particular puppet – a mouse! I bought it wondering what I would do with it and had I wasted my money? As I introduced it to the children they were instantly taken with it and wanted to include it in their play. There were the inevitable disputes – one puppet for 28 children – but they seemed to cope and were content to share this special item. However, because of my concern that they might not get an equal opportunity to experiment with this puppet, I decided we would try sending it home, allowing children opportunity and time to play with it by themselves and really explore puppetry. The results were certainly unexpected and far surpassed my expectations and imagined outcomes! It was this which gave me confidence to try using dolls, giving them a persona, to teach the children about Indigenous Australians.

As part of the research project I was involved with, I became concerned with the prevailing dominant view of Indigenous Australians, that is, that they are poor, primitive people, 'the other', and lesser than the dominant Anglo-European culture (Cannella 1997, 1999), and the impact of this view on children learning about Indigenous Australians. 'Othering' is a concept to describe how we position ourselves in relation to other groups of people as being different and distinct from us. This can occur in many situations including the parent–teacher relationship or the teacher–child relationship. We may construct ourselves as superior, or more expert, and simultaneously construct the 'other' as deficit in the relationship (Cannella 1999; Hughes and Mac Naughton 1999). This was a view I did not want to perpetuate in my work with children and parents.

What issues did I need to explore?
In selecting dolls for my project, there was a need to find dolls that were accessible and to dress them in regular clothing so that they could be introduced to the children as something familiar and recognizable. I decided to purchase Aboriginal dolls, but finding the right doll was difficult. Many of the dolls I was shown were hard, unattractive and seemed to be almost caricatures of Indigenous Australians. I knew that the dolls had to be attractive and cuddly for the children and families to accept them, so that the project would have the greatest chance of success. I finally found some dolls by accident that were soft plastic, had the familiar, powdery smell of a 'real' baby, were cuddly, and had realistic faces with Aboriginal features. I also made the choice to have dolls with light brown skin colouring rather than the dark brown skin colouring because the Koories in our local community were not dark skinned. I also felt that these would be less 'confronting' for both children and families after judging the reaction to the dark skinned dolls by my co-worker. I was concerned that this skin choice might offend the Koories I would be working with, but they agreed with my choice and the reasoning behind it. As I wanted the dolls to be seen as no different to the children in the group, I selected 'Baby Born' clothes so that they were presented to the children in contemporary ways, rather than reinforcing a traditional style of dress for Indigenous Australians. It might be argued that I made them fit the dominant culture and I was not emphasizing the importance of their own culture – I wanted them to be like me as an Anglo-Australian (Cannella 1997). However, this was not my intent. I wanted to portray the dolls as similar to the Koories that I knew and I hoped that this would be the view that I could put across to the children and families.

I needed real stories and families in order to create the doll's personas/stories. I could have read books and used my understandings to create stories for the dolls as others have done (Hanley 1995), but I felt that it was important to get their stories from Indigenous Australians. It seemed important to ask and find out about their story and life. I did not want to be like those who found Victor, the wild child, yet never asked about his life in the woods as they set about changing him (Cannella 1997). I sought assistance from many people. Finally I came into contact with a family that was prepared to let me use their children's names and their family details as a way of developing the stories behind the dolls and introducing the dolls to the children. This gave meaning and context to the dolls.

What happened with the children and their families?
The children instantly connected with these two dolls (there was one for each group of 28 children). Initially, introducing them caused some laughter. The children found their names (Ngurung-aeta and Karla-ngarra) strange and funny-sounding and they were unfamiliar with the terms 'Koori', 'Aboriginal' and 'tribe'. But this did not stop them from wanting to take them home. One boy, at first, said he didn't want to take the doll home, which I said was fine, he would not have to, but only a few days later he was begging to have his turn! They were also very quick at working out that the best day to have their turn was the last session for the week as they then had the doll home for the weekend! These dolls were, in turn, loved by not only the children, but siblings, families and even extended families. Participation was possible for *all* and all children desired to be a participant, regardless of language, ability, gender and culture (Atwater *et al.* 1994). Each had a turn. Only a couple of families did not write in the book and it seemed to be those families from non-English speaking backgrounds who had limited access to support with the English language (since then, I have made use of the interpreter available to explain to families about the concept and what is required and participation is now 100 per cent). Most families took what seemed to be a lot of time and effort to write, draw and place photographs in the books and it never seemed to become competitive between families. What I did find, though, was that when I showed these books to other colleagues, they would often make comments like, 'But a 4-year-old could never have drawn that', which had the effect of making me feel as if I was doing the wrong thing. But then I thought, 'So what? Surely the fact that someone from the family had sat down with the child and together constructed and presented their "story" had just as much importance and value?'

For the first ten weeks (how long it took for the doll to visit each child at home), not much information was provided to the children about Indigenous Australians other than what follows:

Hello,

My name is Ngurung-aeta (pronounce jurrun gaita)/*Karla-ngarra (pronounced Karla-nuhgurra)*. I am Koorie (Aboriginal – Indigenous Australian) and I am from the Gunditjmara people. My name is a Gunditjmara word which means: 'The wise or head man of the tribe'/*'Fire (Karla) Dance (ngarra)'*. I have a Mum who is Aboriginal from a tribe in NSW near Byron Bay. My Mum's tribe is Arakwal people. My Dad is from the Gunditjmara people. I have 1/2 brother(s) and 4/3 sisters and 1 cat.

I am very excited that I am coming to stay at your house.

I will enjoy having something to eat with you. I like to pretend I eat all kinds of foods and like to try new things.

I will enjoy meeting your family, playing with your toys and other friends. I even like going to the shops or the park. You can take my photo or draw a picture in my book (please record and date what I did at your house in my book so I can share it with the other children).

Before I go to bed, please wash me with a face washer and don't forget to brush my teeth. (I don't think I should go in the bath, although I would love it, as I might get wet inside.) I like to be cuddled when we have a story and I would like to go to bed at 8.00pm, or earlier, as I do get very tired from my busy days.

I know you will take good care of me,

From Ngurung-aeta/*Karla-ngarra*.

It was purely an introductory time of getting to know the dolls and each other (through the diaries) and for families to get used to this process, which was unfamiliar to them.

After each child had had their first turn, the dolls had holidays! They spent a week with me where I was able to share details of my home life with the children and families – to reciprocate some of the private details that families revealed about themselves to the group through my entries in the diary.

Again not much happened for us today. Geoff went to work, Diana slept in, but not for too long, and then did, you guessed it – more washing!!!! (And, of course, more ironing!). She also cleaned the house and then spent most of the afternoon working in the study on the top floor, doing all kinds of things for the kindergarten – the program, newsletter, committee report, PSQA report, emails – it was all really quite boring for us, but she seemed very happy about it all. She made lots of phone calls to organise buses and things for excursions – it looks as if we shall have a busy term with lots of fun things planned for us to do

(Karla's Holiday Book 2000)

I found that sharing aspects of my life with parents was really important. They responded extremely positively to my stories where I revealed myself and I feel that they felt they came to know me a bit more.

The dolls then went and spent time with their *real* family (who provided the initial identities and stories). This family included the dolls in their family life, took photos, wrote up a diary and presented it back to our children in the centre. Included in this was information about Indigenous culture which introduced the children to concepts such as Elders, responsibility for the land, Koori Children's Day, traditional dance, Indigenous art, the Aboriginal flag and colours, and what the colours mean to Indigenous Australians.

That night, at home, Uncle Norm came for dinner and he gave me lots of cuddles. Uncle Norm is Aunty Delta's brother and he explained that they are from the 'Arakwal' people who are part of a larger tribe called the 'Bundjalong Nation'. They come from Byron Bay (see the photo) and there is a photo of the elders too. They are the custodians of Byron Bay. The lady in the purple top is Aunty Delta's Nan and her name is Linda, all the other women are Aunty Delta's Aunties (it's not as confusing as it seems!). They have a totem and their totem is the dolphin. That means they must never harm their totem. I was very impressed to learn all this stuff about my family and Aboriginal people. I have a lot more to learn though.

(Karla's Holiday Book 2000)

The dolls were returned with presents of clap sticks, made by local Koories, Koori headbands and a necklace and Aboriginal Flag badges.

The dolls went home for a second time with each child, this time with a second book containing all the information as well as all the artefacts and a Dreamtime story book, *How the birds got their colours*, to allow children and families the opportunity to look at and discuss the importance or significance of these real objects in a meaningful context. They also went home with a second letter.

Hello,

Last time I visited your house, I had so much fun playing and doing special things. Thank you for that.

Today I have brought a special 'Dreamtime' story for us to read. I hope someone will be able to read it to you, if you can't read it yourself. It's called *How the birds got their colours*. I read it in a bookstore called Readers Feast.

When I was on holidays, I was given some clap sticks which were made in Victoria by some Koorie people, and I've got a special badge of the Aboriginal Flag. Please read my holiday book to find out about it. You can also look through my old book and read all my adventures.

Please draw more pictures, and write what we do in my book, as I really like that. I like to go out too!

I hope we have lots more fun.

From Ngurung-aeta/*Karla-ngarra*.

Through the information and artefacts that were returned with the dolls, children and families were challenged to rethink their ideas of a globalized childhood and its universal truths (Cannella 1997). Children were introduced to new concepts including: speaking about adults in a different way, respecting certain adults as Elders, charged with the responsibility to care for the land through the symbol of a totem. Children, families and staff were introduced to new and non-universal ways of thinking about the world in which we all live. I had wanted the children to get an understanding about children around the country and around the world having similarities as well as differences, such as the Dreamtime and the connection with the land being of vital importance for Indigenous Australians, something I still don't fully understand myself. Although Karla and Ngurung were in many ways similar to the children in the centre as shown to them through stories and photos of the dolls, provided by the Indigenous family of the family at McDonalds, going grocery shopping, playing Playstation and going to daycare – there were also some differences. Those differences included marching for NAIDOC week, seeing Indigenous art, observing traditional dance, as well as different words to talk about common events such as 'Kooni' (pooh).

Simultaneously, in the centre, the children were involved in many more learning experiences that increased their knowledge and understandings of Indigenous Australians and their culture. This ranged from reading a variety of books, making Johnny Cakes, watching an Indigenous Australian perform traditional dance (and being involved with those dances when invited) and experimenting with Indigenous art techniques and symbols. These activities, when first considered, might be seen to follow the 'Tourist Approach', but because they happened in the teaching of the doll's stories, they had contextual meaning and relevance for the children. I, along with the children and families, had limited knowledge of Indigenous cultures, but together, with the support of the Indigenous family who had given names and stories to the dolls, we learnt more about those cultures.

Importantly, there was a shift in the notion of me as a teacher having and imparting the knowledge, and therefore the power, which works to 'other' not only children, but also the parents (Lubeck 1994). Learning together was no longer occurring in the usual hierarchical, linear way, where adults have more knowledge and power simply because they are older (Cannella 1997). By sharing the dolls' stories and constructing them, with each other, and myself, all stakeholders/participants were placed on a more equal footing, able to choose information to share.

I could not control what was written in the book, what was done with the dolls, what the families and children did. I hoped that they would use the books and accompanying information to learn more about Indigenous Australians – but they might not. Families did many different things with the dolls. Some did use the small amount of information included in the doll's story to increase and extend their own and their child's knowledge and information about Indigenous Australians:

> Today Ngurung came to Jessica's house. Jessica had some friends come over for a play. All afternoon Jessica, Joshua, Stephanie and Emily played with Jessica's toys. But Ngurung got tired so he had a rest in the cot of Jessica's baby Nellie. When he awoke he felt much better so he helped the kids pack away all the toys. Then he waved goodbye to Jessica's friends before coming inside to warm up and watch a little TV. Once everyone had had a bath Ngurung had some tea. Ngurung had mashed baby food and a bottle of milk. Before bed we read some stories about Aboriginal children and looked up Byron Bay on the map to see where Ngurung's mum was from.
>
> (*Ngurung* Book 1 (2000))

Other families shared their own cultural background and food preferences with the doll and thereby with the rest of the group:

> Today, Cindy brought Ngurung home with her on Tuesday 23th [sic] May. First she gave him a bottle of milk, then had a bath with Ngurung and changed his nappy. After that we all went to St Albans Market for a while, and when we came home, we had dinner with Ngurung, he was very much enjoying the Chinese food. After dinner we watched a little TV and read a story to Ngurung. At 8: pm [sic] it was bed time. Cindy got ready to go bed with Ngurung and washed him with a face washer and brushed his teeth and they both went to bed. It has been lots of fun with Ngurung. Thankyou for visited us, Cindy and family.
>
> (*Ngurung* Book 1 (2000))

Families developed an interest in finding out what other families did with the dolls. I think it developed a sense of community – one family shared the fact that their recently born child had a disability and were going to be involved in a special education programme with him:

> Welcome again Ngurung-aeta. You've come to spend yet another night with us. This will be the last time you spend in our home – enjoy! Joshua again is glad to have you over. Today is a busy day, lots to do, so I hope you have fun. Firstly we have to take Joshua's baby brother, Tyler, to the doctor for his immunization. Joshua reassures his brother during this time . . . Tomorrow morning [Wednesday] we are going to visit Tyler's 'special school' for next year. Joshua's excited to see this 'school' (more like a kinder for babies). You will come with us. I'm sure all the children there would love to meet you. From there we will be going straight to kinder and you will be going to another loving home for a visit
>
> (*Ngurung* Book 3 (2000))

Another family shared their particular cultural background (told through Karla's own words):

> Finally the day had arrived for me to go visit Kaajal's family. I could tell by the look on Kaajal's face that she couldn't wait till kinder was over so that she could take me home. I was also excited and a bit nervous as well, not knowing what kind of reception I would get at Kaajal's. Our long wait was over when Kaajal's Dad (Monte) came to pick us up at 4pm. Kaajal introduced me to her father and off we went. I was a bit shy at first but as we got talking, I got relaxed and comfortable. In the car I sat with Kaajal and Monte drove off to Footscray to pick up Kaajal's little brother, Karan, from the carer's. It took about 30 minutes to get there and the ride was fantastic because Monte had some Indian [sic] music playing in the car all the way. Kaajal was singing along and I hummed along with Kaajal even though the songs didn't make any sense to me. We picked up Karan and came back to . . . Kaajal's place . . .
>
> (*Karla* Book 1 (2000))

To complete and bring closure to the project, we collated all the information from the four books and created a 'story' entitled, *Ngurung's/Karla's Adventures*. These were illustrated by a local artist and then professionally printed in a small book form. Each child received a copy of the book at the end of the kindergarten year. Families were enthusiastic about the books and pleased that the work they had put into the stories came to be recorded in a form they could keep.

Some concluding reflections

I did not set out to build a dialogue about Indigenous cultures with parents of the children in my service, children in the service and Indigenous families. It evolved. What continues now is not that specific conversation but a deep interest in relationships between teachers, parents and children in building curriculum.

Initially in my work as a teacher, I had great relationships with the children, but my interactions with parents were very poor. It was only through growing older and experiencing more of life that these interactions improved and more genuine relationships developed. Through this improvement I began to realize the importance and value of parents in my work and I began to fear parents less. I could feel that a sense of community was developing through the genuine involvement of parents in the programme. The parents made it quite clear that they did not feel their role was in the setting of goals for the curriculum, rather they wanted to be welcome to contribute ideas and resources to enhance and extend the program as they understood it. Through my changing relationships with parents I came to know and understand individual children, their needs and quirks and I felt that finally I was achieving more authentic relationships.

There are also many other things that I do now that support the development of communities in my curriculum. At the start of each term I provide each family with a broad outline of the focus we plan to investigate and some ideas on how we might achieve or work through the investigation. By doing this I have found that parents are able to consider and contribute their own ideas which develop the program further through including their ideas. For example, when a father who is also an artist came in and drew for the children, explaining techniques, colours, light, dark, shadows, shape, form and line, the children were fascinated and were later inspired to attempt shading in their own drawings. He returned later in the year and drew again, and the children were recalling his previous visit, much of what he had said and again were inspired to draw. We displayed their drawings and when he came to collect his child and saw them on display, he was visibly pleased to think his 'small' contribution had made such an impact.

My frequent newsletters contain information about the programme, requests for junk materials and information about special events, but also they share and acknowledge the celebrations and sorrows of others within our community. We celebrate the births of children to families in the kindergarten, we offer condolences to families who are grieving over the death of a special person, and we thank individuals and families for their contributions of resources, ideas and assistance. I open myself up and reveal myself so that they may be able to understand me, who I am and how I think. For instance, they know which football team I support and they use the books of the dolls to tease and have fun, taking photos of the dolls in clothing from other football teams, including the words to the team song and so on.

I make myself available to visit children and families in the home when invited. I used to have a plan but with the past few years of experience, I go without expectations and let the visit just unfold as the personalities of child, parent and teacher allow! Sometimes I am busy attempting to master a game on Playstation, other times I am involved in deep and meaningful educational conversations with parents.

Sadly I feel utterly drained from this – building communities and relationships is hard work on top of everything else that has to be done as a teacher/director. It takes time as well as physical and emotional energy, so I understand why some teachers are reluctant to do such things. I continue to do it because I find it incredibly rewarding, but can I sustain it? Would it help if I only taught no more than 30 children a week instead of the current 76? Would it help if I worked with another trained teacher so the load of 76 could be shared? (I believe that it is unfair to expect an untrained assistant on low pay to do all this.)

So what can be done to ensure that appropriate resources are available to educators to build and develop authentic relationships with parents and build meaningful curriculum communities? My hope for those reading this case study is that they will take aspects of it that make sense for the community in which they find themselves and the resources they have available to them.

Reflecting on where you are now: in the community as an early childhood professional

The combination of respect for children's families, ability to listen to both children and their parents, and the use of learning projects that actively involve and empower children can go far in helping future teachers find 'promise' even in the most desolate 'inner city' landscapes because they engage as allies with young excited learners.

(Blue Swadner 2000: 132)

It is clear that it will be crucial for the field to continue to critically analyze how privileged ones and more powerful elements have influenced the direction of the field toward the scientific-driven epistemologies and the sacred Western lens. Who stands to benefit from the overreliance on Western ways of seeing the world? Why has it been so difficult for the field to examine the Western canon? Where are our ethical concerns?

(Diaz Soto 2000: 200)

Having clarified 'where you are' and 'where you could go' in relation to your positions on your relationships with key participants in the early childhood curriculum, the third step is to reflect critically on these ideas and their implications for your work. You are now invited to reflect critically on your position on the place of children, parents, the wider community and your own professional knowledge base in your curriculum:

- Are there any particular thinkers that you share core ideas with about the place of parents and the wider community in the early childhood curriculum?
- Which thinkers did you share least in common with about the possible roles for children, parents, the wider community and your own professional knowledge in the curriculum?
- To what extent is your current position on how best to contextualize the early childhood curriculum linked with a conforming, reforming, or transforming position on being a professional?
- Whose interests does your position benefit?

Reflection sheet 14.1 links these questions with the ones that we began this chapter with to help you to critically reflect on your position on the role of early childhood services in society.

Reflection sheet 14.1 Critically reflecting on the role of knowledge–power relationships in the early childhood curriculum

Reflection questions	My ideas	Thinkers whose ideas I share
What do I want for my relationships with parents?		
What do I want for my relationships with children?		
What do I want for my relationships with myself as a professional?		
What do I want for my relationships with the wider community?		
Is my position conforming, reforming or transforming?		
Equity implications – whose interests does my position benefit?		

Ideas clarification exercises 14.1 Some simple starting points to building a philosophy on knowledge–power relationships in early childhood curriculum

Review the ideas in the chapters in Part 3 and then attempt one or more of the following tasks to help you to 'get started' on developing your relationship positions:

1 Create a 'Questions' and 'I believe' board. You can do this alone or with colleagues. Generate a set of questions that you would like addressed in your individual, centre or staff group's position on knowledge–power relationships in the curriculum. People can then be invited to make an 'I believe' statement in

response to the question. These can then be used to write a summary for discussion.

2   Write a story of an ideal set of knowledge–power relations between you as an early childhood educator and your local community. Use Diana's story to help you in this process. What does your story say about what you believe knowledge–power relationships should look like in early childhood programmes?

3   Reflect on the following question: what do you see now as the main reasons for community building in early childhood settings?

4   Generate a metaphor. Try to find a metaphor that captures how you and/or your team see your work with parents. Then play with and extend the metaphor through words, poems, images and sounds to build a 'picture' of your position on knowledge–power relations with parents.

5   Read the statements in Ideas gallery 14.1 about knowledge–power relationships in the early childhood curriculum. Once you have read the statements reflect on them using the following questions: what position on knowledge–power relations between staff, parents, children and/or the early childhood profession is implied in each statement? What is similar and what is different between these position statements and the key ideas within your own?

Ideas gallery 14.1 Statements on knowledge–power relations in early childhood

From a USA early childhood scholar:

'The lingering question for us is how issues of power have affected the politics of early childhood education. Abundant evidence indicates that decades of Western ways of early childhood eduction have not led us to a safe and peaceful society. Is there knowledge and wisdom that we can gain from the other, from the feminist, from the critical?.' (Diaz Soto 2000: 201)

From an Australian text on ethics in early childhood:

'Justice is about taking decisions that are fair to others and promote common interests. Justice depends on the benefits and disadvantages of decisions being spread across others equitably on the basis of effort or merit, including reference to issues about diversity and disadvantage in the community.' (Newman and Pollintz 2002: 9)

From an article about Brazilian education:

'According to Freire (1970) education is not politically netural: it is directly related to societal organisation and structural reproduction. Educators must always face the challenge of redefining their insights.' (Rossato 2001: 369)

From an article about early education in refugee camps in Thailand:

'The . . . teachers share the students' culture. This local connection has the following benefits: the program conforms to the culture's interpersonal norms; the teachers are themselves familiar with local traditions, songs, games, and dances, and will be able to add them to the program; students' trust and resilience is buoyed by ongoing relationships with supportive teachers; and the program benefits spill over to other areas of the community.' (Tillman 2001)

At this point, you may want to review your initial beliefs and values about knowledge–power relationships in the early childhood curriculum.

Change occurs because we do something new, think differently and plan to go beyond what we already do and know. The following reflective questions build on the questions you have already faced in this chapter and in Chapters 12 and 13.

- What hopes and visions for community building in early childhood settings will guide your actions?
- What research and thinking might help you to enact your hopes and visions?
- What policy support will help you to enact your hopes and visions?
- To what extent do you know other practitioners who can and do share your hopes and visions?
- What are the issues you currently face or think you might face in enacting your visions and hopes for community building in early childhood settings?
- What are the challenges that you feel will confront you enacting your visions and hopes for community building in early childhood settings?
- What are three promising practices you could 'test out' to begin enacting your visions and hopes for community building in early childhood settings?

Ideas gallery 14.1 offers some ways to reflect critically on how to build equitable relationships between yourself and the family and community contexts in which you work.

Equity and knowledge–power relationships in early childhood communities

In Reflection sheet 14.2, Equity and knowledge–power relationships in early childhood communities, you will find ideas gathered as follows:

- Questions for beginning community building.
- Questions for reflection on equity issues in your community.
- Some final inspirations for reflection about the contexts of early childhood education and its knowledge base.

Reflection sheet 14.2 Equity and knowledge–power relationships in early childhood communities

Questions for beginning community building

The following reflective questions will help you to build an early childhood curriculum–based community. Action planning:

- What is one small step you could take in your current position to form an equitable early childhood curriculum community?
- What support will you need in taking this action?
- Who will you need to involve?

- How will you involve them?
- How and who will you document what happens?
- How will you check the effects of your actions on others?

Questions for reflection on equity issues in your community

Questions that may help you and others in your community to think again about issues that you face in the daily life of your community include:

Gender
- What do researchers and theorists say about how children understand and practise gender? What are the similarities and differences that you see between what is said and what is happening in your classroom?
- Where and how do boys and girls play together, or apart?
- How do boys and girls challenge and resist gendered stereotypes, gender bias and gendered practices?

Culture and 'race'
- What do researchers and theorists say about how children understand and practise meanings of culture and 'race'? What are the similarities and differences that you see between what is said and what is happening in your classroom?
- Are there 'racist' statements used by children or teachers to influence who is able to play in a group, and who is not?
- How is your culture and 'race' part of the way that you understand and practise yourself, as a teacher?

Sexualities
- What do researchers and theorists say about how children understand and practise sexuality? What are the similarities and differences that you see between what is said and what is happening in your classroom?
- What policies does the centre or organization have in place to ensure that there is no discrimination linked with different sexualities?
- How are different sexualities presented and portrayed in children's stories and other visual arts used in the centre or organization?

Class
- What do researchers and theorists say about how children understand and practise wealth and status? What are the similarities and differences that you see between what is said and what is happening in your classroom?
- What commodities do children desire, value and use in their dramatic play?
- Who has access to knowledge about these commodities, and who does not?

Age
- What do researchers and theorists say about how children understand and practise age? What are the similarities and differences that you see between what is said and what is happening in your classroom?
- In what ways do children, teachers and families talk about the very young and the elderly?
- How has the early childhood service invited and valued the contributions of the very young and the elderly in the daily programme?

Some final inspirations for reflection about contexts of early childhood education and its knowledge base

---

Ideas gallery 14.2 Reflections on contexts of early childhood

From UK and Australian writing on identity and diversity in the early years:

'Parents are not a homogeneous group and can therefore hold different culturally conceived ideas about the role of education and the teacher. . . . It is sensible for staff not to make assumptions about parents' knowledge, beliefs or experiences but to create a friendly atmosphere where parents can talk openly about their experiences and feelings.' (Siraj-Blatchford and Clarke 2000: 105)

From Brazialian educator, Anna:

'A child is like a plant inside a room [that] turns around to face and embrace the sunlight, as the sun is crucial for its revitalization, survival and growth. By the same token, a child may feel connected or disconnected from the learning experience, depending on the pedagogical approaches used.' (Friere, in Rossato 2001: 369)

From a USA writing on sexuality in the early years:

'Although schools cannot change a sex-phobic society, they can place questions of the body in the context of a curriculum that values multiple ways of knowing the world. And moral panics can been seen for what they are, obsessions with our own repressed sexuality.' (Silin 1997: 232)

From an article on peace building in South Africa:

'Cultural knowledge is a key resource in both the creation and development of peacebuilding models and must be appropriate to a given setting. This respect for cultural knowledge embraces the indigenous knowledge of participants, their ways of being and doing, their immediate situation, past heritage, and language.' (McKay and Rey 2001: 229)

From an article about an early childhood centre in New Zealand:

'Our project is truly a community affair. Two years ago the Rockdale Park Kindergarten . . . approached the Invercargill Licensing Trust to see if some of its land could be used to extend our playground . . . They were very generous and we were soon on our way to having an extra 1002 sq. m. The focus of turning the additional land into a viable and environmentally useful garden has been enthusiastically supported by our local community groups, the families and the *whanau*, and the children of the kindergarten. The principles and strands of *Te Whāriki*, the early childhood curriculum, has been the focus behind children's involvement and provided a rich dimension for their learning.' (Hayward and Sycamore 1999: 41)

From a USA early childhood scholar:

'When educators rely on psychologies for their knowledge base, they may be avoiding difficult philosophical and social issues while believing themselves to be acting in a "professional" manner. They may also be succumbing to a subtle, but nonetheless potent, form of technical-mindedness because they are taking educational decision making out of the realm of moral and political consideration, where it more properly belongs.' (Silin 1995: 92)

From a US early childhood text:

'Basing the curriculum on an in-depth understanding of child development and learning is often referred to as developmentally appropriate practice. Rather than focusing first on what is to be learned, in a developmentally appropriate classroom, the teacher begins by working hard to understand the developmental abilities of his class and then makes decisions about what should be taught. This philosophical approach to teaching and learning is at the heart of most early childhood classrooms.' (Henniger 1999: 80)

From French research on play in early childhood:

'Providing children with early opportunities for a meeting of minds with others . . . both adults and peers, favours the development of a sense of togetherness and a feeling of belonging in a community. More generally, it favours a blossoming of young children and presumably contributes to preventing learning difficulties and early forms of social exclusion.' (Rayna 2001: 114–15)

Further reading and online resources

Critical reflections on being a contextualized professional

Dahlberg, G., Moss, P. and Pence, A. (1999) *Beyond Quality in Early Childhood Education and Care: Postmodern Perspectives*, chapter 6. London: Falmer Press.

Jones, E. and Nimmo, J. (1999) Collaboration, conflict and change: thoughts on education as collaboration, *Young Children*, 54(1): 5–11.

Lubeck, S. and Post, J. (2000) Creating a Head Start community of practice, in L. Soto Diaz (ed.) *The Politics of Early Childhood Education*, pp. 33–58. New York: Peter Lang Publishers.

Newman, L. and Pollnitz, L. (2002) *Ethics in Action: Introducing the Ethical Response Cycle*. Canberra: Australian Early Childhood Association.

Sumison, J. (2002) Revisiting the challenge of staff recruitment and retention in children's services, *Australian Journal of Early Childhood*, 27(1): 8–13.

Tobin, J. (ed.) (1999) *Making a Place for Pleasure in Early Childhood Education*. New Haven: Yale University Press.

Whalley, M. and the Pen Green Team (2001) *Involving Parents in their Children's Learning*. London: Sage Publications.

Yanez, L. and Moreno de Yanez, A. (2001) Young children, communities and learning – a model for the public management of childhood programmes built upon local strengths and diversities, in T. David (ed.) *Promoting Evidence-based Practice in Early Childhood Education: Research and Its Implications: Advances in Applied Early Childhood Education*, Vol. 1, pp. 43–75. Oxford: Elsevier Science.

References

Aaron, R.I. (1971) *John Locke*. Oxford: Oxford University Press.

Aboud, F. and Doyle, A. (1996) Does talk of race foster prejudice or tolerance in children? *Canadian Journal of Behavioural Science*, 28(3): 161–70.

ACSA (Australian Curriculum Studies Association) (1995) Early childhood curriculum and teaching: an Australian Curriculum Studies Association policy statement, *Curriculum Perspectives*, 15(2): 53–4.

Aguado, T. and Jimenez Frias, R. (1999) Early childhood education: research in Spain, in T. David (ed.) *Researching Early Childhood Education: European Perspectives*.

Alloway, N. (1995) *Foundation Stones: The Construction of Gender in Early Childhood*. Carlton: Curriculum Corporation.

Alloway, N. (1997) Early childhood education encounters the postmodern: what do we know? What can we count as true?, *Australian Journal of Early Childhood*, 22(2): 1–5.

Alpert, H. (ed.) (1988) *We are Everywhere: Writings By and About Lesbian Parents*. California: The Crossing Press.

Alvestad, M. and Samuelsson, I.P. (1999) A comparision of the national preschool curricula in Norway and Sweden, *Early Childhood Research and Practice*, 1(2).

Anderson, G.L. and Herr, K. (1999) The New Paradigm Wars: is there room for rigorous practitioner knowledge in schools and universities?, *Educational Researcher*, 28(5): 12–21, 40.

Anning, A. (1998) Appropriateness or effectiveness in the early childhood curriculum in the UK: some research evidence, *International Journal of Early Years Education*, 6(3): 299–314.

Anthony, L. (2002) *The National Agenda for Early Childhood*. Press release from the Minister for Children and Youth, Commonwealth Government, Canberra, Australia.

Archard, D. (1993) *Children: Rights and Childhood*. London: Routledge.

Ariès, P. (1962) *Centuries of Childhood*. London: Cape.

Arthur, L., Beecher, B., Dockett, S., Farmer, S. and Death, E. (1996) *Programming and Planning in Early Childhood Settings*, 2nd edn. Sydney: Harcourt Brace and Company.

Atmore, E. (1998) Reconstructing early childhood development services in South Africa: from apartheid to democracy, *International Journal of Early Years Education*, 6(3): 291–8.

Atwater, J., Carta, J., Schwarz, I. and McConnell, S. (1994) Blending developmentally appropriate practice and early childhood special education, in B. Mallory and R. New (eds) *Diversity and Developmentally Appropriate Practices*, pp.185–201. New York: Teachers College Press.

Australian Early Childhood Association (1991) Code of Ethics. Watson, ACT: Australia.

Averhart, C.J. and Bigler, R.S. (1997) Shades of meaning: skin tone, racial attitudes, and constructive memory in African American children, *Journal of Experimental Child Psychology*, 67: 363–88.

Baker, L., Allen, J., Shockley, B. *et al.* (1996) Connecting school and home: constructing partnerships to foster reading development, in L. Baker, P. Afflerbach and D. Reinking (eds) *Developing Engaged Readers in School and Home Communities*, pp.21–41. New Mahwah, NJ: Lawrence Erlbaum Associates.

Balcombe, J. and Tansey, J. (1996) Childcare workers who are parents, *Rattler*, 37: 8–11.

Bandura, A. (1977) *Social Learning Theory*. Englewood Cliffs, NJ: Prentice Hall.

Barbour, N. (1986) Teachers can make decisions, *Childhood Education*, May/June: 322–4.

Barnett, J. and Walsh, J. (1999) Academic literacy: it warrants explicit teaching, in B. Johnson and A. Reid (eds) *Contesting the Curriculum*, pp.124–35. Sydney: Social Science Press.

Battersby, C. (1998) Stages on Kant's way: aesthetics, morality, and the gendered sublime, in N. Zack, L. Shrage and C. Sartwell (eds) *Race, Class, Gender and Sexuality: The Big Questions*, pp.227–47. Massachusetts: Blackwell Publishers.

Beattie, M. (1997) Negotiating the curriculum: whose agenda? Keynote address presented to the Australian Curriculum Studies Associate Biennial Conference, June.

Beaty, J. (1986) *Observing Development of the Young Child*. Columbus, O.H.: C.E. Merrill Publishing Company.

Beaty, J. (1992) *Preschool Appropriate Practices*. San Antonio: Harcourt Brace Jovanovich College Publishers.

Becker, J. and Varelas, M. (2001) Piaget's early theory and the role of language in intellectual development: a comment on DeVries's account of Piaget's social theory, *Educational Researcher*, 30(6): 22–3.

Bellamy, C. (2001) *The State of the World's Children*, p.25. New York: UNICEF.

Bennett, N. and Wood, E. (2000) Changing theories, changing practice: exploring early children's teachers' professional learning, *Teaching and Teacher Education*, 16(5–6): 635–47.

Bentzen, W. (1985) *Seeing Young Children: A Guide to Observing and Recording Behaviour*. New York: Delmar Publishers.

Berger, E.H. (1995) *Parents as Partners in Education: Families and Schools Working Together*, 4th edn. Englewood Cliffs, NJ: Prentice-Hall.

Bernard van Leer Foundation (1994) *Why Children Matter: Investing in Early Childhood Care and Development*. The Hague: Bernard van Leer Foundation.

Bertens, H. (1995) *Postmodernism: A History*. London: Routledge.

Black-Gutman, D. and Hickson, F. (1996) The relationship between racial attitudes and social-cognitive development in children: an Australian study, *Developmental Psychology*, 32(3): 448–56.

Bleakley, A. (1999) From reflective practice to holistic reflexivity, *Studies in Higher Education*, 24: 315–30.

Bloch, M. (1992) Critical perspectives on the historical relationship between child development and early childhood education research, in S. Kessler and B. Blue Swadner (eds) *Reconceptualizing the Early Childhood Curriculum: Beginning the Dialogue*. New York: Teachers College Press.

Bloch, M. (2000) Restructuring governing in Eastern Europe, in J. Jipson and R. Johnson (eds) *Representation and Resistance in Early Childhood Research, Theory and Practice*. New York: Peter Lang Publishers.

Blue Swadner, B. (2000) 'At risk' or 'at promise'? From deficit constructions of the 'other childhood' to possibilities for authentic alliances with children and families, in L. Diaz Soto (ed.) *The Politics of Early Childhood Education*. New York: Peter Lang Publishers.

Blyth, A. (2002) Outcomes, standards and benchmarks, *Curriculum Perspectives*, 22(3): 13–22.

Boud, D., Keogh, R. and Walker, D. (1985) What is reflection in learning? in D. Boud, R. Keogh and D. Walker (eds) *Reflection: Turning Experience into Learning*. London: Kogan Page.

Bredekamp, S. (1987) *Developmentally Appropriate Practices in Early Childhood Programs Serving Children from Birth through Age 8*. Washington, DC: National Association for the Education of Young Children.

Bredekamp, S. and Copple, C. (eds) (1997) *Developmentally Appropriate Practice in Early Childhood Programs*. Washington, DC: National Association for the Education of Young Children.

Brennan, D. (1994) *The Politics of Australian Childcare: From Philanthropy to Feminism*. Cambridge: Cambridge University Press.

Brennan, D. and O'Donnell, C. (1986) *Caring for Australia's Children: Political and Industrial Issues in Childcare*. Sydney: Allen & Unwin.

Broinowski, I. (1997) *Working Creatively with Young Children*. Tasmania: Broinowski Publications.

Brookfield, S.D. (1995) *Becoming a Critically Reflective Teacher*. San Francisco: Jossey-Bass.

Brostom, S. (2001) Constructing the early childhood curriculum: the example of Denmark, in T. David (ed.) *Promoting Evidence-based Practice in Early Childhood Education: Research and Its Implications: Advances in Applied Early Childhood Education, Vol 1*. Oxford: Elsevier Science.

Brown, B. (1998) *Unlearning Discrimination in the Early Years*. London: Trentham Books.

Bruer, J. (1999) In search of brain-based education, *Phi Delta Kappan*, 80(9): 648–654.

Bruer, J. (2002) An interview with John Bruer: http://www.pbs.org/wgbh/pages/frontline/shows/teenbrain/interviews/bruer.html

Bruner, J. (1972) The nature and uses of immaturity, *American Psychologist*, 27: 687–708.

Bruner, J. (1996) *The Culture of Education*. Cambridge, MA: Harvard University Press.

Bryant, D., Peisner-Feinberg, E. and Miller-Johnson, S. (2000) Head Start parents' roles in the educational lives of their children. Paper presented at the Annual Conference of the American Educational Research Association, New Orleans, LA, 24–8 April, ED446835.

Burman, E. (1994) *Deconstructing Developmental Psychology*. Routledge: London.

Cairney, R. (1997) Parents and literacy learning: new perspectives, *Every Child*, 3(2): 4–5.

Campbell, S. (1999) Making the political pedagogical in early childhood education, *Australian Journal of Early Childhood*, 24(4): 21–6.

Campbell, S. (2001) *The Description and Definition of a Justice Disposition in Young Children*. Unpublished doctoral thesis, University of Melbourne, Australia.

Campbell, S., Davis, K., Mac Naughton, G. and Smith, K. (2000) Reinventing knowledge/power relations in pedagogical practices: dimensions of action research for equity in early childhood education. Research seminar presented to the Complexity, Diversity and Multiple Perspectives in Early Childhood: the 10th European Conference on Quality in Early Childhood Education, London, 29 August–1 September.

Campbell, S. and Smith, K. (2001) Equity observation and images of fairness, in S. Grieshaber and G.S. Cannella (eds) *Embracing Identities in Early Childhood Education: 'Diversity and Possibilities'*. New York: Teachers College Press.

Cannella, G.S. (1997) *Deconstructing Early Childhood Education: Social Justice and Revolution*. New York: Peter Lang.

Cannella, G. (1999) The scientific discourse of education: predetermining the lives of others – Foucault, education and children, *Contemporary Issues in Early Childhood*, 1(1): 36–44.

Cannella, G. (2000a) Natural born curriculum: popular culture and the representation of childhood, in J. Jipson and R. Johnson (eds) *Representation and Resistance in Early Childhood Research, Theory and Practice*. New York: Peter Lang Publishers.

Cannella, G. (2000b) Critical and feminist reconstructions of early childhood education: continuing the conversations, *Contemporary Issues in Early Childhood*, 1(2): 215–20.

Cannella, G.S. and Grieshaber, S. (2001) Identities and possibilities, in S. Grieshaber and G. Cannella (eds) *Embracing Identities in Early Childhood Education: 'Diversity and Possibilities'*. New York: Teachers College Press.

Cantwell, N. (1995) *United Nations Convention on the Rights of the Child: International Standards Concerning the Rights of the Child*. Geneva: Defence for Children International.

Carlsson Paige, N. and Levin, D. (1990) *Who's Calling the Shot?* New York: New Society Publishers.

Carr, M. (1998) Assessing children's experiences in early childhood. Final report to the Ministry of Education, Wellington, New Zealand.

Carr, M. (2001) *Assessment in Early Childhood Settings: Learning Stories*. London: Paul Chapman Publishing.

Carr, W. and Kemmis, S. (1986) *Becoming Critical: Knowing Through Action Research*. Geelong, Victoria: Deakin University Press.

Castillo, G. (2002) Teaching as the practice of freedom, in A. Darder (ed.) *Reinventing Paulo Friere: A Pedagogy of Love*. Boulder, CO: Westview Press.

Catherwood, D. (1994) Changing views on cognition in early childhood: putting some sacred cows to rest, *Australian Journal of Early Childhood*, 19(4): 25–9.

Catherwood, D. (1999) New views on the young brain: offerings from developmental psychology to early childhood education, *Contemporary Issues in Early Childhood*, 1(1): 23–35.

CETal (2002) http://www.utep.edu/cetal/portfoli/philos.htm

Chabris, C. (1999) Braintwisters, *Commentary*, 108(5): 74–7.

Chang, H., Muckleroy, A., Pulido-Tobiassen, D. and Dowell, C. (2000) Redefining childcare and early education in a diverse society: dialogue and reflection, in L. Diaz Soto (ed.) *The Politics of Early Childhood Education*. New York: Peter Lang Publishers.

Children's Services Office (1991) *Planning for Learning: A Framework for Planning Curriculum in Children's Services*. South Australia: Education Department of South Australia.

China Welfare Institute (2001) *CWI Brochure*. Shanghai: China Welfare Institute.

Clark, A. (2000) Listening to young children: perspectives, possibilities and problems. Paper presented at the 10th European Conference on Quality in Early Childhood Education, Institute of Education, London, 29 August–1 September.

Clarke-Stewart, A. (1982) *Day Care*. London: Fontana Books.

Clift, S., Stagnitti, K. and DeMello, L. (2000) A developmentally appropriate test of kinder/school readiness, *Australian Journal of Early Childhood*, 25(4): 22–6.

Cohen, M. and Martin, L. (1976) *Growing Free: Ways to Help Children Overcome Sex-Role Stereotypes*. Washington, DC: ACEI.

Coleman, M. and Churchill, S. (1997) Challenges to family involvement, *Childhood Education*, 73(3): 144–9.

Collins, P.H. (1990) *Black Feminist Thought: Knowledge, Consciousness, and the Politics of Empowerment*. New York: Routledge.

Cone, K. (1993) Ready to learn: a mandate for the nation, *Workbook*, 18(2): 67–9.

Connell, R. (1987) *Gender and Power*. Sydney: Allen & Unwin.

Connell, R. (1995) *Maculinities*. Sydney: Allen & Unwin.

Cooter, R., Mills-House, E., Marrin, P. and Mathews, B. (1999) Family and community involvement: the bedrock of reading success, *The Reading Teacher*, 52(8): 891–6.

Corrie, L. (2000) Enrichment programs: low-cost fix for high-risk children? *Every Child*, 6(1): 6–7.

Crain, W.C. (1985) *Theories of Development: Concepts and Applications*, 2nd edn. Englewood Cliffs, NJ: Prentice-Hall.

Crain, W.C. (1995) *Theories of Development: Concepts and Applications*, 3rd edn. Englewood Cliffs, NJ: Prentice-Hall.

Cranton, P. (1996) *Professional Development as Transformative Learning: New Perspectives for Teachers of Adults*. San Francisco: Jossey-Bass.

Creaser, B. and Dau, E. (eds) (1995) *The Anti-Bias Approach in Early Childhood*. Sydney: Harper Educational.

Croft, C. (2001) Use of diagnostic tools, *Researched News*, 32(2): 3.

Cuffaro, H. (1975) Reevaluating basic premises: curricula free of sexism, *Young Children*, September: 469–78.

Cuffaro, H. (1995) *Experimenting with the World: John Dewey and the Early Childhood Classroom*. New York: Teachers College Press.

Curtis, D. and Carter, M. (2000) *The Art of Awareness: How Observation Can Transform Your Teaching*. St Paul, MN: Redleaf Press.

Dahlberg, G., Moss, P. and Pence, A. (1999) *Beyond Quality in Early Childhood Education and Care: Postmodern Perspectives*. London: Falmer Press.

Darder, A. (ed.) (2002) *Reinventing Paulo Friere: A Pedagogy of Love*. Boulder, CO: Westview Press.

Dau, E. (2001) Introduction, in E. Dau (ed.) *The Anti-Bias Approach in Early Childhood*. Sydney: Prentice Hall.

David, T. (1999) Changing minds: teaching young children, in T. David (ed.) *Teaching Young Children*. London: Paul Chapman Publishing.

Davies, B. (1988) *Gender Equity and Early Childhood*. Canberra: Commonwealth Schools Commission.

Davies, B. (1989) *Frogs and Snails and Feminist Tales: Preschool Children and Gender*. Sydney: Allen & Unwin.

Davies, B. (1993) *Shards of Glass*. Sydney: Allen & Unwin.

Davies, I. (1977) *Objectives in Teaching and Learning: A Perspective*. London: McGraw Hill.

Davis, D. (2001) Response to the Curriculum Working Party of the Children's Services Forum, *Australian Early Childhood Association Victoria Newsletter*, 5(3): 6.

Davis, W. (1979) *Towards a Non-sexist Classroom*. South Australia: Education Department, Women's Advisory Unit.

DEA (Department of Education and the Arts) (1994) *Key Intended Literacy Outcomes. Kindergarten to Year Eight*. Tasmania: DEA.

DECCD (Department of Education, Community and Cultural Development) (1997) *Why We Should Focus on Student Learning Outcomes: Directions for Education*. Tasmania: DECCD.

Deci, E., Koestner, R. and Ryan, R. (2001) Extrinsic rewards and intrinsic motivation in education: reconsiderd once again, *Review of Educational Research*, 71(1): 1–28.

Decker, C. and Decker, J. (1988) *Planning and Administering Early Childhood Programs*, 4th edn. Toronto: Merrill.

Decker, C. and Decker, J. (1992) *Planning and Administering Early Childhood Programs*, 5th edn. New York: Merrill.

De Lair, H.A. and Irwin, E. (2000) Working perspectives within feminism and early childhood education, *Contemporary Issues in Early Childhood*, 1(2): 153–70.

Derman-Sparks, L. (1998) Education without prejudice: goals, principles and practices.

Paper presented to the Respect: Education Without Prejudice, A Challenge for Early Years Educators in Ireland, 16 October. Dublin: Pavee Point Travellers Centre.

Derman-Sparks, L. and the Anti-Bias Task Force (1989) *The Anti-Bias Curriculum*. Washington, DC: National Association for the Education of Young Children.

De Simone, D. (1995) Charlotte Perkins Gilman and the feminization of education, *WILLA*, 4(fall): 1–5.

DETE (Department of Education, Training and Employment) (1998) *Growing and Learning in the Family*. South Australia: DETE.

Dewy, J. (1916) *Democracy and Education. An Introduction to the Philosophy of Education*. New York: Macmillan.

Dewy, J. (1917) *Essays in Experimental Logic*. Chicago, MI: University of Chicago Press.

Diaz Soto, L. (2000) An early childhood dreamspace for social justice and equity, in L. Diaz Soto (ed.) *The Politics of Early Childhood Education*. New York: Peter Lang Publishers.

Dockett, S. (2000) Caring adults: a necessity for optimal brain development, *Every Child*, 6(1): 12–13.

DoE (Department of Education) (1987) *Guidelines for Preschool Curriculum Development*. NSW: Department of Education.

DoE (Department of Education) (1995) *Handbook for Schools, Trial version, The Year 2 Diagnostic Net*. Queensland: Department of Education.

DoE (Department of Education) (2002) *Essential Learnings*. Tasmania: Department of Education.

Donzelot, J. (1979) *The Policing of Families: Welfare versus the State*. London: Hutchinson.

Doyle, A.B. and Aboud, F.E. (1995) A longitudinal study of white children's racial prejudice as a social-cognitive development, *Merrill-Palmer Quarterly*, 41(2): 209–28.

Durham, F. (1978) *Art for the Child Under Seven*, 5th edn. Canberra: Australian Preschool Association.

Dwivedi, K. (1996) Race and the child's perspective, in R. Davie, G. Upton and V. Varma (eds) *The Voice of the Child: A Handbook for Professionals*. London: Falmer.

Early Years Trainers Anti-Racist Network Goals (2001) *Membership leaflet*. London: Early Years Trainers Anti-Racist Network.

Eaton, J. and Shephard, W. (1998) *Early Childhood Environments*. Watson: Australian Early Childhood Association.

Ebbeck, M. (1991) *Early Childhood Education*. Melbourne: Longman Cheshire.

Ebbeck, M. (1996) Children constructing their own knowledge, *International Journal of Early Years Education*, 4(2): 5–27.

Ebbeck, M. and Glover, A. (1998) Immigrant families' expectations of early childhood, *Australian Journal of Early Childhood*, 23(3): 14–19.

Ecclestone, K. (1996) The reflective practitioner: mantra or a model for emancipation? *Studies in the Education of Adults*, 28(2): 146–61.

Elliot, A. (1984) Creating non-sexist day care environments, *Australian Journal of Early Childhood*, 9(2): 18–23.

Elliot, A. (1998) From childcare to school: expectations and perceptions of children and their families, *Australian Journal of Early Childhood*, 23(3): 26–32.

Elliot, A. (1999) Celebrating diversity: promoting intercultural competence, *Every Child*, 5(4): 8.

Elschenbroich, D. (1999) A childhood free of knowledge: reflections on German educational policy for the early years, *International Journal of Early Years Education*, 7(3): 259–64.

Endsley, R., Minish, P. and Zhou, Q. (1993) Parent involvement and quality day care in proprietary centers, *Journal of Research in Childhood Education*, 7(2): 53–61.

ERIC/EECE (1995) Using ideas from Reggio Emilia in America, *ERIC/EECE Newsletter*, 7(1): 1–2.

Ernest, J. (2001) Teachers' and family members' subjective beliefs about developmentally appropiate practices. Paper presented to the Association for Childhood Education International.

ERO (Education Review Office) (1998) *The Use of Te Whāriki*: http://www.ero.govt.nz/Publications/eers1998/TeWhariki/TeWhariki.htm

ERO (Education Review Office) (2000) *In-Service Training for Teachers in New Zealand Schools*, 1. New Zealand: Crown Copyright.

Espinosa, L. (1995) Hispanic Parent Involvement In Early Childhood Programs, *ERIC Digest*, EDO-PS-95-3.

Evans, R. (1996) Cultural and curriculum in England and Wales: tensions and dilemmas for early childhood specialists, *Early Development and Care*, 123: 61–8.

Evans, P. and Fuller, M. (1996) 'Hello, Who am I speaking to?' communicating with pre-school children in educational research settings, *Early Years*, 17(1): 17–20.

Faragher, J. and Mac Naughton, G. (1998) *Working with Young Children*, 2nd edn. Melbourne: RMIT Publications.

Feeney, S.D., Christiansen, D. and Moravcik, E. (1983) *Who Am I in the Lives of Children?* (2nd edn). New York: Macmillan.

Feinberg, W. (1983) *Understanding Education: Toward a Reconstruction of Educational Enquiry*. Cambridge: Cambridge University Press.

Fell, K. (1999) The State of Victoria: preschools and the reform agenda, *Australian Journal of Early Childhood*, 24(1): 1–7.

Fidler, M. (1995) Building a learning community, *Association Management*, 47(5): 40–7.

Filp, J. (1998) From mutual blame towards trust: changing schoolÖfamily relationships in Chile, *Childhood Education*, International Focus Issue, 74(6): 346–50.

Fish, S. (1979) *Is there a Text in this Class? The Authority of Interpretive Communities*. Cambridge, MA: Harvard University Press.

Fleer, M. (ed.) (1995) *DAPcentrism: Challenging Developmentally Appropriate Practice*. Watson: Australian Early Childhood Association.

Fleer, M. (2002) Research evidence with political currency: keeping the early childhood education agenda on the international agenda, *Australian Journal of Early Childhood*, 27(1): 1–7.

Fleer, M. and Williams-Kennedy, D. (2001) Looking in and not seeing yourself mirrored back: investigations of some indigenous family views on education, *Curriculum Perspectives*, 21(3): 52–7.

Fleer, M. and Williams-Kennedy, D. (2001a) *Building Bridges: Literacy Development in Young Indigenous Children*. Watson, ACT: Australian Early Childhood Association.

Fleet, A. and Patterson, C. (1998) Beyond the boxes: planning for real knowledge and live children, *Australian Journal of Early Childhood*, 23(4): 31–5.

Foot, H., Howe, C., Cheyne, B., Terras, M. and Rattray, C. (2002) Parental participation and partnership in preschool provision, *International Journal of Early Years Education*, 10(1): 5–20.

Ford, E. and Coughlin, P. (1999) The Step by Step Program: linking democracy and early childhood education, *Young Children*, 54(4): 32–5.

Foucault, M. (1978) *The History of Sexuality*, Vol 1. An Introduction. New York: Vintage Books.

Foucault, M. (1982) The subject and power, in H. Dreyfus and P. Rabinow (eds) *Michel*

Foucault: Beyond Structuralism and Hermeneutics. Chicago: University of Chicago Press.

Foucault, M. (1986) What is enlightenment, in P. Rabinow (ed.) *The Foucault Reader*. Harmondsworth: Peregrine Books.

Foucault, M. (1997) Truth and power, in C. Gorden (ed.) *Power/Knowledge: Selected Interviews and Other Writings 1972–1977. Michel Foucault*. Sussex: Harvester Press.

Frede, E. (1995) The role of program quality in producing early childhood program benefits, *The Future of Children*, 5(3): 115–32.

Freire, P. (1970) *Cultural Action for Freedom*, trans. Myra Bergman Ramos, Middlesex: Penguin Books.

Freire, P. (1972) *Pedagogy of the Oppressed*, trans. Myra Bergman Ramos, Middlesex: Penguin Books.

Freire, P. (1985) *The Politics of Education, Culture, Power and Liberation*. Basingstoke: Macmillan.

Gallas, K. (1994) *The Languages of Learning: How Children Talk, Write, Dance, Draw and Sing their Understanding of the World*. New York: Teachers College Press.

Gallas, K. (1998) *Sometimes I Can Be Anything: Power, Gender and Identity in a Primary Classroom*. New York: Teachers College Press.

Gargiulo, R. and Graves, S. (1991) Parental feelings: the forgotten component when working with parents of handicapped preschool children, *Childhood Education*, 67(3): 176–8.

Gelfer, J. (1991) Teacher–parent partnerships: enhancing communications, *Childhood Education*, 67(3): 164–9.

Gesell, A. (1952) *Infant Development: The Embryology of Early Human Behaviour*. London: Hamish Hamilton.

Gesell, A. and Ilg, F. (1943) *Infant & Child in the Culture of Today*. New York: Harper.

Ghaudi, L. (1998) *Postcolonial Theory: A Critical Introduction*. Sydney: Allen & Unwin.

Giddens, A. (1991) *Sociology*. London: Polity Press.

Gilligan, C. (1982) *In a Different Voice*. Cambridge, MA: Harvard University Press.

Ginsburg, H. and Opper, S. (1969) *Piaget's Theory of Intellectual Development: An Introduction*. Englewood Cliffs, NJ: Prentice Hall.

Giroux, H. (1988) *Teachers as Intellectuals: Toward a Critical Pedagogy of Learning*. Massachusetts: Bergin and Garvey Publishers.

Giroux, H. (1990) *Curriculum Discourse as Postmodernist Critical Practice*. Geelong, Victoria: Deakin University.

Giroux, H. (1991) Modernism, postmodernism and feminism: rethinking the boundaries of educational discourse, in H.A. Giroux (ed.) *Postmodernism, Feminism and Cultural Politics: Redrawing Educational Boundaries*. New York: State University of New York Press.

Glassman, M. (2003) Dewey and Vygotsky: society, experience, and inquiry in educational practice, *Educational Researcher*, 30(4): 3–14.

Goldstein, C. (2002) Teaching hope to children in special education, in A. Darder (ed.) *Reinventing Paulo Friere: A Pedagogy of Love*. Boulder, CO: Westview Press.

Goldstein, L. (1997) *Teaching with Love: A Feminist Approach to Early Childhood Education*. New York: Peter Lang Publishing.

Gomez, M.L. (1992) Breaking silences: building new stories of classroom life through teacher transformation, in S. Kessler and B. Blue Swadner (eds) *Reconceptualizing the Early Childhood Curriculum: Beginning the Dialogue*. New York: Teachers College Press.

Gonzalez-Mena, J. (1992) Talking a culturally sensitive approach in infant–toddler programs, *Young Children*, 47(2): 4–9.

Goodfellow, J. (2001) Wise practice: the need to move beyond best practice in early childhood education, *Australian Journal of Early Childhood*, 26(1): 1–6.

Gopaul-McNicol, S.A. (1995) A cross-cultural examination of racial identity and racial preference of preschool children in the West Indies, *Journal of Cross-Cultural Psychology*, 26(2): 141–52.

Gore, J. (1991) Neglected practices: a Foundation critique of traditional and radical approaches to pedagogy. Paper presented to the Liberating Curriculum Conference, University of Adelaide, 11–14 July.

Gore, J. (1993) *The Struggle for Pedagogies: Critical and Femininist Discourses as Regimes of Truth*. London: Routledge.

Gore, J. (1999) *Micro-level Techniques of Power in the Classroom Production of Class, Race, Gender and Other Relations*. AARE-Online Publications. http://www.swin.edu.au/aare/98pap/GOR98285.html

Graue, M.E. (1992) Meanings of readiness and the kindergarten experience, in S. Kessler and B. Blue Swadner (eds) *Reconceptualizing the Early Childhood Curriculum: Beginning the Dialogue*. New York: Teachers College Press.

Grieshaber, S. (1997) Back to basics: the Queensland Year 2 Diagnostic Net, *Curriculum Perspectives*, 17(3): 28–38.

Grundy, S. (1987) *Curriculum: Product or Praxis*. London: Falmer Press.

Guttenberg, M. and Bray, H. (1976) *Undoing Sex Stereotypes*. Middlesex: McGraw-Hill.

Habermas, J. (1979) *Communication and the Evolution of Society* (trans. T. McCarthy). London: Heinemann.

Habermas, J. (1981) Modernity versus postmodernity, *New Left Critique*, winter: 22.

Habermas, J. (1989) The tasks of a critical social theory of society, in E. Bronner and D. MacKay Kellner (eds) *Critical Theory and Society: A Reader*. London: Routledge.

Habermas, J. (1990) *Moral Consciousness and Communicative Action*. Cambridge: Polity Press.

Hall, N. (1996) Why Mathematics Is Important, *Every Child*, 2(4): 4–5.

Hanley, A.M. (1995) Persona dolls, in B. Creaser and E. Dau (eds) *The Anti-Bias Approach in Early Childhood*, pp. 161–73. Pymble, NSW: HarperEducational Publishers.

Hanley, S. (1994) *On Constructivism*. Maryland Collaborative for Teacher Preparation, http://www.inform.umd.edu/UMS+State/UMD-Projects/MCTP/Essays/Constructivism.txt

Hannon, P. (1995) *Literacy, Home and School. Research and Practice in Teaching Literacy with Parents*. Bristol: Falmer Press.

Hartley, R. (ed.) (1995) *Families and Cultural Diversity in Australia*. Sydney: Allen & Unwin.

Hayward, J. and Sycamore, J. (1999) Ours is the greatest early childhood centre: Rockdale Park Kindergarten, *R.E.A.L. Magazine*, 3(Oct): 41–3.

Hedges, H. (2000) Teaching in early childhood: time to merge constructivist views so learning through play equals teaching through play, *Australian Journal of Early Childhood*, 25(4): 16–21.

Hendrick, J. (1990) *Total Learning: Developmental Curriculum for the Young Child*. Colombus, OH: Merrill Publishing Company.

Henniger, M. (1999) *Teaching Young Children: An Introduction*. Englewood Cliffs, NJ: Prentice Hall.

Hepworth Berger, E. (1995) *Parents as Partners in Education: Families and Schools Working Together*, 4th edn. Columbus, OH: Merrill Publishing.

Hetherington, E. and Parke, R. (1986) *Child Psychology: A Contemporary Viewpoint*, 3rd edn. New York: McGraw-Hill Book Company.

Hewitt, B. and Maloney, C. (2000) Malaysian parents' ideal and actual perceptions of pre-school education, *International Journal of Early Years Education*, 8(1): 84–92.

Hirschey, S. (1999) Developing partnerships with parents. Paper presented to the Association for Childhood Education International, April, San Antonio, Texas.

Hirschfeld, L.A. (1995) Do children have a theory of race? *Cognition*, 54: 209–52.

Hitz, R. and Wright, D. (1988) Kindergarten issues: a practitioner survey, *Principal*, 67(5): 28–30.

Hohmann, M., Banet, B. and Weikart, D.P. (1979) *Young Children in Action*. Ypsilanti: High/Scope Press.

Holmes, T. (1992) *Toi Te Kupu, Toi Te Mana, Toi Te Whenua*: culturally appropriate early childhood education. Paper presented at the Children at Risk Conference, May, Bergen, Norway.

Holt, J. (1972) *Escape from Childhood: The Needs and Rights of Children*. New York: Pelican Books.

Honig, A. (1983) Sex role socialisation in early childhood. *Young Children*, September: 59.

Honkavaara, P. (1998) Anniversaries in the Finnish kindergarten system: how and why the system was created, *International Journal of Early Childhood*, 28(1): 7–9.

Hoot, J., Parmar, R., Hujula-Huttunen, E., Cao, Q. and Chacon, A. (1999) Cross-national perspectives on developmentally appropriate practices for early childhood programs, *Journal of Research in Childhood Education*, 10(2): 160–9.

Hughes, E. (2002) Planning meaningful curriculum: a mini story of children and teachers learning together, *Childhood Education*, 78(3): 134–9.

Hughes, P. (2001) Paradigms, methods and knowledge, in G. Mac Naughton, S. Rolfe and I. Siraj-Blatchford (eds) *Doing Early Childhood Research*. Sydney: Allen & Unwin.

Hughes, P. and Mac Naughton, G. (1999a) *Communication in Early Childhood Services: A Practical Guide*. Melbourne: RMIT Press.

Hughes, P. and Mac Naughton, G. (1999b) Who's the expert? Reconceptualising parent–staff relations in early education, *Australian Journal of Early Childhood*, 24(4): 27–32.

Hughes, P. and Mac Naughton, G. (2000) Consensus, dissensus or community the politics of parent involvement in early childhood education, *Contemporary Issues in Early Childhood*, 1(3): 241–58.

Hughes, P. and Mac Naughton, G. (2001) Building equitable staff–parent communication in early childhood settings: an Australian case study, *Early Childhood Research and Practice*, 3(2).

Hughes, P. and Mac Naughton, G. (2002) Preparing early childhood professionals to work with parents: the challenges of diversity and dissensus, *Australian Journal of Early Childhood*, 28(2): 14–20.

Hughes, P. and Mac Naughton, G. (2004) Curriculum contexts: parents and communities, in G. Mac Naughton, *Shaping Early Childhood: Learners, Curriculum, Contexts*. Maidenhead: Open University Press (forthcoming).

Huira, N. (1996) Individual communication between parents and teachers. Parent–teacher notebook, *International Journal of Early Childhood*, 28(1): 8–11.

Hulmes, E. (1989) *Education and Cultural Diversity*. London: Longman.

Hutchinson, F.P. (1996) *Educating Beyond Violent Futures*. London: Routledge.

Hyson, M. (1991) Building the hothouse: how mothers construct academic environments, *New Directions for Child Development*, 53: 31.

Imel, S. (1998) *Teaching Critical Reflection: Trends and Issues. ERIC Alerts from the Clearinghouse on Adult Career and Vocational Education*. Champagne, IL: Educational Resources Information Center (ERIC).

Isenberg, J. and Brown, B. (1987) Societal influences on children, *Childhood Education*, June: 341–8.

Izzo, C., Weissberg, R., Kasprow, W. and Fendrich, M. (1999) A longitudinal assessment of teacher perceptions of parent involvement in children's education and school perform-ance, *American Journal of Community Psychology*, 27(6): 817–39.

James, A., Jenks, C. and Prout, A. (1998) *Theorizing Childhood*. New York: Teachers College Press.

James, A. and Prout, A. (eds) (1990) *Constructing and Reconstructing Childhood*. New York: The Falmer Press.

Jilk, B.A. (1999) Schools in the new millennium, *American School and University*, 71(5): 46–7.

Jipson, J. (1998) Developmentally appropriate practice: culture, curriculum, connections, in M. Hauser and J. Jipson (eds) *Intersections: Feminisms/Early Childhoods*. New York: Peter Lang Publishing.

Johnson, B. and Reid, A. (eds) (1999) *Contesting the Curriculum*. Sydney: Social Science Press.

Johnson, D.J. (1992) Racial preference and biculturality in biracial preschoolers, *Merrill-Palmer Quarterly*, 38(2): 233–44.

Johnson, D. (1996) Teaching low income mothers to teach their children, *Early Childhood Research Quarterly*, 11(1): 101–14.

Jones, E. (1999) An emergent curriculum expert offers this afterthought, *Young Children*, 54(4): 16.

Jones, K. (2000) *Critical Teaching: Reconceptualising the Way We Work in the Early Years. A Report on the Critical Teaching Project*. South Australia: Department of Education and Training.

Jones, K. and Mules, R. (2001) Developing critical thinking and activism, in E. Dau (eds) *The Anti-Bias Approach in Early Childhood*. Frenchs Forrest, NSW: Pearson Education Australia.

Jonquiere, H. (1990) My beliefs about teaching, *Childhood Education*, 66(5): 2912–3.

Joseph, R. (1999) Environmental influences on neural plasticity, the limbic system, and emo-tional development and attachment, *Child Psychiatry and Human Development*, 29: 187–203.

Jungck, S. and Marshall, J.D. (1992) Curricual perspectives on one great debate, in S. Kessler and B. Blue Swadner (eds) *Reconceptualizing Early Childhood Curriculum*. New York: Teacher's College Press.

Karwowska-Struczyk, M. (1993) What do parents think about kindergarten? *International Journal of Early Years Education*, 1(2): 33–41.

Kasting, A. (1994) Respect, responsibility and reciprocity: the 3 Rs of parent involvement, *Childhood Education*, 70(3): 146–50.

Katz, L.G. (1995) *Talks with Teachers of Young Children*. New Jersey: Ablex.

Katz, L. and Chard, S. (1996) The contribution of documentation to the quality of early childhood education, *ERIC Digest*, April (EDO-PS-96-2).

Kelly, C. (1995) Parents as partners, *Early Childhood Review*, 1: 1–27.

Kelly, M. and Duckitt, J. (1995) Racial preference and self-esteem in black South African children, *South African Journal of Psychology*, 25(4): 217–23.

Kemmis, S. (1986) *Curriculum Theorising: Beyond Reproduction Theory*. Geelong, Victoria: Deakin University Press.

Kessler, S. and Hauser, M. (2000) Critical pedagogy and the politics of play, in L. de Soto (ed.) *The Politics of Early Childhood Education*. New York: Peter Lang Publishers.

Kessler, S. and McKenna, W. (1982) Developmental aspects of gender, in E. Whitelegg *et al.* (eds) *The Changing Experience of Women*. Oxford: Martin Robertson and the Open University.

Kessler, S. and Swadner, B. (eds) (1994) *Reconceptualising the Early Childhood Curriculum: Beginning the Dialogue*. New York: Teachers College Press.

Killoran, I. (2002) A road less traveled: creating a community where each belongs, *Childhood Education*, 78(6): 371–7.

Kritskaya, O. (1996) An early childhood programme: an approach to developing the whole child through the arts, *Early Childhood Review*, 2 (spring): 9–14.

Kuhn, D. and Martinko, M.J. (1985) The management of organizational behaviour, in D. Voich Jr. and M. Damjanovic (eds) *The Impact of Culture-based Value Systems on Management*, pp. 279Ö99. New York: Praeger Press.

Ladson-Billings, G. (1999) Just what is critical race theory, and what's it doing in a nice field like education? in L. Parker, D. Deyhl and S. Villenas (eds) *Race is . . . Race isn't*. Boulder, CO: Westview Press.

Laishley, J. (1983) *Working with Young Children: Encouraging their Development and Dealing with Problems*. London: Edward Arnold.

Laloumi-Vidali, E. (1996) Parent's views on their involvement in the development of pre-writing skills in their preschool children in Greece, *International Journal of Early Childhood*, 28(1): 12–19.

Laloumi-Vidali, E. (1997) Professional views on parent's involvement at the partnership level in preschool education, *International Journal of Early Childhood*, 29(1): 19–25.

Lambert, B. and Clyde, M. (2000) *Rethinking Early Childhood Theory and Practice*. Sydney: Social Science Press.

Landreth, C. (1969) *Early Childhood: Behaviour and Learning*. New York: Alfred A. Knopf.

Lanyasunya, A.R. and Lesolayia, M.S. (2001) *The El-barta Child and Family Project*. The Hague: Bernard van Leer Foundation.

Latham, G. (1996) Fostering and preserving wonderment, *Australian Journal of Early Childhood*, 21(1): 12–15.

Lather, P. (1991) *Getting Smart: Feminist Research and Pedagogy with/in the Postmodern*. New York: Routledge.

Lawrence, H. (2000) Stress-free environments: promoting healthy brain development, *Every Child*, 6(1): 10–11.

Le Roux, W. (2002) *The Challenges of Change: A Tracer Study of San Preschool Children in Botswana*. The Hague: Bernard van Leer Foundation.

Lee, G. (1997) The characteristics of early childhood education in Korea, *International Journal of Early Childhood*, 29(2): 44–50.

Lee, N. (2001) *Childhood and Society: Growing Up in an Age of Uncertainty*. Buckingham: Open University Press.

Lindsay, G. (1998) Brain research and implications for early childhood education, *Childhood Education*, 75(2): 97–104.

Linke, P. (2000) Infant brain research: what is it and what does it mean? *Every Child*, 6(1): 4–5.

Linke, P. and Fleer, M. (2002) *Babies: Good Beginnings Last Forever*. Watson, ACT: Australian Early Childhood Association.

Liou, T. and Price, G. (2001) Cultural consonance and dissonance of Taiwanese mothers' ideas about child rearing and their use of personal social networks and expert knowledge. Paper presented to the Association for Childhood International Conference, Toronto, Canada,

Liu, K. and Chien, C. (1998) Project approach and parent involvement in Taiwan, *Childhood Education*, 74(4): 213–19.

Lofts, P. (1983) *How the Birds Got Their Colours*. Gosford, NSW: Scholastic.

Longstreet, W. and Shane, H. (1993) *Curriculum for a New Millennium*. Needham Heights, MA: Allyn and Bacon.

Lovat, T. and Smith, D. (1995) *Curriculum: Action on Reflection*, 3rd edn. Sydney: Social Science Press.

Lubeck, S. (2001) Early childhood education and care in cross-national perspective, *Phi Delta Kappa*, 83(3): 213–16.

Lubeck, S. (1994) The politics of developmentally appropriate practice, in B. Mallory and R. New (eds) *Diversity and Developmentally Appropriate Practices*. New York: Teachers College Press.

Lubeck, S. (1996) Deconstructing 'child development knowledge' and 'teacher preparation', *Early Childhood Research Quarterly*, 11: 147–67.

Machel, G. and Mandela, N. *Global Movement for Children*. http://www.unicef.org.uk/news/Globalmovement6may.htm

Mackintosh, C. (1998) Reflection: a flawed strategy for the nursing profession, *Nurse Education Today*, 18: 553–7.

Mac Naughton, G. (1995) A poststructuralist analysis of learning in early childhood settings, in M. Fleer (ed.) *DAPcentrism: Challenging Developmentally Appropriate Practice*. Canberra: Australian Early Childhood Association.

Mac Naughton, G. (1996) Is Barbie to blame? Reconsidering how children learn gender, *Australian Journal of Early Childhood*, 21(4): 18–22.

Mac Naughton, G. (1997) Feminist Praxis and the Gaze in the Early Childhood Curriculum, *Gender and Education*, pp.1–22.

Mac Naughton, G. (1998) Improving one's gender equity 'tools': a case for discourse analyses, in N. Yelland (ed.) *Gender in Early Childhood*. London: Routledge.

Mac Naughton, G. (1998a) Even pink tents have glass ceilings: crossing the gender boundaries in pretend play, in E. Dau (ed.) *Child's Play: Revisiting Play in Early Childhood Settings*. Maclennan and Petty, Sydney.

Mac Naughton, G. (2000) *Rethinking Gender in Early Childhood Education*. Sydney: Allen & Unwin.

Mac Naughton, G. (2001a) 'Blushes and birthday parties': telling silences in young children's constructions of 'race', *Journal for Australian Research in Early Childhood Education*, 8(1): 41–51.

Mac Naughton, G. (2001b) Silences and subtexts in immigrant and non-immigrant children's understanding of diversity, *Childhood Education*, 78(1): 30–6.

Mac Naughton, G. (2001c) Dolls for equity: foregrounding children's voices in learning respect and unlearning unfairness, *New Zealand Council for Educational Research Early Childhood Folio*, 5: 27–30.

Mac Naughton, G. (forthcoming) Tom's gendered bottles: exploring critical constructivist perspectives on children's learning, in M. Fleer and J. Cullen (eds) *Early Childhood Education: Society and Culture*. London: Sage.

Mac Naughton, G., Barnes, S.. and Jones, K. (2000) Re-creating Intellectual Work in Early Childhood: Stories from the Academy and from the Field. Paper presented at the 9th Interdisciplinary Conference, Reconceptualising Early Childhood Education: Research, Theory and Practice Around the World. Brisbane, Australia.

Mac Naughton, G. and Davis, K. (2001) Beyond 'othering': rethinking approaches to teaching young Anglo-Australian children about indigenous Australians, *Contemporary Issues in Early Childhood*, 2(1): 83–93.

Mac Naughton, G., Mortimer, J. and Parish, K. (1986) *Working Together*. London: Greater London Council.

Mac Naughton, G. and Smith, K. (2001) Action research, ethics and the risks of practicing freedom for early childhood professionals, *Australian Journal of Early Childhood*, 26(4): 32–8.

Mac Naughton, G., Smith, K. and Lawrence, H. (2002) *Learning for Life: A Strategic Review of Early Childhood Services*. Melbourne: Uniting Care Victoria.

Mac Naughton, G. and Williams, G. (1998) *Techniques for Teaching Young Children: Choices in Theory and Practice*. Melbourne: Addison-Wesley Longman.

Malaguzzi, L. (1998) History, ideas and basic philosophy: an interview with Lella Gandini, in C.P. Edwards, L. Gandini and G. Forman (eds) *The Hundred Languages of Children: The Reggio Emilia Approach – Advanced Reflections*. Norwood: Ablex Publishing.

Mallory, B. and New, R. (1994) *Diversity and Developmentally Appropriate Practices*. New York: Teachers College Press.

Mandernach, J. (1999) The infant brain: its growth and development, *Baby Talk*, 2(1).

Mason, M. (1992) *New Internationalist*, July: 1.

McCain, M. and Mustard, F.J. (1999) *Reversing the Real Brain Drain: Early Years Study Final Report*. Ontario: Publications Ontario.

McCallum, F. (2001) *Cracks in the Concrete: The Demise of the Teacher's Role in Reporting Child Abuse and Neglect*, Paper presented at the Australian Association for Research in Education (AARE), 2–6 December, Fremantle, Australia.

McCarthy, T. (1979) *The Critical Theory of Jurgen Habermas*. Cambridge: MIT Press.

McClaren, P. (2002) A legacy of hope and struggle, in A. Darder (ed.) *Reinventing Paulo Friere: A Pedagogy of Love*. Boulder, CO: Westview Press.

McConnochie, K., Hollinsworth, D. and Pettman, J. (1988) *Race and Racism in Australia*. Sydney: Social Science Press.

McDonald Ross, M. (1975) Behavioural objectives: a critical review, in M. Golby, J. Greenwald and R. West (eds) *Curriculum Design*. Milton Keynes: Open University.

McGuigan, J. (1996) *Culture and the Public Sphere*. London: Routledge.

McGuinn, N. (2002) Response to education for a better world, in I. Davies, I. Gregory and N. McGuinn (eds) *Key Debates in Education*. London: Continuum.

McKay, S. and Rey, C. (2001) Women's meanings of peacebuilding in post-apartheid South Africa, *Peace and Conflict: Journal of Peace Psychology*, 7(3): 227–42.

McMillan, A. (2001) *Deconstructing Social and Cultural Meanings: A Model for Education Research Using Postmodern Constructs*. Australia: Common Ground Publishing.

McNeil, J. (1977) *Curriculum: A Comprehensive Introduction*. Boston: Little Brown.

McNeil, L. (2002) Private assess or public good: education and democracy at the crossroads, *American Educational Research Journal*, 39(2): 243–8.

Melhuish, E.D. (1993) Pre-school care and education: lessons from the 20th and 21st century, *International Journal of Early years Education*, 1: 19–32.

Melhuish, E., Hennessy, E., Martin, S. and Moss, P. (1991) Does day care affect development over the first six years? Paper presented at the Conference of the International Society for the Study of Behavioural Development, July, Minneapolis.

Mellor, E. (1990) *Stepping Stones: The Development of Early Childhood Services in Australia*. Sydney: Harcourt Brace Jovanovich Publishers.

Merriam, S.B. (1982) Some thoughts on the relationship between theory and practice, in S.B. Merriam (ed.) *Linking Philosophy and Practice*, New Directions for Continuing Education, No. 15. San Francisco: Jossey-Bass.

Mezirow, J. (1981) A critical theory of adult learning and eduction, *Adult Education*, 32: 3–24.

Mezirow, J. (1990) *Fostering Critical Reflection in Adulthood: A Guide to Transformative and Emancipatory Learning*. San Francisco: Jossey-Bass Publishers.

Miller, P.H. (1993) *Theories of Developmental Psychology*, 3rd edn. New York: Freeman.

Mischel, A. (1966) *Down With Stereotypes! Eliminating Sexism from Children's Literature and School Textbooks*. Paris: UNESCO.

MoE (Ministry of Education) (1996) *Te Whāriki: Early Childhood Curriculum*. Auckland: Ministry of Education.

Moncadu, C. (1984) *Early Childhood Education in Minnesota: A Position Paper*, ED 259826.

Montessori, M. (1973) *From Childhood to Adolescence*. New York: Schocken Books.

Moore, M. and Klass, P. (1995) Understanding parent's expectations on hurrying: United States and England, *International Journal of Early Childhood*, 27(2): 30–6.

Morrison, G. (1995) *Early Childhood Education Today*, 6th edn. New Jersey: Merrill.

Morrison, J. and Milner, V. (1997) Early education and care in Jamaica: a grassroots effort, *International Journal of Early Childhood*, 29(2): 51–7.

Moss, P. (2001) Making space for ethics. Keynote address to the Australian Early Childhood Association Biennial Conference, Sydney, New South Wales.

Moyles, J. (1989) *Just Playing: The Role and Status of Play in Early Childhood Education*. Buckingham: Open University Press.

Moyles, J. (1996) Nationally prescribed curricula and early childhood education: the English experience and Australian comparisons – identifying the rhetoric and the reality! *Australian Journal of Early Childhood*, 21(1): 27–31.

Murray, C. and O'Doherty, A. (2001) *'Eist': Respecting Diversity in Early Childhood Care, Education and Training*. Dublin: Pavee Point.

Murray Thomas, M. (1985) *Comparing Theories of Child Development*, 2nd edn. California: Wadsworth Publishing.

Myers, M. (2002) Leaving as part of living: emotional and social challenges in the kindergarten, *Focus on Pre-K & K: A Quarterly Newsletter for the Education Community*, 14(3): 1–7.

Nash, M. (1997) Fertile minds, *Time* 149: 49–56.

Nasper, E. (1981) Why a concern about preschool sex stereotyping? in B. Heathington (ed.) *Breaking Barriers, Overcoming Career Stereotyping in Early Childhood*. ED 225672, p.14.

National Research Council and Institute of Medicine (2000) *From Neurons to Neighbourhoods: The Science of Early Childhood Development*. Washington, DC: National Academy Press.

NCAC (National Childcare Accreditation Council) (1993) *Quality Assurance and Improvement Handbook*. Canberra: Australian Government Publishing Service.

NCAC (National Childcare Accreditation Council) (2000) *Statistics of the QIAS*: http://www.ncac.gov.au/stats/progress.htm

NCAC (National Childcare Accreditation Council) (2001) *QIAS Handbook*. Sydney: NCAC.

New, R. (1994a) Culture, child development and DAP, in B. Mallory and R. New (eds) *Diversity and Developmentally Appropriate Practice*. New York: Teachers College Press.

New, R. (1994b) Cultural variations on developmentally appropriate practice: challenges to theory and practice, in C. Edwards, L. Gandini and G. Forman (eds) *The Hundred Languages of Children: The Reggio Emilia Approach to Early Childhood Education*. Norwood, NJ: Ablex Publishing Corporation.

New, C. and David, M. (1985) *For the Children's Sake: Making Childcare More than Women's Business*. Harmondsworth: Penguin Books.

Newman, L. and Pollintz, L. (2002) *Ethics in Action: Introducing the Ethical Response Cycle*. Canberra: Australian Early Childhood Association.

Nimmo, J. (1994) Emergent curriculum. Paper given at the Challenge of Reggio Emilia: Realising the Potential of Children Conference, University of Melbourne.

Nimmo, J. (2002) Nurturing the spirit to teach: commitment, community and emergent curriculum, *Australian Journal of Early Childhood*, 28(2): 8–12.

Noddings, N. (1992) *The Challenge to Care in Schools: An Alternative Approach to Education*. New York: Teachers College Press.

Novak, J. (ed.) (1995) The progressive education of progressive educators, *Insight: A Publication of the John Dewey Society for the Study of Education and Culture*, 31(1).

NSW (New South Wales) Department of Community Services Office of Childcare (2002) *Curriculum Framework for Children's Services: The Practice of Relationships. Essential Provisions for Children's Services.* New South Wales: Department of Community Services, Office of Childcare.

O'Loughlin, M. (2001) The development of subjectivity in young children: theoretical and pedagogical considerations, *Contemporary Issues in Early Childhood*, 2(1): 49–65.

O'Toole, K. (1999) The development of the Victorian Municipal Preschool Association, *Australian Journal of Early Childhood*, 24(2): 41–6.

Oberheumer, P. and Coleberg-Schrader, H. (1999) The changing practitioners role in early childhood centres: multiple shifts and contradictory forces, *International Journal of Early Years Education*, 7(3): 249–58.

Objisanya, O. (2001) Early childhood intervention programmes in Nigeria, in T. David (ed.) *Promoting Evidence-based Practice in Early Childhood Education: Research and Its Implications: Advances in Applied Early Childhood Education, Vol 1.* Oxford: Elsevier Science.

Ochsner, M. (2001) Developing reciprocity in a multi-method small-scale research study, in G. Mac Naughton, S. Rolfe and I. Siraj-Blatchford (eds) *Doing Early Childhood Research.* Sydney: Allen & Unwin.

Page, J.M. (2000) *Reframing the Early Childhood Curriculum. Educational Imperatives for the Future.* London: RoutledgeFalmer.

Paley, V. (1986) *Mollie is Three: Growing up in School.* Chicago: The University of Chicago Press.

Parker, S. (1997) *Reflective Teaching in the Postmodern World: A Manifesto for Education in Postmodernity.* Buckingham: Open University Press

Parker, C. and Shaikh, S. (1991) *Early Childhood Education: A Handbook for Preschool Teachers.* Karachi, Pakistan: Teachers Resource Centre.

Pease-Windy Boy, J. (1995) Cultural diversity in the higher education system: an American Indian perspective, in C. Sleeter and P. McClaren (eds) *Multicultural Education, Critical Pedagogy and the Politics of Difference.* New York: State University of New York Press.

Perkins, C. (1900) *Concerning Children.* Boston: Small Maynard.

PFIE (1997) *Partnership for Family Involvement in Education (ED).* Washington, DC: PFIE.

Piaget, J. (1995) Logical operations and social life, in L. Smith (ed.) *Sociological Studies.* London: Routledge.

Pinar, W., Reynolds, W., Slattery, P. and Taubman, P. (1995) *Understanding Curriculum.* New York: Peter Lang.

Popekwitz, T. (1992) Cartesian anxiety, linguistic communication and reading texts, *Educational Researcher*, 21(5): 11–15.

Popham, W. (1998) A message to parents: don't judge your child's school by its standardized test scores. Paper to the annual meeting of the American Educational Research Association, 13–17 April, San Diego, CA.

Poulton, G. and James, T. (1975) *Preschool Learning in the Community: Strategies for Change.* London: Routledge & Kegan Paul.

Powderly, K. and Westerdale, K. (1998) Should men be included? *Every Child*, 4(3): 9.

Preschool and Childcare Branch (1996) *Babies, Toddlers and Two Year Olds: A Curriculum Resource for Developing Child Centred Programs for Children under Three – May 1996.* Victoria: Department of Human Services.

Press, F. (1999) The demise of community-owned long day care centres and the rise of the mythical consumer, *Australian Journal of Early Childhood*, 24(1): 20–5.

Puckett, M., Marshall, S. and Davis, R. (1999) Examining the emergence of brain development research, *Childhood Education*, 76(1): 8–12.

QCA and DES (2002) *Foundation Stage Profile: A Handbook.* London: QCA and DES.

Quigg, C. Reflections from Claudia Quigg: On the Infant Brain. http://www.babytalk.org/creflectsinfantbrain.html

Ramazanoglu, C. (1992) What can you do with a man? Feminism and the critical appraisal of masculinity, *Women's Studies International Forum*, 15(3): 340.

Ramsey, P. (1987) *Teaching and Learning in a Diverse World: Multicultural Education for Young Children.* Columbia: Teachers College Press.

Rayna, S. (2001) The very beginning of togetherness in shared play among young children, *International Journal of Early Years Education*, 9(2): 109–16.

Read, K., Gardner, P. and Mahler, B. (1993) *Early Childhood Programs: Human Relationships and Learning*, 9th edn. Florida: Harcourt Brace Jovanovich.

Readdick, C. and Chapman, P. (2000) Young children's perceptions of time out, *Journal of Research in Childhood Education*, 15(1): 81–7.

Reid, A. (1999) The national education agenda and its curriculum effects, in B. Johnson and A. Reid (eds) *Contesting the Curriculum.* Sydney: Social Science Press.

Rescorla, L. (1991) Parent and teacher attitudes about early academics, *New Directions for Child Development*, 53: 13–19.

Rinaldi, C. (1993) The emergent curriculum and social constructivism: an interview with Lella Gandini, in C. Edwards., L. Gandini and G. Foreman (eds) *The Hundred Languages of Children: The Reggio Emilia Approach to Early Childhood Education.* Norwood, NJ: Ablex Publishing Corporation.

Rinehart, N. (2000) Native American perspectives: connected to one another and to the greater universe, in L. Diaz Soto (ed.) *The Politics of Early Childhood Education.* New York: Peter Lang Publishers.

Rintoul, S. (1993) *The Wailing: A National Black Oral History.* Port Melbourne: William Heinemann.

Ritchie, J. (1996) The bicultural imperative within the New Zealand draft curriculum guidelines for early childhood education, *Te Whāriki, Australian Journal of Early Childhood*, 21(3): 28–32.

Rivera, J. and Poplin, M. (1995) Multicultural, critical, feminine and constructive pedagogies seen through the lives of youth: a call for the revisioning of these and beyond: toward a pedagogy for the next century, in C. Sleeter and P. McClaren (eds) *Multicultural Education, Critical Pedagogy and the Politics of Difference.* New York: State University of New York Press.

Robinson, B. and Hobson, C. (1978) Beyond sex-role stereotyping, *Day Care and Education*, Fall: 16–18.

Rose, N. (1999) *Governing the Soul: The Shaping of the Private Self*, 2nd edn. London: Free Association Books.

Rosenthal, D. and Young Sawyers, J. (1996) Building successful home/school partnerships: strategies for parent support and involvement, *Child Education*, 72(4): 194–201.

Rossato, C. (2001) Social transformation and 'popular schooling' in Brazil, *Childhood Education*, 77(6): 373.

Rousseau, J.-J. ([1762] 1968) *The Social Contract.* London: Penguin Books.

Rousseau, J.-J. ([1762] 1991) *Emile.* London: Penguin Books.

Rousseau, J.-J. (1773) *Emiluis: Or, A Treatise of Education*, 3 volumes. Edinburgh: W. Coke.

Rufai, R. (1996) Day care in Nigeria, *International Journal of Early Childhood*, 30(1): 30–7.

Ryan, S. and Oschner, M. (1999) Traditional practices: New possibilities. Transforming dominant images of early childhood teachers, *Australian Journal of Early Childhood*, 24(4): 14–20.

Ryan, S., Oschner, M. and Genishi, C. (2001) Miss Nelson is missing! Teacher sightings in research on teaching, in S. Grieshaber and G. Cannella (eds) *Embracing Identities in Early Childhood Education*. New York: Teachers College Press.

Salkind, N.J. (1981) *Theories of Human Development*, 2nd edn. New York: J. Wiley and Sons.

Salkind, N. (1985) *Theories of Human Development*, 3rd edn. New York: J. Wiley and Sons.

Sanchez Medina, J., Lozono, V. and Goudena, P. (2001) Conflict management in preschoolers: a cross cultural perspective, *International Journal of Early Years Education*, 9(2): 153–60.

Sandfort, J. and Coleman Selden, S. (2001) Blurring the boundaries: local collaborations among Head Start, preschool and childcare programs, *Policy and Practice of Public Human Services*, 59(1): 18–23.

Sandstrom, S. (1999) Dear Simba is dead forever, *Young Children*, 54(6): 14–15.

Sato, N. (1993) Teaching and learning in Japanese elementary schools, *Peabody Journal of Education*, 68(4): 111–47.

Sayers, J. (1987) Psychology and gender divisions, in G. Weiner and M. Arnot (eds) *Gender Under Scrutiny: New Inquiries in Education*. Milton Keynes: The Open University.

SCAA (School Curriculum and Assessment Authority) *Nursery Education Desirable Outcomes for Children's Learning on Entering Compulsory Education*. London: Department for Education and Employment.

Scarr, S. and Dunn, J. (1982) *Mother Care, Other Care: The Childcare Dilemma for Women and Children*. London: Pelican Books.

Schreiber, M. (1999) Time out for toddlers: is our goal punishment or education? *Young Children*, 54(4): 22–5.

Scott, L. and Altman, R. (1984) *Standardized Curriculum: Early Childhood*. Philadelphia School District, PA ED 288 624.

SEDL (Southwest Educational Development Laboratory) (1996) The practice implications of constructivism, *Southwest Educational Development Laboratory Newsletter*, IX(3): 1–2.

Segura-Mora, A. (2002) Friere and the education of young children, in A. Darder (ed.) *Reinventing Paulo Friere: A Pedagogy of Love*. Boulder, CO: Westview Press.

Shuba (1991/92) *Shuba: Newsletter on Women and Development*, summer: 9.

Silber, K. (1965) *Pestalozzi: The Man and His Work* (2nd edn). London: Schocken Books.

Silin, J. (1995) *Sex, Death and the Education of Children: Our Passion for Ignorance in the Age of AIDS*. New York: Teachers College Press.

Silin, J. (1997) The pervert in the classroom, in J. Tobin (ed.) *Making a Place for Pleasure in Early Childhood Education*. New Haven: Yale University Press.

Silin, J. (1998) Becoming knowledgeable professionals, in B. Spodek, O. Saracho and D. Peters (eds) *Professionalism and the Early Childhood Practitioners*, pp. 117–34. New York: Teachers College Press.

Silin, J. (1999) Speaking up for silence, *Australian Journal of Early Childhood*, 24(4): 41–5.

Singer, E. (1992) *Childcare and the psychology of development*. London: Routledge.

Siraj-Blatchford, I. (1996) *Learning Technology, Science and Social Justice: An Integrated Approach for 3–13 year olds*. London: Education Now.

Siraj-Blatchford, I. and Clarke, P. (2000) *Supporting Identity, Diversity and Language in the Early Years*. Buckingham: Open University Press.

Slee, J. (1998) Understanding and responding to children's anti-social behaviour, *Every Child*, 4(2): 8–9.

Sleeter, C. and Grant, C. (1999) *Making Choices for Multicultural Education: Five Approaches to Race, Class and Gender*. Columbus, OH: Merrill.

Sleeter, C. and McClaren, P. (1995) Introduction: exploring connections to build a critical multiculturalism, in C. Sleeter and P. McClaren (eds) *Multicultural Education, Critical Pedagogy and the Politics of Difference*. New York: State of New York Press.

Sloan Cannella, G. (1997) *Deconstructing Early Childhood Education: Social Justice and Revolution*. New York: Peter Lang Publishers.

Smith, C. (1982) *Promoting the Social Development of Young Children*, p. 32. Mountain View, CA: Mayfield Publishing Company.

Smith, D. and Lovat, T. (1990) *Curriculum: Action on Reflection*. Sydney: Social Science Press.

Smith, D. and Lovat, T. (1991) Tracking the critical curriculum in teacher practice. Paper presented to the Liberating the Curriculum Conference, University of Adelaide, 11–14 July.

Smith, K. (2000) Reconceptualising the role of parents in observation, *Australian Journal of Early Childhood*, 25(2): 18–21.

Smith, K. (2001) Reconstructing quality services through changes to relationships between teachers and parents. Paper presented to the Australian Early Childhood Association Biennial Conference, Excellence for Children, Sydney, 18–21 July.

Smith, S.R. (1997) Partnerships, community building, and local government, *National Civic Review*, 86(2): 167–75.

Solomon, J. (1976) *Encounters: A Resource Schedule for Early Childhood*. Perth: Child Study Publications.

Spaggari, S. (1993) The community–teacher partnership in the governance of the schools, in C. Edwards, L. Gandini and G. Forman (eds) *The Hundred Languages of Children: The Reggio Emilia Approach to Early Childhood Education*. Norwood, NJ: Ablex Publishing Corporation.

Spencer, L. and Krauze, A. (2000) *Introducing the Enlightenment*. Cambridge: Icon Books.

Spodek, B. (1987) The knowledge base of kindergarten education. Paper presented to five year-olds in School Conference. East Lansing, MI, 9 January.

Spodek, B. (1988) *The Early Childhood Professional and the Definition of Knowledge*. ERIC Document, ED 293657.

Spodek, B. (2002) *Current Directions in Early Childhood Education*. Opening address to Pacific Early Childhood Education Research Association Third Conference and Meeting: Early Childhood Education in Cultural Context, Shanghai, China, 23–25 July.

Spodek, B. and Saracho, O. (1994) *Right from the Start: Teaching Children Ages Three to Eight*. Boston: Allyn and Bacon.

Statham, J. (1986) *Daughters and Sons: Experiences of Non-sexist Child Rearing*. London: Basil Blackwell.

Stephen, H. (1993) *Conflict Resolution with Young Children*. Canberra: Australian Early Childhood Association.

Stipik, D. *et al.* (1994) Making parents your allies, *Young Children*, 49(3): 4–9.

Stonehouse, A. (1988) One perspective on programming for toddlers, in A. Stonehouse (ed.) *Trusting Toddlers: Programming for One to Three Year Olds in Childcare Centres*. Canberra: Australian Early Childhood Association.

Studer, J. (1993/94) Listen so that parents will speak, *Childhood Education*, 70(2): 74–7.

Sumison, J. (2002) Revisiting the challenge of staff recruitment and retention in children's services, *Australian Journal of Early Childhood*, 27(1): 8–13.

Swick, K., Boutte, G. and van Scoy, I. (1995) Family involvement in early multicultural learning, *ERIC Digest*, EDO-PS-95-2.

Sylva, K., Blatchford, I.S. and Johnson, S. (1992) The impact of the UK national curriculum on pre-school practice, *International Journal of Early Childhood*, 24(1): 41–51.

Taba, H. (1962) *Curriculum Development: Theory and Practice*. New York: Harcourt Brace & World Inc.

Tamaki, T. (2000) A new activity model theory for anti-bias education of young children in Japan. Paper presented to the Australian Early Childhood Association Biennial Conference, Darwin, Australia, July.

Tanner, D. and Tanner, L. (1975) *Curriculum Development: Theory into Practice*. New York: Macmillan.

Tate, W. (1996) Critical race theory, *Review of Research in Education*, 22: 201–47.

Thompson, P. (1999) How doing justice got boxed in, in B. Johnson and A. Reid (eds) *Contesting the Curriculum*. Sydney: Social Science Press.

Thompson, R. (2001) Development in the first years of life, *The Future of Children*, 11(1): 21–33.

Thornley, C. and Graham, S. (2001) Curriculum integration: an implicit integration model, *Curriculum Perspectives*, 21(2): 31–7.

Tillman, D. (2001) Educating for a culture of peace in refugee camps, *Childhood Education*, 77(6): 375–8.

Tinworth, S. (1997) Whose good idea was it? Child initiated curriculum, *Australian Journal of Early Childhood*, 22(3): 24–9.

Townsend-Cross, M. (2002) Respecting children's voices, *Every Child*, 8(3): 8–9.

Trepanier-Street, M., McNair, S. and Donegan, M. (2001) The views of teachers on assessment: a comparison of lower and upper elementary teachers, *Journal of Research in Childhood Education*, 15(2): 234–41.

Tsumori, M. (1998) Education and care for children with special needs, *International Journal of Early Childhood*, 30(1): 79–82.

Tyler, R.W. (1949) *Basic Principles of Curriculum and Instruction*. Chicago, MI: University of Chicago Press.

Unteregger-Mattenberger, J. (1995) Mothers and teachers look at preschool differently, *International Journal of Early Childhood*, 27(2): 59–64.

Van Ausdale, D. and Feagin, J.R. (1996) Using racial and ethnic concepts: the critical case of very young children, *American Sociological Review*, 61: 779–93.

van Scoy, I. (1995) Trading the three R's for the four E's: transforming curriculum, *Childhood Education*, 72(1): 19–23.

Vandenbroeck, M. (1999) *The View of the Yeti: Bringing up Children in the Spirit of Self-Awareness and Kindredship*. The Hague: Bernard van Leer Foundation.

Velickaite-Katiniene, A. (1998) Development of child's musical culture at a preschool institution, *International Journal of Early Childhood*, 28(1): 71–8.

Viruru, R. and Cannella, G.S. (2001) Postcolonial ethnography, young children, and voice, in S. Grieshaber and G. Cannella (eds) *Embracing Identities in Early Childhood Education: Diversity and Possibilities*. New York: Teachers College Press.

Vygotsky, L. (1929) The problem of the cultural development of the child, *Journal of Genetic Psychology*, 36: 415–34.

Wagner, P., Baadsgaard, M. and Neessen, V. (1995) *The Third Hand*. Melbourne: Swinburne University.

Wah, E. (1992) K2 children's learning of national identity in Singapore, *Singapore Journal of Education*, 12(2): 59–63.

Walker, A. (1989) *The Temple of My Familiar*. London: Penguin Books.

Walkerdine, V. (1982) *Girls and Mathematics*. London: Virago.

Walkerdine, V. (1988) *The Mastery of Reason: Cognitive Development and the Production of Rationality*. London: Routledge.

Walkerdine, V. (1992) Progressive pedagogy and political struggle, in C. Luke and J. Gore (eds) *Feminisms and Critical Pedagogy*. London: Routledge.

Walkerdine, V. (1999) Violent boys and precocious girls: regulating childhood at the end of the millennium, *Contemporary Issues in Early Childhood*, 1(1): 3–22.

Walkerdine, V. and Lucey, H. (1989) *Democracy in the Kitchen: Regulating Mothers and Socialising Daughters.* London: Virago.

Wallance, M. (1998) Conference opening address. Paper presented to the Respect: Education Without Prejudice, a Challenge for Early Years Educators in Ireland Conference, 16 October.

Watson, J. (1997) Children's construction of 'fair' representations of one-third, *Australian Journal of Early Childhood*, 22(2): 34–8.

Watson, J.B. (1924) *Behaviourism.* New York: Norton.

Watson, J.B. (1928) *Psychological Care of Infant and Child.* New York: Norton.

Weber, E. (1984) *Ideas Influencing Early Childhood Education.* Columbia, OH: Teachers College Press.

Weedon, C. (1997) *Feminist Practice and Poststructuralist Theory*, 2nd edn. Oxford: Basil Blackwell.

Weikart, D. (1995/96) High/Scope in action: the milestones, *High/Scope Resource*, Special Edition: 4–6.

Weikart, D. and Schweinart, L. (1987) The High/Scope cognitively orientated curriculum in early childhood, in J. Roopnaarina (ed.) *Approaches to Early Childhood Curriculum.* Columbia, OH: Merrill Publishing Company.

Weikart, D. and Schweinhart, L. (1991) Disadvantaged children and curriculum effects, *New Directions for Child Development*, 53: 57–64.

Whalley, M. and the Pen Green Team (2001) *Involving Parents in their Children's Learning.* London: Sage.

Williams, G. (1983) The denial of minority rights, *New Internationalist*, October: 7–11.

Williams, R. (1976) *Keywords: A Vocabulary of Culture and Society.* London: Fontana.

Witherell, C. and Noddings, N. (eds) (1991) *Stories Lives Tell: Narrative and Dialogue in education.* New York: Teachers College Press.

Woodhead, M. (1999) Reconstructing developmental psychology: some first steps, *Children and Society*, 13: 3–19.

World Bank Group (2002) *Why invest in ECD?* http://www. worldbank.org/children/whyinvest/

Wright Sexton, A. (1996) Sowing and reaping: the seeds of parent involvement in a pre-K co-op, *Focus on Early Childhood*, 9(2): 1–4.

Yang, O.S. (2001) An epistemological and ethical categorization of perspectives on early childhood curriculum, *International Journal of Early Childhood*, 33(1): 1–8.

Yonetani, M., Takasugi, G. and Muto, N. (2001) Development of a two-way system for sharing of information with guardians in kindergartens and future challenges. Paper presented to the Association for Childhood Education International Conference, Toronto, Canada.

Yost, D., Sentner, S. and Forlenza-Bailey, A. (2000) An examination of the construct of critical reflection: implications for teacher education programming in the 21st century, *Journal of Teacher Education*, 51: 39–49.

Young, R. (1990) *A Critical Theory of Education: Habermas and our Children's Future.* New York: Teachers College Press.

Zack, N. (1998) Mixed black and white race and public policy, in N. Zack, L. Shrage and C. Sartwell (eds) *Race, Class, Gender and Sexuality: The Big Questions.* Boston: Blackwell Publishers.

Index

Aboriginals, Australian, 106, 290,
    291–2
    personal dolls project, 304–13
abuse, mandatory reporting of, 287–8
'acceleration' curriculum, 225
acting, 297, 299
action research, 296–9
    planning cycle, 193, 236
    and professional activism, 296–7
    for transforming practice, 98–103
active behaviour management programme,
    134
adult literacy education, 185
advocacy, 294
Afro-American History Site, 120
age, 317
agencies, community as, 256–64, 279
Aguado, T., 192
Alloway, N., 74, 103
Alvestad, M., 132
Andrew, Y., 148, 213–19
anecdotal observations, 136–7, 138
Anning, A., 141, 177
Anthony, L., 122
anti-bias curriculum, 190–2, 234
Anti-Bias Curriculum Task Force, 190
anti-bias gaze, 179–80
anti-biased communication, 275–6
art, 55
artefacts, collecting, 173
ASCA, 156, 170
assessment, 119–20
    case study on, 227–33

conforming curriculum, 140–3, 144,
    149–53
equity and, 149–53, 179–80, 209–10
reforming curriculum, 170–5, 176, 179–80
transforming curriculum, 202–6, 207,
    209–10
assimilationism, 20–1
Atmore, E., 163
attachment, 54, 151–2
audio-taping, 172
Australia, 106, 122, 156, 259, 266
    Early Childhood Code of Ethics, 288–9
    goals for children's learning, 235
    indigenous Aboriginal children, 106, 290,
        291–2
    national profiles and statements, 140–1
    persona dolls project, 304–13
    QIAS, 269, 284–5, 291
    Victoria, 265

babies, respectful interactions with, 238
back-to-school nights, 268
Bandura, A., 32, 33
Barbie, 86
Barbour, N., 146
Barnett, J., 22
Battersby, C., 57
Beattie, M., 222
Beaty, J., 139
behaviour management programme, 134
behavioural objectives, 126
behaviourism, 24–31, 124, 132, 134
    see also social learning theory

Bell, D., 187
Bellamy, C., 2, 183, 219
Bentzen, W., 135–6
Berger, E.H., 258, 260, 261, 265, 266, 268–9
Bernard van Leer Foundation, 274
bias
    children's constructions of 'race', 46–7
    reinforcing biases, 149
Bloch, M., 17, 49, 135
Blue Sage Community Partners, 274
Blyth, A., 140
Bobbit, F., 124
book corner, 227–8
Bowlby, J., 52, 151–2
'brain research', 61–2, 123, 152
    see also neuroscience
Bredekamp, S., 282, 305
Brennan, D., 259
broad guiding principles, 160–3
Broinowski, I., 163
Broström, S., 236
Brown, B., 235
Brown, 156
Bruer, J., 65, 66
Bruner, J., 40, 43, 45, 114, 130
Burman, E., 70, 75
Buruku people (Japan), 192
'business as usual' approach, 21–2, 47–8

'calendar' curriculum, 225
Campbell, S., 88, 203, 205
Canada, 106
Cannella, G.S., 49, 50, 75, 76, 87, 261, 295
care, ethic of, 186, 295–6
Carlsson-Paige, N., 235
Carr, M., 174
Carr, W., 161, 164
Carter, M., 174
Castillo, G., 197
Catherwood, D., 61, 63
CETaL, 114
Chabris, 62
Chang, H., 274
change orientated goals, 189
Chapman, P., 27
child-centred education, 84, 163, 165, 175, 176–7, 319
child psychology, 16–17
childhood, 9–10

children, 9–10
    constructions of 'race', 46–7
    contexts, 248–52
    disempowering, 146–7, 149–50
    experiences, 214–15
    and gender development, 47–8
    interaction with, 197
    involving in programme planning, 99–100
    many truths of the child, 74
    participation and learning, 238
    reflecting with families and, 295
    rights see rights, children's
    transforming their world, 197–8
    underestimating, 150
    see also learner, models of
China, 236
Chugani, 65
citizenship, 264
Clark, A., 170
Clarke, P., 277–8, 318
Clarke-Stewart, A., 257
class, 317
    relationships with parents and communities, 261–2
Clift, 140
co-construction of meaning, 179
codes of practice, 288–92
cognitive interactionism, 42
    see also constructivism
Coleberg-Schrader, H., 221
collaboration
    collaborative dialogic pedagogies, 199–202
    educator-parent, 265–9
collecting artefacts, 173
College Ten, 120
colonization, 290–1
Comenius, J.A., 107, 156–7
communication, 260
    learning community, 272–3, 274–7
communities, 248–52, 255–81
    case study of relationships with, 303–13
    conforming position, 255, 256–64, 279
    equity issues in, 317
    reforming position, 255, 265–9, 280
    transforming position, 255, 269–79, 280
communities of learners, 265–9, 271, 279, 280
community building, 272, 279–80, 316–17
community involvement, 272, 279–80

conforming positions, 4
  curriculum, 121–54,
    models of learner, 10, 14–39, 93–5
    parents and communities, 255, 256–64,
     279
    professionalism, 283–92
Connell, R., 37, 82
conservative cultural values, reinforcing,
  176–7
construction site play, 88
constructivism, 40–52
consumer, 264
content
  conforming curriculum, 127, 129–32
  conforming models of learner, 19, 28, 35
  reforming curriculum, 160, 162, 166–7
  reforming models of learner, 46, 56, 64
  transforming curriculum, 190, 195–8
  transforming models of learner, 78, 91
contexts, curriculum *see* relationships
Copple, C., 282, 305
Corrie, L., 66, 67
Council of Economic Advisors Report,
  122–3
Crain, W.C., 15, 25, 26, 32, 44
Creative Perception process, 163
crime, 122–3
criteria-referenced interpretation, 139
critical activism, 295–9
critical analysis table, 204
critical anti-racists, 187–8
critical approach to curriculum, 188–207
critical community, 293
critical constructivists, 48, 49
critical dialogue, 5–6
critical educational theory, 184–5
  critical multiculturalism, 187–8
  feminists and social reconstructionism,
   185–7
critical friend, 239
critical interests, 4
  see also transforming positions
critical multiculturalism, 187–8
critical race theory, 187–8, 195–6
critical reflection, 1–6
  in action research, 297, 299
  curriculum, 113–20, 213–43
  defining, 2–3
  models of the learner, 9–13, 93–109
  relationships, 247–54, 302–19

time for not structured into educator's
  days, 208–9
Critical Teaching Project, 96, 97–8, 196
critical theory, 72
Croft, C., 138
cross-cultural communication, respectful,
  277
cross-cultural partnerships, 278
cultural feminists, 185–6
cultural transmission, 123–4
  implications for early childhood
   curriculum, 125–44
culturally narrow goals, 177–8
culture, 14, 317
  conforming to, 24–38
  conforming to dominant culture, 145
  of learning, 240
curriculum, 111–243
  conforming position, 121–54
  critical reflection, 113–20, 213–43
  in early childhood settings, 235–41
  implications of conforming models of
   learner, 17–19, 26–8, 33–5
  implications of reforming models of
   learner, 43–6, 54–6, 63–4
  implications of transforming models of
   learner, 75–8, 87–9
  reforming position, 155–81
  shaping through goals *see* goals
  shaping through observervation and
   assessment *see* assessment; observation
  shaping through philosophy *see*
   philosophies of education
  shaping through plans *see* planning
  transforming position, 182–212
curriculum contexts *see* relationships
curriculum documents, 288–9
curriculum packages, 131
Curtis, D., 174

Dahlberg, G., 76–7, 106, 273, 291
daily communication with parents, 276
Darder, A., 184, 202
Dau, E., 191, 192
David, M., 258
Davies, B., 36, 80, 85, 200
Davies, I., 126
Davis, D., 139
Davis, K., 305
Deci, E., 27

Decker, C., 132, 258, 260
Decker, J., 132, 258, 260
deficit model of the child, 150, 214
DeMello, 140
democracy, 208, 209–10
Denmark, 236
Department for Education and Skills (DES)
    (UK), 142
Derman-Sparkes, L., 177–8, 190–1
Desirable Objectives and Practices (DOPs),
    142
DETE, *Growing and Learning in the Family*,
    259
developmental approach, 164–5, 214
    disempowering educators, 151–2
    problematic, 75
    see also maturationism
developmentally appropriate practice
    (DAP), 84, 163, 165, 175, 176–7, 319
Dewey, J., 108, 155, 158, 158–60, 171, 175
dialogue
    creating opportunities for regular dialogue
        with parents, 274–5
    critical, 5–6
    transforming curriculum, 199–202
Diaz Soto, L., 76, 313, 315
disability, 278–9
disciplines, 130
discourse, 80–3
    learning in, 81–2
    learning in discourse and power, 82–3
    learning in discourses and their power
        effects, 83
    learning in discourse and subjectivity,
        82
disempowerment
    educator, 146–7, 150–3
    learner, 146–7, 149–50
diversity/difference, 20–3
    abnormal, 20–1
    bringing diversity into curriculum
        community, 304–13
    cultural construction, 74
    natural, 21–2
Diversity in Early Childhood Education and
    Training (DECET), 294
documenting, 297, 299
dolls, as teaching tool, 304–13
dominant culture
    conforming to, 145

reinforcement of dominant cultural values
    by standards and codes, 289–91
Dreamtime, 309
Dunn, J., 259
Durham, F., 55

early childhood organizations, 294, 300–1
Early Years Trainers Anti-Racist Network,
    UK, 183
Ebbeck, M., 44, 159, 267
Education Review Office (ERO) (New
    Zealand), 142
educators/teachers
    and child's failure to learn, 66
    disempowerment of, 146–7, 150–3
    distancing from child, 151–3
    see also pedagogical relationships
'egg carton' curriculum, 225
Elliot, A., 36, 149
Elschenbroich, D., 223
emancipatory interests, 4
    see also transforming positions
emergent curriculum, 167, 171–3
emotion, 88
emotional climate, 240
empiricism, 136
empowerment, 199–202
    see also disempowerment
Enlightenment, 16, 156–60
enrichment programmes, 66
environment, 63
equity
    conforming curriculum and, 145–53
    conforming models of learner and, 20–4,
        29–31, 35–8
    and knowledge-power relationships in
        early childhood communities,
        316–19
    parents and communities, 261–4, 268–9,
        274–9
    professionalism and, 289–92, 299–300
    reforming curriculum and, 176–80
    reforming models of learner and, 46–52,
        56–9, 64–7
    transforming curriculum and, 207–10
    transforming models of learner and,
        78–80, 89–91
Erikson, E., 52, 53–4
ethics, 288–92
ethnicity, 278

ethnocentrism
    dominance of ethnocentric knowledge, 263
    privileging ethnocentric individualistic
        goals, 177–8
Eurocentrism, 146
European Commission Network on
    Childcare, 223
European Enlightenment, 16, 156–60
evaluation of teaching and learning, 238–9
event sampling, 137
experiences, children's, 214–15

families, reflecting with, 295
    see also parents
family centres, 258
Faragher, J., 149
favourite sayings, 105, 221
Feagan, J.R., 79
Feeney, 136
Fell, K., 264
feminism
    'feminist' in poststructuralism, 85–7
    and social reconstructionism, 185–7
feminist poststructuralism, 80–91, 186–7
Fidler, M., 271
fields of inquiry, 130
fighting games, 230–1
'fill in the blanks' curriculum, 225
Finland, 156
Fleer, M., 226, 238, 273
Foucault, M., 83–5, 87, 228, 289–90
Foundation Areas of Learning, 259
Foundation Stage Profile, 142
four 'e's, 234
Frankfurt School of Critical Theory, 4, 195,
    271
Frede, E., 262–3
free play, 55, 58
Freeman, A., 187
Freire, P., 78, 182, 184–5, 187–8, 197, 199,
    201, 206, 318
Freud, A., 54
Freud, S., 52, 53, 57, 59
friendship patterns, 240–1
Froebel, F., 108, 152, 156–7, 159, 258
futures education, 302–3

Gallas, K., 293
Gargiulo, R., 279
Gelfer, J., 265

gender, 317
    behaviourism and equity, 29
    children and gender development, 47–8
    dynamics, 232–3, 239, 240
    identity and psychodynamics, 56–8, 59
    natural differences, 21
    reforming curriculum and equity, 178, 179
    social learning theory and gender roles,
        35–6, 37–8
genital identity, 57
Gesell, A., 14, 15, 16, 135
Giddens, A., 86
Gilligan, C., 186
Gilman, C.P., 108
Ginsburg, H., 44
Giroux, H., 124, 182, 185, 207
goal-based interpretation, 139–40
goal orientated communication, 275
goals, 116–17, 235–6
    conforming curriculum, 125–8, 143–4,
        146–8
    critical reflections, 222–4
    equity and, 146–8, 177–8, 207–8
    reforming curriculum, 160–5, 175, 177–8
    transforming curriculum, 188–92, 206–7,
        207–8
Goldstein, C., 189, 190, 208–9
Goldstein, L., 186, 199
Gomez, M.L., 170
Goodfellow, J., 147, 166, 169–70
Goodwin, F., 62
Gore, J., 84
grand narratives, 290
Grant, C., 2, 20–1, 37, 187, 197–8, 199, 219,
    222, 272
Graue, M.E., 21, 22
Graves, S., 279
Grieshaber, S., 50, 76, 150
group dynamics, 232–3, 240
group experiences, planning, 236–7
group meetings, 100–2
group time, 97–8
Grundy, S., 160, 201
guiding principles, broad, 160–3

Habermas, J., 1, 3, 4, 16, 195, 271
Hall, N., 131
Hampstead War Nursery, 54
Hanley, 41
Hartley, R., 145

Hauser, M., 37
Hayward, J., 318
Head Start programmes, 258, 259, 261, 266, 286
Hedges, 106
Hendrick, J., 54, 59, 167, 260
Henniger, M., 45, 132, 138, 151, 163, 165, 319
Hepworth Berger, E., 258, 260, 261, 265, 266, 268–9
Hetherich, D., 303, 304–13
Hetherington, E., 29
Hewitt, B., 277
High/Scope programme, 95–6, 233
Holmes, T., 177
Holt, J., 106
home corner, 55
home visits, 258, 313
Honig, A., 47
Honkavaara, P., 156
Hubel, D., 60, 61
Hughes, E., 173–4
Hughes, P., 17, 37–8, 72, 171, 202, 249–50, 257, 263–4, 270, 275–6
Hulmes, E., 20
hurried child syndrome, 256

ideal speech, 271
identification, gender, 56–8, 59
independent thinkers, 158–60
indigenous Australians *see* Aboriginals, Australian
individual children, planning for, 129, 237–8
individual constructivism, 42
individualism
    behaviourism and equity, 29
    reforming curriculum, 177–8
initial interviews, 276
inputs, equity of, 64–5
institutions
    power and discourses, 75, 82
    regimes of truth, 84
integrated curriculum planning, 167, 168
intention-based interpretation, 175
interaction, 40
    with children and generating meaningful content, 197
    between nature and culture, 40–69
interactionism, 72

interpretation of observations, 139–40, 175, 203–4
interpretive communities, 273–4
interpretivism, 171–2
Investigating Partnerships in Early Childhood Education (I-PIECE) project, 286
Isenberg, J., 156
Italy, 173–4, 233, 270, 285–6

Jamaica, 159–60
Japan, 107, 192
jewellery, 100–2
Jilk, B.A., 271
Johnson, B., 208
Jones, E., 168–9
Jones, K., 196
Jonquiere, 17–18
journal writing, 172, 239
Jungck, S., 182

Kant, I., 41
Katz, L.G., 253
Kemmis, S., 123–4, 129, 161, 164, 166
Kenya, 106, 122
Kessler, S., 35–6, 37, 57
Killoran, I., 106
Klass, P., 256, 257
knowledge
    acknowledging parents' knowledge of their children, 277–8
    critical approaches to, 2–3
    curriculum planning, 128, 144, 165, 176, 193
    multiple sources, 299–300
    and power *see* knowledge-power relationships
    socially constructed and problematic, 195–6
    specialized and professionalism, 293
    specialized and wise and just practices, 291–2
    uncertainty despite scientific research, 262–3
knowledge interests, 4–5
knowledge-power relationships, 250–1, 255–81, 315–16
    conforming to, 255, 256–64, 279
    equity and, 316–19
    reforming, 255, 265–9, 280
    transforming, 255, 269–79, 280

Kohlberg, 47
Korea, 122
Kritskaya, O., 267
Kuhn, 127

Lady Gowrie Child Centres, 259
Laishley, J., 43, 138
Landreth, C., 20
language, 42
    goals, 127, 162, 190
Lanyasunya, A.R., 106, 122, 226
Lather, P., 74
Lawrence, H., 239
learner, models of, 7–109
    conforming models, 10, 14–39, 93–5
    critical reflection, 9–13, 93–109
    position statement, 10–12, 103–6
    reforming models, 10, 40–69, 95–6
    transforming models, 10, 70–92,
        96–103
learner centred approach, 84, 163, 165, 175,
    176–7, 319
learners, communities of, 265–9, 271, 279,
    280
learning areas, 141
learning communities, 269–79, 280
learning difficulties, 65–6
learning episodes, 134
learning outcomes, 140–3, 150–1, 205–6
learning resources, 128, 144, 165, 176, 193
learning stories, 172–3
Lee, G., 122
Lee, N., 151
legislation, 283–9
    and equity, 289–92
Lesolayia, M.S., 106, 122, 226
Levin, D., 235
liberal feminists, 185
liberalism, 78, 156–60
    implications for early childhood
        curriculum, 160–76
Linke, P., 238
listening, pedagogy of, 169–70
literacy education, adult, 185
Lithuania, 156
Locke, J., 16, 25–6, 107
Longstreet, W., 185
Lovat, T., 3, 114, 126, 129, 195, 198
love, 186
Lubeck, S., 77

Lucey, H., 85
Lyotard, F., 290

Machel, G., 222
Mac Naughton, G., 2, 5, 25, 37–8, 58–9, 89,
    149, 150, 178, 179–80, 196, 205,
    249–50, 257, 263–4, 270, 275–6, 305
Malaguzzi, L., 285–6
Maloney, C., 277
mandated curricula, 1
    and marginalization of critical pedagogues,
        207–8
mandatory reporting, 287–8
Mandela, N., 222
Mandernach, J., 61
Margaret Trembarth Project, 5–6
Marshall, J.D., 182
Martinko, 127
Marx, K., 48
materials
    conforming models of learner, 19, 28, 34
    reforming models of learner, 45, 56, 64
    structuring space and, 134, 169, 199
    transforming models of learner, 77, 90–1
    see also learning resources
maternal deprivation, 151–2
maturationism, 14–24, 165
McCain, M., 60, 61–2, 65
McClaren, P., 183, 185, 195, 207
McKay, S., 318
McKenna, W., 35–6, 57
McMillan, A., 72
McMillan, M., 108, 158, 159
McNeil, L., 149
meetings with parents, 276
metaphors, 221, 315
    for curriculum planning, 225
    for learning, 104–5
middle class parents, 261–2
Miller, P.H., 32
Milner, V., 159–60
models of learner see learner, models of
modernism, 71–2, 73
Montessori, M., 93–5, 158, 159, 226
Moore, M., 256, 257
Morrison, G., 95
Morrison, J., 159–60
Moss, P., 76–7
mouse puppet, 305–6
Moyles, J., 169, 260, 267

Mules, R., 196
multiple perspectives, 299–300
Murray, C., 192
Murray Thomas, M., 24
Mustard, F.J., 60, 61–2, 65
Myers, M., 248–9

narratives, 173
    see also story writing
Nash, 62
Nasper, E., 56–7
National Childcare Accreditation Council
        (NCAC) (Australia), 284
national profiles and outcome statements,
        140–1
natural differences, 21–2
nature, 14
    conforming to, 14–24, 93–5
    interaction between nature and culture,
        40–69
    transforming culture and, 70–92
Neal, D., 148, 213–19
neoclassical curriculum, 129
networking, 294
neuroscience, 60–7, 123, 152
New, C., 258
New, 224
New, R., 22, 177
new sociology of childhood, 71
New Zealand, 106, 235, 290–1
    learning outcomes, 142
    PAFT programme, 272
    Te Whāriki, 142, 215, 234, 236, 286, 289,
        291
Newman, B., 148, 213–19
Newman, L., 315
Nigeria, 122, 235
Nimmo, J., 197, 205
Noddings, N., 186, 199
non-interference, 58–9
norm-referenced interpretation, 139
normalization, 20
Norway, 132
NSW Department of Community Services,
        282

Oberheumer, P., 221
objectives-based goal development, 126
objectives-based planning, 128–9, 148
Objisanya, O., 235

observation, 119–20, 239–41
    case studies, 227–33
    conforming curriculum, 134–40, 144,
        149–53
    equity and, 149–53, 179–80, 209–10
    interpreting, 139–40, 175, 203–4
    reforming curriculum, 170–5, 176, 179–80
    transforming curriculum, 202–6, 207,
        209–10
O'Doherty, A., 192
O'Loughlin, 82
Ontario studies, 64–5
Open-Air Nursery, 158
Open Society Institute (OSI), 221
Opper, S., 44
optimal production procedures, 127
osmosis theories of gendering, 36, 85
othering, 306
outcomes-based assessment, 140–3, 150–1,
        205–6

Paley, V., 18, 226
parent education, 258, 260, 268
parent-staff meetings, 260
parents, 248–52, 255–81
    acknowledgement of parents' knowledge of
        children, 277–8
    case study of relationships with, 303–13
    conforming position, 255, 256–64, 279
    reforming position, 255, 265–9, 280
    transforming position, 255, 269–79, 280
Parents As First Teachers (PAFT)
        programme, 272
Parke, R., 29
Parker, C., 159
Pavlov, I., 24, 26
Pease-Windy Boy, J., 198
pedagogical relationships
    conforming curriculum, 133–4, 151–3
    conforming models of learner, 23–4,
        29–31, 38
    reforming curriculum, 168–70
    reforming models of learner, 50–2, 59,
        66–7
    transforming curriculum, 198–202
    transforming models of learner, 79–80,
        89–90
pedagogy of listening, 169–70
Pen Green Centre, 269, 271, 286
Pence, A., 76–7

people
   conforming curriculum, 128, 144
   conforming models of learner, 19, 28, 35
   reforming curriculum, 165, 176
   reforming models of learner, 45, 56, 64
   transforming curriculum, 192
   transforming models of learner, 78, 91
Perkins Gilman, C., 223
persona dolls, 304–13
Pestalozzi, J., 107–8, 152, 156–7, 159
philosophies of education, 114–16, 214–15
   building a position statement, 220–2
   conforming curriculum, 122–4, 143,
      145–6
   equity and, 145–6, 176–7, 207–8
   reforming curriculum, 156–60, 175, 176–7
   transforming curriculum, 183–8, 206,
      207–8
Piaget, J., 40, 41, 42, 43, 44, 74, 95
Pinar, W., 124, 126
plan-do-review learning sequence, 95
planning, 118, 236–8
   action research, 296–7, 299
   case studies on, 213–19
   conforming curriculum, 128–33, 144, 148
   conforming models of learner, 18–19,
      27–8, 34–5
   equity and, 148, 178–9, 208–9
   position statement on, 224–6
   process, 128–9, 165–6, 193–4
   reforming curriculum, 165–8, 175–6,
      178–9
   reforming models of learner, 45–6, 55–6,
      63–4
   transforming curriculum, 192–5, 207,
      208–9
   transforming models of learner, 77–8, 90–1
play, 55, 58, 319
pleasure principle, 53
Plowden Report, 258
policy, 233–4, 249–50
politics of 'truth' and knowledge, 75
Pollintz, L., 315
Popekwitz, 145
Popham, W., 256
Poplin, M., 186, 200
position statement
   child as learner, 10–12, 103–6
   curriculum, 219–26
   relationships, 313–16

postmodernism, 3, 70–80
poststructuralism, 72, 73, 74, 83–5, 202
   feminist, 80–91, 186–7
power, 89
   conforming curriculum and Eurocentric
      power relations, 146
   constructivists and power relations, 48–9
   institutional, 75, 82
   knowledge-power relationships see
      knowledge-power relationships
   learning in discourse and power, 82–3
   learning in discourses and their power
      effects, 83
   liberalism and, 157
   play and power relations, 58
   reforming curriculum and privileging
      voices and meanings of the powerful,
      179–80
   transforming curriculum and power
      relations, 207–8
practical approach to curriculum, 160–76
practical interests, 4
   see also reforming positions
practical judgements in action, 160, 163–4
praxis, 201–2
pre-packaged curricula, 131
Preschool and Childcare Branch, 139
Press, F., 264
problem-posing approach, 184–5
professionalism, 282–301
   conforming position, 283–92
   critical reflection, 252–4, 313–19
   transforming position, 292–300
programme planning, involving child in,
   99–100
progressive education, 84, 163, 165, 175,
   176–7, 319
project based curriculum, 167
psyche, 53
psychodynamics, 52–9
psycho-social crises, 54

QCA, 142
quality assurance, 284–6
Quality in Diversity in Early Learning, 234
Quality Improvement and Accreditation
   System (QIAS), 269, 284–5, 291
'Questions' and 'I believe' board, 104, 220,
   314–15
Quigg, C., 62

'race', 22, 179, 317
  children's constructions of, 46–7
  critical race theory, 187–8, 195–6
  critical reflections on 'race' in relationships
    with parents and community, 278
  inability of specialized knowledge to
    prevent racism, 291–2
Ramazanoglu, C., 37
rating scales, 137–8
rationality, 124, 125
  goal development, 126–7
Rayna, 319
Read, K., 131–2, 134–5, 159, 265
Readdick, C., 27
reciprocity, 88–9
reconnaissance, 296–7, 298
record keeping, 276
reforming positions, 4
  curriculum, 155–81
  models of the learner, 10, 40–69, 95–6
  relationships, 255, 265–9, 280
refugee camps, Thailand, 315
Reggio Emilia, Italy, 173–4, 233, 270, 285–6
regimes of truth, 84–5, 289–90
regulations, 283–6, 287–8
Reid, A., 19, 208
reinforcement, 26, 27, 29, 134
  vicarious, 32
relationships, 247–319
  critical reflections, 247–54, 302–19
  equity and knowledge-power relationships,
    316–19
  parents and communities, 248–52,
    255–81, 303–13
  pedagogical see pedagogical relationships
  professionalism, 252–4, 282–301, 313–16
resistance, 37
resources
  equity in, 64–5
  learning resources, 128, 144, 165, 176, 193
  see also materials
respectful cross-cultural communication, 277
Rey, C., 318
rights, children's, 286–7
  undermined by formal assessment, 209–10
Rinaldi, C., 167, 169, 170
Rinehart, N., 274
risk-minimization plan, 201
Rivera, J., 186, 200
Roach, A., 290

Rockdale Park Kindergarten, 318
role modelling, 32–8
Romanticism, 15–16
Rosenthal, D., 267
Rossato, C., 201, 221, 315
Rousseau, J.-J., 15–16, 25–6, 107, 156–7
Rufai, R., 122
Rugg, H., 176
running records, 137
Ryan, O., 88

Saitta, S., 98–102
Salkind, N., 33
Samuelsson, I.P., 132
Sandstrom, S., 162
Sato, N., 107, 223
scaffolding, 43
Scarr, S., 259
schedule, 132–3, 167–8, 198
School Curriculum and Assessment
    Authority (SCAA) (UK), 141, 143
school projects, 269
Schreiber, M., 33
Schwab, J., 164
Schweinhart, L., 95
science, 16–17
  role of scientific thinking and cultural
    transmission, 124
  scientific research and uncertainty, 262–3
scientific management theory, 127
SEDL, 41
Segura-Mora, A., 189
self-governing child, 155, 158, 265
September, 11 2001 terrorist attacks, 2
sex roles, 32–3
sexuality, 88, 317, 318
Shaikh, S., 159
Shane, H., 185
shared meanings, 272–3
Shumaker, A., 176
Silin, J., 147, 151, 152–3, 318
Singer, E., 157–8, 259, 261
Siraj-Blatchford, I., 277–8, 318
Siraj-Blatchford, J., 147
Skinner, B.F., 24
Slee, J., 27
Sleeter, C., 2, 20–1, 37, 183, 187, 195, 197–8,
    199, 219, 222, 272
Sloan Cannella, G., 49
Smith, 47

Smith, D., 3, 114, 126, 129, 195, 198
Smith, K., 88, 203, 205, 227–31
Smith, S.R., 264
Smith Hill, P., 176
social activism, 183–4, 272
   critical educational theory as, 184–5
   see also social reconstructionism
'social consciousness', 4
social constructionism, 42–3, 70–80
social learning theory, 32–8, 185
social reconstructionism, 183–4
   equity, 207–10
   feminists and, 185–7
   implications for early childhood
     curriculum, 188–207
social relationships, 240
   reforming curriculum and masking, 178–9
social reproduction, 122–3
social structures, 85–7
   see also under individual structures
social utility, 122–3
socialization theory, 80, 85
society
   conforming to, 121–54
   reforming, 155–81
   role of early childhood education in,
     219–22
   transforming, 182–212
Solomon, J., 43
space
   conforming curriculum, 128, 134, 144
   conforming models of learner, 19, 28, 35
   reforming curriculum, 165, 169, 176
   reforming models of learner, 45, 56, 64
   structuring, 134, 169, 199
   transforming curriculum, 193, 199
   transforming models of learner, 78, 91
Spaggari, S., 270
Spodek, B., 176
Stagnitti, 140
standardized curriculum, 126
standardized testing, 150, 256
standards, 288–91
Start Right programme, 269
state
   conforming relationships and helping state
     to abdicate from its responsibilities,
     263–4
   policy, 233–4, 249–50
Statham, 32

Stenhouse, L., 164
Step by Step Program, 221
stereotypes, reinforcing, 147–8
stimulation, 63
Stonehouse, A., 139
story writing, 104, 172–3, 221, 315
stress-free environments, 239
stresses, child, 249
subjectivity, 82
Sumison, J., 292
Sure Start programme, 269
Swadner, 313
Sweden, 106, 291
Swedish Childcare Commission (SOU), 106,
   226
Sycamore, J., 318

Taba, H., 126
Tamaki, T., 150, 192
Tanner, D., 115
Tanner, L., 115
Taylor, F., 127
Te Whāriki, 142, 215, 234, 236, 286, 289, 291
teaching strategies, structuring, 134, 169–70,
   199–202
technical approach to curriculum, 124,
   125–44, 146–7, 161
technical interests, 4
   see also conforming positions
teddy bears, 305
Test of Pretend Play (ToPP), 140
theory-based interpretation, 140, 175
thinking
   children's and adults', 46, 48, 49
   developmental stages exist in specific times
     and cultures, 48, 49–50
Thompson, P., 63, 197
Thompson, R., 11, 17, 53, 152
Tillman, 315
time
   conforming curriculum, 128, 144
   conforming models of learner, 19, 28, 34
   reforming curriculum, 165, 175
   reforming models of learner, 45, 56, 64
   transforming curriculum, 192
   transforming models of learner, 77, 90–1
time out, 27, 29
time sampling, 137, 240
Tinworth, S., 167
'Tourist Approach', 304–5

Townsend-Cross, M., 106, 146
transforming positions, 4
    curriculum, 182–212
    models of learner, 10, 70–92, 96–103
    parents and communities, 255, 269–79,
        280
    professionalism, 292–300
Trembarth Project, 5–6
Trepanier-Street, M., 150
Tsumori, M., 174
Tyler, R., 121

uncertainty, 74
    despite scientific research, 262–3
underestimation of children, 150
United Kingdom (UK), 235, 265, 266, 272
    family centres, 258
    outcomes-based assessment, 141–2
    Pen Green Centre, 269, 271, 286
    Quality in Diversity in Early Learning, 234
United Nations Convention on the Rights of
    the Child, 286–7
United States (US), 106, 156, 235
    Head Start, 258, 259, 261, 266, 286
    High/Scope, 95–6, 233
    parent education programmes, 258
    reforming approach to parent involvement,
        266
units of study, 130
universal theories, 50

values, 215
    reinforcing conservative values, 176–7
Van Ausdale, D., 79
Vandenbroeck, M., 223
Velickaite-Katiniene, A., 156
vicarious reinforcement, 32

Vico, G., 41
videoing, 172
Viruru, R., 49
vocationally orientated curriculum, 129
volunteering, 257–8, 263–4
Vygotsky, L., 40, 41, 42–3, 74

Wagner, P., 27
Wah, E., 130
Walker, A., 116
Walkerdine, V., 80, 85, 88, 178
Wallance, M., 183
Walsh, J., 22
Walters, R., 33
Watson, J., 169
Watson, J.B., 24, 25, 26
Weedon, C., 88
Weikart, D., 95, 96
Weisel, T., 60, 61
Whalley, M., 269, 286
Williams, G., 25, 179, 207–8
Williams-Kennedy, D., 226, 273
'windows of opportunity' for learning, 66,
    67
wise practice, 166
    inability to ensure with codes and
        specialized knowledge, 291–2
Women's History Site, 120
Woodhead, M., 50, 71
working class parents, 261–2
World Bank Group, 60–1
written communication, 276

Yang, O.S., 136
Young Sawyers, J., 267

zone of proximal development (ZPD), 43

OBSERVING HARRY
CHILD DEVELOPMENT AND LEARNING 2–5

Cath Arnold

This book is about Harry, a determined little boy, who is intrinsically motivated to explore his world from an early age. His parents and grandparents find him so fascinating that they keep a written and video diary of Harry's play from when he is 8 months to 5 years. The author offers theories about how children learn and applies the theories to the observations of Harry.

The book demonstrates how effectively Harry accesses each area of the curriculum through his interests. It shows how Harry develops coping strategies when the family experiences major changes. It also highlights the contribution made by Harry's parents and his early years educators to his early education. Much of what we learn about Harry's early learning can be applied to many other young children.

This book about one child's early development and learning will be of interest to all who are fascinated by how young children learn – nursery practitioners, early years teachers, parents, students and advisers.

Contents
Introduction – Background about the book and using observation to assess children's development and learning – Getting to know Harry and his family – Using theory to understand Harry's development and learning – Harry's physical development – Harry's personal, social and emotional development – Harry learns to communicate, to use language and to become literate – Harry's mathematical development – Harry's creative development – Harry gains knowledge and understanding of the world – Harry's story – Reflections and making connections – References – Index.

160pp   0 335 21301 4 (Paperback)   0 335 21302 2 (Hardback)

THE FOUNDATIONS OF LEARNING

Julie Fisher

The introduction of the Foundation Stage for children aged 3 to becoming 6 has had a profound impact on policy and practice in early education in the UK. The choice of the word 'foundation' to describe this first stage of learning has emphasized the importance of children's earliest experiences in underpinning all their subsequent attitudes and achievements. In this innovative and challenging book, Julie Fisher has brought together some of the country's leading early years specialists to explore how educators can establish firm foundations for young children's learning. The themes in the book are stimulated by the metaphor of 'foundations', with an introduction by an architect who explains the principles of establishing firm foundations for buildings. Each of these established engineering principles is then creatively explored from an educational perspective as the authors seek to question how the foundations laid for buildings can offer fresh insights into the principles for creating firm foundations for learning.

Contents

Acknowledgements – Introduction – Foundations take longer to create than buildings – The higher the building, the firmer the foundations have to be – The more stress a building is likely to face, the more flexible the foundations need to be – When building on poor ground, the foundations must be strengthened to compensate – If new buildings are to be added to existing buildings, making the right connections between the foundations is crucial – When testing foundations, early strength is not a reliable predictor of later strength – If foundations are inadequate, it is very, very expensive to underpin them later on – Conclusion – References – Index.

160pp   0 335 20991 2 (Paperback)   0 335 20992 0 (Hardback)

FROM BIRTH TO ONE
THE YEAR OF OPPORTUNITY

Maria Robinson

The first year of life is the year of opportunity. It is when the foundations for our emotional and social well-being, together with our motivation and ability to learn, begin to be laid down by an ongoing interplay of physical, neurological and psychological processes.

Maria Robinson draws upon up-to-date research to illuminate this process and highlights the importance of understanding the meaning and influence of adult interactions, reactions and behaviour towards their child and the child's impact on the adult. She indicates how the outcomes of early experience can influence the direction of future development, so providing insight into the potential reasons for children's behavioural responses.

The powerful nature of working with babies and young children is addressed in a separate section which encourages practitioners to reflect on how personal attitudes, beliefs and values can influence professional practice.

This fascinating book is a valuable resource for all early years practitioners including teachers, social workers and health visitors who wish to understand behaviour within a context of early developmental processes.

Contents

Introduction – Part one: Development in the first year – Making connections: a perspective on development – Setting the scene: parents and parenting – Starting out: from birth to 3 months – From smiling to waving: 3 months–7 months – Peek a boo and where are you?: 7 months–12 months – Unhappy babies – Part two: Reflections on professional practice and personal emotions – The personal in the professional – When dreams go awry – The year of opportunity – References – Index.

208pp   0 335 20895 9 (Paperback)   0 335 20896 7 (Hardback)